Photo Identification—Page 311

THE CLASSICS OF GOLF

Edition of

THE COMPLETE GOLFER

Edited by

Herbert Warren Wind

with an Introduction by

Robert T. Jones, Jr.

Foreword by Herbert Warren Wind
Afterword by Frank Hannigan

For my brother and sisters
Martha, Jack, Git, and Rhody

"The Complete Golfer", a golf anthology originally published in 1954, was, in a way, a delayed dividend for the months I had spent in 1946 and 1947 doing the research for the "The Story of American Golf". That period of intensive reading was a helpful start in becoming acquainted with the many important golf books and articles that had been produced over the previous sixty-five years in Scotland and England beginning in the 1880s. Baseball and boxing have inspired a good deal of first-class writing, as have a number of field sports, fox hunting and freshwater fishing in particular, but golf may have the finest literature of any game.

I happened to grow up in a golf-oriented town—Brockton, Massachusetts—an old shoe-manufacturing center which had a population of about sixty-three thousand people at the close of the First World War. It had two eighteen-hole golf courses, one of them a wonderful layout, and two nine-hole courses. As a boy I was a devout reader of The American Golfer, a monthly that may well have been the best golf magazine of all time. In my first year in college, as part of the course in Freshman English that all students were required to take, we had to write a thesis of approximately four-thousand words. I asked the professor who taught the particular three-times-a-week class I was in whether it would be possible to write a brief history of golf. He told me that would be quite all right. My research consisted entirely of reading the long and detailed article on golf in the Encyclopaedia Britannica. I got a good grade on my paper, and I remember distinctly the professor's written comment: "What I like most about your history of golf is that it is completely different from anything that one might find in the Encyclopaedia Britannica."

"The Complete Golfer" was published in 1954. The period following the close of the Second World War, very much like the years we are living in today at the start of the last decade of the twentieth century, was a time when golf was enjoying a colossal boom. Only a few years earlier, a man walking through Grand Central Station with a bag of golf clubs slung over his shoulder would have been an object of derision because of his obvious attachment to a game that was played mainly by rich people and sissies. This attitude vanished overnight when it became known that the most popular American of the day, General Dwight D. Eisenhower, who was shortly to become President Eisenhower, was crazy about golf. During the Eisenhower administration, the Vacation White House or the Little White House was "Mamie's Cabin", a modest wooden structure situated near the large practice green at the Augusta National Golf Club, in Augusta, Georgia. Robert T. (Bobby) Jones, Jr. had founded the club shortly after his retirement from competitive golf in 1930 following his Grand Slam of the four major championships. He had designed the course in 1931 in association with Alister MacKenzie, the brilliant British golf-course architect. Three years later, in 1934, the club's annual spring invitational tournament, which quickly came to be known as the Masters, was inaugurated. By the early 1950s, the tournament had reached that stage in its growth where it was on the verge of joining the U.S. Open, the British Open, and our P.G.A. Championship as one of golf's four major events. Most golf authorities are agreed that the Masters probably reached this exalted status in April, 1954, when the two best golfers in the world, Ben Hogan and Sam Snead, tied for first in the Masters and played off for the title the following morning over eighteen holes. Snead edged out Hogan by a stroke, 70 to 71.

Sensing the new wave of interest in golf, I attempted, in 1951, to interest the publishing house of Simon & Schuster in bringing out a collection of the best golf cartoons that had appeared in newspapers, magazines, and books in this country and in Britain since the turn of the century. The editor I dealt with at S. & S. was Peter Schwed, who, among his duties then, handled the books on sports. Peter wasn't all that enthusiastic about doing a book of golf cartoons. He wondered if it were possible to do a really first-class golf anthology. I returned many months later with a tentative table of contents. Peter liked it, and I continued to search for outstanding pieces over a fairly good period of time. Briefly, the completed collection opened with a section made up of five short stories. This was followed by a section devoted to golf cartoons, forty-one of them. The third section, The Spirit of the Game, was a mixture of Reminiscence, Comment, History, and Humor down through the years. The fourth zeroed in on the Great Players and Historic Moments. The fifth, The Masters' Voices, presented the views of the great players and teachers on the theory and technique of the modern golf swing and sound shotmaking. The sixth and last section reflected the growing interest in golf-course architecture. Robert Trent Jones, the young architect who had come to the fore with his daring revisions of Oakland Hills and other courses he had prepared specifically for the United States Open, discussed the qualities that a modern championship course should possess in order to provide a suitable test for the world's best golfers.

A word at this point about the title, "The Complete Golfer". It had been used in 1905 for an instruction book that Harry Vardon wrote with Henry Leach, one the top golf writers of that day. A half-century later, few if any people were still aware of that book. Bob Jones was, not surprisingly. I had written to him to ask if he would be kind enough to write an introduction to the anthology. He said that he would be pleased to do this. Then, characteristically, he inquired whether or not I was aware that the title, "The Complete Golfer", had been used by Harry Vardon at the turn of the century. He wanted to be sure that I knew this so that I wouldn't get into any trouble over international copyright law.

In retrospect, the weakest part of the anthology undoubtedly was the first section, the Short Stories. Of the five, one of them, "The Clicking of Cuthbert" by P. G. Wodehouse, has always struck me as the best of Wodehouse's many dazzling golf stories. No one else is in his class. Two of the other short stories selected were pretty good, but the remaining two, looking back at them years later, are just plain mediocre. I wonder why I ever chose them. Today I know of four or five other golf short stories that are far superior to them. I can only conclude that, if they existed in the early 1950s, I simply did not know about them. Speaking of Wodehouse, relatively early in his career he began to turn out those superlative stories that are introduced by the Oldest Member, and while many other writers have, consciously or unconsciously, produced stories that echo Wodehouse's closely in their characters, plot construction, and general point of view, none of them possesses anything like the arrant magic of the genuine article.

The second section, the Cartoons, has stood up well over the years. Some of Clare Briggs's beauties and most of the cartoons from The New Yorker still come right off the page.

The third section, The Spirit of the Game may have actually improved with age. There are many delightful and discerning pieces. Let me mention just a few. "The Birth of the Linksland Courses", by Sir Guy Campbell, comes from that distinguished collection, "A History of Golf in Britain", which came out in 1952. It is a thrilling blend of scholarship and inspired descriptive writing which stays with the reader forever. (Sir Guy, by the way, is seldom given appropriate credit for one of the wittiest spontaneous comments in the long history of golf. When a new captain of the Royal & Ancient drives himself into office in late September on the first tee of the Old Course, the caddies take up their positions on the first fairway at the spots where they think the drive will be hit, for it is traditional for the caddie who fields the ball to receive a golden sovereign on returning it to the incoming captain. In 1950, when Sir Guy was asked where the caddies had positioned themselves in 1922 when the Duke Of Windsor, then the Prince of Wales, had driven himself into office, he twinkled his blue eyes a second and then answered, "I'm afraid they stood disloyally close.") "Some of the Humors of Golf", by the Right Honorable A. J. Balfour, later the highly respected Prime Minister, is a shortened version of his contribution to the Badminton Library's celebrated 1890 edition of "Golf". The piece is best remembered by many readers for its transcript of a conversation by Old Tom Morris, the sage of St. Andrews, on New Year's Day in 1886, but it seems to me that the opening paragraph is an almost peerless evaluation of the special charms of golf. ("Care may sit behind the horseman, she never presumes to walk with the caddie.") "The Prospect for 1930" by Grantland Rice is another ageless piece. It is Rice's uncanny prediction of Jones's Grand Slam that year. (The closing sentence goes like this: "And at twenty-eight, with fifteen years of tournament experience back of him, with his swing better controlled than it ever was before, there is at least a first-class chance that this will be the best year he has ever had.") Another one of the evergreen pieces in this section is "The Golfomaniac" by Stephen Leacock, a professor of Political Economy at McGill University in Montreal, who achieved a nice balance in his life by devoting a portion of his spare time to writing humorous pieces. For some unfathomable reason, a large number of people seem to fancy themselves as being exceptionally gifted at perceiving and presenting the funny side of golf. One can only comment that bringing this off is a much more difficult feat than they evidently appreciate.

Great Players, Historic Moments, the fourth section, offers three selections by Bernard Darwin (1876–1961), the Englishman who practically invented golf writing. In the first of these pieces, Darwin introduces The Triumvirate of Harry Vardon, John Henry Taylor, and James Braid, who, among them, won sixteen British Open championships between 1894 and 1914. Three of nature's noblemen, they played tournament golf with an implicit sportsmanship that elevated the game to a popularity that hadn't been dreamt of. Darwin's second piece takes you right onto the links of Hoylake on the afternoon of the fourth round of the 1924 British Open as he describes Walter Hagen's great rush down the last nine holes that won him the second of his four British crowns. In his third piece, Darwin looks carefully at Jones. He thought the world of him because he was able to play the draining game of competitive golf with a beauty and resolution that hid the ever-accumulating strain he was under. In addition, he understood the subtler sides of Jones's make-up. I should also like to direct your attention to "Little, at Prestwick and St. Annes", by Peter Lawless. The longtime golf correspondent of the London Morning Post, Lawless was an astute judge of golfers and a writer with a lucid and congenial style. In 1936, he brought out the first modern golf anthology I know of, "The Golfer's Companion", a very sound piece of work. This section also provides some interesting studies of Ralph Guldahl, Byron Nelson, Sam Snead, and Ben Hogan, signalling their arrival as the new wave of American champions.

The fifth section, The Masters' Voices—Their Views on Theory, Technique, Learning, and Playing, is a symposium conducted by some of the ablest golf minds from Willie Park, Jr., who in 1896 became the first golf professional to write an instructional book, to Tommy Armour, who in 1953 brought out what has proved to be the game's all-time best-selling instruction book, "How To Play Your Best Golf All the Time". Another high point is the key chapter from "On Learning Golf", the profound and highly readable book written during the Second World War by Percy Boomer, for decades the teaching pro at the St. Cloud Golf Club, outside Paris. Shorly before the war, the stop-action camera had been perfected. It provided Boomer with the evidence

he needed to corroborate his theories of what really happens in the golf swing.

The sixth and last section, Golf-Course Architecture, came off much better than I had originally hoped for. After the war, like many American golfers, I set out to learn something about golf-course architecture. I was very fortunate. I got to know Robert Trent Jones, the rising young architect, who lived in Montclair, New Jersey, and maintained an office in New York City at that time. He was just getting to be known nationally for the revolutionary new courses he was designing and for his daring revisions of a number of old courses on which the U.S. Open was played at this time. In addition to providing "The Complete Golfer" with a landmark article called "From St. Andrews to the Modern American Golf Courses", Trent had his office staff pr are maps of Pine Valley, Merion, Pinehurst No. 2, Pebble Beach, Augusta National, and Jones's controversial revision of Oakland Hills, the venue of the 1951 U.S. Open, to supplement the famous Alister MacKenzie map of the Old Course in St. Andrews and the much-admired E. J. Raisz map of C. B. Macdonald's National Golf Links in Southampton, Long Island, the first great American golf course. The actual execution of the maps was done by a young member of Jones's staff, Frank Duane, who went on to become a very successful golf-course architect. On top of this, Tom Bevans, one of the co-chiefs of the production department at Simon & Schuster—the other was Helen Barrow—turned the maps into fine art with the clarity of his layouts and his dramatic use of color. The whole book, indeed, was handsomely laid out and produced.

By the way, Peter Schwed went on to become the Editor-in-Chief of Simon & Schuster, and he enjoyed a long and prestigious career at the helm.

It should be noted that a main reason "The Complete Golfer" gained a measure of success was the enthusiatic support it received from Joseph S. F. Murdoch, a businessman and golf scholar who makes his home in Lafayette Hill, outside Philadelphia. In the early 1950s, Murdoch became so enamored of the history of golf that he decided to collect golf books as a hobby. He threw himself into this with his customary ardor. In 1968, at length, he brought out the most thoroughgoing guide to golf literature and golf writing ever produced. It was entitled "The Library of Golf, 1743–1966" and was subtitled *A Bibliography of Golf Books, Indexed Alphabetically, Chronologically, and by Subject Matter.* It was published by the Gale Research Company in Detroit, and Richard Kinney, who designed it, did a very good job handling the complicated format.

In 1977, Murdoch brought "The Library of Golf" up to date. A man who enjoys the company of a wide range of people, he had earlier become the founding father of the Golf Collectors Society. He had noted that an ever-increasing number of Americans was collecting golf books, antique clubs and balls, golf art, and assorted memorabilia. A natural organizer, he arranged for the first meetings at which diverse collectors were able to get together, exchange knowledge, and buy or sell pieces of value.

Some years ago, Murdoch began to limit his active participation and stepped down as the head of the Golf Collectors Society. In the 1980s, however, he assisted his friend Richard E. Donovan, of Endicott, New York, in assembling a more widely researched bibliography of golf literature, "The Game of Golf and the Printed Word, 1566–1985". In recent years, when the golf boom has at times seemed to be getting out of hand, it has been reassuring that responsible men like Joe Murdoch have been keeping a patriarchal eye on things.

Frank Hannigan, one of the most knowledgable persons in golf, has written an observant and witty Afterword for this book.

A brief word about Hannigan. He was born in 1931 on Staten Island, a part of New York City, and graduated in 1951 from Wagner College, which is situated on the island. He majored in English. Growing up, he worked in the summer on the maintenance crew at one of the island's three public courses, took up the game and learned to play it well, and went on to write the Monday morning golf page for the Staten Island Advance. (He covered what had happened on Saturday in the competitions at the three public courses and the one private course.) After completing college, he served as Wagner's Public Relations Director. He was hoping to find more interesting work.

Hannigan's big break came in 1961 when he answered a blind ad—Golf Editor Wanted—in the New York Times. The head of the employment agency was impressed by his background and sent him to see Joseph C. Dey, Jr., the Executive Director of the United States Golf Association at the U.S.G.A.'s old headquarters on East 38th Street in Manhattan. Dey needed a young man to assist him in putting out the Golf Journal, and Hannigan was just the sort of aide he was looking for. Hannigan was also appointed Director of Public Information and Curator of the U.S.G.A. Museum. He gradually went up the ladder during this period when the association was greatly expanding its functions and services, and, at length, in 1983 he was appointed Executive Director. He stepped down in 1989 after six years in that office and was succeeded by David B. Fay.

At the present time, the bulk of Hannigan's time is devoted to his duties as the Editorial Advisor of the production unit that is responsible for the American Broadcasting Company's golf telecasts. A member as well of the announcing crew on these shows, he is a gifted interviewer because of his wide knowledge of golf and his skill in listening to people. At the present time, Frank also writes a stimulating monthly column, "Loose Impediments", for Golf magazine.

Herbert Warren Wind

TABLE OF CONTENTS

·I·

SHORT STORIES

·II·

CARTOONS
PAGE 45

·III·

THE SPIRIT OF THE GAME
Reminiscence, Comment, History, and Humor

·IV·

GREAT PLAYERS, HISTORIC MOMENTS

· V ·

THE MASTERS' VOICES

Their Views on Theory, Technique, Learning and Playing

· VI ·

GOLF COURSE ARCHITECTURE

INTRODUCTION

BACK IN THE DAYS *when all Americans were both notoriously rich and, for the most part, bad golfers, one of our countrymen is supposed to have visited St. Andrews, the cradle of the game, and played the Old Course. He had assigned to him one of the picturesque (and picaresque) old caddies, so commonly encountered there, who know the game from beginning to end and are quite frankly impatient of any trifling with it.*

Our friend played very badly and, as the round progressed, the relationship between him and his caddie became more and more strained. Finally, with great relief he put his ball into the hole of the home green, and, thinking to recapture some of his caddie's esteem, he handed the old boy a tip of a gold sovereign, remarking as light-heartily as he could,

"Well, caddie, golf is a funny game, isn't it?"

"Aye," responded the Old Scot, eyeing the gold coin and wagging his head ruefully, "but it was nae meant to be."

No one knows what kind of a game golf was "meant to be." The game did not spring full-blown from any Jovian skull, but evolved slowly over several centuries. Probably the most fortunate circumstance of all, affecting the good of the game for the vast numbers who play it, is that its trustees, on both sides of the Atlantic, have ever been slow to legislate changes in the rules and conditions of play.

Nevertheless, golf is a funny game. It is also a tantalizing, frustrating, fascinating game. Tournament golf can be heroic or tragic, a play of forces in which players and spectators alike may experience drama equal to that on any stage. And in any kind of golf, pathetic and ludicrous situations may succeed one another with kaleidoscopic rapidity.

I suppose the one saving grace is that we soon forget our disappointments and learn to remember and to laugh at our own foolishness. And in tournament play the heroic successes are always longer remembered than the tragic failures.

Golf is also a game of temperament and, for some of us, even of temper. The whole thing seems so simple, and our better performances seem so easy. Invariably we become convinced that our best shots are merely normal and that our lowest rounds represent that thing we call our "game." Any regression from this standard is therefore intolerable.

I remember that I was a very young man when I first played East Lake, my home course, in 63. Afterward, I confided to my father that I had mas-

tered the secret of the game and that I should never go above 70 again. Next day I had to work my head off to get around in 77.

Yes, golf is astoundingly many-sided. It can be played and enjoyed by children and elderly people, but it is neither "child's play" nor an "old man's game." Golf has more than enough in it to command the respect of any man whatever his physical or mental stature.

It has been inevitable, of course, that a game such as this should develop a considerable literature. History, humor, curiosities, stories of championships, essays on method—literally by the hundreds—are available. And every golfer, I think, owes it to himself to have some acquaintance with this literature.

The present anthology is an effort to provide a broad sampling of these writings on or related to golf, to make this acquaintance easy to come by. I am sure it will lead many to further browsings in a fascinating field.

From the wealth of material available it is certain that not every anthologist would make the same choices. It is therefore a particularly happy circumstance that in the present volume we have the tasteful guidance of Herbert Warren Wind.

Herb Wind is devoted to golf. He is a fine, sensitive writer on the game whose works range from essays of the most accurately appreciative kind to some of the finest golf reporting I have ever read. Anyone familiar with his truly monumental Story of American Golf will attest to his thoroughness. I know that his search has been wide and that his selections have been made with high intelligence and integrity.

ROBERT T. JONES, JR.

Atlanta, Georgia

"Fore!"

A. B. FROST
From *The Golfer's Alphabet*, by
W. G. Van Tassel Sutphen,
Harper & Brothers.

PREFACE

EVER SINCE GOLF BEGAN—Scottish historians have settled on the
year 1100 as a reasonable date of birth—the game has been an
enigma. For those who have steered clear of its clutches, the devotion it commands from its followers looms as one of the great
absurdities of the human race's supposed progress. There are
moments when every golfer agrees with this verdict. If he could
only have back in one lump all the time, money, energy, and
anguish he has spent on golf and invest it toward some sensible
goal, why, there is no knowing the heights of happiness he might
reach. Then he plays a good round in congenial company on a
sunny morning, and his golfer's balance returns. If there is one
thing he is certain he has done right in his life, it has been to
play golf, and his only regret is that he hasn't given the game more
time. He might have become better.

Beyond the fact that it is a limitless arena for the full play of
human nature, there is no sure accounting for golf's fascination.

Obviously yet mysteriously, it furnishes its devotees with an intense, many-sided, and abiding pleasure unlike that which any other form of recreation affords. Perhaps it is, as Andrew Carnegie once claimed, an "indispensable adjunct of high civilization." Perhaps it is nothing more than the best game man has ever devised.

In comparatively modern times, the spread of golf's popularity has come on by waves. The first big one broke just about a century ago—in 1848—when the gutta-percha ball was introduced and rapidly replaced the "feathery," the leather-cased ball packed tight with feathers, for centuries the standard equipment. Until the coming of the "gutty," Scots living in Scotland had been the only golfers, but the new ball changed all that. It made golf a much better game. A player no longer had to be a technician of considerable skill to nudge the ball nicely off the ground and send it flying a good distance in a relatively straight line. The gutty required a powerful swing and a well-timed hit, but when it was struck cleanly, it could be propelled tens of yards farther than the feathery, and the essential thrill of "distance" entered the game for the first time. This revitalized kind of golf swept south of the Scottish border into England, then to the European playgrounds of the international set of that day, and, by the turn of the century, it had made its way to every continent. Wherever golf was taken, it took. It arrived in the United States in 1888—that, in any event, was the year the first American golf club was founded—and so instant was its contagiousness that twelve years later the number of American golfers exceeded a quarter of a million.

Golf—gutty golf—undoubtedly would have gained more and more adherents, but it is questionable if it would have made quite the conquest of man's leisure hours as did the rubber-core ball, the revolutionary modification of the gutty which made its appearance in 1898. This new ball—its core wound tightly with strips of rubber, the cover of gutta-percha—was the impetus behind golf's second great wave of popularity and ushered in the present version of golf, the game eight million people play today. The new ball was superior to the solid glob of gutta-percha in almost precisely the same respects which the gutty had been to the feathery: it would, on the average, go some fifteen yards farther when struck correctly, and, more important, it would go *someplace* when not struck right on the button. It was just what was needed to make the average player feel like a golfer and not like a well-dressed laborer. The invention of the rubber-core ball is usually credited to Coburn Haskell, of Cleveland, and for all that American ingenuity later did for the game, it undoubtedly stands as our outstanding technical contribution to the advancement of golf.

Then the waves began to come closer to each other. There was a mighty one in 1913. In our National Open Championship that

September, an unknown homegrown amateur, Francis Ouimet, a remarkable twenty-year-old ex-caddie from a family of medium means, astounded the golf world as it has never been astounded before or afterwards by first tieing and then defeating in a dramatic play-off two acknowledged masters from Great Britain, Harry Vardon and Ted Ray. Until Francis' epochal victory, most nongolfers in America had viewed the game with hostility as the pampered pastime of the wealthy, the elderly, the would-be Continental, the unrugged—and they were welcome to it. After Francis' victory, this stigma was removed once and for all, and the base was laid for golf's development in this country as a genuinely democratic sport, whatever the inevitable social overtones of the clubhouse. Hundreds of thousands of reformed golf-haters rushed to the golf courses, and it was only a matter of months before they viewed with suspicion anyone who didn't play their game.

The majestic personalities of the twenties completed golf's ascendancy to the status of a major American sport. First there came Walter Hagen. Until Walter made the British Open his personal property—he won it first in 1922 and three times later—British golfers, despite Ouimet's one breakthrough, had continued to rule supreme in international competition. Walter's exploits abroad and at home eradicated our national inferiority complex, and they were achieved with a dash and bravado that captivated the Great American Sports Fan

CLARE BRIGGS
From *The Duffer's Handbook of Golf,* by Grantland Rice. Copr., The Macmillan Company.

who had been bred on baseball, football, and boxing heroes. Hagen was a guy he could understand, and he took to golf through him. Another dimension was added when Gene Sarazen, the son of an immigrant carpenter from Italy, came bolting out of complete obscurity to win the National Open in 1922, the first of his many championships. And then there was Jones—Robt. T. Jones, Jr., Atlanta, Ga. Even in the Golden Age of the twenties when every sport had its heroic-sized champion, its Ruth or its Dempsey or its Tilden, there was no other athlete who was consistently the champion that Bobby Jones was on and off the fairway. The beauty of it was that Jones's qualities were recognized by everyone instinctively.

Golf is presently on the crest of another wave, the first that has rolled in since Jones's Grand Slam. From the close of World War II on, the game has made tens of thousands of converts annually. The increase in leisure time available to the average man and woman has been a major factor in this recent expansion. In a way, so has Ben Hogan, by all odds *the* dominant sports personality of the postwar world, the champion who came back after his near-fatal accident and had the stuff to make himself an even greater champion. In the process he became a national hero of such proportions that, during his assault on the British Open in 1953, nongolfers, so green about the game that they first confused Carnoustie with a new wax for automobiles, followed his progress with the same proud concern that veteran golfers did. And, of course, a good measure of the game's increasing popularity derives from the presence in the White House of a man for whom golf is, no question about it, an "indispensable adjunct of high civili-

ALAIN
By permission. Copr., 1953, The
New Yorker Magazine, Inc.

zation." Today well over five million Americans play some golf every year and there are not nearly enough courses to take care of everyone who would like to play.

Part and parcel of this upsurge of enthusiasm has been a burgeoning interest in what has been written about the game. A great deal has, which is not too surprising. Whatever else it may be, golf is the most ruminative of recreations. Play it and you will talk it endlessly and chew upon it at the oddest hours and, apparently, if you have the dormant urge to put your thoughts on paper, golf will bring it out. Over the years, as a result, a vast body of writing about golf has accumulated which far surpasses any other game's for sheer quantity. Forgetting the countless magazines and pamphlets, golf books alone run into the thousands—how-to guides, collections of short stories, poetry (usually of the class that leaves Milton's position intact), memoirs and biographies, diaries, critical essays, involved psychological disquisitions, formal histories, one-act and three-act plays, all varieties of humor, travel reports, over a score of full-length novels, and "golf translations" of Shakespeare, Horace and Omar Khayyám. While a large part of this outpouring falls a good distance short of that standard of writing we call literature, no other game has acquired a literature that compares with golf's. Men write extremely well about it, and sometimes wonderfully. What we have attempted to do in this anthology is to gather together under one cover, somewhat in the fashion of those dream courses composed of fine individual holes from many courses, a representative cross-section of the best writing on all phases of the game. Some of the selections are undoubtedly literature, some are first-rate journalism, and some are simply good golf.

CLARE BRIGGS
From *The Duffer's Handbook of Golf*, by Grantland Rice. Copr., The Macmillan Company.

Quite soon after the job of foraging for likely material was begun, it was decided that it would be advisable not to include a spread of newspaper columns and reports. Even the liveliest newspaper pieces, because of the very nature of the assignment, are bound to have a certain incompleteness and perishability. In any event, the line-up includes only six pieces which originally appeared in newspapers, each of them well off the beaten track —like Sam McKinlay's account for the Glasgow *Herald* of the ceremonies at St. Andrews the brisk September morn in 1951 when Francis Ouimet drove himself into office as the first "overseas" captain of the Royal and Ancient. For the rest, the selections have been culled from books and magazines, with the one exception of Robert Trent Jones's article on golf course architecture which was written specifically for this collection. Jones's article, illustrated with his superb maps of six of the classic courses and two other maps obtained from other sources, forms the book's sixth section. The other five suggested themselves as natural categories early in the research, and we found they worked as well as any other format. The first section, fiction, contains five short stories, four of them humorous in vein and one of them a detective story. The second section is a selection of the outstanding golf cartoons of the last fifty years, arranged in a roughly chronological sequence. The third, called "The Spirit of the Game," is a potpourri of short-length articles and extracts, from Tobias Smollett, that inadvertent pioneer among golf writers, down to Stephen Potter, the father of Gamesmanship. Accounts of memorable individual matches and championships make up the bulk of the fourth section, "Great Players, Historic Moments." The fifth, "The Masters' Voices," has to do with instruction. It is, however, not so much a catalogue of how-to homilies as a forum in which top-rank players and teachers describe their thoughts on all aspects of that very difficult business of learning how to hit good golf shots and hit them regularly. All down the line an effort has been made to strike a happy balance in several directions—between the old and the new, the humorous and the straightaway, the British and the American. In this last connection, American golfers who haven't yet made the acquaintance of such British writers as Henry Longhurst and the incomparable Bernard Darwin have a genuine treat in store for them.

One other thing. One of the pleasures of editing an anthology is the matchless opportunity it affords to speak up for certain pieces which, for strictly personal reasons, have always been dear to the editor's heart. Like many people who "discovered" golf in the mid-1920's, I was impressed by two books above all others: *Down the Fairway* by Bob Jones and O. B. Keeler, and *The Duffer's Handbook of Golf* by Grantland Rice and Clare Briggs. They were always around the house and you dipped into them whenever you had time on your hands and didn't know what to do with it. It has been hard keeping down to three the number of selections from *Down the Fairway,* for when I reread the book these days, it strikes me, as it did from the first, as possessing the perfect golf flavor along with an unbeatable charm and candor. Similarly, I have included more cartoons by Clare Briggs than by any other artist, and perhaps there should have been still more. He also still seems to me to be in a class by himself in capturing the spirit of golf and golfers. Essentially, over the century from the first wave down through the current one, this spirit has changed hardly at all.

HERBERT WARREN WIND

New York City
August 1954

·I·

SHORT STORIES

The Clicking of
Cuthbert

by

P. G. WODEHOUSE

1922 — FROM *WODEHOUSE ON GOLF*

THE YOUNG MAN came into the smoking-room of the clubhouse, and flung his bag with a clatter on the floor. He sank moodily into an armchair and pressed the bell.

"Waiter!"

"Sir?"

The young man pointed at the bag with every evidence of distaste.

"You may have these clubs," he said. "Take them away. If you don't want them yourself, give them to one of the caddies."

Across the room the Oldest Member gazed at him with a grave sadness through the smoke of his pipe. His eye was deep and dreamy—the eye of a man who, as the poet says, has seen Golf steadily and seen it whole.

"*You* are giving up golf?" he said.

He was not altogether unprepared for such an attitude on the young man's part: for from his eyrie on the terrace above the ninth green he had observed him start out on the afternoon's round and had seen him lose a couple of balls in the lake at the second hole after taking seven strokes at the first.

"Yes!" cried the young man fiercely. "Forever, dammit! Footling game! Blanked infernal fatheaded silly ass of a game! Nothing but a waste of time."

The Sage winced.

"Don't say that, my boy."

"But I do say it. What earthly good is golf? Life is stern and life is earnest. We live in a practical age. All round us we see foreign competition making itself unpleasant. And we spend our time playing golf! What do we get out of it? Is golf any *use*? That's what I'm asking you. Can you name me a single case where devotion to this pestilential pastime has done a man any practical good?"

The Sage smiled gently.

"I could name a thousand."

"One will do."

"I will select," said the Sage, "from the innumerable memories that rush to my mind, the story of Cuthbert Banks."

"Never heard of him."

"Be of good cheer," said the Oldest Member. "You are going to hear of him now."

It was in the picturesque little settlement of Wood Hills (said the Oldest Member) that the incidents occurred which I am about to relate. Even if you have never been in Wood Hills, that suburban paradise is probably familiar to you by name. Situated at a convenient distance from the city, it combines in a notable manner the advantages of town life with the pleasant surroundings and healthful air of the country. Its inhabitants live in commodious houses, standing in their own grounds, and enjoy so many luxuries—such as gravel soil, main drainage, electric light, telephone, baths (h. and c.), and company's own water, that you might be pardoned for imagining life to be so ideal for them that no possible improvement

3

could be added to their lot. Mrs. Willoughby Smethurst was under no such delusion. What Wood Hills needed to make it perfect, she realized, was Culture. Material comforts are all very well, but if the *summum bonum* is to be achieved, the Soul also demands a look in, and it was Mrs. Smethurst's unfaltering resolve that never while she had her strength should the Soul be handed the loser's end. It was her intention to make Wood Hills a center of all that was most cultivated and refined, and, golly! how she had succeeded. Under her presidency the Wood Hills Literary and Debating Society had tripled its membership.

But there is always a fly in the ointment, a caterpillar in the salad. The local golf club, an institution to which Mrs. Smethurst strongly objected, had also tripled its membership; and the division of the community into two rival camps, the Golfers and the Cultured, had become more marked than ever. This division always acute, had attained now to the dimensions of a Schism. The rival sects treated one another with a cold hostility.

Unfortunate episodes came to widen the breach. Mrs. Smethurst's house adjoined the links, standing to the right of the fourth tee: and, as the Literary Society was in the habit of entertaining visiting lecturers, many a golfer had foozled his drive owing to sudden loud outbursts of applause coinciding with his downswing. And not long before this story opens a sliced ball, whizzing in at the open window, had come within an ace of incapacitating Raymond Parsloe Devine, the rising young novelist (who rose at that moment a clear foot and a half) from any further exercise of his art. Two inches, indeed, to the right and Raymond must inevitably have handed in his dinner pail.

To make matters worse, a ring at the front door bell followed almost immediately, and the maid ushered in a young man of pleasing appearance in a sweater and baggy knickerbockers who apologetically but firmly insisted on playing his ball where it lay, and what with the shock of the lecturer's narrow escape and the spectacle of the intruder standing on the table and working away with a niblick, the afternoon's session had to be classed as a complete frost. Mr. Devine's determination, from which no argument could swerve him, to deliver the rest of his lecture in the coal cellar

gave the meeting a jolt from which it never recovered.

I have dwelt upon this incident, because it was the means of introducing Cuthbert Banks to Mrs. Smethurst's niece, Adeline. As Cuthbert, for it was he who had so nearly reduced the muster roll of rising novelists by one, hopped down from the table after his stroke, he was suddenly aware that a beautiful girl was looking at him intently. As a matter of fact, everyone in the room was looking at him intently, none more so than Raymond Parsloe Devine, but none of the others were beautiful girls. Long as the members of Wood Hills Literary Society were on brain, they were short on looks, and, to Cuthbert's excited eye, Adeline Smethurst stood out like a jewel in a pile of coke.

He had never seen her before, for she had only arrived at her aunt's house on the previous day, but he was perfectly certain that life, even when lived in the midst of gravel soil, main drainage, and company's own water, was going to be a pretty poor affair if he did not see her again. Yes, Cuthbert was in love: and it is interesting to record, as showing the effect of the tender emotion on a man's game, that twenty minutes after he had met Adeline he did the short eleventh in one, and as near as a toucher got a three on the four-hundred-yard twelfth.

I will skip lightly over the intermediate stages of Cuthbert's courtship and come to the moment when—at the annual ball in aid of the local Cottage Hospital, the only occasion during the year on which the lion, so to speak, lay down with the lamb, and the Golfers and the Cultured met on terms of easy comradeship, their differences temporarily laid aside —he proposed to Adeline and was badly stymied.

That fair, soulful girl could not see him with a spyglass.

"Mr. Banks," she said, "I will speak frankly."

"Charge right ahead," assented Cuthbert.

"Deeply sensible as I am of —"

"I know. Of the honor and the compliment and all that. But, passing lightly over all that guff, what seems to be the trouble? I love you to distraction —"

"Love is not everything."

"You're wrong," said Cuthbert, earnestly. "You're right off it. Love —" And he was about to dilate on the theme when she interrupted him.

"I am a girl of ambition."

"And very nice, too," said Cuthbert.

"I am a girl of ambition," repeated Adeline, "and I realize that the fulfillment of my ambitions must come through my husband. I am very ordinary myself —"

"What!" cried Cuthbert. "You ordinary? Why, you are a pearl among women, the queen of your sex. You can't have been looking in a glass lately. You stand alone. Simply alone. You make the rest look like battered repaints."

"Well," said Adeline, softening a trifle, "I believe I am fairly good-looking —"

"Anybody who was content to call you fairly good-looking would describe the Taj Mahal as a pretty nifty tomb."

"But that is not the point. What I mean is, if I marry a nonentity, I shall be a nonentity myself forever. And I would sooner die than be a nonentity."

"And, if I follow your reasoning, you think that lets *me* out?"

"Well, really, Mr. Banks, *have* you done anything, or are you likely ever to do anything worth while?"

Cuthbert hesitated.

"It's true," he said, "I didn't finish in the first ten in the Open, and I was knocked out in the semifinal of the Amateur, but I won the French Open last year."

"The—what?"

"The French Open Championship. Golf, you know."

"Golf! You waste all your time playing golf. I admire a man who is more spiritual, more intellectual."

A pang of jealousy rent Cuthbert's bosom.

"Like What's-his-name Devine?" he said, sullenly.

"Mr. Devine," replied Adeline, blushing faintly, "is going to be a great man. Already he has achieved much. The critics say that he is more Russian than any other young American writer."

"And is that good?"

"Of course it's good."

"I should have thought the thing would be to be more American than any other young American writer."

"Nonsense! Who wants an American writer to be American? You've got to be Russian or Spanish or something to be a real success. The mantle of the great Russians has descended on Mr. Devine."

"From what I've heard of Russians, I should hate to have that happen to *me*."

"There is no danger of that," said Adeline, scornfully.

"Oh! Well, let me tell you that there is a lot more in me than you think."

"That might easily be so."

"You think I'm not spiritual and intellectual," said Cuthbert, deeply moved. "Very well. Tomorrow I join the Literary Society."

Even as he spoke the words his leg was itching to kick himself for being such a chump, but the sudden expression of pleasure on Adeline's face soothed him; and he went home that night with the feeling that he had taken on something rather attractive. It was only in the cold, gray light of the morning that he realized what he had let himself in for.

I do not know if you have had any experience of suburban literary societies, but the one that flourished under the eye of Mrs. Willoughby Smethurst in Wood Hills was rather more so than the average. With my feeble powers of narrative, I cannot hope to make clear to you all that Cuthbert Banks endured in the next few weeks. And, even if I could, I doubt if I should do so. It is all very well to excite pity and terror, as Aristotle recommends, but there are limits. In the ancient Greek tragedies, it was an ironclad rule that all the real rough stuff should take place off stage, and I shall follow this admirable principle. It will suffice if I say merely that J. Cuthbert Banks had a thin time. After attending eleven debates and fourteen lectures on *vers libre*, Poetry, the Seventeenth-Century Essayists, the Neo-Scandinavian Movement in Portuguese Literature, and other subjects of a similar nature, he grew so enfeebled that, on the rare occasions when he had time for a visit to the links, he had to take a full iron for his mashie shots.

It was not simply the oppressive nature of the debates and lectures that sapped his vitality. What really got right in amongst him was the torture of seeing Adeline's adoration of Raymond Parsloe Devine. The man seemed to have made the deepest possible impression upon her plastic emotions. When he spoke, she leaned forward with parted lips and looked at him. When he was not speaking—which was seldom—she leaned back and looked at him. And when he happened to take the next seat to her, she leaned sideways and looked at him. One glance at Mr. Devine would have been more than enough for Cuthbert; but Adeline found him a spectacle that never palled. She could not have gazed at him with a more rapturous intensity if she had been a small child and he a saucer of ice cream. All this Cuthbert had to witness while still endeavoring to retain the possession of his faculties sufficiently to enable him to duck and back away if somebody suddenly asked him what he thought of the somber realism of Vladimir Brusiloff. It is little wonder that he tossed in bed, picking at the coverlet, through sleepless nights, and had to have all his waistcoats taken in three inches to keep them from sagging.

This Vladimir Brusiloff to whom I have referred was the famous Russian novelist, and, owing to the fact of his being in the country on a lecturing tour at the moment, there had been something of a boom in his works. The Wood Hills Literary Society had been studying them for weeks, and never since his first entrance into intellectual circles had Cuthbert Banks come nearer to throwing in the towel. Vladimir specialized in gray studies of hopeless misery, where nothing happened till page three hundred and eighty, when the moujik decided to commit suicide. It was tough going for a man whose deepest reading hitherto had been Vardon on the Push-Shot, and there can be no greater proof of the magic of love than the fact that Cuthbert stuck it without a cry. But the strain was terrible, and I am inclined to think that he must have cracked, had it not been for the daily reports in the papers of the internecine strife which was proceeding so briskly in Russia. Cuthbert was an optimist at heart, and it seemed to him that, at the rate at which the inhabitants of that interesting country were murdering one another, the supply of Russian novelists must eventually give out.

One morning, as he tottered down the road for the short walk which was now almost the only exercise to which he was equal, Cuthbert met Adeline. A spasm of anguish flitted through all his nerve centers as he saw that she was accompanied by Raymond Parsloe Devine.

"Good morning, Mr. Banks," said Adeline.

"Good morning," said Cuthbert, hollowly.

"Such good news about Vladimir Brusiloff."

"Dead?" said Cuthbert, with a touch of hope.

"Dead? Of course not. Why should he be? No, Aunt Emily met his manager after his lecture at Carnegie Hall yesterday, and he has promised that Mr. Brusiloff shall come to her next Wednesday reception."

"Oh, ah!" said Cuthbert, dully.

"I don't know how she managed it. I think she must have told him that Mr. Devine would be there to meet him."

"But you said he was coming," argued Cuthbert.

"I shall be very glad," said Raymond Devine, "of the opportunity of meeting Brusiloff."

"I'm sure," said Adeline, "he will be very glad of the opportunity of meeting you."

"Possibly," said Mr. Devine. "Possibly. Competent critics have said that my work closely resembles that of the great Russian masters."

"Your psychology is so deep."

"Yes, yes."

"And your atmosphere."

"Quite."

Cuthbert, in a perfect agony of spirit, prepared to withdraw from this love-feast. The sun was shining brightly, but the world was black to him. Birds sang in the tree tops, but he did not hear them. He might have been a moujik for all the pleasure he found in life.

"You will be there, Mr. Banks?" said Adeline, as he turned away.

"Oh, all right," said Cuthbert.

When Cuthbert had entered the drawing room on the following Wednesday and had taken his usual place in a distant corner where, while able to feast his gaze on Adeline, he had a sporting chance of being overlooked or mistaken for a piece of furniture, he perceived the great Russian thinker seated in the midst of a circle of admiring females. Raymond Parsloe Devine had not yet arrived.

His first glance at the novelist surprised Cuthbert. Doubtless with the best motives, Vladimir Brusiloff had permitted his face to become almost entirely concealed behind a dense zareba of hair, but his eyes were visible through the undergrowth, and it seemed to

Cuthbert that there was an expression in them not unlike that of a cat in a strange back yard surrounded by small boys. The man looked forlorn and hopeless, and Cuthbert wondered whether he had had bad news from home.

This was not the case. The latest news which Vladimir Brusiloff had had from Russia had been particularly cheering. Three of his principal creditors had perished in the last massacre of the bourgeoisie, and a man whom he owed for five years for a samovar and a pair of overshoes had fled the country, and had not been heard of since. It was not bad news from home that was depressing Vladimir. What was wrong with him was the fact that this was the eighty-second suburban literary reception he had been compelled to attend since he had landed in the country on his lecturing tour, and he was sick to death of it. When his agent had first suggested the trip, he had signed on the dotted line without an instant's hesitation. Worked out in rubles, the fees offered had seemed just about right. But now, as he peered through the brushwood at the faces round him, and realized that eight out of ten of those present had manuscripts of some sort concealed on their persons, and were only waiting for an opportunity to whip them out and start reading, he wished that he had stayed at his quiet home in Nijni-Novgorod, where the worst thing that could happen to a fellow was a brace of bombs coming in through the window and mixing themselves up with his breakfast egg.

At this point in his meditations he was aware that his hostess was looming up before him with a pale young man in horn-rimmed spectacles at her side. There was in Mrs. Smethurst's demeanor something of the unction of the master-of-ceremonies at the big fight who introduces the earnest gentleman who wishes to challenge the winner.

"Oh, Mr. Brusiloff," said Mrs. Smethurst, "I do so want you to meet Mr. Raymond Parsloe Devine, whose work I expect you know. He is one of our younger novelists."

The distinguished visitor peered in a wary and defensive manner through the shrubbery, but did not speak. Inwardly he was thinking how exactly Mr. Devine was like to the eighty-one other younger novelists to whom he had been introduced at various hamlets throughout the country. Raymond Parsloe Devine bowed courteously, while Cuthbert, wedged into his corner, glowered at him.

"The critics," said Mr. Devine, "have been kind enough to say that my poor efforts contain a good deal of the Russian spirit. I owe much to the great Russians. I have been greatly influenced by Sovietski."

Down in the forest something stirred. It was Vladimir Brusiloff's mouth opening, as he prepared to speak. He was not a man who prattled readily, especially in a foreign tongue. He gave the impression that each word was excavated from his interior by some up-to-date process of mining. He glared bleakly at Mr. Devine, and allowed three words to drop out of him.

"Sovietski no good!"

He paused for a moment, set the machinery working again, and delivered five more at the pithead.

"I spit me of Sovietski!"

There was a painful sensation. The lot of a popular idol is in many ways an enviable one, but it has the drawback of uncertainty. Here today, gone tomorrow. Until this moment Raymond Parsloe Devine's stock had stood at something considerably over par in Wood Hills intellectual circles, but now there was a rapid slump. Hitherto he had been greatly admired for being influenced by Sovietski, but it appeared now that this was not a good thing to be. It was evidently a rotten thing to be. The law could not touch you for being influenced by Sovietski, but there is an ethical as well as a legal code, and this it was obvious that Raymond Parsloe Devine had transgressed. Women drew away from him slightly, holding their skirts. Men looked at him censoriously. Adeline Smethurst started violently, and dropped a teacup. And Cuthbert Banks, doing his popular imitation of a sardine in his corner, felt for the first time that life held something of sunshine.

Raymond Parsloe Devine was plainly shaken, but he made an adroit attempt to recover his lost prestige.

"When I say I have been influenced by Sovietski, I mean, of course, that I was once under his spell. A young writer commits many follies. I have long since passed through that phase. The false glamor of Sovietski has ceased to dazzle me. I now belong wholeheartedly to the school of Nastikoff."

There was a reaction. People nodded at one another sympathetically. After all, we cannot expect old heads on young shoulders, and a lapse at the outset of one's career should not be held against one who has eventually seen the light.

"Nastikoff no good," said Vladimir Brusiloff, coldly. He paused, listening to the machinery.

"Nastikoff worse than Sovietski."

He paused again.

"I spit me of Nastikoff!" he said.

This time there was no doubt about it. The bottom had dropped out of the market, and Raymond Parsloe Devine Preferred were down in the cellar with no takers. It was clear to the entire assembled company that they had been all wrong about Raymond Parsloe Devine. They had allowed him to play on their innocence and sell them a pup. They had taken him at his own valuation and had been cheated into admiring him as a man who amounted to something, and all the while he had belonged to the school of Nastikoff. You never can tell. Mrs. Smethurst's guests were well-bred, and there was consequently no violent demonstration, but you could see by their faces what they felt. Those nearest Raymond Parsloe jostled to get further away. Mrs. Smethurst eyed him stonily through a raised lorgnette. One or two low hisses were heard, and over at the other end of the room somebody opened the window in a marked manner.

Raymond Parsloe Devine hesitated for a moment, then, realizing his situation, turned and slunk to the door. There was an audible sigh of relief as it closed behind him.

Vladimir Brusiloff proceeded to sum up.

"No novelists any good except me. Sovietski—yah! Nastikoff—bah! I spit me of zem all. No novelists anywhere any good except me. P. G. Wodehouse and Tolstoi not bad. Not good, but not bad. No novelists any good except me."

And, having uttered this dictum, he removed a slab of cake from a near-by plate, steered it through the jungle, and began to champ.

It is too much to say that there was a dead silence. There could never be that in any room in which Vladimir Brusiloff was eating cake. But certainly what you might call the general chit-chat was pretty well down and out. Nobody liked to be the first to speak. The members of the Wood Hills Literary Society looked at one another timidly. Cuthbert, for his part, gazed at Adeline; and Adeline gazed into space. It was plain that the girl was deeply stirred. Her eyes were opened wide, a faint flush crimsoned her cheeks, and her breath was coming quickly.

Adeline's mind was in a whirl. She felt as if she had been walking gaily along a pleasant path and had stopped suddenly on the very brink of a precipice. It would be idle to deny that Raymond Parsloe Devine had attracted her extraordinarily. She had taken him at his own valuation as an extremely hot potato, and her hero-worship had gradually been turning into love. And now her hero had been shown to have feet of clay. It was hard, I consider, on Raymond Parsloe Devine, but that is how it goes in this world. You get a following as a celebrity, and then you run up against another bigger celebrity and your admirers desert you. One could moralize on this at considerable length, but better not, perhaps. Enough to say that the glamor of Raymond Devine ceased abruptly in that moment for Adeline, and her most coherent thought at this juncture was the resolve, as soon as she got up to her room, to burn the three signed photographs he had sent her and to give the autographed presentation set of his books to the iceman.

Mrs. Smethurst, meanwhile, having rallied somewhat, was endeavoring to set the feast of reason and flow of soul going again.

"And how do you like America, Mr. Brusiloff?" she asked.

The celebrity paused in the act of lowering another segment of cake.

"Damn good," he replied, cordially.

"I suppose you have traveled all over the country by this time?"

"You said it," agreed the Thinker.

"Have you met many of our great public men?"

"Yais—Yais—Quite a few of the nibs—The President, I meet him. But—" Beneath the matting a discontented expression came into his face, and his voice took on a peevish note. "But I not meet your *real* great men—your Volterragin, your Veener Sirahzen—I not meet them. That's what gives me the pipovitch.

8

Have *you* ever met Volterragin and Veener Sirahzen?"

A strained, anguished look came into Mrs. Smethurst's face and was reflected in the faces of the other members of the circle. The eminent Russian had sprung two entirely new ones on them, and they felt that their ignorance was about to be exposed. What would Vladmir Brusiloff think of the Wood Hills Literary Society? The reputation of the Wood Hills Literary Society was at stake, trembling in the balance, and coming up for the third time.

In dumb agony Mrs. Smethurst rolled her eyes about the room searching for someone capable of coming to the rescue. She drew a blank.

And then, from a distant corner, there sounded a deprecating cough, and those nearest Cuthbert Banks saw that he had stopped twisting his right foot round his left ankle and his left foot round his right ankle and was sitting up with a light of almost human intelligence in his eyes.

"Er —" said Cuthbert, blushing as every eye in the room seemed to fix itself on him, "I think he means Walter Hagen and Gene Sarazen."

"Walter Hagen and Gene Sarazen?" repeated Mrs. Smethurst, blankly. "I never heard of —"

"Yais! Yais! Most! Very!" shouted Vladimir Brusiloff, enthusiastically. "Volterragin and Veener Sirahzen. You know them, yes, what, no, perhaps?"

"I've played with Walter Hagen often, and I was partnered with Gene Sarazen in last year's Open."

The great Russian uttered a cry that shook the chandelier.

"You play in ze Open? Why," he demanded reproachfully of Mrs. Smethurst, "was I not been introduced to this young man who play in Opens?"

"Well, really," faltered Mrs. Smethurst. "Well, the fact is, Mr. Brusiloff —"

She broke off. She was unequal to the task of explaining, without hurting anyone's feelings, that she had always regarded Cuthbert as a piece of cheese and a blot on the landscape.

"Introduct me!" thundered the Celebrity.

"Why, certainly, certainly, of course. This is Mr. —" She looked appealingly at Cuthbert.

"Banks," prompted Cuthbert.

"Banks!" cried Vladimir Brusiloff. "Not Cootaboot Banks?"

"*Is* your name Cootaboot?" asked Mrs. Smethurst, faintly.

"Well, it's Cuthbert."

"Yais! Yais! Cootaboot!" There was a rush and swirl, as the effervescent Muscovite burst his way through the throng and rushed to where Cuthbert sat. He stood for a moment eyeing him excitedly, then, stooping swiftly, kissed him on both cheeks before Cuthbert could get his guard up. "My dear young man, I saw you win ze French Open. Great! Great! Grand! Superb! Hot stuff, and you can say I said so! Will you permit one who is but an eighteen-handicap player at Nijni-Novgorod to salute you once more?"

And he kissed Cuthbert again. Then, brushing aside one or two intellectuals who were in the way, he dragged up a chair and sat down.

"You are a great man!" he said.

"Oh, no," said Cuthbert modestly.

"Yais! Great. Most! Very! The way you lay your approach putts dead from anywhere!"

"Oh, I don't know."

Mr. Brusiloff drew his chair closer.

"Let me tell you one vairy funny story about putting. It was one day I play in Nijni-Novgorod with the pro against Lenin and Trotsky, and Trotsky had a two-foot putt for the hole. But, just as he addresses the ball, someone in the crowd he tries to assassinate Lenin with a rewolver—you know that is our great national sport, trying to assassinate Lenin with rewolwers—and the bang puts Trotsky off his stroke and he goes five yards past the hole, and then Lenin, who is rather shaken, you understand, he misses again himself, and we win the hole and match and I clean up three hundred and ninety-six thousand rubles, or fifty cents in your money. Some gameovitch! And now let me tell you one other vairy funny story —"

Desultory conversation had begun in murmurs over the rest of the room, as the Wood Hills intellectuals politely endeavored to conceal the fact that they realized that they were about as much out of it at this reunion of twin souls as cats at a dog show. From time to time they started as Vladimir Brusiloff's laugh boomed out. Perhaps it was a consolation to them to know that he was enjoying himself.

As for Adeline, how shall I describe her emotions? She was stunned. Before her very eyes the stone which the builders had rejected had become the main thing, the hundred-to-one shot had walked away with the race. A rush of tender admiration for Cuthbert Banks flooded her heart. She saw that she had been all wrong. Cuthbert, whom she had always treated with a patronizing superiority, was really a man to be looked up to and worshipped. A deep, dreamy sigh shook Adeline's fragile form.

Half an hour later Vladimir and Cuthbert Banks rose.

"Goot-a-bye, Mrs. Smet-thirst," said the Celebrity. "Zank you for a most charming visit. My friend Cootaboot and me we go now to shoot a few holes. You will lend me clobs, friend Cootaboot?"

"Any you want."

"The niblicksky is what I use most. Goot-a-bye, Mrs. Smet-thirst."

They were moving to the door, when Cuthbert felt a light touch on his arm. Adeline was looking up at him tenderly.

"May I come, too, and walk round with you?"

Cuthbert's bosom heaved.

"Oh," he said, with a tremor in his voice, "that you would walk around with me for life!"

Her eyes met his.

"Perhaps," she whispered softly, "it could be arranged."

And so (concluded the Oldest Member), you see that golf can be of the greatest practical assistance to a man in Life's struggle. Raymond Parsloe Devine, who was no player, had to move out of the neighborhood immediately, and is now, I believe, writing scenarios out in California for the Flicker Film Company. Adeline is married to Cuthbert, and it was only his earnest pleading which prevented her from having their eldest son christened Francis Ouimet Ribbed-Faced Mashie Banks, for she is now as keen a devotee of the great game as her husband. Those who know them say that theirs is a union so devoted, so —

The Sage broke off abruptly, for the young man had rushed to the door and out into the passage. Through the open door he could hear him crying passionately to the waiter to bring back his clubs.

Mr. Frisbie

by

RING LARDNER

1929 — FROM *ROUND-UP*

I AM Mr. Allen Frisbie's chauffeur. Allen Frisbie is a name I made up because they tell me that if I used the real name of the man I am employed by that he might take offense and start trouble though I am sure he will never see what I am writing as he does not read anything except *The American Golfer,* but of course some of his friends might call his attention to it. If you knew who the real name of the man is, it would make more interesting reading as he is one of the 10 most wealthiest men in the United States and a man who everybody is interested in because he is so famous and the newspapers are always writing articles about him and sending high salary reporters to interview him but he is a very hard man to reproach or get an interview with and when they do he never tells them anything.

That is how I come to be writing this article because about two weeks ago a Mr. Kirk had an appointment to interview Mr. Frisbie for one of the newspapers and I drove him to the station after the interview was over and he said to me your boss is certainly a tough egg to interview and getting a word out of him is like pulling turnips.

"The public do not know anything about the man," said Mr. Kirk. "They know he is very rich and has got a wife and a son and a daughter and what their names are but as to his private life and his likes and dislikes he might just as well be a monk in a convent."

"The public knows he likes golf," I said.

"They do not know what kind of a game he plays."

"He plays pretty good," I said.

"How good?" said Mr. Kirk.

"About 88 or 90," I said.

"So is your grandmother," said Mr. Kirk.

He only meant the remark as a comparison but had either of my grandmothers lived they would both have been over 90. Mr. Kirk did not believe I was telling the truth about Mr. Frisbie's game and he was right though was I using real names I would not admit it as Mr. Frisbie is very sensitive in regards to his golf.

Mr. Kirk kept pumping at me but I am used to being pumped at and Mr. Kirk finally gave up pumping at me as he found me as closed mouth as Mr. Frisbie himself but he made the remark that he wished he was in my place for a few days and as close to the old man as I am and he would then be able to write the first real article which had ever been written about the old man. He called Mr. Frisbie the old man.

He said it was too bad I am not a writer so I could write up a few instance about Mr. Frisbie from the human side on account of being his caddy at golf and some paper or magazine would pay me big. He said if you would tell me a few instance I would write them up and split with you but I said no I could not think of anything which would make an article but after Mr. Kirk had gone I got to thinking it over and thought to myself maybe I could be a writer if I tried and at least there is no harm in trying so for the week after Mr. Kirk's visit I spent all my spare time writing down about Mr. Frisbie only at first I used his real name but when I showed the article they said for me not to use real names but the public would guess who it was anyway and that was just as good as using real names.

So I have gone over the writing again and

changed the name to Allen Frisbie and other changes and here is the article using Allen Frisbie.

When I say I am Mr. Frisbie's chauffeur I mean I am his personal chauffeur. There are two other chauffeurs who drive for the rest of the family and run errands. Had I nothing else to do only drive I might well be turned a man of leisure as Mr. Frisbie seldom never goes in to the city more than twice a week and even less oftener than that does he pay social visits.

His golf links is right on the place an easy walk from the house to the first tee and here is where he spends a good part of each and every day playing alone with myself in the roll of caddy. So one would not be far from amiss to refer to me as Mr. Frisbie's caddy rather than his chauffeur but it was as a chauffeur that I was engaged and can flatter myself that there are very few men of my calling who would not gladly exchange their salary and position for mine.

Mr. Frisbie is a man just this side of 60 years of age. Almost 10 years ago he retired from active business with money enough to put him in a class with the richest men in the United States and since then his investments have increased their value to such an extent so that now he is in a class with the richest men in the United States.

It was soon after his retirement that he bought the Peter Vischer estate near Westbury, Long Island. On this estate there was a 9 hole golf course in good condition and considered one of the best private 9 hole golf courses in the United States but Mr. Frisbie would have had it plowed up and the land used for some other usage only for a stroke of chance which was when Mrs. Frisbie's brother came over from England for a visit.

It was during while this brother-in-law was visiting Mr. Frisbie that I entered the last named employee and was an onlooker when Mr. Frisbie's brother-in-law persuaded his brother-in-law to try the game of golf. As luck would have it Mr. Frisbie's first drive was so good that his brother-in-law would not believe he was a new beginner till he had seen Mr. Frisbie shoot again but that first perfect drive made Mr. Frisbie a slave of the game and without which there would be no such instance as I am about to relate.

I would better explain at this junction that I am not a golfer but I have learned quite a lot of knowledge about the game by cadding for Mr. Frisbie and also once or twice in company with my employer have picked up some knowledge of the game by witnessing players like Bobby Jones and Hagen and Sarazen and Smith in some of their matches. I have only tried it myself on a very few occasions when I was sure Mr. Frisbie could not observe me and will confide that in my own mind I am convinced that with a little practise that I would have little trouble defeating Mr. Frisbie but will never seek to prove same for reasons which I will leave it to the reader to guess the reasons.

One day shortly after Mr. Frisbie's brother-in-law had ended his visit I was cadding for Mr. Frisbie and as had become my custom keeping the score for him when a question arose as to whether he had taken 7 or 8 strokes on the last hole. A 7 would have given him a total of 63 for the 9 holes while a 8 would have made it 64. Mr. Frisbie tried to recall the different strokes but was not certain and asked me to help him.

As I remembered it he had sliced his 4th. wooden shot in to a trap but had recovered well and got on to the green and then had taken 3 putts which would make him a 8 but by some slip of the tongue when I started to say 8 I said 7 and before I could correct myself Mr. Frisbie said yes you are right it was a 7.

"That is even 7s," said Mr. Frisbie.

"Yes," I said.

On the way back to the house he asked me what was my salary which I told him and he said well I think you are worth more than that and from now on you will get $25.00 more per week.

On another occasion when 9 more holes had been added to the course and Mr. Frisbie was playing the 18 holes regular every day he came to the last hole needing a 5 to break 112 which was his best score.

The 18th. hole is only 120 yards with a big green but a brook in front and traps in back of it. Mr. Frisbie got across the brook with his second but the ball went over in to the trap and it looked like bad business because Mr. Frisbie is even worse with a niblick than almost any other club except maybe the No. 3 and 4 irons and the wood.

Well I happened to get to the ball ahead of him and it laid there burred in the deep sand about a foot from a straight up and down bank 8 foot high where it would have been impossible for any man alive to oust it in one stroke but as luck would have it I stumbled and gave the ball a little kick and by chance it struck the side of the bank and stuck in the grass and Mr. Frisbie got it up on the green in one stroke and was down in 2 putts for his 5.

"Well that is my record 111 or 3 over 6s," he said.

Now my brother had a couple of tickets for the polo at Meadowbrook the next afternoon and I am a great lover of horses flesh so I said to Mr. Frisbie can I go to the polo tomorrow afternoon and he said certainly any time you want a afternoon off do not hesitate to ask me but a little while later there was a friend of mine going to get married at Atlantic City and Mr. Frisbie had just shot a 128 and broke his spoon besides and when I mentioned about going to Atlantic City for my friend's wedding he snapped at me like a wolf and said what did I think it was the xmas holidays.

Personally I am a man of simple tastes and few wants and it is very seldom when I am not satisfied to take my life and work as they come and not seek fear or favor but of course there are times in every man's life when they desire something a little out of the ordinary in the way of a little vacation or perhaps a financial accommodation of some kind and in such cases I have found Mr. Frisbie a king amongst men provide it one uses discretion in choosing the moment of their reproach but a variable tyrant if one uses bad judgment in choosing the moment of their reproach.

You can count on him granting any reasonable request just after he has made a good score or even a good shot where as a person seeking a favor when he is off his game might just as well ask President Coolidge to do the split.

I wish to state that having learned my lesson along these lines I did not use my knowledge to benefit myself alone but have on the other hand utilized same mostly to the advantage of others especially the members of Mr. Frisbie's own family. Mr. Frisbie's wife and son and daughter all realized early in my employment that I could handle Mr. Frisbie better than anyone else and without me ever exactly divulging the secret of my methods they just naturally began to take it for granted that I could succeed

with him where they failed and it became their habit when they sought something from their respective spouse and father to summons me as their adviser and advocate.

As an example of the above I will first sight an example in connection with Mrs. Frisbie. This occurred many years ago and was the instance which convinced her beyond all doubt that I was a expert on the subject of managing her husband.

Mrs. Frisbie is a great lover of music but unable to perform on any instrument herself. It was her hope that one of the children would be a pianiste and a great deal of money was spent on piano lessons for both Robert the son and Florence the daughter but all in vain as neither of the two showed any talent and their teachers one after another gave them up in despair.

Mrs. Frisbie at last became desirous of purchasing a player piano and of course would consider none but the best but when she brooched the subject to Mr. Frisbie he turned a deaf ear as he said pianos were made to be played by hand and people who could not learn same did not deserve music in the home.

I do not know how often Mr. and Mrs. Frisbie disgust the matter pro and con.

Personally they disgust it in my presence any number of times and finally being a great admirer of music myself and seeing no reason why a man of Mr. Frisbie's great wealth should deny his wife a harmless pleasure such as a player piano I suggested to the madam that possibly if she would leave matters to me the entire proposition might be put over. I can no more than fail I told her and I do not think I will fail so she instructed me to go ahead as I could not do worse than fail which she had already done herself.

I will relate the success of my plan as briefly as possible. Between the house and the golf course there was a summer house in which Mrs. Frisbie sat reading while Mr. Frisbie played golf. In this summer house she could sit so as not to be visible from the golf course. She was to sit there till she heard me whistle the strains of "Over There" where at she was to appear on the scene like she had come direct from the house and the fruits of our scheme would then be known.

For two days Mrs. Frisbie had to console herself with her book as Mr. Frisbie's golf was terrible and there was no moment when I felt like it would not be courting disaster to summons her on the scene but during the 3rd. afternoon his game suddenly improved and he had shot the 1st. 9 holes in 53 and started out on the 10th. with a pretty drive when I realized the time had come.

Mrs. Frisbie appeared promptly in answer to my whistling and walked rapidly up to Mr. Frisbie like she had hurried from the house and said there is a man at the house from that player piano company and he says he will take $50.00 off the price if I order today and please let me order one as I want one so much.

"Why certainly dear go ahead and get it dear," said Mr. Frisbie and that is the way Mrs. Frisbie got her way in regards to a player piano. Had I not whistled when I did but waited a little longer it would have spelt ruination to our schemes as Mr. Frisbie took a 12 on the 11th. hole and would have bashed his wife over the head with a No. 1 iron had she even asked him for a toy drum.

I have been of assistance to young Mr. Robert Frisbie the son with reference to several items of which I will only take time to touch on one item with reference to Mr. Robert wanting to drive a car. Before Mr. Robert was 16 years of age he was always after Mr. Frisbie to allow him to drive one of the cars and Mr. Frisbie always said him nay on the grounds that it is against the law for a person under 16 years of age to drive a car.

When Mr. Robert reached the age of 16 years old however this excuse no longer held good and yet Mr. Frisbie continued to say Mr. Robert nay in regards to driving a car. There is plenty of chauffeurs at your beckon call said Mr. Frisbie to drive you where ever and when ever you wish to go but of course Mr. Robert like all youngsters wanted to drive himself and personally I could see no harm in it as I personally could not drive for him and the other 2 chauffeurs in Mr. Frisbie's employee at the time were just as lightly to wreck a car as Mr. Robert so I promised Mr. Robert that I would do my best towards helping him towards obtaining permission to drive one of the cars.

"Leave it to me" was my bequest to Mr. Robert and sure enough my little strategy turned the trick though Mr. Robert did not have the patience like his mother to wait in the summer house till a favorable moment arrived so it was necessary for me to carry through the entire proposition by myself.

The 16th. hole on our course is perhaps the most difficult hole on our course at least it has always been a variable tartar for Mr. Frisbie.

It is about 350 yards long in lenth and it is what is called a blind hole as you can not see the green from the tee as you drive from the tee up over a hill with a direction flag as the only guide and down at the bottom of the hill there is a brook a little over 225 yards from the tee which is the same brook which you come to again on the last hole and in all the times Mr. Frisbie has played around the course he has seldom never made this 16th. hole in less than 7 strokes or more as his tee shot just barely skins the top of the hill giving him a down hill lie which upsets him so that he will miss the 2d. shot entirely or top it and go in to the brook.

Well I generally always stand up on top of the hill to watch where his tee shot goes and on the occasion referred to he got a pretty good tee shot which struck on top of the hill and rolled half way down and I hurried to the ball before he could see me and I picked it up and threw it across the brook and when he climbed to the top of the hill I pointed to where the ball laid the other side of the brook and shouted good shot Mr. Frisbie. He was overjoyed and beamed with joy and did not suspect anything out of the way though in reality he could not hit a ball more than 60 yards if it was teed on the summit of Pike's Peak.

Fate was on my side at this junction and Mr. Frisbie hit a perfect mashie shot on to the green and sunk his 2d. putt for the only 4 of his career on this hole. He was almost delirious with joy and you may be sure I took advantage of the situation and before we were fairly off the green I said to him Mr. Frisbie if you do not need me tomorrow morning do you not think it would be a good time for me to learn Mr. Robert to drive a car.

"Why certainly he is old enough now to drive a car and it is time he learned."

I now come to the main instance of my article which is in regards to Miss Florence Frisbie who is now Mrs. Henry Craig and of course Craig is not the real name but you will soon see that what I was able to do for her was no such childs play like gaining consent for Mr. Robert to run a automobile or Mrs. Frisbie to purchase a player piano but this was a matter of the up most importance and I am sure the reader will not consider me a vain bragger when I claim that I handled it with some skill.

Miss Florence is a very pretty and handsome girl who has always had a host of suiters who paid court to her on account of being pretty as much as her great wealth and I believe there has been times when no less than half a dozen or more young men were paying court to her at one time. Well about 2 years ago she lost her heart to young Henry Craig and at the same time Mr. Frisbie told her in no uncertain turns that she must throw young Craig over board and marry his own choice young Junior Holt or he would cut her off without a dime.

Holt and Craig are not the real names of the two young men referred to though I am using their real first names namely Junior and Henry. Young Holt is a son of Mr. Frisbie's former partner in business and a young man who does not drink or smoke and has got plenty of money in his own rights and a young man who any father would feel safe in trusting their daughter in the bands of matrimony. Young Craig at that time had no money and no position and his parents had both died leaving nothing but debts.

"Craig is just a tramp and will never amount to anything," said Mr. Frisbie. "I have had inquiries made and I understand he drinks when anyone will furnish him the drinks. He has never worked and never will. Junior Holt is a model young man from all accounts and comes of good stock and is the only young man I know whose conduct and habits are such that I would consider him fit to marry my daughter."

Miss Florence said that Craig was not a tramp and she loved him and would not marry anyone else and as for Holt he was terrible but even if he was not terrible she would never consider undergoing the bands of matrimony with a man named Junior.

"I will elope with Henry if you do not give in," she said.

Mr. Frisbie was not alarmed by this threat as Miss Florence has a little common sense and would not be lightly to elope with a young man who could hardly finance a honeymoon trip on the subway. But neither was she showing any signs of yielding in regards to his wishes in regards to young Holt and things began to take on the appearance of a dead lock between father and daughter with neither side showing signs of yielding.

Miss Florence grew pale and thin and spent most of her time in her room instead of seeking enjoyment amongst her friends as was her custom. As for Mr. Frisbie he was always a man of iron will and things began to take on the appearance of a dead lock with neither side showing any signs of yielding.

It was when it looked like Miss Florence was on the verge of a serious illness when Mrs. Frisbie came to me and said we all realize that you have more influence with Mr. Frisbie than anyone else and is there any way you can think of to get him to change his status towards Florence and these 2 young men because if something is not done right away I am afraid of what will happen. Miss Florence likes you and has a great deal of confidence in you said Mrs. Frisbie so will you see her and talk matters over with her and see if you can not think up some plan between you which will put a end to this situation before my poor little girl dies.

So I went to see Miss Florence in her bedroom and she was a sad sight with her eyes red from weeping and so pale and thin and yet her face lit up with a smile when I entered the room and she shook hands with me like I was a long lost friend.

"I asked my mother to send you," said Miss Florence. "This case looks hopeless but I know you are a great fixer as far as Father is concerned and you can fix it if anyone can. Now I have got a idea which I will tell you and if you like it it will be up to you to carry it out."

"What is your idea?"

"Well," said Miss Florence, "I think that if Mr. Craig the man I love could do Father a favor why Father would not be so set against him."

"What kind of a favor?"

"Well Mr. Craig plays a very good game of golf and he might give Father some pointers which would improve Father's game."

"Your father will not play golf with anyone and certainly not with a good player and besides that your father is not the kind of a man that wants anyone giving him pointers. Personally I would just as leaf go up and tickle him as tell him that his stance is wrong."

"Then I guess my idea is not so good."

"No," I said and then all of a sudden I had a idea of my own. "Listen Miss Florence does the other one play golf?"

"Who?"

"Young Junior Holt."

"Even better than Mr. Craig."

"Does your father know that?"

"Father does not know anything about him or he would not like him so well."

Well I said I have got a scheme which may work or may not work but no harm to try and the first thing to be done is for you to spruce up and pretend like you do not feel so unkindly towards young Holt after all. The next thing is to tell your father that Mr. Holt never played golf and never even saw it played but would like to watch your father play so he can get the hang of the game.

And then after that you must get Mr. Holt to ask your father to let him follow him around the course and very secretly you must tip Mr. Holt off that your father wants his advice. When ever your father does anything wrong Mr. Holt is to correct him. Tell him your father is crazy to improve his golf but is shy in regards to asking for help.

There is a lot of things that may happen to this scheme but if it should go through why I will guarantee that at least half your troubles will be over.

Well as I said there was a lot of things that might have happened to spoil my scheme but nothing did happen and the very next afternoon Mr. Frisbie confided in me that Miss Florence seemed to feel much better and seemed to have changed her mind in regards to Mr. Holt and also said that the last named had expressed a desire to follow Mr. Frisbie around the golf course and learn something about the game.

Mr. Holt was a kind of a fat pudgy young man with a kind of a sneering smile and the first minute I saw him I wished him the worst.

For a second before Mr. Frisbie started to play I was certain we were lost as Mr. Frisbie remarked where have you been keeping yourself Junior that you never watched golf before. But luckily young Holt took the remark as a joke and made no reply. Right afterwards the storm clouds began to gather in the sky. Mr. Frisbie sliced his tee shot.

"Mr. Frisbie," said young Holt, "there are several things the matter with you then but the main trouble was that you stood too close to the ball and cut across it with your club head and besides that you swang back faster than Alex Smith and you were off your balance and you gripped too hard and you jerked instead of hitting with a smooth follow through."

Well, Mr. Frisbie gave him a queer look and then made up his mind that Junior was trying to be humorous and he frowned at him so as he would not try it again but when we located the ball in the rough and Mr. Frisbie asked me for his spoon young Holt said Oh take your mashie Mr. Frisbie never use a wooden club in a place like that and Mr. Frisbie scowled and mumbled under his breath and missed the ball with his spoon and missed it again and then took a midiron and just dribbled it on to the fairway and finally got on the green in 7 and took 3 putts.

I suppose you might say that this was one of the quickest golf matches on record as it ended on the 2d. tee. Mr. Frisbie tried to drive and sliced again. Then young Holt took a ball from my pocket and a club from the bag and said here let me show you the swing and drove the ball 250 yards straight down the middle of the course.

I looked at Mr. Frisbie's face and it was puffed out and a kind of a purple black color. Then he burst and I will only repeat a few of the more friendlier of his remarks.

"Get to hell and gone of my place. Do not never darken my doors again. Just show up around here one more time and I will blow out what you have got instead of brains. You lied to my girl and you tried to make a fool out of me. Get out before I sick my dogs on you and tear you to pieces."

Junior most lightly wanted to offer some word of explanation or to demand one on his own account but saw at a glance how useless same would be. I heard later that he saw Miss Florence and that she just laughed at him.

"I made a mistake about Junior Holt," said Mr. Frisbie that evening. "He is no good and must never come to this house again."

"Oh Father and just when I was beginning to like him," said Miss Florence.

Well like him or not like him she and the other young man Henry Craig were married soon afterwards which I suppose Mr. Frisbie permitted the bands in the hopes that same would rile Junior Holt.

Mr. Frisbie admitted he had made a mistake in regards to the last named but he certainly was not mistaken when he said that young Craig was a tramp and would never amount to anything.

Well I guess I have rambled on long enough about Mr. Frisbie.

The Sweet Shot

by

E. C. BENTLEY

1938 — FROM *TRENT'S CASE BOOK*

"No, I HAPPENED TO BE abroad at the time," Philip Trent said. "I wasn't in the way of seeing the English papers, so until I came here this week I never heard anything about your mystery."

Captain Royden, a small, spare, brown-faced man, was engaged in the delicate—and forbidden—task of taking his automatic telephone instrument to pieces. He now suspended his labors and reached for the tobacco jar. The large window of his office in the Kempshill clubhouse looked down upon the eighteenth green of that delectable golf course, and his eye roved over the whin-clad slopes beyond as he called on his recollection.

"Well, if you call it a mystery," he said as he filled a pipe. "Some people do, because they like mysteries, I suppose. For instance, Colin Hunt, the man you're staying with, calls it that. Others won't have it, and say there was a perfectly natural explanation. I could tell you as much as anybody could about it, I dare say."

"As being secretary here, you mean?"

"Not only that. I was one of the two people who were in at the death, so to speak—or next door to it," Captain Royden said. He limped to the mantelshelf and took down a silver box embossed on the lid with the crest and mottoes of the Corps of Royal Engineers. "Try one of the cigarettes, Mr. Trent. If you'd like to hear the yarn, I'll give it you. You have heard something about Arthur Freer, I suppose?"

"Hardly anything," Trent said. "I just gathered that he wasn't a very popular character."

"No," Captain Royden said with reserve. "Did they tell you he was my brother-in-law? No? Well, now, it happened about four months ago, on a Monday—let me see—yes, the second Monday in May. Freer had a habit of playing nine holes before breakfast. Barring Sundays—he was strict about Sunday—he did it most days, even in the beastliest weather, going round all alone usually, carrying his own clubs, studying every shot as if his life depended on it. That helped to make him the very good player he was. His handicap here was two, and at Undershaw he used to be scratch, I believe.

"At a quarter to eight he'd be on the first tee, and by nine he'd be back at his house—it's only a few minutes from here. That Monday morning he started off as usual—"

"And at the usual time?"

"Just about. He had spent a few minutes in the clubhouse blowing up the steward about some trifle. And that was the last time he was seen alive by anybody—near enough to speak to, that is. No one else went off the first tee until a little after nine, when I started round with Browson—he's our local padre; I had been having breakfast with him at the vicarage. He's got a game leg, like me, so

17

we often play together when he can fit it in.

"We had holed out on the first green, and were walking on to the next tee, when Browson said, 'Great Scott! Look there. Something's happened.' He pointed down the fairway of the second hole; and there we could see a man lying sprawled on the turf, face down and motionless. Now there is this point about the second hole—the first half of it is in a dip in the land, just deep enough to be out of sight from any other point on the course, unless you're standing right above it—you'll see when you go round yourself. Well, on the tee, you *are* right above it; and we saw this man lying there. We ran to the spot.

"It was Freer, as I had known it must be at that hour. He was dead, lying in a disjointed sort of way no live man could have lain in. His clothing was torn to ribbons, and it was singed too. So was his hair—he used to play bareheaded—and his face and hands. His bag of clubs was lying a few yards away, and the brassie, which he had just been using, was close by the body.

"There wasn't any wound showing, and I had seen far worse things often enough, but the padre was looking sickish, so I asked him to go back to the clubhouse and send for a doctor and the police while I mounted guard. They weren't long coming, and after they had done their job the body was taken away in an ambulance. Well, that's about all I can tell you at first hand, Mr. Trent. If you are staying with Hunt, you'll have heard about the inquest and all that, probably."

Trent shook his head. "No," he said. "Colin was just beginning to tell me, after breakfast this morning, about Freer having been killed on the course in some incomprehensible way, when a man came to see him about something. So, as I was going to apply for a fortnight's run of the course, I thought I would ask you about the affair."

"All right," Captain Royden said. "I can tell you about the inquest anyhow—had to be there to speak my own little piece, about finding the body. As for what had happened to Freer, the medical evidence was rather confusing. It was agreed that he had been killed by some tremendous shock, which had jolted his whole system to pieces and dislocated several joints, but had been not quite violent enough to cause any visible wound. Apart

from that, there was a disagreement. Freer's own doctor, who saw the body first, declared he must have been struck by lightning. He said it was true there hadn't been a thunder storm, but that there had been thunder about all that week-end, and that sometimes lightning did act in that way. But the police surgeon, Collins, said there would be no such displacement of the organs from a lightning stroke, even if it did ever happen that way in our climate, which he doubted. And he said that if it had been lightning, it would have struck the steel-headed clubs; but the clubs lay there in their bag quite undamaged. Collins thought there must have been some kind of explosion, though he couldn't suggest what kind."

Trent shook his head. "I don't suppose that impressed the court," he said. "All the same, it may have been all the honest opinion he could give." He smoked in silence a few moments, while Captain Royden attended to the troubles of his telephone instrument with a camel-hair brush. "But surely," Trent said at length, "if there had been such an explosion somebody would have heard the sound of it."

"Lots of people would have heard it," Captain Royden answered. "But there you are, you see—nobody notices the sound of explosions just about here. There's the quarry on the other side of the road there, and any time after 7:00 A.M. there's liable to be a noise of blasting."

"A dull, sickening thud?"

"Jolly sickening," Captain Royden said, "for all of us living near by. And so that point wasn't raised. Well, Collins is a very sound man; but as you say, his evidence didn't really explain the thing, and the other fellow's did, whether it was right or wrong. Besides, the coroner and the jury had heard about a bolt from a clear sky, and the notion appealed to them. Anyhow, they brought it in death from misadventure."

"Which nobody could deny, as the song says," Trent remarked. "And was there no other evidence?"

"Yes; some. But Hunt can tell you about it as well as I can; he was there. I shall have to ask you to excuse me now," Captain Royden said. "I have an appointment in the town. The steward will sign you on for a fortnight, and probably get you a game too, if you want one today."

Colin Hunt and his wife, when Trent returned to their house for luncheon, were very willing to complete the tale. The verdict, they declared, was tripe. Dr. Collins knew his job, whereas Dr. Hoyle was an old footler, and Freer's death had never been reasonably explained.

As for the other evidence, it had, they agreed, been interesting, though it didn't help at all. Freer had been seen after he had played his tee-shot at the second hole, when he was walking down to the bottom of the dip towards the spot where he had met his death.

"But according to Royden," Trent said, "that was a place where he couldn't be seen, unless one was right above him."

"Well, this witness *was* right above him," Hunt rejoined. "Over one thousand feet above him, so he said. He was an R.A.F. man, piloting a bomber from Bexford Camp, not far from here. He was up doing some sort of exercise, and passed over the course just at that time. He didn't know Freer, but he spotted a man walking down from the second tee, because he was the only living soul visible on the course. Gossett, the other man in the plane, is a temporary member here, and he did know Freer quite well—or as well as anybody cared to know him—but he never saw him. However, the pilot was quite clear that he saw a man just at the time in question, and they took his evidence so as to prove that Freer was absolutely alone just before his death. The only other person who saw Freer was another man who knew him well; used to be a caddie here, and then got a job at the quarry. He was at work on the hillside, and he watched Freer play the first hole and go on to the second—nobody with him, of course."

"Well, that was pretty well established then," Trent remarked. "He was about as alone as he could be, it seems. Yet something happened somehow."

Mrs. Hunt sniffed skeptically, and lighted a cigarette. "Yes, it did," she said. "However, I didn't worry much about it, for one. Edith—Mrs. Freer, that is: Royden's sister—must have had a terrible life of it with a man like that. Not that she ever said anything—she wouldn't. She is not that sort."

"She is a jolly good sort, anyhow," Hunt declared.

"Yes, she is; too good for most men. I can tell you," Mrs. Hunt added for the benefit of Trent, "if Colin ever took to cursing me and knocking me about, my well-known loyalty wouldn't stand the strain for very long."

"That's why I don't do it. It's the fear of exposure that makes me the perfect husband, Phil. She would tie a can to me before I knew what was happening. As for Edith, it's true she never said anything, but the change in her since it happened tells the story well enough. Since she's been living with her brother she has been looking far better and happier than she ever succeeded in doing while Freer was alive."

"She won't be living with him for very long, I dare say," Mrs. Hunt intimated darkly.

"No. I'd marry her myself if I had the chance," Hunt agreed cordially.

"Pooh! You wouldn't be in the first six," his wife said. "It will be Rennie, or Gossett, or possibly Sandy Butler—you'll see. But perhaps you've had enough of the local tittle-tattle, Phil. Did you fix up a game for this afternoon?"

"Yes; with the Jarman Professor of Chemistry in the University of Cambridge," Trent said. "He looked at me as if he thought a bath of vitriol would do me good, but he agreed to play me."

"You've got a tough job," Hunt observed. "I believe he is almost as old as he looks, but he is a devil at the short game, and he knows the course blindfold, which you don't. And he isn't so cantankerous as he pretends to be. By the way, he was the man who saw the finish of the last shot Freer ever played—a sweet shot if ever there was one. Get him to tell you."

"I shall try to," Trent said. "The steward told me about that, and that was why I asked the professor for a game."

*   *   *

Colin Hunt's prediction was fulfilled that afternoon. Professor Hyde, receiving five strokes, was one up at the seventeenth, and at the last hole sent down a four-foot putt to win the match. As they left the green he remarked, as if in answer to something Trent had that moment said, "Yes; I can tell you a curious circumstance about Freer's death."

Trent's eye brightened; for the professor had not said a dozen words during their game, and Trent's tentative allusion to the subject after the second hole had been met merely by an intimidating grunt.

"I saw the finish of the last shot he played," the old gentleman went on, "without seeing the man himself at all. A lovely brassie it was, too—though lucky. Rolled to within two feet of the pin."

Trent considered. "I see," he said, "what you mean. You were near the second green, and the ball came over the ridge and ran down to the hole."

"Just so," Professor Hyde said. "That's how you play it—if you can. You might have done it yourself today, if your second shot had been thirty yards longer. I've never done it; but Freer often did. After a really good drive you play a long second, blind, over the ridge; and with a perfect shot, you may get the green. Well, my house is quite near that green. I was pottering about in the garden before breakfast, and just as I happened to be looking towards the green a ball came hopping down the slope and trickled right across to the hole. Of course, I knew whose it must be—Freer always came along about that time. If it had been anyone else, I'd have waited to see him get his three, and congratulate him. As it was, I went indoors, and didn't hear of his death until long afterwards."

"And you never saw him play the shot?" Trent said thoughtfully.

The professor turned a choleric blue eye on him. "How the deuce could I?" he said huffily. "I can't see through a mass of solid earth."

"I know, I know," Trent said. "I was only trying to follow your mental process. Without seeing him play the shot, you knew it was his second—you say he would have been putting for a three. And you said, too—didn't you—that it was a brassie shot."

"Simply because, my young friend"—the professor was severe—"I happened to know the man's game. I had played that nine holes with him before breakfast often, until one day he lost his temper more than usual, and made himself impossible. I knew he practically always carried the ridge with his second—I won't say he always got the green—and his brassie was the only club that would do it.

It is conceivable, I admit," Professor Hyde added a little stiffly, "that some mishap took place and that shot in question was not actually Freer's second; but it did not occur to me to allow for that highly speculative contingency."

On the next day, after those playing a morning round were started on their perambulation, Trent indulged himself with an hour's practice, mainly on the unsurveyed stretch of the second hole. Afterwards he had a word with the caddie-master; then visited the professional's shop, and won the regard of that expert by furnishing himself with a new mid-iron. Soon he brought up the subject of the last shot played by Arthur Freer. A dozen times that morning, he said, he had tried, after a satisfying drive, to reach the green with his second; but in vain. Fergus MacAdam shook his head. Not many, he said, could strike the ball with yon force. He could get there himself, whiles, but never for certainty. Mr. Freer had the strength, and he kenned how to use it forbye.

What sort of clubs, Trent asked, had Freer preferred? "Lang and heavy, like himsel'. Noo ye mention it," MacAdam said, "I hae them here. They were brocht here after the ahccident." He reached up to the top of a rack. "Ay, here they are. They shouldna be, of course; but naebody came to claim them, and it juist slippit ma mind."

Trent, extracting the brassie, looked thoughtfully at the heavy head with the strip of hard white material inlaid in the face. "It's a powerful weapon, sure enough," he remarked.

"Ay, for a man that could control it," MacAdam said. "I dinna care for yon ivorine face mysel'. Some fowk think it gies mair reseelience, ye ken; but there's naething in it."

"He didn't get it from you, then," Trent suggested, still closely examining the head.

"Ay, but he did. I had a lot down from Nelsons while the fashion for them was on. Ye'll find my name," MacAdam added, "stampit on the wood in the usual place, if yer een are seein' right."

"Well, I don't—that's just it. The stamp is quite illegible."

"Tod! Let's see," the professional said, taking the club in hand. "Guid reason for its being illegible," he went on after a brief scrutiny. "It's been obleeterated—that's easy seen.

Who ever saw sic a daft-like thing! The wood has juist been crushed some gait—in a vise, I wouldna wonder. Noo, why would onybody want to dae a thing like yon?"

"Unaccountable, isn't it?" Trent said. "Still, it doesn't matter, I suppose. And anyhow, we shall never know."

It was twelve days later that Trent, looking in at the open door of the secretary's office, saw Captain Royden happily engaged with the separated parts of some mechanism in which coils of wire appeared to be the leading motive.

"I see you're busy," Trent said.

"Come in! Come in!" Royden said heartily. "I can do this any time—another hour's work will finish it." He laid down a pair of sharp-nosed pliers. "The electricity people have just changed us over to A.C., and I've got to re-wind the motor of our vacuum cleaner. Beastly nuisance," he added, looking down affectionately at the bewildering jumble of disarticulated apparatus on his table.

"You bear your sorrow like a man," Trent remarked; and Royden laughed as he wiped his hands on a towel.

"Yes," he said, "I do love tinkering about with mechanical jobs, and if I do say it my-self, I'd rather do a thing like this with my own hands than risk having it faultily done by a careless workman. Too many of them about. Why, about a year ago the company sent a man here to fit a new main fuse box, and he made a short-circuit with his screw-driver that knocked him right across the kitch-en and might very well have killed him." He reached down his cigarette box and offered it to Trent, who helped himself; then looked down thoughtfully at the device on the lid.

"Thanks very much. When I saw this box before, I put you down for an R.E. man. *Ubique*, and *Quo fas et gloria ducunt*. H'm! I wonder why Engineers were given that motto in particular."

"Lord knows," the captain said. "In my experience, Sappers don't exactly go where right and glory lead. The dirtiest of all the jobs and precious little of the glory—that's what they get."

"Still, they have the consolation," Trent pointed out, "of feeling that they are at home in a scientific age, and that all the rest of the Army are amateurs compared with them. That's what one of them once told me, any-how. Well now, Captain, I have to be off this evening. I've looked in just to say how much I've enjoyed myself here."

"Very glad you did," Captain Royden said. "You'll come again, I hope, now you know that the golf here is not so bad."

"I like it immensely. Also the members. And the secretary." Trent paused to light his ciga-rette. "I found the mystery rather interest-ing, too."

Captain Royden's eyebrows lifted slightly. "You mean about Freer's death? So you made up your mind it *was* a mystery."

"Why, yes," Trent said. "Because I made up my mind he had been killed by somebody, and probably killed intentionally. Then, when I had looked into the thing a little, I washed out the 'probably.'"

Captain Royden took up a penknife from his desk and began mechanically to sharpen a pencil. "So you don't agree with the coroner's jury?"

"No: as the verdict seems to have been meant to rule out murder or any sort of human agency, I don't. The lightning idea, which apparently satisfied them, or some of them, was not a very bright one, I thought. I was told what Dr. Collins had said against it at the inquest; and it seemed to me he had disposed of it completely when he said that Freer's clubs, most of them steel ones, were quite undamaged. A man carrying his clubs puts them down, when he plays a shot, a few feet away at most; yet Freer was supposed to have been electrocuted without any notice having been taken of them, so to speak."

"H'm! No, it doesn't seem likely. I don't know that that quite decides the point, though," the captain said. "Lightning plays funny tricks, you know. I've seen a small tree struck when it was surrounded by trees twice the size. All the same, I quite agree there didn't seem to be any sense in the lightning notion. It was thundery weather, but there wasn't any storm that morning in this neigh-borhood."

"Just so. But when I considered what had been said about Freer's clubs, it suddenly oc-curred to me that nobody had said anything about *the* club, so far as my information about the inquest went. It seemed clear, from what you and the parson saw, that he had just played a shot with his brassie when he was struck down; it was lying near him, not in the bag. Besides, old Hyde actually saw the ball he had hit roll down the slope onto the green. Now, it's a good rule to study every little detail when you are on a problem of this kind. There weren't many left to study, of course, since the thing had happened four months before; but I knew Freer's clubs must be somewhere, and I thought of one or two places where they were likely to have been taken, in the circumstances, so I tried them. First, I reconnoitred the caddie-master's shed, asking if I could leave my bag there for a day or two; but I was told that the regular place to leave them was the pro's shop. So I went and had a chat with MacAdam, and sure enough it soon came out that Freer's bag was still in his rack. I had a look at the clubs, too."

"And did you notice anything peculiar about them?" Captain Royden asked.

"Just one little thing. But it was enough to set me thinking, and next day I drove up to London, where I paid a visit to Nelsons, the sporting outfitters. You know the firm, of course."

Captain Royden, carefully fining down the point of his pencil, nodded. "Everybody knows Nelsons."

"Yes; and MacAdam, I knew, had an account there for his stocks. I wanted to look over some clubs of a particular make—a brassie, with a slip of ivorine let into the face, such as they had supplied to MacAdam. Freer had purchased one of them from him."

Again Royden nodded.

"I saw the man who shows clubs at Nelsons. We had a talk, and then—you know how little things come out in the course of conversation—"

"Especially," put in the captain with a cheerful grin, "when the conversation is being steered by an expert."

"You flatter me," Trent said. "Anyhow, it did transpire that a club of that particular make had been bought some months before by a customer whom the man was able to remember. Why he remembered him was because, in the first place, he insisted on a club of rather unusual length and weight—much too long and heavy for himself to use, as he

was neither a tall man nor of powerful build. The salesman had suggested as much in a delicate way; but the customer said no, he knew exactly what suited him, and he bought the club and took it away with him."

"Rather an ass, I should say," Royden observed thoughtfully.

"I don't think he was an ass, really. He was capable of making a mistake, though, like the rest of us. There were some other things, by the way, that the salesman recalled about him. He had a slight limp, and he was, or had been, an Army officer. The salesman was an ex-Service man, and he couldn't be mistaken, he said, about that."

Captain Royden had drawn a sheet of paper towards him, and was slowly drawing little geometrical figures as he listened. "Go on, Mr. Trent," he said quietly.

"Well, to come back to the subject of Freer's death. I think he was killed by someone who knew Freer never played on Sunday, so that his clubs would be—or ought to be, shall we say?—in his locker all that day. All the following night, too, of course—in case the job took a long time. And I think this man was in a position to have access to the lockers in this clubhouse at any time he chose, and to possess a master key to those lockers. I think he was a skillful amateur craftsman. I think he had a good practical knowledge of high explosives. There is a branch of the Army"—Trent paused a moment and looked at the cigarette box on the table—"in which that sort of knowledge is specially necessary, I believe."

Hastily, as if just reminded of the duty of hospitality, Royden lifted the lid of the box and pushed it towards Trent. "Do have another," he urged.

Trent did so with thanks. "They have to have it in the Royal Engineers," he went on, "because—so I'm told—demolition work is an important part of their job."

"Quite right," Captain Royden observed, delicately shading one side of a cube.

"*Ubique!*" Trent mused, staring at the box-lid. "If you are 'everywhere,' I take it you can can be in two places at the same time. You could kill a man in one place, and at the same time be having breakfast with a friend a mile away. Well, to return to our subject yet once more; you can see the kind of idea I was led to form about what happened to Freer. I believe that his brassie was taken from his locker on the Sunday before his death. I believe the ivorine face of it was taken off and a cavity hollowed out behind it; and in that cavity a charge of explosive was placed. Where it came from I don't know, for it isn't the sort of thing that is easy to come by, I imagine."

"Oh, there would be no difficulty about that," the captain remarked. "If this man you're speaking of knew all about H.E., as you say, he could have compounded the stuff himself from materials anybody can buy. For instance, he could easily make tetranitroaniline—that would be just the thing for him, I should say."

"I see. Then perhaps there would be a tiny detonator attached to the inner side of the ivorine face, so that a good smack with the brassie would set it off. Then the face would be fixed on again. It would be a delicate job, because the weight of the clubhead would have to be exactly right. The feel and balance of the club would have to be just the same as before the operation."

"A delicate job, yes," the captain agreed. "But not an impossible one. There would be rather more to it than you say, as a matter of fact; the face would have to be shaved down thin, for instance. Still, it could be done."

"Well, I imagine it done. Now, this man I have in mind knew there was no work for a brassie at the short first hole, and that the first time it would come out of the bag was at the second hole, down at the bottom of the dip, where no one could see what happened. What certainly did happen was that Freer played a sweet shot, slap on to the green. What else happened at the same moment we don't know for certain, but we can make a reasonable guess. And then, of course, there's the question what happened to the club—or what was left of it; the handle, say. But it isn't a difficult question, I think, if we

remember how the body was found."

"How do you mean?" Royden asked.

"I mean, by whom it was found. One of the two players who found it was too much upset to notice very much. He hurried back to the clubhouse; and the other was left alone with the body for, as I estimate it, at least fifteen minutes. When the police came on the scene, they found lying near the body a perfectly good brassie, an unusually long and heavy club, exactly like Freer's brassie in every respect—except one. The name stamped on the wood of the clubhead had been obliterated by crushing. That name, I think, was not F. Mac-Adam but W. J. Nelson; and the club had been taken out of a bag that was not Freer's —a bag which had the remains, if any, of Freer's brassie at the bottom of it. And I believe that's all." Trent got to his feet and stretched his arms. "You can see what I meant when I said I found the mystery interesting."

For some moments Captain Royden gazed thoughtfully out of the window; then he met Trent's inquiring eye. "If there was such a fellow as you imagine," he said coolly, "he seems to have been careful enough—lucky enough too, if you like—to leave nothing at all of what you could call proof against him. And probably he had personal and private reasons for what he did. Suppose that somebody whom he was much attached to was in the power of a foul-tempered, bullying brute; and suppose he found that the bullying had gone to the length of physical violence; and suppose that the situation was hell by day and by night to this man of yours; and suppose there was no way on earth of putting an end to it except the way he took. Yes, Mr. Trent; suppose all that!"

"I will—I do!" Trent said. "That man—if he exists at all—must have been driven pretty hard, and what he did is no business of mine anyway. And now—still in the conditional mood —suppose I take myself off."

The Ooley-Cow

by

CHARLES E. VAN LOAN

1918 — FROM *FORE!*

AFTER THE EXPLANATION, and before Uncle Billy Poindexter and Old Man Sprott had been able to decide just what had hit them, Little Doc Ellis had the nerve to tell me that he had seen the fuse burning for months and months. Little Doc is my friend and I like him, but he resembles many other members of his profession in that he is usually wisest after the post mortem, when it is a wee bit late for the high contracting party.

And at all times Little Doc is full of vintage bromides and figures of speech.

"You have heard the old saw," said he. "A worm will turn if you keep picking on him, and so will a straight road if you ride it long enough. A camel is a wonderful burden bearer, but even a double-humped ship of the desert will sink on your hands if you pile the load on him a bale of hay at a time."

"A worm, a straight road, a camel and a sinking ship," said I. "Whither are we drifting?"

Little Doc did not pay any attention to me. It is a way he has.

"Think," said he, "how much longer a camel will stand up under punishment if he gets his load straw by straw, as it were. The Ooley-cow was a good thing, but Uncle Billy and Old Man Sprott did not use any judgment. They piled it on him too thick."

"Meaning," I asked, "to compare the Ooley-cow with a camel?"

"Merely a figure of speech," said Little Doc; "but yes, such was my intention."

"Well," said I, "your figures of speech need careful auditing. A camel can go eight days without a drink—"

Little Doc made impatient motions at me with both hands. He has no sense of humor, and his mind is a one-way track, totally devoid of spurs and derailing switches. Once started, he must go straight through to his destination.

"What I am trying to make plain to your limited mentality," said he, "is that Uncle Billy and Old Man Sprott needed a lesson in conservation, and they got it. The Ooley-cow was the easiest, softest picking that ever strayed from the home pasture. With care and decent treatment he would have lasted a long time and yielded an enormous quantity of nourishment, but Uncle Billy and Old Man Sprott were too greedy. They tried to corner the milk market, and now they will have to sign tags for their drinks and their golf balls the same as the rest of us. They have killed the goose that laid the golden eggs."

"A minute ago," said I, "the Ooley-cow was a camel. Now he is a goose—a dead goose, to be exact. Are you all done figuring with your speech?"

"Practically so, yes."

"Then," said I, "I will plaster up the cracks in your argument with the cement of information. I can use figures of speech myself. You

24

are barking up the wrong tree. You are away off your base. It wasn't the loss of a few dollars that made Mr. Perkins run wild in our midst. It was the manner in which he lost them. Let us now dismiss the worm, the camel, the goose and all the rest of the menagerie, retaining only the Ooley-cow. What do you know about cows, if anything?"

"A little," answered my medical friend.

"A mighty little. You know that a cow has hoofs, horns and a tail. The same description would apply to many creatures, including Satan himself. Your knowledge of cows is largely academic. Now me, I was raised on a farm, and there were cows in my curriculum. I took a seven-year course in the gentle art of acquiring the lacteal fluid. Cow is my specialty, my long suit, my best hold. Believe it or not, when we christened old Perkins the Ooley-cow we builded better than we knew."

"I follow you at a great distance," said Little Doc. "Proceed with the rat killing. Why did we build better than we knew when we did not know anything?"

"Because," I explained, "Perkins not only looks like a cow and walks like a cow and plays golf like a cow, but he has the predominant characteristic of a cow. He has the one distinguishing trait which all country cows have in common. If you had studied that noble domestic animal as closely as I have, you would not need to be told what moved Mr. Perkins to strew the entire golf course with the mangled remains of the two old pirates before mentioned. Uncle Billy and Old Man Sprott were milking him, yes, and it is quite likely that the Ooley-cow knew that he was being milked, but that knowledge was not the prime cause of the late unpleasantness."

"I still follow you," said Little Doc plaintively, "but I am losing ground every minute."

"Listen carefully," said I. "Pin back your ears and give me your undivided attention. There are many ways of milking a cow without exciting the animal to violence. I speak now of the old-fashioned cow—the country cow—from Iowa, let us say."

"The Ooley-cow is from Iowa," murmured Little Doc.

"Exactly. A city cow may be milked by machinery, and in a dozen different ways, but the country cow does not know anything about new-fangled methods. There is one thing—and one thing only—which will make the gentlest old mooley in Iowa kick over the bucket, upset the milker, jump a four-barred fence and join the wild bunch on the range. Do you know what that one thing is?"

"I haven't even a suspicion," confessed Little Doc.

Then I told him. I told him in words of one syllable, and after a time he was able to grasp the significance of my remarks. If I could make Little Doc see the point, I can make you see it too. We go from here.

Wesley J. Perkins hailed from Dubuque, but he did not hail from there until he had gathered up all the loose change in Northeastern Iowa. When he arrived in sunny Southern California he was fifty-five years of age, and at least fifty of those years had been spent in putting aside something for a rainy day. Judging by the diameter of his bankroll, he must have feared the sort of a deluge which caused the early settlers to lay the ground plans for the Tower of Babel.

Now it seldom rains in Southern California—that is to say, it seldom rains hard enough to produce a flood—and as soon as Mr. Perkins became acquainted with climatic conditions he began to jettison his ark. He joined an exclusive downtown club, took up quarters there and spent his afternoons playing dominoes with some other members of the I've-got-mine Association. Aside from his habit of swelling up whenever he mentioned his home town, and insisting on referring to it as "the Heidelberg of America," there was nothing about Mr. Perkins to provoke comment, unfavorable or otherwise. He was just one more Iowan in a country where Iowans are no novelty.

In person he was the mildest-mannered man that ever foreclosed a short-term mortgage and put a family out in the street. His eyes were large and bovine, his mouth dropped perpetually and so did his jowls, and he moved with the slow, uncertain gait of a venerable milch cow. He had a habit of lowering his head and staring vacantly into space, and all these things earned for him the unhandsome nickname by which he is now known.

"But why the Ooley-cow?" someone asked one day. "It doesn't mean anything at all!"

"Well," was the reply, "neither does Perkins."

But this was an error, as we shall see later.

It was an increasing waistline that caused the Ooley-cow to look about him for some form of gentle exercise. His physician suggested golf, and that very week the board of directors of the Country Club was asked to consider his application for membership. There were no ringing cheers, but he passed the censors.

I will say for Perkins that when he decided to commit golf he went about it in a very thorough manner. He had himself surveyed for three knickerbocker suits, he laid in a stock of soft shirts, imported stockings and spiked shoes, and he gave our professional *carte blanche* in the matter of field equipment. It is not a safe thing to give a Scotchman permission to dip his hand in your change pocket, and MacPherson certainly availed himself of the opportunity to finger some of the Dubuque money. He took one look at the novice and unloaded on him something less than a hundredweight of dead stock. He also gave him a lesson or two, and sent him forth armed to the teeth with wood, iron and aluminum.

Almost immediately Perkins found himself in the hands of Poindexter and Sprott, two extremely hard-boiled old gentlemen who have never been known to take any interest in a financial proposition assaying less than seven per cent, and that fully guaranteed. Both are retired capitalists, but when they climbed out of the trenches and retreated into the realm of sport they took all their business instincts with them.

Uncle Billy can play to a twelve handicap when it suits him to do so, and his partner in crime is only a couple of strokes behind him; but they seldom uncover their true form, preferring to pose as doddering and infirm invalids, childish old men, who only think they can play the game of golf, easy marks for the rising generation. New members are their victims; beginners are just the same as manna from heaven to them. They instruct the novice humbly and apologetically, but always with a small side bet, and no matter how fast the novice improves he makes the astounding discovery that his two feeble old tutors are able

to keep pace with him. Uncle Billy and Old Man Sprott are experts at nursing a betting proposition along, and they seldom win any sort of a match by a margin of more than two up and one to go. Taking into account the natural limitations of age they play golf very well, but they play a cinch even better—and harder. It is common scandal that Uncle Billy has not bought a golf ball in ten years. Old Man Sprott bought one in 1915, but it was under the mellowing influence of the third toddy and, therefore, should not count against him.

The Ooley-cow was a cinch. When he turned up, innocent and guileless and eager to learn the game, Uncle Billy and his running mate were quick to realize that Fate had sent them a downy bird for plucking, and in no time at all the air was full of feathers.

They played the Ooley-cow for golf balls, they played him for caddie hire, they played him for drinks and cigars, they played him for luncheons and they played him for a sucker—played him for everything, in fact, but the locker rent and the club dues. How they came to overlook these items is more than I know. The Ooley-cow would have stood for it; he stood for everything. He signed all the tags with a loose and vapid grin, and if he suffered from writer's cramp he never mentioned the fact. His monthly bill must have been a thing to shudder at, but possibly he regarded this extra outlay as part of his tuition.

Once in a while he was allowed to win, for Poindexter and Sprott followed the system practiced by other confidence men; but they never forgot to take his winnings away from him the next day, charging him interest at the rate of fifty per cent for twenty-four hours. The Ooley-cow was so very easy that they took liberties with him, so good-natured about his losses that they presumed upon that good nature and ridiculed him openly; but the old saw sometimes loses a tooth, the worm turns, the straight road bends at last, so does the camel's back, and the prize cow kicks the milker into the middle of next week. And, as I remarked before, the cow usually has a reason.

One morning I dropped into the downtown club which Perkins calls his home. I found him sitting in the reception room, juggling a newspaper and watching the door. He seemed somewhat disturbed.

"Good morning," said I.

"It is not a good morning," said he. "It's a bad morning, Look at this."

He handed me the paper, with his thumb at the head of the Lost-and-Found column, and I read as follows:

LOST—*A black leather wallet, containing private papers and a sum of money. A suitable reward will be paid for the return of same, and no questions asked. Apply to W.J.P., Argonaut Club, City.*

"Tough luck," said I. "Did you lose much?"

"Quite a sum," replied the Ooley-cow. "Enough to make it an object. In large bills mostly."

"Too bad. The wallet had your cards in it?"

"And some papers of a private nature."

"Have you an idea where you might have dropped it? Or do you think it was stolen?"

"I don't know what to think. I had it last night at the Country Club just before I left. I know I had it then, because I took it out in the lounging room to pay a small bet to Mr. Poindexter—a matter of two dollars. Then I put the wallet back in my inside pocket and came straight here—alone in a closed car. I missed it just before going to bed. I telephoned to the Country Club. No sign of it there. I went to the garage myself. It was not in the car. Of course it may have been there earlier in the evening, but I think my driver is honest, and —"

At this point we were interrupted by a clean-cut looking youngster of perhaps seventeen years.

"Your initials are W.J.P., sir?" he asked politely.

"They are."

"This is your ad in the paper?"

"It is."

The boy reached in his pocket and brought out a black leather wallet. "I have returned your property," said he, and waited while the Ooley-cow thumbed a roll of yellow-backed bills.

"All here," said Perkins with a sigh of relief. Then he looked up at the boy, and his large bovine eyes turned hard as moss agates. "Where did you get this?" he demanded abruptly. "How did you come by it?"

The boy smiled and shook his head, but his eyes never left Perkins' face. "No questions were to be asked, sir," he said.

"Right!" grunted the Ooley-cow. "Quite right. A bargain's a bargain. I—I beg your pardon, young man — Still, I'd like to know — Just curiosity, eh? — No? — Very well then. That being the case"—he stripped a fifty-dollar note from the roll and passed it over—"would you consider this a suitable reward?"

"Yes, sir, and thank you, sir."

"Good day," said Perkins, and put the wallet into his pocket. He stared at the boy until he disappeared through the street door.

"Something mighty queer about this," mused the Ooley-cow thoughtfully. "Mighty queer. That boy—he looked honest. He had good eyes and he wasn't afraid of me. I couldn't scare him worth a cent. Couldn't bluff him — Yet if he found it somewhere, there wasn't any reason why he shouldn't have told me. He didn't steal it—I'll bet on that. Maybe he got it from someone who did. Oh, well, the main thing is that he brought it back — Going out to the Country Club this afternoon?"

I said that I expected to play golf that day.

"Come out with me then," said the Ooley-cow. "Poindexter and Sprott will be there too. Yesterday afternoon I played Poindexter for the lunches today. Holed a long putt on the seventeenth green, and stuck him. Come along, and we'll make Poindexter give a party—for once."

"It can't be done," said I. "Uncle Billy doesn't give parties."

"We'll make him give one," chuckled the Ooley-cow. "We'll insist on it."

"Insist if you want to," said I, "but you'll never get away with it."

"Meet me here at noon," said the Ooley-cow. "If Poindexter doesn't give the party, I will."

I wasn't exactly keen for the Ooley-cow's society, but I accepted his invitation to ride out to the club in his car. He regaled me with a dreary monologue, descriptive of the Heidelberg of America, and solemnly assured me that the pretty girls one sees in Chicago are all from Dubuque.

It was twelve-thirty when we arrived at the Country Club, and Uncle Billy and Old Man Sprott were there ahead of us.

"Poindexter," said Perkins, "you are giving

a party today, and I have invited our friend here to join us."

Uncle Billy looked at Old Man Sprott, and both laughed uproariously. Right there was where I should have detected the unmistakable odor of a rodent. It was surprise number one.

"Dee-lighted!" cackled Uncle Billy. "Glad to have another guest, ain't we, Sprott?"

Sprott grinned and rubbed his hands. "You bet! Tell you what let's do, Billy. Let's invite everybody in the place—make it a regular party while you're at it!"

"Great idea!" exclaimed Uncle Billy. "The more the merrier!" This was surprise number two. The first man invited was Henry Bauer, who has known Uncle Billy for many years. He sat down quite overcome.

"You shouldn't do a thing like that, Billy," said he querulously. "I have a weak heart, and any sudden shock—"

"Nonsense! You'll join us?"

"Novelty always appealed to me," said Bauer. "I'm forever trying things that nobody has ever tried before. Yes, I'll break bread with you, but—why the celebration? What's it all about?"

That was what everybody wanted to know and what nobody found out, but the luncheon was a brilliant success in spite of the dazed and mystified condition of the guests, and the only limit was the limit of individual capacity. Eighteen of us sat down at the big round table, and sandwich-and-milk orders were sternly countermanded by Uncle Billy, who proved an amazing host, recommending this and that and actually ordering Rhine wine cup for all hands. I could not have been more surprised if the bronze statue in the corner of the grill had hopped down from its pedestal to fill our glasses. Uncle Billy collected a great pile of tags beside his plate, but the presence of so much bad news waiting at his elbow did not seem to affect his appetite in the least. When the party was over he called the head waiter. "Mark these tags paid," said Uncle Billy, capping the collection with a yellow-backed bill, "and hand the change to Mr. Perkins."

"Yes sir," said the head waiter, and disappeared.

I looked at the Ooley-cow, and was just in time to see the light of intelligence dawn in his big soft eyes. He was staring at Uncle

Billy, and his lower lip was flopping convulsively. Everybody began asking questions at once.

"One moment, gentlemen," mooed the Ooley-cow, pounding on the table. "One moment!"

"Now don't get excited, Perkins," said Old Man Sprott. "You got your wallet back, didn't you? Cost you fifty, but you got it back. Next time you won't be so careless."

"Yes," chimed in Uncle Billy, "you oughtn't to go dropping your money round loose that way. It'll teach you a lesson."

"It will indeed." The Ooley-cow lowered his head and glared first at one old pirate and then at the other. His soft eyes hardened and the moss-agate look came into them. He seemed about to bellow, paw up the dirt and charge.

"The laugh is on you," cackled Poindexter, "and I'll leave it to the boys here. Last night our genial host dropped his wallet on the floor out in the lounging room. I kicked it across under the table to Sprott and Sprott put his foot on it. We intended to give it back to him today, but this morning there was an ad in the paper—reward and no questions asked—so we sent a nice bright boy over to the Argonaut Club with the wallet. Perkins gave the boy a fifty-dollar note—very liberal, I call it—and the boy gave it to me. Perfectly legitimate transaction. Our friend here has had a lesson, we've had a delightful luncheon party, and the joke is on him."

"And a pretty good joke, too!" laughed Old Man Sprott.

"Yes," said the Ooley-cow at last, "a pretty good joke. Ha, ha! A mighty good joke." And place it to his credit that he managed a very fair imitation of a fat man laughing, even to the shaking of the stomach and the wrinkles round the eyes. He looked down at the tray in front of him and fingered the few bills and some loose silver.

"A mighty good joke," he repeated thoughtfully, "but what I can't understand is this—why didn't you two jokers keep the change? It would have been just that much funnier."

The Ooley-cow's party was generally discussed during the next ten days, the consensus of club opinion being that someone ought to teach Poindexter and Sprott the difference between humor and petty larceny. Most of the playing members were disgusted with the two old skinflints, and one effect of this sentiment manifested itself in the number of invitations that Perkins received to play golf with real people. He declined them all, much to our surprise, and continued to wallop his way round the course with Uncle Billy and Old Man Sprott, apparently on as cordial terms as ever.

"What are you going to do with such a besotted old fool as that?" asked Henry Bauer. "Here I've invited him into three foursomes this week—all white men, too—and he's turned me down cold. It's not that we want to play with him, for as a golfer he's a terrible thing. It's not that we're crazy about him personally, for socially he's my notion of zero minus; but he took his stinging like a dead-game sport and he's entitled to better treatment than he's getting. But if he hasn't any better sense than to pass his plate for more, what are you going to do about it?"

" 'Ephraim is joined to idols,' " quoted Little Doc Ellis. "Let him alone!"

"No, it's the other way round," argued Bauer. "His idols are joined to him—fastened on like leeches. The question naturally arises, how did such a man ever accumulate a fortune? Who forced it on him, and when, and where, and why?"

That very afternoon the Ooley-cow turned up with his guest, a large, loud person, also from the Heidelberg of America, who addressed Perkins as "Wesley" and lost no time in informing us that Southern California would have starved to death but for Iowa's capital. His name was Cottle—Calvin D. Cottle—and he gave each one of us his card as he was introduced. There was no need. Nobody could have forgotten him. Some people make an impression at first sight—Calvin D. Cottle made a deep dent. His age was perhaps forty-five, but he spoke as one crowned with Methuselah's years and Solomon's wisdom, and after each windy statement he turned to the Ooley-cow for confirmation.

"Ain't that so, Wesley? Old Wes knows, you bet your life! He's from my home town!"

It was as good as a circus to watch Uncle Billy and Old Man Sprott sizing up this fresh victim. It reminded me of two wary old dogs circling for position, maneuvering for a safe hold. They wanted to know something about his golf game—what was his handicap, for instance?"

"Handicap?" repeated Cottle. "Is that a California idea? Something new, ain't it?"

Uncle Billy explained the handicapping theory.

"Oh!" said Cottle. "You mean what do I go round in—how many strokes. Well, sometimes I cut under a hundred; sometimes I don't. It just depends. Some days I can hit 'em, some days I can't. That's all there is to it."

"My case exactly," purred Old Man Sprott. "Suppose we dispense with the handicap?"

"That's the stuff!" agreed Cottle heartily. "I don't want to have to give anybody anything; I don't want anybody to give me anything. I like an even fight, and what I say is, may the best man win! Am I right, gentlemen?"

"Absolutely!" chirped Uncle Billy. "May the best man win!"

"You bet I'm right!" boomed Cottle. "Ask Old Wes here about me. Raised right in the same town with him, from a kid knee-high to a grasshopper! I never took any the best of it in my life, did I, Wes? No, you bet not! Remember that time I got skinned out of ten thousand bucks on the land deal? A lot of fellows would have squealed, wouldn't they? A lot of fellows would have hollered for the police; but I just laughed and gave 'em credit for being smarter than I was. I'm the same way in sport as I am in business. I believe in giving everybody credit. I win if I can, but if I can't—well, there's never any hard feelings. That's me all over. You may be able to *lick* me at this golf thing—likely you will; but you'll never *scare* me, that's a cinch. Probably you gentlemen play a better game than I do—been at it longer; but then I'm a lot younger than you are. Got more strength. Hit a longer ball when I do manage to land on one right. So it all evens up in the long run."

Mr. Cottle was still modestly cheering his many admirable qualities when the Perkins party went in to luncheon, and the only pause he made was on the first tee. With his usual caution Uncle Billy had arranged it so that Dubuque was opposed to Southern California, and he had also carefully neglected to name any sort of a bet until after he had seen the stranger drive.

Cottle teed his ball and stood over it, gripping his driver until his knuckles showed white under the tan. "Get ready to ride!" said he. "You're about to leave this place!"

The clubhead whistled through the air, and I can truthfully say that I never saw a man of his size swing any harder at a golf ball—or come nearer cutting one completely in two.

"Topped it, by gum." ejaculated Mr. Cottle, watching the maimed ball until it disappeared in a bunker. "Topped it! Well, better luck next time! By the way, what are we playing for? Balls, or money, or what?"

"Whatever you like," said Uncle Billy promptly. "You name it."

"Good! That's the way I like to hear a man talk. Old Wes here is my partner, so I can't bet with him, but I'll have a side match with each of you gentlemen—say, ten great, big, smiling Iowa dollars. Always like to bet what I've got the most of. Satisfactory?"

Uncle Billy glanced at Old Man Sprott, and for an instant the old rascals hesitated. The situation was made to order for them, but they would have preferred a smaller wager to start with, being petty larcenists at heart.

"Better cut that down to five," said Perkins to Cottle in a low tone. "They play a strong game."

"Humph!" grunted his guest. "Did you ever know me to pike in my life? I ain't going to begin now. Ten dollars or nothing!"

"I've got you," said Old Man Sprott.

"This once," said Uncle Billy. "It's against my principles to play for money; but yes, this once."

And then those two old sharks insisted on a foursome bet as well.

"Ball, ball, ball," said the Ooley-cow briefly, and proceeded to follow his partner into the bunker. Poindexter and Sprott popped conservatively down the middle of the course and the battle was on.

Battle, did I say? It was a massacre of the innocents, a slaughter of babes and sucklings. Our foursome trailed along behind, and took note of Mr. Cottle, of Dubuque, in his fruitless efforts to tear the cover off the ball. He swung hard enough to knock down a lamppost, but he seldom made proper connections, and when he did the ball landed so far off the course that it took him a dozen shots to get back again. He was hopelessly bad, so bad that there was no chance to make the

side matches close ones. On the tenth tee Cottle demanded another bet—to give him a chance to get even, he said. Poindexter and Sprott each bet him another ten dollar note on the last nine, and this time Uncle Billy did not say anything about his principles.

After it was all over Cottle poured a few mint toddies into his system and floated an alibi to the surface.

"It was those confounded sand greens that did it," said he. "I'm used to grass, and I can't putt on anything else. Bet I could take you to Dubuque and flail the everlasting daylights out of you!"

"Shouldn't be surprised," said Uncle Billy. "You did a lot better on the last nine—sort of got into your stride. Any time you think you want revenge —"

"You can have it," finished Old Man Sprott, as he folded a crisp twenty-dollar note. "We believe in giving a man a chance—eh, Billy?"

"That's the spirit!" cried Cottle enthusiastically. "Give a man a chance; it's what I say, and if he does anything, give him credit. You beat me today, but I never saw this course before. Tell you what we'll do: Let's make a day of it tomorrow. Morning and afternoon both. Satisfactory? Good! You've got forty dollars of my dough and I want it back. Nobody ever made me quit betting yet, if I figure to have a chance. What's money? Shucks! My country is full of it! Now then, Wesley, if you'll come out on the practice green and give me some pointers on this sand thing, I'll be obliged to you. Ball won't run on sand like it will on grass—have to get used to it. Have to hit 'em a little harder. Soon as I get the hang of the thing we'll give these Native Sons a battle yet! Native Sons? Native Grandfathers! Come on!" Uncle Billy looked at Old Man Sprott and Old Man Sprott looked at Uncle Billy, but they did not begin to laugh until the Ooley-cow and his guest were out of earshot. Then they clucked and cackled and choked like a couple of hysterical old hens.

"His putting!" gurgled Uncle Billy. "Did he have a putt to win a hole all the way round?"

"Not unless he missed count of his shots. Say, Billy!"

"Well?"

"We made a mistake locating so far west. We should have stopped in Iowa. By now we'd have owned the entire state!"

I dropped Mr. Calvin D. Cottle entirely out of my thoughts; but when I entered the locker room shortly after noon the next day something reminded me of him. Possibly it was the sound of his voice.

"Boy! Can't we have 'nother toddy here? What's the matter with some service? How 'bout you, Wes? Oh, I forgot—you never take anything till after five o'clock. Think of all the fun you're missing. When I get to be an old fossil like you maybe I'll do the same. Good rule—You gentlemen having anything? No? Kind of careful, ain't you? Safety first, hey?— Just one toddy, boy, and if that mint ain't fresh, I'll— Yep, you're cagey birds, you are, but I give you credit just the same. And some cash. Don't forget that. Rather have cash than credit any time, hey? I bet you would! But I don't mind a little thing like that. I'm a good sport. You ask Wes here if I ain't. If I ain't a good sport I ain't anything— Still, I'll be darned if I see how you fellows do it! You're both old enough to have sons in the Soldiers' Home over yonder, but you take me out and lick me again—lick me and make me like it! A couple of dried-up mummies with one foot in the grave, and I'm right in the prime of life! Only a kid yet! It's humiliating, that's what it is, humiliating! Forty dollars apiece you're into me—and a flock of golf balls on the side! Boy! Where's the mint toddy? Let's have a little service here!"

I peeped through the door leading to the lounging room. The Dubuque-California foursome was grouped at a table in a corner. The Ooley-cow looked calm and placid as usual, but his guest was sweating profusely, and as he talked he mopped his brow with the sleeve of his shirt. Uncle Billy and Old Man Sprott were listening politely, but the speculative light in their eyes told me that they were wondering how far they dared go with this outlander from the Middle West.

"Why," boomed Cottle, "I can hit a ball twice as far as either one of you! 'Course I don't always know where it's going, but the main thing is I got the *strength*. I can throw a golf ball farther than you old fossils can hit one with a wooden club, yet you lick me easy as breaking sticks. Can't understand it at all— Twice as strong as you are— Why, say, I bet I can take one hand and outdrive you! *One hand!*"

"Easy, Calvin," said the Ooley-cow reprovingly. "Don't make wild statements."

"Well, I'll bet I can do it," repeated Cottle stubbornly. "If a man's willing to bet his money to back up a wild statement, that shows he's got the right kind of a heart anyway. I ought to be able to stick my left hand in my pocket and go out there and trim two men of your age. I ought to, and I'll be damned if I don't think I can!"

"Tut, tut!" warned the Ooley-cow. "That's foolishness."

"Think so?" Cottle dipped his hand into his pocket and brought out a thick roll of bills. "Well, this stuff here says I can do it—at least I can *try*—and I ain't afraid to back my judgment."

"Put your money away," said Perkins. "Don't be a fool!"

Cottle laughed uproariously and slapped the Ooley-cow on the back.

"Good old Wes!" he cried. "Ain't changed a bit. Conservative! Always conservative! Got rich at it, but me I got rich taking chances. What's a little wad of bills to me, hey? Nothing but chicken-feed! I'll bet any part of this roll—I'll bet *all* of it—and I'll play these sun-dried old sports with one hand. Now's the time to show whether they've got any sporting blood or not. What do you say, gentlemen?"

Uncle Billy looked at the money and moistened his lips with the tip of his tongue.

"Couldn't think of it," he croaked at length.

"Pshaw!" sneered Cottle. "I showed you too much—I scared you!"

"He ain't scared," put in Old Man Sprott. "It would be too much like stealing it."

"I'm the one to worry about that," announced Cottle. "It's my money, ain't it? I made it, didn't I? And I can do what I damn please with it—spend it, bet it, burn it up, throw it away. When you've worried about everything else in the world, it'll be time for you to begin worrying about young Mr. Cottle's money! This slim little roll—bah! Chicken-feed! Come get it if you want it!" He tossed the money on the table with a gesture which was an insult in itself. "There it is—cover it! Put up or shut up!"

"Oh, forget it!" said the Ooley-cow wearily. "Come in and have a bite to eat and forget it!"

"Don't want anything to eat!" was the stubborn response. "Seldom eat in the middle of

31

the day. But I'll have 'nother mint toddy — Wait a second, Wes. Don't be in such a rush. Lemme understand this thing. These—these gentlemen here, these two friends of yours, these dead-game old Native Sons have got eighty dollars of my money—not that it makes any difference to me, understand, but they've got it—eighty dollars that they won from me playing golf. Now I may have a drink or two in me and I may not, understand, but anyhow I know what I'm about. I make these—gentlemen a sporting proposition. I give 'em a chance to pick up a couple of hundred apiece, and they want to run out on me because it'll be like stealing it. What kind of a deal is that, hey? Is it sportsmanship? Is it what they call giving a man a chance? Is it —"

"But they know you wouldn't have a chance," interrupted the Ooley-cow soothingly. "They don't want a sure thing."

"They've had one so far, haven't they?" howled Cottle. "What are they scared of now? 'Fraid I'll squeal if I lose? Tell 'em about me, Wes. Tell 'em I never squealed in my life. I win if I can, but if I can't—'s all right. No kick coming. There never was a piker in the Cottle family, was there, Wes? No, you bet not! We're sports, every one of us. Takes more than one slim little roll to send us up a tree! If there's anything that makes me sick, it's a cold-footed, penny-pinching, nickel-nursing, sure-thing player!"

"Your money does not frighten me," said Uncle Billy, who was slightly nettled by this time. "It is against my principles to play for a cash bet —"

"But you and your pussy-footed old side-partner got into me for eighty dollars just the same!" scoffed Cottle. "You and your principles be damned!"

Uncle Billy swallowed this without blinking, but he did not look at Cottle. He was looking at the roll of bills on the table.

"If you are really in earnest —" began Poindexter, and glanced at Old Man Sprott.

"Go ahead, Billy," croaked that aged reprobate. "Teach him a lesson. He needs it."

"Never mind the lesson," snapped Cottle. "I got out of school a long time ago. The bet is that I can leave my left arm in the clubhouse safe—stick it in my pocket—and trim you birds with one hand."

"We wouldn't insist on that," said Old Man Sprott. "Play with both hands if you want to."

"Think I'm a welsher?" demanded Cottle. "The original proposition goes. 'Course I wouldn't really cut the arm off and leave it in the safe, but what I mean is, if I use two arms in making a shot, right there is where I lose. Satisfactory?"

"Perkins," said Uncle Billy, solemnly wagging his head, "you are a witness that this thing has been forced on me. I have been bullied and browbeaten and insulted into making this bet —"

"And so have I," chimed in Old Man Sprott. "I'm almost ashamed —"

The Ooley-cow shrugged his shoulders.

"I am a witness," said he quietly. "Calvin, these gentlemen have stated the case correctly. You have forced them to accept your proposition —"

"And he can't blame anybody if he loses," finished Uncle Billy as he reached for the roll of bills.

"You bet!" ejaculated Old Man Sprott. "He was looking for trouble, and now he's found it. Count it, Billy, and we'll each take half."

"That goes, does it?" asked Cottle.

"Sir?" cried Uncle Billy.

"Oh, I just wanted to put you on record," said Cottle, with a grin. "Wesley, you're my witness too. I mislaid a five-hundred-dollar note the other day, and it may have got into my change pocket. Might as well see if a big bet will put these safety-first players off their game! Anyhow, I'm betting whatever's there. I ain't sure how much it is."

"I am," said Uncle Billy in a changed voice. He had come to the five-hundred-dollar bill, sandwiched in between two twenties. He looked at Old Man Sprott, and for the first time I saw doubt in his eyes.

"Oh, it's there, is it?" asked Cottle carelessly. "Well, let it all ride. I never backed out on a gambling proposition in my life—never pinched a bet after the ball started to roll. Shoot the entire works—'s all right with me!"

Uncle Billy and Old Man Sprott exchanged significant glances, but after a short argument and some more abuse from Cottle they toddled over to the desk and filled out two blank checks—for five hundred and eighty dollars apiece.

"Make 'em payable to cash," suggested Cottle. "You'll probably tear 'em up after the game. Now the next thing is a stakeholder —"

"Is that—necessary?" asked Old Man Sprott.

"Sure!" said Cottle. "I might run out on you. Let's have everything according to Hoyle—stakeholder and all the other trimmings. Anybody'll be satisfactory to me; that young fellow getting an earful at the door; he'll do."

So I became the stakeholder—the custodian of eleven hundred and sixty dollars in coin and two checks representing a like amount. I thought I detected a slight nervousness in the signatures, and no wonder. It was the biggest bet those old petty larcenists had ever made in their lives. They went in to luncheon—at the invitation of the Ooley-cow, of course—but I noticed that they did not eat much. Cottle wandered out to the practice green, putter in hand, forgetting all about the mint toddy which, by the way, had never been ordered.

"You drive first, sir," said Uncle Billy to Cottle, pursuing his usual system. "We'll follow you."

"Think you'll feel easier if I should hit one over into the eucalyptus trees yonder?" asked the man from Dubuque. "Little nervous, eh? Does a big bet scare you? I was counting on that— Oh, very well, I'll take the honor."

"Just a second," said Old Man Sprott, who had been prowling about in the background and fidgeting with his driver. "Does the stakeholder understand the terms of the bet? Mr. Cottle is playing a match with each of us individually —"

"Separately and side by each," added Cottle.

"Using only one arm," said Old Man Sprott.

"If he uses both arms in making a shot," put in Uncle Billy, "he forfeits both matches. Is that correct, Mr. Cottle?"

"Correct as hell! Watch me closely, young man. I have no mustache to deceive you—nothing up my sleeve but my good right arm. Watch me closely!"

He teed his ball, dropped his left arm at his side, grasped the driver firmly in his right hand and swung the club a couple of times in tentative fashion. The head of the driver described a perfect arc, barely grazing the top of the tee. His two-armed swing had been a thing of violence—a baseball wallop, constricted, bound up, without follow-through or timing, a combination of brute strength and awkwardness. Uncle Billy's chin sagged as he

watched the easy, natural sweep of that wooden club—the wrist-snap applied at the proper time, and the long graceful follow-through which gives distance as well as direction. Old Man Sprott also seemed to be struggling with an entirely new and not altogether pleasant idea.

"Watch me closely, stakeholder," repeated Cottle, addressing the ball. "Nothing up my sleeve but my good right arm. Would you gentlemen like to have me roll up my sleeve before I start?"

"Drive!" grunted Uncle Billy.

"I'll do that little thing," said Cottle, and this time he put the power into the swing. The ball, caught squarely in the middle of the clubface, went whistling toward the distant green, a perfect screamer of a drive without a suspicion of hook or slice. It cleared the cross-bunker by ten feet, carried at least a hundred and eighty yards before it touched grass, and then bounded ahead like a scared rabbit, coming to rest at least two hundred and twenty-five yards away. "You like that?" asked Cottle, moving off the tee. "I didn't step into it very hard or I might have had more distance. Satisfactory, stakeholder?" And he winked at me openly and deliberately.

"What—what sort of a game is this?" gulped Old Man Sprott, finding his voice with an effort.

"Why," said Cottle, smiling cheerfully, "I wouldn't like to say offhand and so early in the game, but you might call it golf. Yes, call it golf, and let it go at that."

At this point I wish to go on record as denying the rumor that our two old reprobates showed the white feather. That first tee shot, and the manner in which it was made, was enough to inform them that they were up against a sickening surprise party; but, though startled and shaken, they did not weaken. They pulled themselves together and drove the best they knew how, and I realized that for once I was to see their true golfing form uncovered.

Cottle tucked his wooden club under his arm and started down the course, and from that time on he had very little to say. Uncle Billy and Old Man Sprott followed him, their heads together at a confidential angle, and I brought up the rear with the Ooley-cow, who had elected himself a gallery of one.

The first hole is a long par four. Poindexter

33

and Sprott usually make it in five, seldom getting home with their seconds unless they have a wind behind them. Both used brassies and both were short of the green. Then they watched Cottle as he went forward to his ball.

"That drive might have been a freak shot," quavered Uncle Billy.

"Lucky fluke, that's all," said Old Man Sprott, but I knew and they knew that they only hoped they were telling the truth.

Cottle paused over his ball for an instant, examined the lie and drew a wooden spoon from his bag. Then he set himself, and the next instant the ball was on its way, a long, high shot, dead on the pin.

"And maybe that was a fluke!" muttered the Ooley-cow under his breath. "Look! He's got the green with it!"

From the same distance I would have played a full mid-iron and trusted in Providence, but Cottle had used his wood, and I may say that never have I seen a ball better placed. It carried to the little rise of turf in front of the putting green, hopped once, and trickled close to the cup. I was not the only one who appreciated that spoon shot.

"Say," yapped Old Man Sprott, turning to Perkins, "what are we up against here? Miracles?"

"Yes, what have you framed up on us?" demanded Uncle Billy vindictively.

"Something easy, gentlemen," chuckled the Ooley-cow. "A soft thing from my home town. Probably he's only lucky."

The two members of the Sure-Thing Society went after their customary fives and got them, but Cottle laid his approach putt stone dead at the cup and holed out in four. He missed a three by the matter of half an inch. I could stand the suspense no longer. I took Perkins aside while the contestants were walking to the second tee.

"You might tell a friend," I suggested. "In strict confidence, what are they up against?"

"Something easy," repeated the Ooley-cow, regarding me with his soft, innocent eyes. "They wanted it and now they've got it."

"But yesterday, when he played with both arms —" I began.

"That was yesterday," said Perkins. "You'll notice that they didn't have the decency to offer him a handicap, even when they felt

morally certain that he had made a fool bet. Not that he would have accepted it—but they didn't offer it. They're wolves, clear to the bone, but once in a while a wolf bites off more than he can chew." And he walked away from me. Right there I began reconstructing my opinion of the Ooley-cow.

In my official capacity as stakeholder I saw every shot that was played that afternoon. I still preserve the original score card of that amazing round of golf. There are times when I think I will have it framed and present it to the club, with red-ink crosses against the thirteenth and fourteenth holes. I might even set a red-ink star against the difficult sixth hole, where Cottle sent another tremendous spoon shot down the wind, and took a four where most of our Class-A men are content with a five. I might make a notation against the tricky ninth, where he played a marvellous shot out of a sand trap to halve a hole which I would have given up as lost. I might make a footnote calling attention to his deadly work with his short irons. I say I think of all these things, but perhaps I shall never frame that card. The two men most interested will never forget the figures. It is enough to say that Old Man Sprott, playing such golf as I had never seen him play before, succumbed at the thirteenth hole, six down and five to go. Uncle Billy gave up the ghost on the fourteenth green, five and four, and I handed the money and the checks to Mr. Calvin D. Cottle, of Dubuque. He pocketed the loot with a grin.

"Shall we play the bye-holes for something?" he asked. "A drink—or a ball, maybe?" And then the storm broke. I do not pretend to quote the exact language of the losers. I merely state that I was surprised, yes, shocked at Uncle Billy Poindexter. I had no idea that a member of the Episcopal church—but let that pass. He was not himself. He was the biter bitten, the milker milked. It makes a difference. Old Man Sprott also erupted in an astounding manner. It was the Ooley-cow who took the center of the stage.

"Just a minute, gentlemen," said he. "Do not say anything which you might afterward regret. Remember the stakeholder is still with us. My friend here is not, as you intimate, a crook. Neither is he a sure-thing player. We have some sure-thing players with us, but he is not one of them. He is merely the one-armed golf champion of Dubuque—and the Middle West."

Imagine an interlude here for fireworks, followed by pertinent questions.

"Yes, yes, I know," said Perkins soothingly. "He can't play a lick with two arms. He never could. Matter of fact, he never learned. He fell off a haystack in Iowa—how many years ago was it, Cal?"

"Twelve," said Mr. Cottle. "Twelve next July."

"And he broke his left arm rather badly," explained the Ooley-cow. "Didn't have the use of it for—how many years, Cal?"

"Oh, about six, I should say."

"Six years. A determined man can accomplish much in that length of time. Cottle learned to play golf with his right arm—fairly well, as you must admit. Finally he got the left arm fixed up—they took a piece of bone out of his shin and grafted it in—new-fangled idea. Decided there was no sense in spoiling a one-armed star to make a dub two-armed golfer. Country full of 'em already. That's the whole story. You picked him for an easy mark, a good thing. You thought he had a bad bet and you had a good one. Don't take the trouble to deny it. Gentlemen, allow me to present the champion one-armed golfer of Iowa and the Middle West!"

"Yes," said Cottle modestly, "when a man does anything, give him credit for it. Personally I'd rather have the cash!"

"How do you feel about it now?" asked the Ooley-cow.

Judging by their comments, they felt warm—very warm. Hot, in fact. The Ooley-cow made just one more statement, but to me that statement contained the gist of the whole matter.

"This," said he, "squares us on the wallet proposition. I didn't say anything about it at the time, but that struck me as a scaly trick. So I invited Cal to come out and pay me a visit — Shall we go back to the clubhouse?"

I made Little Doc Ellis see the point; perhaps I can make you see it now.

Returning to the original simile, the Ooley-cow was willing to be milked for golf balls and luncheons and caddie hire. That was legitimate milking, and he did not resent it. He would have continued to give down in great abundance, but when they took fifty dollars from him, in the form of a bogus reward, he kicked over the bucket, injured the milkers and jumped the fence.

Why? I'm almost ashamed to tell you, but did you ever hear of a country cow—an Iowa cow—that would stand for being milked from the wrong side?

I think this will be all, except that I anticipate a hard winter for the golfing beginners at our club.

Golf Is a
Nice Friendly Game

by

PAUL GALLICO

1942 — FROM *GOLF IS A FRIENDLY GAME*

WHEN THE BUZZER on my desk snarled three times, meaning that old A. R., Argyle Rutherford Mallow, president of Mallow & Co., makers of Far-Fli woods, Tru-Distance irons and the Tuff-Hide and Thunderbolt golf balls was yearning to bend my ear, I paused just long enough to bid a fond farewell to the rest of the staff before stepping in onto the carpet to get the can tied to me. Your Uncle William was a sure thing to get fired. Of what use was a sales-promotion manager to a golf equipment company when pretty soon there wasn't going to be anything to sell?

Sooner or later, of course, Uncle Sam was going to hand me one of those Garands that can hole out at a thousand yards, but while I was waiting for my number to come up it was nice to go on eating.

True, I'd read in the papers where the Priorities Board had released a small quantity of second-grade rubber to be rationed to the four leading makers of golf balls, in the interest of morale. But when a golf ball gets that rare, you don't need a top promotion guy to figure out ways to get rid of them. Well, what was going to happen to me was no worse than what had happened to a lot of others.

Oh, yeah?

You could have knocked me over with a score card when I walked into A. R.'s office. Instead of being parked behind his desk scowling at reports, he was swinging a mashie in the middle of the floor.

"Ha! Har-r-r-rumph!" he barked, missing the chandelier by an inch. "Come in, Fowler. Don't stand there gawking."

I flattened up against the wall. So the Old Man had finally fallen for the game. Every time I came in to see him I had to listen to his beef about what a bunch of no-good loafers our pros were, and why couldn't they win every tournament, since that was what they were paid for? Maybe he'd be a little easier to handle now. Which gives you an idea of William Fowler's skullwork.

"I—I didn't know you had taken up golf, A. R."

"Lot of things you don't know, Fowler. Started four months ago. Doctor's orders. Not getting enough exercise. Simple game. Mastered it at once. Sit down; sit down, Fowler. Want to talk to you."

I figured, *Here it comes, and there I go.* But it was just as easy to take it sitting down as standing up. I wouldn't have so far to fall.

A. R. sat down too. He was a little bit of a guy, no bigger than a pepper box, but twice as sharp. He had Antarctic eyes and a mouth like the edge of a No. 3 iron.

"Joined the Skipping Brook Country Club, Fowler. Learned golf. Ridiculously easy game. Confirmed a suspicion I have entertained for many years. Those professionals on our pay roll—bunch of good-for-nothing, lazy loafers. Absolutely no excuse for them to lose. Look at me. Play only Saturdays and Sundays. Completely familiar with the rudimentary science of the sport. No doubt if I were to devote my entire time to it, as they do, I would become perfect. Lot of fakers and idlers, those professionals. Lame excuses about nerves and strain. Outrageous!"

Well, now, I don't go much for that hero stuff about golfers, but I've got a pretty fair idea what some of the lads go through trying to knock off a big championship, or just win eating money, for that matter, and I couldn't let him get by with that, so I started to say, "Aw, now, A. R. —"

"Humph! Never mind, Fowler. We'll discuss that some other time. Do you know Fairfield Greenly?"

"Sure. He's president of Fairgreen Company." They were our big rivals in the golf equipment field, making the Shoor-out sand wedge and the Accu-Putt ball—the one they claimed had a diamond chip in the center.

"Humph! Exactly! Pompous ass. Always bragging and blowing. Sickening. Play with him on Sundays. Member at Skipping Brook. Doesn't know first rudiments of golf. Just lucky. Had to take him down a peg, eh, Fowler, my boy?"

Beware of the boss when he calls you "my boy." I ventured, "Did you beat him sir?"

"Eh? Har-r-rumph! Well, not exactly. That is to say, on skill and knowledge, of course, but he's damnably lucky. Crows afterwards. Had to fix his kite, once and for all. Challenged him, Fowler, that's what I did. That's where you come in."

I thought, *Oh, oh. Careful, Fowler.* Out loud I said, "Me, sir?"

"Precisely. You know all those indolent, incompetent pros I have been supporting. Want you to pick the best of a bad lot and have him at Skipping Brook next Sunday morning. Relying upon your choice."

"I don't exactly get the picture, A. R."

"Har-r-rumph! Well, perhaps we were all imbibing a bit. Customary at the end of a round. Wasn't enough I paid Greenly his money. Had to listen to his blowing. Fairgreen clubs! Fairgreen professionals! Got sick of it. Challenged him. Myself and best Mallow professional against Greenly and a Fairgreen pro. Scotchman's four ball —"

"You mean a Scotch foursome, sir?"

"Eh? That's what I said. Strict rules. Eighteen holes. Play our own equipment. Made a wager on it. That will fix him. Now, you get me a man who can win."

Did I breathe a sigh of relief! Here I was expecting to be fired, and all it was about was a grudge match between a couple of old coots. They'd probably agreed on a five-dollar Nassau, which wasn't going to hurt anybody.

Still, just for the record, I asked, "How much is the bet, A. R.?"

I should have known something was coming, because he didn't answer right away, but fiddled with stuff on his desk, hemming and hawing and getting red.

"Har-r-rumph! oh, yes. The wager. Well, now, Fowler, it was necessary to put him in his place. We—ah-hroomph—agreed that the stakes should be our share of the—ah—rubber allotment we are getting from the —"

"The what!"

"Now, now, Fowler! Don't shout. I can hear you. It was Greenly's idea. Naturally, I couldn't let him bluff —"

"But great Jehoshaphat, A. R.! If we lose, we might as well go out of business. We won't be able to make a golf ball."

A. R. gave me that icebox stare. "Exactly, Fowler. You know our professionals. It's up to you to see that we don't lose, or else —"

He didn't have to finish that "or else." That was a dilleroo, wasn't it? We had a lot of ace pros on our pay roll, but Fairgreen was a sure thing to play Angus McDonough, their Open champion. And what did I know about A. R.'s game, or Greenly's either, for that matter?

I said, "Gee, A. R., this is a pretty important match. What kind of a score do you shoot? Maybe we'd better play a round together some day this week, so that I could study your —"

"Eh? What for, Fowler? Wholly unnecessary. It isn't the figures that count. Told you there's nothing about golf I don't understand."

I had to use bait. "It's just plain strategy, A. R. For instance, if you're a long hitter, I'd naturally assign you a pro with the best approach shots"—I had the decency to blush— "ah—someone who will back up your game."

He swallowed it. "Well, if you put it that way, Fowler. Wouldn't want a man who would hold me down. Supposing you come up to Skipping Brook next Wednesday morning. Might be able to give you a few pointers. That's all."

But when I got to the door, he called me back. "Ah, Fowler! Just one moment. Do you know of a golf professional by the name of Lane—Jimmy Lane?"

"Jimmy Lane? Sure, A. R. He's a kid we signed up last year. Hasn't had a chance to do much yet, but he sure raised hell around Texas, where he comes from. Lot of the boys think he'll grab the Open in a couple of years. We were lucky to —"

Now, what had I done? A. R. was looking as black as a tar pit. That blade mouth of his was set like a trap.

"On my pay roll, eh? Well, then, you just tell him to stay away from my niece Eleanor, do you hear? I'm responsible for her and I don't intend having her take up with a lazy, good-for-nothing golf loafer. Tell him if I catch him hanging around her again, he's fired. Har-r-rumph!"

Did I tell you that your Uncle William is the guy everything happens to? Or do I have to?

Believe me, by the time I hit the third tee with A. R. out at Skipping Brook in Westchester on the following Wednesday, I had forgotten about Jimmy Lane and Mallow's niece and everything else. I had troubles of my own.

I won't try to describe A. R.'s game, beyond saying the way he played it would have taken him three years of solid practice to work up to where he could be called a duffer.

Brethren, now that it can be told, it was to weep. He sliced, he jabbed, he jumped, he hacked, he sclaffed, he shanked, he dribbled, he dug, he gouged, he shimmied, he whiffed, he pressed and depressed, he jounced and jiggled, he swayed and swiveled, he bent at the knees, and likewise at the instep, the thighs and the fourth vertebra; he closed his eyes, he looked up, he slashed, swooped, leaped, lurched, ducked, bobbed, heaved and wrenched.

But that wasn't even the worst. He was convinced he knew all about the game, and never stopped saying so. That bevel-edged mouth of his didn't quit working from tee to green, between alibiing his shots, giving me instruction, blasting the pros who made such a fuss over a simple game, and jawing the caddies. As near as I can remember without stenographic notes, a sample hole went something like this:

"Hoop! . . . Know what I did then? Didn't keep my elbow out . . . Ugh! . . . Dratted car going along the road disturbed me . . . Wagh! . . . Caddie, you rattled those clubs. Do it again and back you go to the clubhouse . . . Fowler, you're getting too much shoulder into your swing. Here, watch me! . . . Ooops! . . . Had it right, but the club slipped that time . . . Come on, Fowler, hurry up and hit it. Don't keep me waiting . . . There. See how that one went? It's because I don't break my wrists. Own discovery. Those crazy pros tell you to break your wrists.

Lot of fakers . . . Bah! There was a lump of dirt back of the ball. That's why I didn't hit it right . . . Fowler, you're standing wrong . . . Wunh! . . . Had something in my eye that time. Couldn't see the ball."

But you get the idea. Bob Jones, the year he made the Grand Slam, couldn't have beaten a couple of three-year-old kids, teamed with a guy like that. And your Uncle William was supposed to dig up a Mallow pro who would bring home the rubber.

As we plowed up the fourth fairway, we could see across to number nine, where it looked like one of those war photos in the picture magazines, when a land mine goes up. Chunks of the scenery were leaping into the air.

A. R. grunted and said, "There you are. That's Greenly. Look at him. Man like that ought to stay off a golf course."

When some of the dust of battle settled, I could see there was a man involved in the scene, a long, thin, dried-up guy with a fine badminton swing. It was a minor comfort to ascertain that Mr. Greenly was the second worst golfer in the world. And not even that comfort lasted. I hadn't seen anything yet.

I won't insult your intelligence by asking you to guess who walked out of the bushes back of the sixth tee, using a club for a walking stick, his patent-leather hair looking like one of those "Try Slicko" ads, his lemon-meringue puss parted in the middle to show four fangs. It was the smile that curdles, and its owner was the one guy in the world that I can do without in large quantities—J. Sears Hammett, sales-promotion manager of the Fairgreen Company.

And did he move in!

"How-de-do, Mr. Mallow. Enjoying a little healthful exercise again, I see. Making some fine shots too. Watched you coming up the fifth." He twitched that flea-bite mustache of his and gave that half strangle, half sneeze he used in place of a laugh. "Ha-a-a-argh! Must say the company you're in won't help your game much . . . Ah, there, Fowler."

"Oh, yeah?" I said. "Oh, yeah?"

Yes, sir, a regular Fred Allen for repartee, that's your Uncle William. I'm the guy who comes up with the right crack about three hours later.

"Hah!" said A. R. "You've noticed those shots, eh, Hammett? New discovery of mine.

Don't keep your eye on the ball. Keep it on the line of flight. See where it's going that way. The pros don't know anything at all."

"You're absolutely right, Mr. Mallow," said J. Sears Hammett, doing a double smirk. "Those pros will put you off your game. You do it your own way."

It wasn't even any use trying to tip A. R. off to what Hammett was trying to put over on him. It was obvious that they had become palsy-walsy. J. Sears kept buttering A. R., supporting him in his revolting theories about the game and egging him on to try new stances, grips and swings. The old fool just lapped it up.

Then the louse did just the thing I was afraid of. He said, "You see that Fowler assigns you a good man to play against Angus McDonough, the Open champion, Mr. Mallow. Bill's got some awful lemons on his list . . . Ah-ah, Fowler, too much left hand on that shot. Just as Mr. Mallow told you. That's why you knocked it out of bounds."

I said, "Oh, is that so?" That was a killer, wasn't it?

Coming up to the sixteenth, Mallow went into a deep bunker alongside the green and started excavating. He had taken eight socks at it and even his alibis were growing weaker when Hammett said, "Here, Mr. Mallow, try this one," and handed down the club he had been using for a walking stick. A. R. took one gorblimey swipe and out popped the ball and dropped onto the carpet.

"Hah! Knew there was something the matter with my niblick all the time. Thanks, young man." He started to hand the club back, when Hammett gave a magnanimous wave of his hand.

"Oh, that's all right, Mr. Mallow. Just stick it in your bag and keep it. I could see from here that club you were using wasn't properly balanced for you."

Walking up to the home hole, A. R. said to me, "Fine chap, that Hammett, Fowler. Knows his stuff. Alert. Keen. Suggest you try to emulate him a little more."

I didn't even bat an eye at that one. I had other worries. You didn't forget about that rubber, did you? Who was I going to assign to A. R. to play against Greenly and Angus McDonough?

Well, who? You know the list of A. R. Mallow professionals as well as I. Freddy McRae,

our best shot maker? Ever see him in a tournament? Hair-trigger nerves. If somebody sneezes in the gallery, he starts to shake. A. R. would drive him stark, raving mad in two minutes.

Elmer Brown and Jed Scraggins were two even-tempered guys, but they were both in Florida. I didn't dare give him Archie Crobb. Archie is a poisonous, dried-up, misanthropic old Scotsman who believes that dubs and duffers shouldn't be allowed to desecrate golf courses. He once threw a niblick at a kid in the gallery who was jiggling a balloon. I know, I know—Whitey Brompton. But what you don't know is that Whitey had had some kind of run-in with A. R. and hated his shadow. Pete Clary? No good. Great iron player, nasty, sarcastic tongue. One crack out of A. R. and Pete would tear him to pieces. And I couldn't use Reggie Ring, because Angus McDonough had the Indian sign on him.

What I needed was a guy with Craig Wood's tee-shots, the short game of Paul Runyan and the disposition of a saint. There wasn't any such animal. Classmates, I was low, walking back to the clubhouse from the eighteenth green. The match was in the bag for Fairgreen, and so was William Fowler, Esquire, and the firm, unless we could figure some way to make golf balls out of chewing gum.

I was so low I didn't even care when A. R. and Hammett, their arms about each other's shoulders, went into the grillroom for a drink and didn't ask me to come along. I needed solitude. I went into the locker room and ordered a long one.

After the third, when I discovered I had left my change of clothes in the car, I figured maybe the air would do me some good, so I went to get the bag myself instead of sending the Senegambian.

It was surprising how much one car looked like another at that point, so the only thing to do was try them all. I was just about to crawl into the back of the fifth when I heard a voice that was familiar on account of the Texas in it, saying, "Gee, Eleanor, I jes' cain't help telling you. I'll bust ef I don't. I—I jes' love you, that's all."

Oh, oh, Fowler, I said to myself. *Blow.*

But you know how it is. I just couldn't resist taking a gander. Yop! You guessed it. It was the crusher too. I told you I'd forgotten about A. R. warning me about Jimmy Lane, our kid pro, and his niece Eleanor. When I have trouble, it comes like asparagus, in bunches.

They were in the front seat, and when I peeked again, she was in his arms, and for keeps too. Friends, it was Capital El-Oh-Vee-Eee, except that your old partner William wasn't exactly in the mood. She was pretty, too, a soft little brunette with doe eyes. I couldn't see the mouth, because it was occupied. Now, why couldn't I have found out that A. R. had a looker like that in the family?

Then, all of a sudden, they were apart and the girl had begun to cry. Well, you wouldn't expect me to check out at that point, would you? That's like tearing up the magazine with the last installment in it.

I heard her say, "Oh, Jim, I'm so miserable. I don't know what to do about Uncle Argyle. He can make everything so unpleasant. Oh, Jim—Jim—"

Yeah, and a nice little package I had wrapped up for Jim too. The old heave-o. But he was still blissfully unaware of that.

He just looked at her and said, "Honey, I'll jes' make that man like me. I'll make him. There's nothing I won't do for you, darling. I'll try anything to win him over, El. I know I cain do it. Why, I'd plumb go through hell for you, honey."

She said, "Oh, Jim, I know you will," and got back into his arms again, at which point little Willie snuck away from there.

I could hardly wait to get back to that locker room. I wanted to be somewhere alone where I could hug myself. I've told you about me, haven't I? I don't get ideas often, but when I do, it's frightening.

That kid was so eager to go plumb through hell for his girl that I was going to fix it for him. I was just going to let him play eighteen holes of Scotch foursome with Argyle Rutherford Mallow, Inc.

Simple, wasn't it? In that frame of mind, there was nothing he wouldn't take from A. R. for the sake of the girl. And by the time I got through steaming him up, he might even bring home the latex for her too. I had another shot of formula in the locker room before going into the grill. You see, I still had to sell it to A. R.

Whew! X marks the spot where he hit the ceiling when I told him I had picked Jimmy Lane to play with him. Even Hammett was scared, and helped pour a couple of drinks into him while I talked fast.

I told him that McRae had broken his ankle in a blackout, that Brompton was in jail and Reggie Ring was at the bedside of his ailing grandmother. I gave him fast alibis for Pete and Archie and all the rest, and then got down to business.

"Look, A. R.," I said, "I know all about what you said with regard to Jim in the office that day, but this is a time to put personal prejudices aside for the good of the Mallow team. He's young, but he's a fine golfer and, above all, he'll take advice and instruction. He's not like those old mossback know-it-alls. You'll be able to teach that kid."

I could see that part of it appealed to A. R., but he wasn't sold by a long shot. Then what do you think happened? You could have knocked me flat with a whisk broom when Hammett suddenly turned those tomcod eyes of his on A. R., and said, "Ah-hem! I think perhaps Fowler has something there, Mr. Mallow, if I may say so. Lane is a comer. Best natural swing in years. Wish we had him signed up. Couldn't make a better choice myself."

Of course, I got Hammett's angle. Jim was still a year or so away from top tournament golf and figured to be a soft touch for an old hand like Angus McDonough. But wouldn't you think A. R. would have more sense? Well, the dew was still on his beautiful friendship with J. Sears Hammett.

He turned to me and said, "Young man, I have a great deal of faith in Mr. Hammett's judgment. Wish I could say the same for you. In this instance I shall take his advice. You may tell Lane to be here at two o'clock on Sunday afternoon. Har-r-rumph!"

Anyway, I was in. Uh-huh. Right up to my ears.

You've played a Scotch foursome, haven't you? Two men on a side, and you play alternate strokes. It's a variation of golf invented to try men's souls, with a perfect record of having busted up more deep and lasting friendships than women. When your partner fluffs the ball into a trap or hooks it into a brier patch and leaves you to play it out, you find your love and respect for him cooling rapidly.

Well, there we were, the six of us, on the first tee on Sunday afternoon; Hammett all tricked out in white flannels, and Angus looking like one of those red-faced Scotsmen they use on whisky ads. Fairfield Greenly was a long, jittery gent with a sour face. When he stood next to A. R., they looked like Mutt and Jeff. Jim Lane was a nice-looking kid with a bony nose and plenty of chin. He had do-or-die written all over his face. I had the shakes. That was our party.

I suppose it was purely by accident that Eleanor Mallow, dressed up in one of those fluffy, pink Angora things, wandered over from the practice tee just as we were about to start.

A. R. didn't even speak to Jim on the tee, but just stood there giving him sour looks, with one eye on Eleanor to see that she didn't get too close to him.

We won the toss, and Jim knelt down to tee up his ball when A. R. barked, "What do you think you're doing, young man? I'm driving first."

Jim gave him a nice smile. "Sure, Mr. Mallow. I just thought —"

"Hroomph! I'll do the thinking. Stand back out of my way now . . . You, Fowler, stop moving your feet . . . Everybody quiet now."

He took a swing like a man with a wasp under his shirt and his pants on fire, trying to impale a butterfly on the end of a scythe. The ball flew up into the air and settled in some rosebushes in front of the clubhouse on the right.

"Ga-a-ah! I hit it perfectly. . . . You put me off, Lane—you and your butting in to drive. I ought to get another one." He turned to Hammett for confirmation, but J. Sears happened to be looking out the window.

"I'm terribly sorry, sir," Jim began. "I didn't mean —"

"Go on, you old bluffer," Greenly rasped pleasantly. "Get off the tee. You know the rules."

It was going to be a lovely match. And listen. If you think Eleanor's brown eyes weren't shooting sparks, I'm telling you.

After Angus poled a honey right down the middle, I went over with Jim to inspect the extent of the disaster. It was a nasty lie. The kid laid hold of a No. 3 iron and whaled. He took out about eighteen dollars' worth of yellow-flowering *Rosa lutea*, but it was a

magnificent shot, and the ball wound up in the fairway not more than thirty yards behind Angus' drive.

When we got to it, A. R. glared at it and then at Jim. "Why aren't we up to where they are?" he demanded. "What did you use there —an iron? You should have used a wooden club. Hereafter you consult me what club you're to use. Understand?"

Jim gave him a smile like an angel. "Why, yes, sir. Surely I'll be glad to take yore advice."

Greenly, who was too nervous to wait, twitched at the ball, topping it, but it scuttered along the ground to the edge of the green.

"Of all the luck!" snorted A. R. He had an easy approach, but he shanked the ball off to the right into some knee-high weeds. "Ugh! Ball was lying in a hole. Partner's fault. Couldn't get at it . . . All right, Lane. What are you staring at? Hit it up onto the green."

The kid did, too, a sweetheart of a niblick out that dropped the ball eight inches from the cup. Angus ran his chip up to within three feet, but Greenly blew the putt. A. R. sank the eight-incher and then looked around as though he had made a hole in one.

"Fine putt, Mr. Mallow!" Jim applauded. "We halved them!"

"Bah!" snarled A. R., "We could have won the hole if you had played it right! A half isn't good enough!"

"I'll try to do better next time, sir." The boy was just like honey. And was William Fowler, Esquire, tickled with his brainwork. Lane was right in there, pitching for that girl. The only thing that worried me at the moment was how long Eleanor was going to be able to hold out. That girl had spirit, and she was plenty sore.

And she kept getting madder and madder as the match went on, until I began to feel pretty rotten at having done that to her and young Jimmy. The farther we went, the worse A. R. got. He griped and squawked and bullied the kid, and when he wasn't picking on Lane, he was handing it out to pros in general. Lane just kept on taking it and coming back for more.

Love must be a wonderful thing, because that boy performed miracles. A. R. was making him play woods out of midfairway bunkers, misjudging distances to greens and forcing him to use pitch clubs on shots that called for long irons. Once he even made him change his swing.

All Lane would do was smile and say, "Guess you're right, Mr. Mallow. You sure know a lot about golf."

And then I noticed a funny thing when we turned the tenth. Eleanor was still hopping mad, but it wasn't at A. R. any more. It was at Jim. I caught her looking at him and saw her lip curl. After a while she dropped back and walked with Hammett. I thought maybe I'd better say something, so, crossing the bridge over the brook at twelve, I stepped alongside and murmured, "It's a shame what Jimmy has to take from A. R., but he's doing a great job."

She gave me one of those smiles right down from Greenland, and said, "If you are referring to Mr. Lane, I haven't the slightest interest in what he is doing."

And four days ago she was in his arms, crying over him. You figure 'em out.

The match was a seesaw dingdonger. Luckily, Greenly was jittery and almost as bad as Mallow. Angus was playing that smooth, perfect golf that made him Open champion, and not saying much. Then we hit a bad streak and were three down at the twelfth. A. R. was fit to be tied.

"What's the matter, Lane?" he bawled. "Haven't you any guts? That's why you professionals blow up! Yellow!"

I didn't dare look at Eleanor. And for once Jimmy lost his sweet smile and didn't say anything. Luckily, Angus ran into a streak of bad putting, and our side picked up three holes in a row before Angus changed their ball and apparently got his touch back.

We went one down on fifteen. I thought we were going to blow another on sixteen, when Jimmy hit into a bunker because A. R. made him use a No. 8 iron on a shot that called for a No. 5. My heart was rattling against my teeth when Mallow went down into the pit. But I have to hand it to A. R. He made the only good stroke of his whole round, and how we needed it there. He swung. The ball sailed out and dropped a foot from the can, for Jim to tap in for the half.

Even old Angus said, "Weel played, sor. A bonnie hit," while Jim beamed. "Splendid, sir. Wonderful shot."

A. R. just glared at the kid and said, "Some-body's got to know how to play this game. I don't need you to tell me when I make a good shot."

But I felt pretty sick when we came to the eighteenth, because we were still one down. We had to win the hole to keep the match alive. A half would mean we were licked. Old Greenly was getting more and more nervous, but I couldn't count on that. Even Eleanor came up close with Hammett to see what would happen.

I would rather not go into details about that eighteenth, but when the smoke cleared away, Fairgreen's ball lay on the green, four inches from the cup in six, for a sure seven. We were on the green, too, in five, but about nine feet from the hole. Lane had played the greatest shot I ever saw, with the ball an inch underwater at the edge of the pond, where Mallow had dumped it.

And it was Mallow's and Greenly's turn to putt.

A. R. marched right up to the ball and began to sight it. I had to give him credit. I didn't know he had that much nerve.

Then I heard an unpleasant rasping noise which I identified as the voice of J. Sears Hammett, "You've got to sink this one, Mallow, old boy!"

A. R. looked up, frowning. "Eh?" he said. "What for? We're five to your six."

J. Sears parted that lemon he uses for a face. "If you miss it, all you can get is a half. We're one up now, and that means we win. That's what for."

A. R. turned as white as his collar. "Wha-what? What do you mean?"

Greenly gave a snort like a horse. "It means, you old buzzard, that you've run out of holes. And rubber, too. Haw-haw-haw. This is the eighteenth. There aren't any more. If you sink it, we play an extra hole. If you don't —" He made that pretty gesture of the finger across the throat.

A lot of the bounce had suddenly gone out of A. R. He stared at the ball, then at the hole, and finally at Jim and me. "D-do I really have to s-sink it?" he quavered.

I said, "Guess you do, sir, but Hammett ought to have kept his big mouth shut."

Jim encouraged him, "There's nothing to it, sir. It's a straight putt. Just step right up and knock it into the bucket. The hole looks as big as a washtub."

"H'm'm'm," said A. R. But it wasn't the old Mallow snort any more. It was a plaintive moan that sounded like first cousin to a whine.

Did you ever see a man who is really frightened? Not pretty, is it? That putt meant bucks, and more. It meant maybe we were going out of business. And as it finally dawned on him, Argyle Rutherford Mallow began to come apart at the seams.

As he studied the putt, he began to shake so his teeth chattered. He turned from white to a beautiful pea-green color. I thought his eyes were going to pop right out of his head. His chest heaved up and down; his knees knocked together. He examined the ball, the grass, the hole, the putter; and the longer he took, the worse he got.

Greenly, Angus and Hammett had big grins on their faces, but I noticed that Jim Lane wasn't smiling any more as he watched A. R. Instead, he had a queer expression on his face, one I had never seen there before.

Days turned into weeks and weeks into months, and still A. R. hadn't putted. He wiped his sweaty hands. He loosened his collar and walked around. He lit a cigarette, threw it away and put the match in his mouth. He was quaking so he couldn't hold the putter on the ground.

Gee, nobody wanted to see Mallow & Co. win more than I, but I could have cheered at that moment. The Old Man was learning something about golf when the chips are down.

I've talked to the boys. I knew just what he was going through. That hole looked as big as a pea, and a thousand miles away. The close-cropped green was a jungle and every irregularity in the ground was Mount Everest.

Sweat began to pour from his face. All he had to do was tap the ball in a straight line and it would roll into the hole. But what was the line? And how hard to tap it? And how to hit a smooth, even stroke when every nerve in his body was screaming? If he could have done something explosive at that point, like hit a drive, it might have been different. But what was called for was a little bit of a delicate movement. On the complete accuracy and control of that movement everything depended.

A quivering wreck, A. R. tried to line up the putt again. I felt like hollering, "So you want to know why pros blow up in a big-money tournament, do you?" I knew what he was thinking. As long as he hadn't putted, he still had a chance. But if he missed—and he had to putt. He saw the ball short, over, past the cup on one side or the other, but never in. Why, oh, why, did everything—honor, money, victory or defeat—have to hang on that one damnable movement that he couldn't bring himself to make?

All of a sudden, A. R. gave a horrible groan, closed his eyes and putted. Oh, it was a lulu! He took up a foot of turf and the ball moved exactly one inch. Then his legs gave way and he fell right down on his knees, while Hammett and Angus McDonough patted each other's backs and whooped. It was all over.

With a fine disregard for rules, Fairfield Greenly stepped up to tap his four-incher into the cup and addressed it carefully. Nobody stopped him.

"EASY, NOW, MR. GREENLY!"

The rasping voice of J. Sears Hammett exploded on the quiet like a concealed four-inch rifle. Greenly jumped as though somebody had stabbed him in the rear, and knocked the ball ten feet past the hole.

"Dod blast you for a triple-plated clown!" he roared at Hammett. "Look what you made me do!"

"Hah!" shouted A. R., still on his knees. "You missed! We've got another chance . . . Come on, Jim. Putt it in. You can do it."

I couldn't figure out what was coming from Jim. He stood there for a moment, looking down at A. R. with that queer expression on his face.

Then he said evenly, "I cain, Mr. Mallow, but I ain't agoin' to."

"What the devil do you mean?"

Jim turned and gazed at Eleanor for a moment in a sort of sad way, and then said to A. R., "Exactly what I said. I'm not agoin' to hit thet putt for you. I'm goin' back to the clubhouse and leave it lay. Yo're no golfer, no sportsman, no gentleman. Yo're just a disgrace to golf. You been pickin' on me and all the other boys who play the game for you. I'd have taken it if you'd showed the courage of a mouse when the blue chips was down. But you folded up just like an old woman. I don't care for you, or the doggone rubber, or the match, or the job either. An' that's that."

He turned to Eleanor, whose sweet eyes

were shining like headlamps out of her white face. "Honey, I'm sorry. Lawd knows, I love yo' an' tried hard, but I got to go on living with myself and lookin' myself in the face. I wasn't made to be a doormat. I jes' had to tell him. I guess it's good-by."

She got to him before he had taken more than three steps. "Darling! Darling! Oh, you're wonderful! I was so afraid you weren't going to do that! I was simply furious with you for letting him walk all over you! Oh, I adore you now!" Her arms were around his neck. His were pretty busy too.

But that ball of ours was still about nine feet from the hole. And A. R. was still kneeling on the green looking like a man who has been hit by lightning.

"Jim, darling," Eleanor said suddenly, when they had got through making up. "You said everything you had to. Won't you sink it now —for me?"

Lane walked over to Mallow. Gee, he could look tough. "Is there going to be any more trouble about Eleanor and me?"

The experience of the putt had taken all the fight out of A. R. He just moaned and shook his head.

"Are you ever agoin' to say again that pros have no guts and are lazy, good-for-nothing —"

"No-no, no, my boy. I was wrong. Pay no attention. Wonderful set of fellows."

"Okay!" Jim stepped up to the ball, gave it a careless once-over and tapped it. Boy, I never heard a sweeter sound than it made clattering into the bottom of that can. "Come on!" I whooped. "We'll get 'em at the next hole!"

A. R. got up with a moan. His knees were still shaking. "Another hole? Don't know if I can make it. All unstrung. Terrible experience."

J. Sears Hammett stepped forward. His voice dripped oil and treacle. He said, "I think I can spare you that trouble, Mallow, old boy. I claim the match and the bet for Fairgreen."

"You what? What are you talking about?"

Hammett looked at A. R. coldly. "You know the terms of the bet. Play your own equipment. The fine shot you hit out of that bunker on sixteen was made with that Fairgreen Shoor-Out sand wedge I gave you last Wednesday. Here it is in your bag."

Smart old Fowler! Will I never learn that

J. Sears Hammett always has an edge? I had forgotten all about the Fairgreen club that louse had planted on A. R. We were sunk!

Mallow turned on Hammett and shouted, "You are a villain, sir! I trusted you!" when Jim cut him short.

"Skip it, A. R. . . . And you, too, Hammett. If you're going to stick that close to the terms of the bet, we'll jes' cancel it out. Angus McDonough there has been playing the A. R. Mallow Thunderbolt ball for the last six holes."

Did we make a dive for those golf balls! It was true. They were both Thunderbolts. A. R. looked at Jim with a new respect in his eyes.

Now it was Greenly's turn to scream, "McDonough, what the devil does this mean? I pay you to play with —"

Friends, there was mutiny in the air. Angus cut Greenly off with a cold stare. "It means, sor, that I canna play wi' your blosted ball. Thot domned diamond chip rottlin' aroond inside it makes me nairvous, and ye can take it or leave it. As for your bet —"

"Hah!" I yelled. "The bet!" They weren't to keep William Fowler, Esquire, out of that insurrection, if it cost me my job. And all that squawking about sticking to the terms of the bet had popped off an idea in my skull.

"The bet! It's all over. The terms of the match were eighteen holes. Well, you've played eighteen and you're all even. Nothing was said about extra holes. Outside of being the two lousiest golfers in the world, you're a couple of old fools trying to cut each other's throats for a little bit of rubber, at a time when we all ought to be pulling together and trying to help each other out. Go on, shake hands, you two, and let's get out of here."

The pair of them looked just like a couple of kids caught in the cooky jar. A. R. heaved a sigh of relief like the Overland Limited blowing off steam.

"Gad!" he said. "Damned relieved. Couldn't play another stroke."

"Whew!" grunted Greenly. "Neither could I." They shook.

"Fowler," said A. R., "proud of you. You're a genius. I'll buy a drink."

"You bet you will," I said.

It wasn't that I was still being fresh. It just made me so darned happy to see Jim and Eleanor, their arms around each other, disappearing past the corner of the clubhouse.

· II ·

CARTOONS

EDWARD PENFIELD
By permission, P. F. Collier & Son.

CHARLES DANA GIBSON

ADVICE TO CADDIES
You will save time by keeping your eye on the ball, not on the player.

From old *Life*; Copr., 1900, Life Publishing Co.

PROFESSIONAL (AT INDOOR SCHOOL OF GOLF): *"Are you going to have a lesson, Madam?"*
MADAM: *"No, but my friend is. I learnt last week."*

By permission of the Proprietors of *Punch.*
Copr., Bradbury, Agnew & Company, Ltd.

SMALL GIRL (AS GOLFER PAUSES FOR BREATH): *"He's stopped beating it, Mummy. I think it must be dead."*

TRY OUR CORK-TIPPED GOLF BAG—IT FLOATS!—AND OUR COMBINATION SPOON-MASHIE PADDLE.

From *The Duffer's Handbook of Golf,* by Grantland Rice.
Copr., The Macmillan Company.

From *The Duffer's Handbook of Golf,* by Grantland Rice.
Copr., The Macmillan Company.

From *The Duffer's Handbook of Golf,* by Grantland Rice.
Copr., The Macmillan Company.

IS THERE SUCH A THING AS A HAPPY GOLFER?

THIS GOLFER MADE
A SCORE OF 112
AND IS SORE
BECAUSE HE
THINKS HE
SHOULD HAVE
MADE 108 -

THIS ONE BROKE
100 AND IS VERY
UNHAPPY BECAUSE
HE SHOULD HAVE
MADE A 94 -

HE MADE AN 89
AND IS PERFECTLY
MISERABLE BECAUSE
HE DIDN'T GO
AROUND IN 84 -

THIS UNHAPPY WRETCH
MADE A 79 BUT
HIS WHOLE NATURE
IS SOURED BECAUSE
HE THINKS HE
SHOULD HAVE DONE
IT IN 76 -

THIS MAN
DOESN'T
PLAY
GOLF !

By permission of the artist. Copr., Rube Goldberg.

WHAT THE WELL DRESSED GOLFER SHOULD WEAR

THE CORRECT
SHOE FOR GOLFERS
WHO SPEND MOST
OF THEIR TIME IN
TRAPS — THE TWO
LITTLE DRAIN-PIPES
AT EITHER END OF
THE SHOE LET OUT
THE SAND AND
INSURE COM-
FORTABLE WALKING.

THE FORM-FITTING
COUCH ON WHICH
THE TIRED PLAYER
CAN RECLINE WHILE
WAITING FOR A
DEAD FOURSOME TO
GET OFF THE GREEN.

THE MAGNETIC SHIRT-
THIS SHIRT IS
GUARANTEED NOT TO
CREEP UP OUT OF THE
TROUSERS- IRON
GARTERS MUST BE
WORN TO ATTRACT
THE MAGNETS.

THE GOLFERS' AWNING
ELIMINATES ALL
WORRY ABOUT
RAIN— IT CAN
BE USED OVER
YOUR DELICATESSEN
STORE DURING
THE WEEK.

WHEN THE GOLFER
FEELS HIMSELF
GETTING SORE AND
DISGUSTED, HE SLIPS
THIS OVER HIS FACE
AND HIS REPUTATION
AS A GOOD SPORT
IS INSURED.

RUBE GOLDBERG

By permission of the artist. Copr., Rube Goldberg.

A RULING PASSION

MR. MEENISTER MACGLUCKY (of the Free Kirk, after having given way more than usual to an expression "a wee thing strong"—despairingly). *"Oh! Aye! Ah, w-e-el! I'll hae ta gie 't up!"*
MR. ELDER MACNAB. *"Wha-at, man, gie up gowf?"*
MR. MEENISTER MACGLUCKY. *"Nae, nae! Gie up the Meenistry!"*

TOONERVILLE FOLKS

From *The Duffer's Handbook of Golf*, by Grantland Rice.
Copr., The Macmillan Company.

TOONERVILLE FOLKS

By permission of the artist. Copr., 1953, Fontaine Fox

"No, No, Galsworthy! You're pronating the supinator longus—
I said extend the capri radialis and flex the deltoid."

Copr., 1953, *Golf Digest* Magazine

"If you don't mind my saying so, your right hand is too far under the shaft."

Copr., 1941, *Golfing*

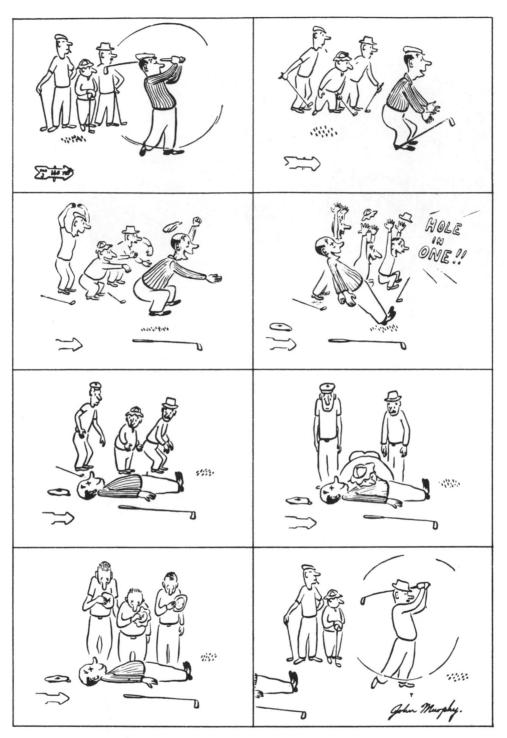

Copr., 1948, *Golfing*

Copr., 1922, *The American Golfer*

"May we play through?"

By permission, *True* Magazine. Copr., Fawcett Publishing Co., Inc.

"Mebbe 'tis, mebbe 'tisn't. Your name Spalding?"

"Now you and I are going to share a little secret."

By permission. Copr., 1940, 1968, *The New Yorker* Magazine, Inc.

"*Well, there goes Junior.*"

SUNDAY MORNING GOLF.

"Could we ask you not to cash this check until next Monday?"

63

"Fore!"

By permission of the artist. From *The Saturday Evening Post*. Copr., 1950, Charles E. Martin.

By permission of the artist. Copr., 1949, *This Week* Magazine.

"*Fore!*"

By permission of the artist. Copr., 1951, *This Week* Magazine.

"Awful lot of Sunday drivers out today."

"*Oh, for goodness sake, forget it, Beasley. Play another one.*"

HOW TO TORTURE YOUR HUSBAND

"How many on that last one—roughly?"

"Now, when the club comes down, shift that weight of yours to your left foot."

"Have either of you gentlemen seen anything of a little white ball?"

"Well, I told you I hadn't played this course in a couple of years."

"*Mind if I play through? My wife's having a pretty tricky operation and
I'd like to get to the hospital as soon as I can.*"

"This is the big one, folks.... Now he's sighting the putt.... Now he's
bending over and addressing the ball.... Now he's glaring in my direction...."

· III ·

THE SPIRIT
OF THE GAME

Reminiscence, Comment, History, and Humor

The Links of Leith

by

TOBIAS SMOLLETT

1771 — FROM THE NOVEL, *THE EXPEDITION OF HUMPHREY CLINKER*

HARD BY, in the fields called the Links, the citizens of Edinburgh divert themselves at a game called Golf, in which they use a curious kind of bats tipped with horn, and small elastic balls of leather, stuffed with feathers, rather less than tennis balls, but of a much harder consistence. These they strike with such force and dexterity from one hole to another, that they will fly to an incredible distance. Of this diversion the Scots are so fond, that, when the weather will permit, you may see a multitude of all ranks, from the senator of justice to the lowest tradesman, mingled together, in their shirts, and following the balls with the utmost eagerness. Among others, I was shown one particular set of golfers, the youngest of whom was turned of fourscore. They were all gentlemen of independent fortunes, who had amused themselves with this pastime for the best part of a century, without having ever felt the least alarm from sickness or disgust; and they never went to bed without having each the best part of a gallon of claret in his belly. Such uninterrupted exercise, cooperating with the keen air from the sea, must, without all doubt, keep the appetite on edge, and steel the constitution against all the common attacks of distemper.

The Birth of the Linksland Courses

by

SIR GUY CAMPBELL

1952 — FROM *A HISTORY OF GOLF IN BRITAIN*

BRITISH GOLF was first played over links or "green fields." The earliest of them were sited at points up and down the eastern seaboard of Scotland, of which Dornoch, Montrose, Barry, Scotscraig, St. Andrews, Elie, Leven, Musselburgh, North Berwick, and Dunbar were, and Dornoch, Barry (Carnoustie), and North Berwick are typical. Nature was their architect, and beast and man her contractors.

In the formation and over-all stabilization of our island coastlines, the sea at intervals of time and distance gradually receded from the higher ground of cliff, bluff and escarpment to and from which the tides once flowed and ebbed. And as during the ages, by stages, the sea withdrew, it left a series of sandy wastes in bold ridge and significant furrow, broken and divided by numerous channels up and down which the tides advanced and retired, and down certain of which the burns, streams and rivers found their way to sea.

As time went on, these channels, other than those down which the burns, streams and rivers ran, dried out and by the action of the winds were formed into dunes, ridges, and knolls, and denes, gullies and hollows, of varying height, width and depth.

In the course of nature these channel-threaded wastes became the resting, nesting and breeding places for birds. This meant bird droppings and so guano or manure, which,

with the silt brought down by the burns, streams and rivers, formed tilth in which the seeds blown from inland and regurgitated from the crops of the birds germinated and established vegetation. Thus eventually the whole of these areas became grass-covered, from the coarse marram on the exposed dunes, ridges and hillocks, and the finer bents and fescues in the sheltered dunes, gullies and hollows, to the meadow grasses round and about the river estuaries and the mouths of the streams and burns. Out of the spreading and intermingling of all these grasses which followed, was established the thick, close-growing, hard-wearing sward that is such a feature of true links turf wherever it is found.

On these areas in due course and where the soil was suitable, heather, whins, broom and trees took root and flourished in drifts, clumps, and coverts; terrain essentially adapted to attract and sustain animal life.

Nature saw to this. First came the rabbits or "cunninggis" as an ancient St. Andrews charter describes them; and after the "cunninggis" as naturally came the beasts of prey, followed inevitably by man.

This sequence had a definite effect on these wastes or warrens. In them the rabbits bred and multiplied. They linked up by runs their burrows in the dunes and ridges with their feeding and frolicking grounds in the straths and sheltered oases flanked and backed by whins and broom. The runs were then gradually worn into tracks by foxes, and man the hunter in his turn widened the tracks into paths and rides. Generations later when man the sportsman, having adopted golf as a pastime, went in search of ground suitable for its pursuit, he found it waiting for him, in these warrens, almost ready to hand. In form it was certainly primitive but it supplied lavishly what today are regarded as the fundamental and traditional characteristics of golfing terrain.

The rides leading from one assembly place to another made the basis of each fairway; the wild and broken country over which the rides threaded their way provided the rough and hazards—rough and hazards that would now bring a blanch to the faces of the most accurate and phlegmatic of our "Professors," and the sheltered *enclaves* used by the "cunninggis" for their feeding halls and dancing floors presented the obvious sites for greens.

Shortly the original layout of nature, interpreted and completed by beast and man, not only hallmarked golf as a point-to-point game, but from then on became the blueprint and sealed pattern for every links and course constructed by intention; indeed it remains today the ideal of all quality design.

As a complete and concentrated example of these "combined operations," the alliance between nature, beast and man (the foundation of our first links with a governing influence on their descendants here and all over the world), the area known as St. Andrews links is outstanding. Its coastline back in the dim ages started from the cliffs guarding the Scores, then ran inland and below what is now known as the Station Hill, and continued along under the high ground of the Strathtyrum estate policies to where the River Eden makes its break for the sea at Guard Bridge —a perimeter extending from east through south, southwest, west to northwest. As the sea retreated from it the process of natural reclamation progressed until today the links area is bounded by a long belt of fertile farmland, an expanse of saltings, the Eden estuary and St. Andrews Bay.

What is now the Old Course was primitively in existence when the University was founded in 1414. As today, it then "pointed" generally north by west and south by east

in the shape of a hill-hook. Then, however, it occupied the narrowest of strips between the arable land on the west and a dense mass of whins that spread east to the high ridge of dunes flanking the sands. So narrow a strip that until towards the middle of the nineteenth century there was room only for single greens; at first eleven and later nine. Accordingly in the full round, eventually of eighteen holes, golfers had to play to the same holes both going out and coming home, with priority in approaching to, and putting on them, at the call of those homeward bound. The nine holes all had names which were used both going out and coming home, i.e., "The Heather Hole out," "The High Hole home," a custom that still continues.

With the advent of the gutta ball the game became so popular that the old method, as it were, of flow and return along the same pipe, became impossible. Consequently six of the nine greens were extended laterally so as to allow two holes to be cut upon them, thus establishing the double greens for which the Old Course has so long been famous. A new site for the seventeenth green was established due north of the Road hole and just west of the Swilken Burn.

The three single-hole greens were and are the first, the ninth or End, and the eighteenth or Home. When the eighteen separate holes were first played the original nine holes were used on the outward half, and the six holes on the extended greens and the newly sited seventeenth green on the return journey. This caused two "crosses" in play, one between the first and Home holes, and the other between the seventh or High hole out and the short eleventh or High hole home. Before long the course was sampled in the reverse order, or "right-handed" going out and coming home. Leaving only one "cross," between the seventh and eleventh holes, was found so satisfactory that this layout—the right-hand course—came to be accepted as the "official" presentation for all major events, although up to the First World War the right-hand and left-hand courses were used alternately a week at a time, except during the high season.

In this connection and as a fact historically interesting, the Amateur Championship of 1886, won by Horace Hutchinson, was played at St. Andrews over the left-hand course. It happened by chance. The week for the great event coincided with the turn of the left-hand course, the Old Course was so prepared, and play in the tournament was begun over it, before authority was aware what had occurred. Accordingly, the Amateur was continued and completed over the left-hand course for the first and only time. This has been recorded by Jack Tait—Freddy Tait's eldest brother—who was himself a competitor, and for the occasion acted as the special correspondent of the *Times*.

Incidentally this "alteration" of course presentation was due chiefly to the representations of Old Tom Morris, the curator of the links, who declared the "switch" was necessary to prevent constant wear and tear in defined areas—the Old Tom who said to a golfer deploring the taboo on Sunday golf, "Weel, sir, the links want a rest on the Sabbath, even if you don't."

This "spreading" of the Old Course (for the width of the fairways was also extended sufficiently to provide a distinct route for both the outward and homeward journeys) was not the only change that time and the increasing popularity of the game brought to St. Andrews links. In 1894 the New Course running parallel to and east of the Old Course was constructed out of the mass of whins already mentioned, but leaving a belt—now steadily and regrettably disappearing—to separate it from its ancient neighbor. Three years later a number of additional holes were made east of the New Course and close to the dunes or sandhills, which became the exercising ground of children and beginners under the name of the Jubilee Course.

Golf continued to gain fresh adherents year by year in such numbers that in 1912 the Town Council of St. Andrews had a fourth course constructed on each side of the railway line, west of the Old Course and between it and the farmland, and the Eden estuary. This was named the Eden Course and is today a representative expression of modern golf architecture.

And year by year while all this was happening, the sea continued its retreat. Up till the First World War this was so gradual as to rouse little if any attention. But in the interval between the first and second cataclysms, the pace quickened at such a rate that by 1939 an entirely fresh tract of golfing ground had formed between the sandhills and high-water mark. A case for St. Andrews links of *ein Drang nach Osten*. On this freshly surrendered expanse the Town Council prepared another full eighteen-hole course, during the Second World War, incorporating the holes of the former Jubilee Course under which name this latest extension is now known. Thus, thanks to nature, the cooperation of beast and man, and finally of man alone, nine-tenths of St. Andrews links as today existing is devoted to golf, and supports four full-sized eighteen-hole courses—two of them used in championships— and three putting courses of eighteen holes and generous dimensions.

This may seem a somewhat lengthy description accorded to one place, but it is justified because it crystallizes the story of the origin, evolution and development of all similar areas in our islands: such as Carnoustie and Machrihanish in Scotland; Westward Ho! and Prince's in England; Harlech and Aberdovey in Wales; Portrush and Portmarnock in Ireland, and many other happy hunting grounds that will quicken the minds of the faithful golfers to and by whom they are known and held in esteem. And it is on such a foundation stone, historical in its laying, that the edifice of British links and courses has been built.

Some of the Humors of Golf

by

THE RT. HON A. J. BALFOUR

1890 — FROM THE BADMINTON LIBRARY'S *GOLF*

ATOLERABLE DAY, a tolerable green, a tolerable opponent, supply, or ought to supply, all that any reasonably constituted human being should require in the way of entertainment. With a fine sea view, and a clear course in front of him, the golfer should find no difficulty in dismissing all worries from his mind, and regarding golf, even it may be indifferent golf, as the true and adequate end of man's existence. Care may sit behind the horseman, she never presumes to walk with the caddie. No inconvenient reminiscences of the ordinary workaday world, no intervals of weariness or monotony interrupt the pleasures of the game. And of what other recreation can this be said? Does a man trust to conversation to occupy his leisure moments? He is at the mercy of fools and bores. Does he put his trust in shooting, hunting, or cricket? Even if he be so fortunately circumstanced as to obtain them in perfection, it will hardly be denied that such moments of pleasure as they can afford are separated by not infrequent intervals of tedium. The ten-mile walk through the rain after missing a stag; a long ride home after a blank day; fielding out while your opponents score 400, cannot be described by the most enthusiastic deer-stalker, fox-hunter, or cricketer as otherwise than wearisome episodes in delightful pursuits. Lawn tennis, again, is not so much a game as an exercise, while in real tennis or in rackets something approaching to equality of skill between the players would seem to be almost necessary for enjoyment. These more violent exercises, again, cannot be played with profit for more than one or two hours in the day. And while this may be too long for a man very hard worked in other ways, it is too short for a man who wishes to spend a complete holiday as much as possible in the open air.

Moreover, all these games have the demerit of being adapted principally to the season of youth. Long before middle life is reached, rowing, rackets, fielding at cricket are a weariness to those who once excelled at them. At thirty-five, when strength and endurance may be at their maximum, the particular elasticity required for these exercises is seriously diminished. The man who has gloried in them as the most precious of his acquirements begins, so far as they are concerned, to grow old; and growing old is not commonly supposed to be so agreeable an operation in itself as to make it advisable to indulge in it more often in a single lifetime than is absolutely necessary.

The golfer, on the other hand, is never old until he is decrepit. So long as Providence allows him the use of two legs active enough to carry him round the green, and of two arms supple enough to take a "half swing," there is no reason why his enjoyment in the game need be seriously diminished. Decay no doubt there is;

long driving has gone forever; and something less of firmness and accuracy may be noted even in the short game. But the decay has come by such slow gradations, it has delayed so long and spared so much, that it is robbed of half its bitterness.

I do not know that I can do much better than close this desultory chapter with a brief autobiography, taken down from his own lips, of perhaps the most distinguished professional of the century—a man known by name to all golfers, even to those who have never visited St. Andrews—Old Tom Morris.

This transcript of a conversation held on New Year's Day, 1886, is not only interesting in itself, but contains much sound golfing philosophy. I give it to the reader precisely in the shape in which it has been given to me:

"A gude new year t'ye, Maister Alexander, an' mony o' them! An' it's come weel in, the year has; for it's just a braw day for a mautch. Lod, sir, it ay seems to me the years, as they rise, skelp fester the tane after t'ither; they'll sune be makin' auld men o've a'. Hoo auold am I, d'ye ask, sir? Weel I was born June 16, 1821; and ye can calc'late that for yoursel'. Aye! as ye say, sir, born and bred in St. Awndrews, an' a gowffer a' ma days. The vera first time, I think, I hae mind o' mysel' I was toddlin' aboot in the short holes, wi' a putter uneath ma bit oxter.

"I was made 'prentice to Allan as a ba'-macker at eighteen, and wrocht wi' him eliven years. We played, Allan and me thegither, some geyan bit mautches—ane in parteecler wi' the twa Dunns, Willie and Jamie, graund players baith, nane better—over fower greens. It was a' through a braw fecht atweens—green and green—but we snoddit 'em bonnie ere the end i't. I canna ca' to mind Allan and me was iver sae sair teckled as that time; though a wheen richt gude pair o' them did their best to pit oor twa noses oot o' joint. But it was na to be dune wi' Allan an' me. An awfu'

player, puir Allan! the cunningest bit body o' a player, I dae think, that iver haun'led cleek an' putter. An' a kindly body tae, as it weel fits me to say, sir, an' wi' a walth o' slee pawky fun aboot him.

"I left Allan to keep the Green at Prestwick, and was there fourteen years. Three years efter Allan deed I cam to keep the Green here; an' here I hae been sin syne. Na! sir, I niver weary o' the gemm; an' I'm as ready noo to play any gentleman as I was in ma best days. I think I can play aboot as weel yet as I did in ma prime. No, may be, drive *jist* sae lang a ba'; but there's not muckle odds e'en in that yet. Jist the day I was sixty-four, I gaed roon' in a single wi' Mr. H. in 81. No that ill for the 'Auld Horse' as they ca' me—it'll tak' the best of the young ones, I reckon, to be mony shots better than *that*.

"An' it had na been for gowff, I'm no sure that at this day, sir, I wad hae been a leevin' man. I've had ma troubles an' ma trials, like the lave; an', whiles, I thocht they wad hae clean wauved me, sae that to 'lay me doun an' dee'—as the song says—lookit aboot a' that was left in life for puir Tam. It was like as if ma vera sowle was a' thegither gane oot o' me. But there's naething like a ticht gude-gowing mautch to soop yer brain clear o' that kin' o' thing; and wi' the help o' ma God an' o' gowff, I've aye gotten warsled through somehow or ither. The tae thing ta'en wi' the tither, I hae na had an ill time o't. I dinna mind that iver I had an unpleasant ward frae ony o' the many gentlemen I've played wi'. I've aye tried —as ma business was, sir—to mak masel' pleesant to them; an' they've aye been awfu' pleesant to me.

"An' noo, sir, to end a long and, maybe, a silly crack—bein' maistly about masel'—ye'll jist come wi' me, an ye'll hae a glass o' gude brandy, and I'll have ma pint o' black strap, an' we'll drink a gude New Year to ane an-ither, an' the like to a' gude gowffers."

Hints to Golfers of Riper Years

by

HORACE G. HUTCHINSON

1886 — FROM *HINTS ON GOLF*

IF YOU HAPPEN to be a really long driver, the fact will be generally admitted without your emphasizing it, to the annoyance and even peril of your neighbors, by always firing off your tee-shot the moment the parties in front of you have struck their seconds. To bear and to forbear is a necessity of golfing existence.

If your adversary is badly bunkered, there is no rule against your standing over him and counting his strokes aloud, with increasing gusto as their number mounts up; but it will be a wise precaution to arm yourself with the niblick before doing so, so as to meet him on equal terms.

Do not get into the habit of pointing out the peculiarly salient blade of grass which you imagine to have been the cause of your failing to hole your putt. You may sometimes find your adversary, who has successfully holed his, irritatingly shortsighted on these occasions. Moreover, the opinion of a man who has just missed his putt, about the state of that particular putting green, is usually accepted with some reserve.

Of course in every match your ultimate success will depend largely upon the terms on which you have arranged to play, before starting. The settling of these conditions is sometimes a nice matter, needing all the wisdom of the serpent in combination with the meekness of the dove. At such times you will perhaps be surprised to hear a person, whom previously you had believed to somewhat overrate his game, now speaking of it in terms of the greatest modesty. These preliminaries once arranged, however, you will find that Richard soon becomes himself again—till next match making begins.

If you are one of the many golfers who overrate their game, and, when constantly beaten by those they imagine to be their inferiors, are in the habit of ascribing their ill success to indisposition, the state of the atmosphere, or even to the Government's foreign policy or the spots on the sun, you really must not be surprised at finding some ill-natured persons disposed to accept the issue of a large number of matches as a tolerably conclusive test of your powers, in preference to attributing the result to any agency in the field of politics or astronomy.

Never, if you can possibly help it, allow yourself to be beaten by a man from whom you generally win. If you do so, you are likely to find that this one particular round, which appears to you of such peculiarly little importance, is more talked of by your opponent than the score or so of matches in which you have previously defeated him.

If your adversary is a hole or two down, there is no serious cause for alarm in his complaining of a severely sprained wrist, or an acute pain, resembling lumbago, which checks his swing. Should he happen to win the next hole, these symptoms will in all probability become less troublesome.

Again, if you hear a man complaining of having "lost all interest" in a match which he has lately played, you will be pretty safe in inferring that he lost it. The winner very seldom experiences this feeling.

Though the henchman who carries your clubs may be a most able adviser, you will seldom, as a beginner, derive much encouragement from his criticism. If he should happen to remark, "Ye learnt your game from Mr. So-and-so, I'm thinking?"—naming the celebrated player from whom as a matter of fact you did receive your first instructions—you must not conclude too hastily, and in misconception of the Scottish idiom, that this comment is an inference from what he has observed of your play. If you should unwarily reply with too great eagerness in the affirmative, the remark which has been known to follow, "Eh! ye've verra little o' his style aboot ye," will quite suffice to show you your mistake.

However unlucky you may be, and however pleasant a fellow your adversary, it really is not fair to expect his grief for your undeserved misfortunes to be as poignant as your own. Remember, too, that it is not altogether impossible for him to have bad luck also, and that with such measure as you mete out sympathy to him, will he be likely, in turn, to show sympathy for you. I do not remember to have met any golfer who did not consider himself on the whole a remarkably unlucky one.

In partnership with a stronger player, it will not be needful for you to make this careful study of the times to advise and the times to refrain from advising. Ask for advice if you want it, but not otherwise. Do not think it necessary, out of deference to your partner, to be continually soliciting his opinion. It is quite sufficient to apologize once for a topped shot. Do not be constantly referring to it, as if such a mistake was a rarity. Nor when you have made what is, for you, a fair shot, apologize to your partner for "having made such a bad one." He will soon form an estimate of your game, quite apart from the effect produced by these remarks—an estimate probably more correct, and possibly lower, than your own.

Try to remember, too, that a person may be a most indifferent golfer, and yet be a good Christian gentleman, and in some respects worthy of your esteem.

When you hear a golfer enlarging upon the cruel ill-treatment which his ball suffered after "one of the finest shots that ever was played," you need not hastily conclude that the stroke was one of any really very transcendent merit. This is generally a mere golfing *façon de parler*, and should be taken to imply no more than that the stroke in question was not a noticeably bad one.

If you find yourself being outplayed by the excellent iron approaches of your adversary, it is sometimes a good plan to say to him, in a tone of friendly interest, "Really you are playing your iron wonderfully well today—better than I ever saw you play it before. Can you account for it in any way?" This is likely to promote a slight nervousness when he next takes his iron in his hand; and this nervousness is likely, if the match is at all a close one, to be of considerable service to you. There is no rule to prevent your doing this; only after a time people will cease playing with you.

Remember that it is always possible to "over-golf" yourself. Two rounds a day is enough for any man with a week or more of solid golf before him—I am speaking of eighteen-hole rounds, of course—and even then your game will probably be improved by your indulging yourself in another *dies non* besides the Sabbath. Two rounds, moreover, occupy most of the ordinary man's day, and leaves but little spare time for the lighter matters of life.

How to Go About Buying a Putter

by

JOHN L. LOW

1903 — FROM *CONCERNING GOLF*

IF YOU WISH a good putter, you will hardly expect to find one in a clubmaker's ready-made stock, far less in a toyshop or a tobacconist's window. The putter must be sought for with care and not hastily, for she is to be the friend, be it hoped, of many years. First, then, find out a workman of repute as a maker of putters—and in these days of "reach-me-down" clubs there are few such artists—and, having found him, proceed warily. It will never do to go and order him to make you a first-class club for your match next morning; you would probably receive only the work of an apprentice. Wait your time and you will find the great man about his shop, or on his doorstep at the dinner hour, and may remark to him that the day is fine; this will be a safe opening, even though rain be falling in torrents, for it will give him the idea that you are a simple fellow and so throw him off his guard.

If a half-empty pipe lies beside him, offer him a cigar, and mention that you are afraid that it is not as good as you would have wished, being the last of the box, at the same time giving him to understand that another box is expected that evening. The cigar having been accepted and lighted, you may, in course of conversation, allude to a very fine putter made by a rival clubmaker which, you will tell your friend, is being much talked about and copied. This will be almost certainly a winning card to play, for there is much jealousy among the profession, and as likely as not the remark will be made that So-and-so—naming the rival maker—has about as much idea of fashioning a putter as he has of successfully solving the problem of aerial navigation. Do not press the matter to a conclusion, but meet your man again in similar manner, this time carelessly holding in your hand the club which you have long felt was the cause of the success of some distinguished player. Almost seem to hide it from the clubmaker, and he will be sure to ask to see it, and probably volunteer to make you one on the same lines with slight improvements of his own.

In time you will get your putter, and it will probably be a good one; in any case it will be good enough to resell if it does not suit you, which is always a point to be considered.

The Old Apple Tree Gang

by

H. B. MARTIN

1936 — FROM *FIFTY YEARS OF AMERICAN GOLF*

THE St. Andrews clubhouse, an imposing and artistically modern edifice, stands majestically on a prominent eminence at Mt. Hope in Westchester County, New York, a fitting monument to American golf. The imperishable fame of the mother club—the first to be organized in this country and to preserve its continuity—will last forever in the history of golf in the United States.

It will be necessary to turn back a few years to a clear crisp winter's day in February, 1888, to ascertain what prompted the organization of that first golf club. It was on February twenty-second, Washington's Birthday to be exact, that John Reid invited some of his cronies to his cowpasture across the street from his home in Yonkers for the purpose of playing a game of golf. The "sticks" brought over by Robert Lockhart, a friend of Mr. Reid's, had already been satisfactorily tested and approved, so the principals who were to play such an important part in that first game were all set and ready to go. Washington's Birthday being a holiday, the men were hanging around the house with not much to do. As the weather was favorable, there was a keen interest exhibited by the participants in the foray and by the gallery that had come to look on. That morning bright and early three improvised holes were laid out, not much in the way of a test, but something that would serve the purpose. There was only one set of clubs, enough for two players by passing them back and forth, so it was decided that John Reid and John B. Upham should play and the others look on.

Had the start been delayed three weeks, the weather would not have been so propitious, as it would have encountered the greatest blizzard in the history of New York—the famous snowstorm of March 12, which tied up traffic for several days. Later, with the coming of the first crocuses of spring and the opportunity to get out on the cowpasture again at hand, enthusiasm was revived and the miniature playground was becoming cramped and inadequate. Some more clubs and balls had been secured, so all who were interested could play. The three short holes did not allow enough room to give vent to the player's feelings, especially when he elected to let out at the ball. The decision was quickly made to move to a larger field around the corner, where they planned to build a real course with both length and breadth. There were thirty acres in the parcel of land that they selected on the northeast corner of Broadway and Shonnard Avenue. It was owned by John C. Shotts, the local butcher, a thrifty German who thought it wise to buy land in the vicinity of New York City and hold on to it. Shotts' thirty acres were preëmpted, but the wise old German made no complaint, as he considered it poor business to exact the meager rent the land would bring from a class of men who were his best customers.

The little band of pioneers was off to a new start and they went about playing the game with a determination and perseverance that must be admired. They withstood the gibes of the populace and turned a deaf ear to criticism. They went on about their recreation, tending strictly to their own affairs. This little group must be given credit for American golf, because they were the first to start the little ball rolling and to keep it rolling through all these years. There had been other attempts to play golf in this country, but none of the other venturesome pioneers had the temerity to follow through.

The new layout on the butcher's meadow offered possibilities. It was rolling terrain and, as it was good pasture land, the turf was highly satisfactory. The main hazard was a road, or footpath, which wound its way through the property. It had not occurred to any of the original players that an old tomato can was about the right size and shape for a golf hole, so the holes were merely scooped out with the blade of a cleek. The greens, once worthy of the name since they had originally a grass surface, were soon worn bare from constant tramping.

The original course on Broadway was all that was needed to secure peace and happiness, filling the cup of joy to overflowing for those early golfers. Discussions came up from time to time about acquiring more land and building a better course, but it was always decided negatively by John Reid, who was first, last and always a conservative. So the old stamping ground remained the home of St. Andrews until encroaching civilization drove them out. They had stuck like leeches for four years and might have remained longer had the city fathers of Yonkers not seen fit to extend Palisade Avenue farther north, right through the heart of the old golf course. There were no chattels except the few sets of clubs, a tent and a wicker demijohn. So like the ancient Arabs they silently folded their tent and stole away although it may not have been in the middle of the night; the following day, however, found them pleasantly located and ready to carry on. The trail had led northward up the newly planned Palisade Avenue about a quarter of a mile. The little band of wanderers found refuge in an apple orchard on the Weston estate.

It required the greater part of one day to lay out the new course, as there was more or less difficulty experienced in adapting the links to the ground available. The holes had to be woven in and out among the apple trees without sacrificing so much as a limb. There were thirty-four acres, so the course could be stretched a little. This land too was preëmpted but the golfers were not unwelcome as they had by this time become necessary evils in the community. It was still thought unnecessary to adopt the tomato can standardization which other early courses had popularized. The original way of making holes was plenty good enough for the apple orchard, so the holes were again scooped out with the cleek. St. Andrews may have been more or less instrumental in selling golf to the rest of the United States, but it could never persuade the new clubs to follow its rather primitive method of making a hole in the green. Some of the other courses had tomato cans, pea cans and flower pots, and one club had imported steel cups from the other side of the Atlantic.

It was on this new course on Palisade Avenue that the players became known as the "Old Apple Tree Gang," a name that seemed to be decidedly appropriate, as apple trees made the principal hazards; one in particular which stood near the first tee became an integral part of the club itself since it served as a locker room and a nineteenth hole. In the crotch of the friendly tree the men in the hot days of summer laid their coats. From one of the branches hung a basket of sandwiches and from another the old wicker demijohn of Scotland's favorite thirst-quencher.

Just thirteen golfers had come up from the old cowpasture course, not altogether an unlucky number as things turned out. Once settled in the new quarters, the club instituted an active membership drive, and in the next two years seven members were added.

The new membership didn't exactly blend with the original thirteen, and the spirit of supreme contentedness began to diminish. There developed dissatisfaction in the ranks, due to certain growing factions. In most clubs there are conservatives and progressives, and this was true of the first club. Reid was a conservative and his closest friends strung along with him. He insisted that it was not the intention of the St. Andrews Club to teach the rest of the United States the game of golf or to establish any precedents or set any standards in golf course construction. He pointed out that the little organization had plenty of honest recreation and no heartaches and that it might be folly to expand. Harry Tallmadge was a decided liberal and was heartily supported by W. D. Baldwin and Walter E. Hodgeman. These men argued that all the other courses of importance had nine holes and Chicago had put in eighteen holes at Wheaton. All of these clubs had at least twice as many members as St. Andrews. Shinnecock Hills had a membership of seventy-five and they too were talking about eighteen holes; they had a fine clubhouse, too. It was this latter club that awakened the Old Apple Tree Gang from its lethargy.

A committee on selecting a new site was organized for action and without much hesitation decided upon the Odell farm at Grey Oaks. Again we pick up the trail of the nomads, which was east by north, about three miles up the Sawmill River Road. The old farm lay between a long stretch of abruptly rising ground called Snake Hill and the Road. Nine holes were laid out and by May eleventh the club was on the move. It was a happy little group that filed out of the old apple orchard with their cherished possessions under their arms to follow the trail northward. At last they were going some place and the twenty members, born of a new spirit, were united and determined to wage war against Colonel Bogey as a single unit. For six years they had never had a clubhouse, but now they were to have a real home, a locker room to shelter them from the Hudson's breezes and a place to store their golfing kits.

There was romance and mystery connected with the new quarters and some apprehension on the part of some of the gang. In taking over the Odell Mansion, the club did so with the full knowledge that the place was supposed to be haunted. A tragedy had been enacted there some time after the War of 1812, and ghosts had made it so uncomfortable for tenants that it was impossbile to keep the property rented. It was one of the oldest farmhouses in Westchester County, originally built by Jacob Odell about 1790. Odell was an American patriot and later fought in the War of 1812. When the story was sprung that the farmhouse was haunted, some of the timid members of the club possessed with more or less of an imagination were not so keen about sharing the new clubhouse with spooks or apparitions. They had looked forward to this important occasion for six long years, and when at last the day and hour had arrived for them to occupy their own home, they wanted it free and clear of spectral visitors. It was pointed out that the little band was composed of just thirteen members when they made the trek up Palisade Avenue to the apple orchard and no hard luck had ever pursued them. Those who entered the premises with any apprehension found their fears allayed, for just as soon as the Old Apple Tree Gang walked in the ghosts walked out. A crowd of golfers, especially when they came as an organized gang, was too much for an honest and intelligent ghost to countenance.

The Old Apple Tree Gang had never found any incentive to dress for golf affairs because red coats didn't seem to go in the cowpasture and the apple orchard. But when the Shinnecock Hills boys and the Newport swells came out in their scarlet melton coats, fancy knickers or flannels, and gaiters resembling elongated spats, it made the Grey Oaks golfers sit up and take notice. St. Andrews then adopted a uniform. The club, to a man, appeared in full golfing regalia after they had taken the most meticulous care in choosing their colors. There was first of all the red coat with the brass buttons; but the St. Andrews dandies in addition wore blue checked waistcoats, pearl-gray hats with blue-and-white bands, gray knickers, Scotch plaid hose, and gray gaiters. A blue checked cap was worn on the course. To make the St. Andrews coat distinctive, the collar was a blue field with the silver cross of St. Andrew on it. One might choose his own tie but there was always the uniform winged collar, the badge of a gentleman of those days.

In the middle of August, '97, the St. Andrews Golf Club was on the move again. There was a rush to join the famous old club and a desire on the part of the golfers to establish an eighteen-hole links with a modern clubhouse where they could take their place under the sun and hold their head as high as other organizations who were boasting about their championship courses.

The club moved straight up the valley this time to Mt. Hope, again following the old Sawmill River Road. In October, St. Andrews opened the new course officially with an inaugural tournament that brought the best amateurs in the country together.

To be a member of St. Andrews is an honor and distinction, as there is a feeling of permanency there that is not merely tradition. The conservatism of John Reid in the beginning has had something to do with a policy that has been followed through these fifty years. Today St. Andrews is as solid as the Rock of Gibraltar and could well serve as a model for all clubs who wish to balance their budgets. The club has a splendid curling rink which is well patronized by the members throughout the winter months. The club is proud of its golf course and has kept up with the march of progress. It has the finest watering system of any club in America, which is an insurance against summer droughts and parched fairways. The castle on the hill which St. Andrews is proud to call its home is a paradise of security. A visitor is impressed with the cordial hospitality of the members and the efficiency of the employees who have been schooled to receive the guest with wholesome honor and respect.

Across the Street from The Country Club

by

FRANCIS OUIMET

1932 — FROM *A GAME OF GOLF*

BORN IN A rather thinly populated section of Brookline, Massachusetts, I have often wondered what my golfing activities would have amounted to if my father had not bought a home bordering on The Country Club. Of one thing I am quite certain and that is I should never have had the opportunity of developing an interest in the game of golf to the same extent that was made possible by close proximity to a fine course. As it was, daily trips from home to a little schoolhouse, built in 1768 and known as the Putterham School, carried me back and forth across the fairways. Not that I was granted any such privileges, but in the role of a trespasser I discovered that this route saved many footsteps, got me to school on time, and, more important, enabled me to get home with the least possible delay.

There was a more intriguing motive, however. Frequently on one of my excursions I ran across a lost ball, of the gutta-percha variety. At the age of seven I had a collection of Silvertowns, Ocobos, Vardon Flyers, Henleys, and other brands popular among golfers in 1900 that would do full credit to the professional's shop.

Long before I ever had a club, I had golf balls enough to last me for years. But the balls without a club were not very useful. Golf was so new to America in 1900 that it was difficult to get clubs. They never got lost, and were rarely discarded. The balls, however, seemed to have plenty of life in them, their varied markings held some sort of fascination for me, and it was fun watching them bound from rocks and other solid substances.

After I had hoarded golf balls enthusiastically for two years, someone gave my brother Wilfred a club. When Wilfred was busy caddying, I helped myself to that club and used it to knock some of my hoard around the back yard. I was careful to put Wilfred's club back in its place before he put in an appearance. Otherwise, I felt, there might have been a family riot. Occasionally a tournament was held at The Country Club and on those days and after school, I would stand on the edge of a fairway and watch the golfers go by. If I saw someone play an exceptional stroke, I watched how he did it and hastened home to take Wilfred's club and set about trying to put into practice what I had seen. Those efforts must have been funny, but they were, after all, the beginnings of my game, such as it is.

I can remember vividly the first Haskell ball I ever found. It was in the fall of 1902, and I was nine years old. Wilfred was a caddie boy at The Country Club, and the ladies were having their national championship. On the way home from school, I picked up a nice new ball. It was unlike any other I had ever seen and seemed much livelier. I showed it to Wilfred and he told me it was one of the new rubber-cored balls. Few had them, and Big Brother tried his best to talk me into parting with it. Nothing doing. I played with it, bounded it, and used it until the paint wore off. I got some white paint and painted it. Mother was baking some bread in a hot oven and I sneaked my repainted Haskell into the oven, thinking the heat would dry the ball.

Mother smelled something burning and went all through the house trying to discover the cause. She found nothing, but the odor was so strong, and she was so worried that the house was burning up, that she kept on searching. Finally she opened the oven door and the most awful smell in the world came out of the newly made batch of bread. It was ruined—and so was my prize, the Haskell. The heat had melted the gutta-percha shell and there was nothing left of the thing but a shriveled-up mass of elastic bands. I learned then and there how Doctor Haskell made his golf balls and why it was that the rubber-cored ball was vastly superior to the solid gutta.

The Haskell crowded the gutta off the courses and made the game much more enjoyable to play. At any rate, I could play the rubber-cored better than the hard ones, and my interest in the game increased. Behind our house was a cowpasture, and here Wilfred, with the mind of a golf architect, built three holes. The first was about a hundred and fifty yards long, with a carry over a brook. The brook was a hundred yards or so from where we drove. When he hit a shot well, Wilfred could drive close to the green, but it was far beyond my reach. As a matter of fact, the very best I could do was to drive into the brook. The second hole was very short, hardly more than fifty yards. The last was a combination of the first two, and brought the player back to the starting point. We used tomato cans for hole rims. As I visualize that old course of ours, it was the most difficult one I have ever played because it contained a gravel pit, swamps, brooks, and patches of long grass. We—or rather Wilfred—had selected only the high and dry pieces of land, which were few and far between, to play over. A shot that traveled three yards off line meant a lost ball, and it was well we had plenty!

Wilfred made trips to Boston from time to time and discovered that Wright and Ditson had a golf department with a man named Alex Findlay in charge. He discovered also that a good club could be got in exchange for used golf balls, and that three dozen would be a fair exchange for the best club made. From one of these visits Wilfred brought me home a mashie, and for the first time in my young life I was independent so far as playing golf was concerned. I had my own club, balls, and a place to play. What more could anyone ask!

A lawnmower kept two of the greens in fair condition, but the one near our house was used so much it was worn bare and had no grass whatsoever on it. You see, while we were waiting for a meal we fiddled around the hole and the grass never had a chance to grow. One advantage, from Mother's point of view, was that she always knew where to look, and it was a simple matter for her to call us into the house. We fooled around that particular spot early in the morning and long after dark, and it was small wonder that my interest in golf increased because, with all this practice, it was natural enough that I should notice some improvement in my play. Mother thought I had gone crazy because golf was the only thing I seemed interested in.

I had more time to devote to the game than Wilfred. He had chores to do around the house and barn and being older, he was the one called upon to go on errands. They say practice makes perfect, and I believe it. After striving for weeks and months to hit a ball over the brook, and losing many, I finally succeeded. A solid year of practice had enabled me to drive accurately, if not far, and one Saturday morning, after trying for an hour, I drove a ball as clean as a whistle beyond the brook.

When I told Wilfred of my accomplishment, he received my story with a good deal of doubt. I had now acquired a brassie to go with the mashie, and I invited my brother out to the pasture to see what I could do with it. Whether I was tired out from my earlier efforts or not, I do not know, but I failed utterly, and Wilfred naturally was more skeptical than ever. The next day was Sunday, and after I returned from Sunday School, I went at it again. This time Wilfred was with me, and I definitely convinced him by hitting two balls out of three over the brook. It soon got to be a habit, and I was quite disgusted with myself when I failed.

A good many tournaments were held at The Country Club and the best golfers gathered to play in them. Soon I was old enough to caddie, and as a youngster of eleven I saw in action such great golfers as Arthur Lockwood, Chandler Egan, Fred Herreshoff, Jerry Travers, and Walter J. Travis among the amateurs, and Alex Campbell, The Country Club professional, Alex Smith, Tom McNamara, Willie Anderson, and many of the prominent professional players. If I noticed anything particularly successful in the play of any of these golfers, I made a mental note of it, and when opportunity afforded, I set out to my private course and practiced the things I had noted.

Therefore, you see, I was brought up in a golfing environment and learned to love the game. I read in magazines or newspapers anything I could find relating to golf, got a few of the boys in the neighborhood interested in the game, and jumped into it head over heels. One day I caddied for a dear old gentleman named Samuel Carr. Mr. Carr was a golfing enthusiast and, furthermore, always most considerate of the boy who carried his clubs. All the boys liked him. Playing the eighteenth or last hole one day, he asked me if I played golf. I told him I did.

He asked me if I had any clubs. I replied that I had two, a brassie and mashie.

"When we finish, I wish you would come to the locker room with me; I may have a few clubs for you," he said.

I took Mr. Carr's clubs downstairs to the caddie shop and hustled back. He came out with four clubs under his arm, a driver with a leather face, a lofter, a mid-iron, and a putter. I think it was the biggest thrill I had ever got up to that time.

Early mornings—and when I say early I mean around four-thirty or five o'clock—I abandoned my own course and played a few holes on that of The Country Club, until a greenskeeper drove me away. Rainy days, when I was sure no one would be around, I would do the same thing. Complaints concerning my activities arrived home, and Mother warned me to keep off the course, usually ending her reprimand by saying that the game of golf was bound to get me into trouble.

I was so wrapped up in the game, however, I just couldn't leave it alone. One summer, tired of my own layout, I talked a companion, Frank Mahan, into going to Franklin Park with me. Franklin Park was a public course and we could go there and play unmolested. We set out one Saturday morning. To get to Franklin Park, we had to walk a mile and a half with our clubs to the car line. Then we rode to Brookline Village, transferred there to a Roxbury Crossing car, arrived at Roxbury Crossing and changed again to a Franklin Park car. After getting out of the last street car, we walked about three quarters of a mile to the clubhouse, checked our coats—that is all we had to check—and then played six full rounds of the nine holes, a total of fifty-four holes.

Then we went home the way we had come, completely exhausted. All this at the age of thirteen!

Golf in Four Acts

by

GEORGE ADE

1897 — FROM THE SEPTEMBER 27 ISSUE OF THE CHICAGO *RECORD*

ONE of the Frohmans has bargained with a Chicago man of literary attainments for a play dealing with the life among the "best people" of Chicago at the present time. This means that the play will concern golf.

Inasmuch as plays full of romantic episode, such as *Under the Red Robe, The Prisoner of Zenda, Prince Rudolph,* etc., are in popular demand at present, it is essential that the Chicago play shall have plenty of melodramatic coloring.

A correspondent sends in an outline of a play and asserts that this outline will be followed, more or less closely, by the Chicago playwrights. For the benefit of the students of the drama the outline is herewith submitted.

ACT I

THE hero, Mr. Arbuckle, and the heroine, Miss Meadows, are discovered in a vast wilderness, playing golf. They have been out two days, and dying of hunger, but they are still playing. The caddie weeps bitterly and asks to be taken home. They see a man crawling out of a sand pit (called a hazard) and they hail him. It proves to be Mr. Riddle, who is Mr. Arbuckle's deadly rival. He is looking for a lost ball, and has a basket of lunch with him. Arbuckle asks him for food. He refuses to part with his lunch, saying he does not know how soon he will find the ball. Arbuckle accuses him of being "no gentleman," and Riddle replies that Arbuckle's father was a pawnbroker before the fire.

They draw their golfsticks and fight. The caddie faints. Arbuckle disarms Riddle and hits him over the head with a bunker. He and Miss Meadows examine the lunch and find that it consists of caviar sandwiches and olives. They know that if they eat the lunch they will be hungrier than before. Arbuckle calls the olives "hors doove." They escape.

The searching party, headed by Mr. Meadows (known on the links as "Old Man Meadows") and his wife, arrive on the scene. The party has followed a trail of broken turf. Mr. Meadows arouses Mr. Riddle, who regains consciousness, and tells a story to the effect that Arbuckle insulted Miss Meadows by accusing her of foozling her approach. He (Riddle) had protested and Arbuckle had struck him in the fairway. Meadows declares that Arbuckle shall never marry his daughter. The caddie recovers, and finding that the two have gone away with the lunch, corroborates the story told by Riddle. Arbuckle and Miss Meadows return. They have eaten the olives and are in a delirious condition. Curse scene— old Mr. Meadows telling Arbuckle that he must never again darken his threshold.

ACT II

IN FRONT of the golf clubhouse, Riddle is using his influence to have Arbuckle's card revoked. He is assisted by Mr. Van Beet, the villain of the play, who has come from the east to be entertained by members of the club, taking them alphabetically. He has been at the club a month and has reached the R's. They order several things and Riddle signs the checks.

The directors of the club assemble on the veranda and the case is laid before them. Four of the seven directors agree that Arbuckle is no longer entitled to the privileges of the club. Van Beet says: "I will not remain here with that man. One of us must go." The formal vote is about to be taken when a caddie rushes in and announces that Arbuckle has made eighteen holes in 82. Arbuckle is immediately elected to full membership.

Cheers heard outside. Arbuckle enters and is greeted as a member. He makes a speech. "I did it because I thought it was my duty."

The second scene shows the night camp of the caddies. They are gathered around the fire, discussing the peculiarities of the people with whom they are compelled to associate day by day. Riddle and Van Beet enter and offer the caddies a dollar apiece if they will lie in ambush at a distant portion of the links and assault Arbuckle when he is at practice. The plot is completed when Miss Meadows, who has been hiding in the background, comes forward and denounces the conspirators. She is seized and locked in the music pavilion. As the curtain falls the caddies are taking the oath of allegiance.

ACT III

THE clubhouse again—Miss Meadows has been missing for eighteen hours, but no anxiety is felt. It is supposed she is going around the holes again. Riddle and Van Beet have started a report that Arbuckle did not make the course in 82, that the man who was keeping score deliberately made a clerical error and omitted a figure, and that the score should have been 182. Arbuckle's business partner, Mr. Short, arrives at the clubhouse. He begs Arbuckle to return to the city. The market is going against the firm and ruin is imminent. Arbuckle replies that he will not leave the golf club until he

has cleared his name of foul suspicion and can stand once more in the open sunlight.

The second scene is a lonely part of the links. The caddies are secreted in the high grass waiting for Arbuckle. They bemoan the fact that the youth of America should be known as "caddies," a Scotch term. It is agreed that the money received from the two villains shall be expended for uniforms, so that they may organize a baseball team and forget their sorrows.

Arbuckle approaches, singing "Edinboro Town." They fall upon him and a fierce battle ensues. This will be one of the best things in the play.

Arbuckle fights fiercely, but he is about to be overpowered when the board of directors comes to the rescue, led by Miss Meadows, who has escaped from the music pavilion. Miss Meadows throws herself into Arbuckle's arms. Riddle and Van Beet arrive. Miss Meadows accuses them of hiring the caddies to assault her Mr. Arbuckle. They deny it. Mr. Meadows comes on the scene. He hears the story, and is about to give his consent to a marriage, when a telegram for Arbuckle is brought from the clubhouse. It informs him that his firm has failed. Another curse scene, Mr. Meadows declaring his daughter shall never marry a pauper.

ACT IV

THE first scene is at the golf links. A great many people sit around and talk about Mr. Arbuckle. There appears to be a growing belief that he did not do the eighteen holes in 82. Mr. Riddle makes love to Miss Meadows. Mr. Van Beet drinks tea. One man is playing golf. It proves to be Arbuckle. Mr. Meadows tells his daughter she must marry Riddle. She weeps and is led away. There is a scene between Riddle and Van Beet. Riddle promises a box of balls and an inlaid brassie if he will kill Arbuckle. Van Beet agrees.

The second scene is at the club stables. Arbuckle is telling his troubles to his polo pony. A very sad scene. "I have no one left but you," etc. Van Beet enters, and attacks Arbuckle with a knife. Arbuckle is wounded in the arm. The faithful polo pony rushes on Van Beet and eats him. Arbuckle is arrested for the crime. He says he is innocent.

The third scene is at the clubhouse. It is evening and everyone is wearing golf clothes and talking about Arbuckle. No one sympathizes with him.

The scene is supposed to show the heartlessness of modern society.

The engagement of Mr. Riddle and Miss Meadows is announced. Miss Meadows smiles sadly when she is congratulated.

A messenger arrives and requests a private conversation with Mr. Meadows. He tells Mr. Meadows that he (Mr. Meadows, not the messenger) is a ruined man. The market has gone in the wrong direction. The firm needs $40,000 immediately.

Mr. Meadows appeals to Riddle for assistance. Riddle refuses, and says he will not marry his (Meadows') daughter. Arrival of Arbuckle with his arm in a sling. He has been acquitted of the charge. He offers to lend $40,000 to Mr. Meadows.

"You are her father," etc.

Meadows is surprised and asks Arbuckle how and where he got so much money. Arbuckle says that when he found himself penniless he was at his wits' end to discover some method of recovering his fortune. Suddenly he remembered the pond in the golf links. He obtained a net and dragged the pond, taking out over $1,000 worth of golf balls that had been knocked into it inadvertently during three seasons. With the $1,000 he speculated carefully, and soon he was wealthier than ever before.

Meadows asks: "And you do this for me?" Arbuckle tells him that he does it for his (Meadows') daughter's sake.

An officer of the law appears and arrests Riddle. The caddies have confessed.

Miss Meadows enters. Arbuckle rushes to her. They embrace. The whole company enters. Arbuckle announces that the wedding is to be at the clubhouse, and that all participants will be expected to wear golf costumes.

Caddying at Edgewater

by

CHICK EVANS

1921 — FROM *CHICK EVANS' GOLF BOOK*

IN THE EARLY history of the Edgewater Club, back in 1898, there was no caddie master and the so-called caddie yard bore no resemblance to those of today. The entrance to the club was on Devon Avenue, with the caddie yard just across the street and car tracks. I am not certain that this ground even belonged to the club. It was more likely a place where the boys "hung out." There was a ridge running through the lots, and in that part of the city the subsoil is of sand (it was this sand that gave the course such wonderful greens) and some of this had been dug out, leaving a big sandy hole that played an important part in the lives of the caddies. There were high board signs, and trees and bushes, and climbing the signs and trees was a favorite sport. There were rabbits there, too, and we frequently chased them. There were many wild violets—which we did not pick. It was a strangely fascinating spot for a boy of my temperament.

The street cars stopped at the club entrance, and from the the lot across the way the caddies emerged and asked the descending clubmen for a job. That is, if they were what caddies considered good men to work for, otherwise there would not be a caddie in sight, all being carefully concealed in the sandhole, among the bushes, or up in the trees.

I was, however, really too young for caddying; even my brother was rather young, boys of twelve and fourteen being preferred. But there is one quality that I possess in abundance, and that is persistence, and from that first day I simply haunted that caddie yard, confident in the belief that sometime I would be allowed to carry the bag that was taller than I. One day when only ladies were playing, my long-looked-for opportunity arrived. It happened that there were few boys out, the older ones, I fancy, having been drawn to a football game of their own, and a caddie was needed. The lady who accepted my services, such as they were, was Miss Amy Jones, daughter of G. I. Jones, one of the five founders of the Edgewater Golf Club, and unless I am mistaken, she, herself, was at the time the woman champion of the club.

I cannot recall now whether I took any interest in Miss Jones's game. I am afraid not, for at that time I was practically unacquainted with golf, and was probably only interested in "pay time." I may have asked (but I hope not), as I have heard many a small boy do, if we were nearly through. The extraordinary interest that I as a caddie always took in the game of my player came later. I became proudly happy over every fine shot, excused all the poor ones, and made of my caddying time a period of great emotions.

The next spring I remember finding a brand new ball by a method that I have always claimed to have originated, but, of course, I may have deceived myself. I saw a player drive into some long grass that separated the then second and third holes. He knew, of course, that it had gone into that strip but although he looked for a long time, neither he nor this caddie could find it. When he left I concluded to try an experiment and went over and lay down where I thought the ball had fallen. Then I rolled over with thoroughness, accompanied, I must confess, by dizziness, all around the spot until some part of my body struck a round, hard object. This, of course, was the ball, which I immediately proceeded to dig out. The method soon made me rich in golf balls, but what was better it gave me a reputation among both members and caddies of never losing a golf ball.

There is a certain skill about caddying and some boys never make good caddies. There is a knack about the carrying of a bag, and in the days when I was caddying the manufacturers did not make the bags as carefully as they do now. They were not well balanced for the shoulders and almost any sort of a bag was good enough. We used to put the niblick, the least used club, heel downward so that the preponderance of weight would not send the bag tipping forward. Without such weight in the bottom of the bag, it was very uncomfortable for the boy. David Maxwell used his niblick so often, however, that his regular caddie kept a little smooth stone that he dropped in the bottom of the bag.

Nearly all of us North End kids had clubs that we kept with us constantly. They were our greatest treasures and it would never have done to leave them around in the caddie yard if we ever expected to see them again. I even took mine to my bedroom at night, partly to keep it from my brother and partly to protect myself from burglars. Not that I had anything that a burglar would care to steal but there was always a chance that he might not know that.

I made a study of caddying, from the beginning, and I tried to do everything that I saw the experienced boy do, and if I could think out anything that seemed better I did that, too. It was easy for me to learn quickly the names of all the clubs, and I noticed, too, that the members had different ways of taking them for the next shot. When they called for them I got so that, without looking, I could just feel for the right club and hand it out. Many caddies pulled out the club and thrust the cold iron into the player's hand. I made a point of dusting off the head of the club and handing the grip to the player.

When it came to shining clubs I was as good as any, if not the best of the crowd. Caddies no longer do this, yet they still think that they are obliged to work too hard. I really liked the polishing. It was sport for me to work on the clubs till they shone.

There was a constant stream of amusing incidents in our world at Edgewater. One I remember vividly took place one day when I was caddying for C. L. Allen. Joe Morheiser had Arthur Dyrenforth, and Joe Harter carried for W. W. Gurley. The latter player did not drive so long a ball as the others, while Mr. Allen always sent a straight ball down the center of the course. I went up to his ball without paying particular attention to the other players, when, all of a sudden, Mr. Gurley's ball came whizzing along and hit me on the arm. Neither he nor I expected so long a shot. I dropped with a yell. The pain was slight, but the surprise was great, and I thought the only thing to do was to cry. I made a good job of it. Everyone gathered around me in sympathy, and poor Mr. Gurley was the most frightened and sympathetic of all. The only thing he could think of doing was to hold out a bright, new dollar bill, saying: "There you are, sonny; don't cry any more." The remedy acted like magic. My tears ceased flowing at once, and from that moment the black-and-blue spot on my arm meant nothing to me. News travels swiftly in a caddie yard, and in an incredibly short space of time every caddie knew the extent of my injury and the balm applied. Within the next two or three weeks an amazing number of caddies were hit. After a time the casualties ceased. Whether the members had caught on or the boys had collected sufficient extra money I do not know.

There is not much that I can say about playing at the early period of caddying which will help other caddies to become good golfers. As soon as I possessed a golf club I kept it in my hand most of the time, and swung it in as close an imitation of the best players as was possible to me, but my method, I regret to say, was wrong, and that meant many a month of discouragement. After all is said, it was my good caddying, not my good playing, that brought me out of the heap of other caddies, and to the attention of the members. Later on I received help and encouragement from them, but I earned it first by toting a bag.

Mr. Dooley on Golf

by

FINLEY PETER DUNNE

1910 — FROM *MR. DOOLEY AT HIS BEST*

"Wurruk is wurruk if ye're paid to do it an' it's pleasure if ye pay to be allowed to do it."

WELL, SIR," said Mr. Dooley, "I don't want to say annything that wud hurt a frind, but I do think th' authorities ar-re very lax in lavin' Hogan at large, as they ar-re doin'."

"An' what ails Hogan?" Mr. Hennessy asked.

"He's got what th' dock calls a fixed deelusion," said Mr. Dooley. "He thinks he's a goluf player. No, he don't play th' game. Nobody does that. They wurruk at it. But Hogan he slaves at it. He don't think iv annything else. He takes it down to th' wather-office with him in th' mornin', an' he carries it home with him at night an' sleeps with it. If ye go over to his house at this minyit ye'll find him in th' front parlor swingin' a poker an' tellin' th' good woman how he played th' eighth hole. There's nawthin' more excitin' to th' mother iv siven at th' end of a complete wash-day thin to listen to an account iv a bum goluf game fr'm th' lips iv her lifemate. 'Tis almost as absorbin' as th' inventory iv a grocery store. I was over there th' other night, an' he broke three panes iv glass showin' me what he calls a mashie shot, an' he near took an ear off his aunt Bridget practisin' with a war-club that he calls a nibbelick. I wuddn't be harsh with him, but a few months or aven years in a well upholstered cell with a ball an' chain on his leg, might restore him to himself an' make him again th' safe an' bashful husband an' father he wanst was.

"But 'tis a gr-reat game, a gr-rand, jolly, hail-fellow-well-met spoort. With th' exciption maybe iv th' theery iv infant damnation, Scotland has given nawthin' more cheerful to th' wurruld thin th' game iv goluf. Whin 'twas first smuggled into this counthry, I cuddn't make out what 'twas like. I thought whin I first read about it that it was intinded f'r people with a hackin' cough, an' that no wan who was robust enough to play 'Twinty Questions' in a wheel-chair, wud engage in it without a blush. I had it in me mind that 'twas played iv a rainy afthernoon in th' front parlor. Th' two athletes got out their needles an' their embroidery canvas, give a shout iv glee an' flew at it. Th' results was submitted to th' *Ladies Home Journal*, an' me frind Eddie Bok decided who was champeen, an' give him a goold thimble f'r a prize.

"But I know betther now. 'Tis a rough an' angry game, full of ondacint remarks an' other manly charakteristics, d'ye mind. . . . At th' end iv ivry goluf match th' player loathes himsilf, is not on speakin' terms with th' fellow he played again, cud kill his own caddie an' his opponent's, an' hates th' criminal that laid out th' coorse, th' game itsilf, th' Jook iv Argyll, each wan iv his clubs, th' little bur-rd that twittered whin he was shootin', th' pretty wild flowers on th' margin iv th' links, an' each separate spear iv grass on th' puttin' green. If that Dutch pote that wrote th' 'Hymn iv Hate' wants to write an-other on th' same subjick with a rale punch in it he ought to larn goluf. 'Twuld help him.

"How's it played, says ye? I don't exactly know. I niver studied law. But ye can get th' rules iv th' game in th' public library, in siven volumes edited be th' Lord Chief Justice iv Scotland. If ye have a dispute over th' rules, th' quickest way to get a decision is to hire a lawyer, make a test case, an' carry it to th' Supreme Coort. In a gin'ral way, all I can say about it is that it's a kind iv a game iv ball that ye play with ye'er own worst inimy which is ye'ersilf, an' a man ye don't like goes around with ye an' gloats over ye, an' a little boy follows ye to carry th' clubs an' hide th' ball af-ther ye've hit it. Th' ball is small, made iv injy rubber an' filled with a pizinous substance, an' if ye hit it a good smash it busts an' puts out ye'er eye. Ye're supposed to smash this little grenade fr'om place to place an' here an' there an' up an' down an' hither an' yon with an enormous insthrument iv wood or iron, ontil in due time ye get to what is called a puttin' green. There's a little hole with a tin can in it in th' middle iv this place, an' whin ye're within a fut or two iv this hole ye take a small hammer out iv th' bag, an' yet hit th' ball four or five times till it tumbles into th' hole. Thin ye wipe th' cold sweat fr'm ye'er brow, write down '5' on a little card, an' walk away a few feet an' do it all over again.

"So far so good. But that ain't nearly all. . . . Ye're told be a frind that ye ought to take a lesson. So ye pick out a bright-faced Scotch lad with a head shaped like a alligator pear an' who can hit th' ball a mile blindfolded an' ye give him what change ye have an' ask him to pint out ye'er faults. He pints out all ye'er wife has told ye about an' manny dark wans besides. I see Hogan takin' a goluf lesson wanst, an' how he iver dared to lift his head agin is more thin I cud undherstand. Afther th' pro-fissyonal has recited th' catalog iv ye'er sins an' vices, an' ye've made an act iv conthri-tion, he tells ye how to hit th' ball. Ye'd think that ought to be aisy. Just go up an' give it a cuff.

"But it ain't annything like as soft as that. There ar-re forty different things ye have to think iv with each shot, an' if ye do wan iv

thim wrong, ye're a lost soul. When ye'er idjication is completed ye go out an' do all th' things he told ye, but nineteen, an' th' ball skips lightly into a pit. Now is ye'er time to escape. If ye lave it lie there, turn ye'er back on it, run to th' parish-house an' ask fr'r th' prayers iv th' congregation, it may not be too late. Ye may be saved. Fly, weak an' wretched man, while ye have th' strenth! But if ye delay, if ye step but wan fut into th' thrap, ye're doomed an' on'y th' kindly hand iv death will release ye fr'm a life iv shame. . . .

"Did I iver see th' game played? Faith, I did. Th' other mornin' I see Hogan go out with his kit iv tools. In other games wan bat is enough, but in goluf ye have to own twinty. All th' money that used to go fr shoes in Hogan's fam'ly now goes fr goluf clubs. If he manages to hit th' ball with a club, he tells ye he wuddn't part with that club fr a hundherd dollars an' asts ye to feel it an' say ain't that a nice club. Whin he misses it he says th' club has gone back on him an' he buys a new wan. He has as manny implymints iv this new thrade iv his as a tinker. He has a hammer to beat th' ball into th' ground with, an' a pick to get it out, an' a little shovel to scrape it fr'm th' sand, an' a little hatchet to knock it into th' hole whin he gets near it. 'Where ar-re ye goin' with th' hardware?' says I. 'Is it to open a safe or build a battleship?' says I. 'I'm goin' to play goluf,' says he angrily. 'This is th' day I hang Larkin's hide on th' fence,' he says.

"So I followed him out to Douglas Park, an' there we met Larkin, who had a bag iv akel size. Hogan used to be champeen caber tosser iv th' ward an' Larkin was a sthructural ir'n-wurruker befure his health give out an' he be-come a horseshoer, but they groaned undher their burdens. Fortchnitly at that moment two bright little boys iv about eight years stepped up an' relieved thim iv their burden. 'What are these pigmies goin' to do with this here year's output iv th' Gary mills?' says I. 'They're goin' to carry thim,' says Larkin. 'They're caddies,' he says. 'Well,' says I, ' 'tis very nice iv th' little toddlers. Th' young can-not start too arly in helpin' th' aged. But,' I says, 'why don't ye get up on their backs an' have thim carry ye around? A little more weight wuddn't make much difference,' says I. 'Hush up,' says Hogan.

"Th' poor fellow was standin' on what they

call th' tee, which is where ye take th' first lick at th' ball. He had a pole in his hand an' was swingin' it at a dandeline an' missin'. Ivinchooly he stepped up to where th' ball roosted on a little pile iv sand, stood with his legs apart like th' statue he calls th' Goloshes iv Rhodes, waggled th' stick in th' air, p'inted it tords th' pole, cried out, 'Stand away, Larkin, get round behind me, Martin, stop shufflin' there, boy,' an' screamed 'Fore' at a fat old gintleman that was at wurruk in a trench three city blocks ahead. Thin he hauled off with th' bat, muttherin' to himsilf: 'Eye on th' ball, slow back, keep th' lift arm sthraight, pivot on th' right foot, folly through.' Up crept th' dhread insthrument slow an' cautious an' down it came with a blow that wud've foorced th' Dardanelles. I expicted to see th' ball splintered into a thousan' pieces or disappear into space. But it didn't. It left th' tee ridin' on a piece iv turf th' size iv ye'er hat, floated lazily off to wan side, dhropped, bounced twice, an' nestled in a bush. 'Watch it, boy,' yells Hogan. 'Watch it. Go right to it. Oh,' says he, 'what did I do that was wrong, what *did* I do?' says he, wringin' his hands. 'Ye dhropped ye're right shouldher,' says Larkin. 'Took ye're eye off it,' says Larkin's caddie. 'Toed it,' says an innocint bystander. 'Ye made a mistake thryin' to hit at all. Ye shud've kicked it,' says I. Hogan stood by, his face convulsed with mortyfication ontil Larkin, a man whose Sundah mornin' recreation used to be raisin' a kag iv beer over his head fifty times, give a lunge at th' ball, done a complete spin an' missed it altogether. Thin a wan smile come to Hogan's lips. 'What ar-re ye haw-hawin' about?' says Larkin. They niver spoke again. Most iv th' time they weren't in speakin' distance iv each other. Fr'm time to time they wud meet be chanst on a puttin' green an' Hogan wud say to himsilf: 'I'm down in twelve,' an' Larkin wud kick his ball over to th' next tee. So they wint rollickin' on. Hogan spoke to me wanst. He said: 'Dammit, stop coughin'.' Whin I left thim at th' sivinth hole th' excitemint was at its hite. Larkin' was lookin' f'r his ball in a geeranyum bush, an' Hogan was choppin' down an evergreen three with wan iv his little axes. 'Where ar-re ye goin'?' says he. 'I don't know,' says I, 'but I may dhrop in at th' morgue an' listen to an inquest,' says I. 'I've got to spend me holiday someway,' says I.

"I see Hogan th' next day an' asked him why he played. 'Why,' says I, 'd'ye make a joke iv ye'ersilf at ye'er time iv life, an' ye a man with a family?' says I. 'That's just it,' says he. 'I do it because iv me time iv life an' me fam'ly cares,' says he. 'I defy anny man in th' wurruld to get a bad lie in a bunker an' think iv annything else. He's that mad all his other sorrows, his debts, his sins, an' his future, disappears,' he says, 'like a summer cloud in a hur'cane. I'm that onhappy nawthin' bothers me. If a man come up an' told me me house was afire I'd not hear him. I don't know what it is,' says he, 'onless,' he says, 'it's th' feelin' that ye're bein' persecuted. It's ye'er sinse iv injustice that's stirred up in ye, that makes ye injye a round,' says he.

"Is th' Prisidint a good goluf player, d'ye know, at all?" asked Mr. Hennessy after a moment of judicial silence.

"As a goluf player he cud give Lincoln a sthroke a hole," said Mr. Dooley.

Merion—First Visit

by

ROBERT T. JONES, JR., and O. B. KEELER

1927 — FROM *DOWN THE FAIRWAY*

MY DEBUT in national championship affairs at the Merion Cricket Club, Philadelphia, in 1916, has given rise to a deal of comment, due to my lack of years, and as the personal statistics have been somewhat mixed I may explain that I was 14 years and six months old, five feet four inches tall, and weighed 165 pounds—a chunky, rather knock-kneed, tow-headed youngster playing in long pants; supremely innocent of the vicissitudes of major tournament golf and the keenness of northern greens—so different from our heavy Bermuda texture in the South; pretty cocky, I suppose, from having at last won a real title, if only a state championship; and simply pop-eyed with excitement and interest. I had two weeks of violet-ray treatments for the lumbago that had tormented me earlier in the season, and it left me, never to return. I never had seen any of the great players who were to compete at Merion—Bob Gardner, then amateur champion, and Chick Evans, who had lately won the Open Championship at Minneapolis, and the others; and so far as I recall, I was not in the least afraid of any of them. I hadn't sense or experience enough to be afraid. Mr. Adair and his son Perry and I stayed at the Bellevue-Stratford hotel in Philadelphia and traveled out to the club on suburban trains. It was my first big trip away from home and I was having a grand time.

We played our first practice round on the West Course—there were, and are, two fine courses at Merion—and I never had seen any such beautiful greens. They looked like billiard tables to me and I was crazy to putt on them. But their speed was bewildering. I remember the sixth hole, then a short pitch down to the green over a brook, the green faced slightly toward the shot. I was thirty feet beyond the hole, which was in the middle of the green. Forgetting all about the faster pace of these new greens, I socked the ball firmly with my little Travis putter and was horrified to see it roll on past the hole, apparently gathering momentum, and trickle into the brook, so that I was playing 4 from the other side of the stream—a most embarrassing *contretemps*.

When the qualifying rounds came on, the field was divided into sections, one playing the morning round on the East Course, the other on the West Course, and both sections changing for the second round. I played the West Course in the morning and turned in a 74 which led the entire field for that round. After luncheon, when I got over to the East Course, word had got about that the new kid from Dixie was breaking up the tournament, and almost the entire gallery assembled to follow me. Gosh—it scared me to death! I fancy I led the field the other way in the afternoon, taking an 89, for a total of 163, about ten strokes more than will get you in, these days, but safe enough then. Perry got in by a play-off at 167, won his first match, and lost the second. I was drawn with Eben Byers for my first match, a former national champion, and everybody in our party began to condole with me. Tough luck, they said, catching a big one in the first round. But Mr. Adair clapped me hard on the back and told me not to mind what they said.

"Remember what old Bob Fitzsimmons used to say," he advised. " 'The bigger they are, the harder they fall!' "

I thought that was a corking line, but as a matter of fact the name of Eben Byers meant nothing to me. I was a fresh kid, and golf as yet didn't have me down—at least, I didn't know it.

Mr. Byers and I played terribly. He was a veteran and I was a youngster, but we expressed our feelings in exactly the same way—when we missed a shot, we threw the club away. This habit later got me no end of critical comment, some of which hurt my feelings deeply, as I continued reading references to my temper long after I had got it under control to the point where there was no outward evidence of it except my ears getting red, which they do to this day—for I still get as mad as ever, missing a simple shot.

These columns I've read about my temper—it seems I got off on the wrong foot, and it was a long time before I was anywhere near in step with the critics, in the matter of disposition and deportment. Even now it strikes me as a bit unreasonable that so much type should have been employed on the gusty vagaries of one petulant youngster, when so little has been printed about the same unaffected displays by great golfers twice his age and more. There was only a whimsical reference to the club-throwing of Mr. Byers, I remember; and since then I have seen more than one national champion rival both of us. Two years ago at Oakmont, I saw a competitor in the National Amateur championship heave his putter into an adjoining wood and forbid his caddy to go after it—and he has been a national title-holder more than once. But nothing was said about it in the papers.

I'm not saying I didn't need some lecturing, mind you. The golf writers have been only too good to me, all along. And I was a sort

of bad boy of golf, I suppose, and required an occasional spanking, such as appeared in a Boston paper of 1918, when Alexa Sterling and Elaine Rosenthal and Perry Adair and I were playing a Red Cross benefit match at Brae-Burn. I kept those spankings in my scrap-book, along with the more pleasant clippings. This one was as follows:

> *Some interesting golf was shown during the match, interspersed with some pranks by Jones, which will have to be corrected if this player expects to rank with the best in the country. Although Jones is only a boy, his display of temper when things went wrong did not appeal to the gallery.*

That was two years after Merion. And I was a year or two more, getting my turbulent disposition in hand. It wasn't an easy matter. It's sort of hard to explain, unless you play golf yourself, and have a temper. You see, I never lost my temper with an opponent. I was angry only with myself. It always seemed, and it seems today, such an utterly useless and idiotic thing to stand up to a perfectly simple shot, one that I *know* I can make a hundred times running without a miss—and then mess up the blamed thing the one time I want to make it! And it's gone forever—an irrevocable crime, that stroke. I think it was Stevenson who said that bad men and fools eventually got what was coming to them, but the fools first. And when you feel so extremely a fool, and a bad golfer to boot, what the deuce can you do, except throw the club away? Well, well—Chick Evans, writing years later, said I had conquered my temper not wisely but too well; that a flare now and then would help me. I liked that of Chick. But I could have told him I get just as mad today. I stopped club-throwing in public, but the lectures didn't stop coincidentally. A bad name sticks. Having quoted one well-merited spanking, let me give an example of how hard it is to live down a wicked reputation.

Four years after Merion, and two years after Brae-Burn, when I had reached the mature age of 18 years and the club-throwing penchant had been completely hammered out of me, I was playing in my first National Open championship, at the Inverness Club, Toledo, qualifying with Harry Vardon. At the last hole I messed up a good round and took a villainous 6, finally missing a putt of about four feet. I was mad—thoroughly mad, certainly. But I didn't mean to show it. I holed out the ball, which lay at the edge of the cup, and tossed the putter to my caddy. He was not looking for it and the club fell on the green. Next day the newspapers said that I was throwing my clubs again, and had hacked up a slice of the eighteenth green in a rage after missing a short putt. That hurt me a lot.

Returning to my first match at Merion in 1916, after this bit of *apologia*—which may not be in the best of taste—I repeat that Mr. Byers and I played very wretchedly and I think the main reason I beat him was because he ran out of clubs first. Somebody playing behind us said later that we looked like a juggling act. At the twelfth hole Mr. Byers threw an iron out of bounds and wouldn't let his caddy go after it. I finally won, 3-1, and felt no elation whatever over my successful debut in a national championship. I knew I was lucky to win, the way I had played, and that I ought to have been well drubbed.

The second match I played better. This was with Frank Dyer, champion of several states and districts, and he started fast, putting me 5 down in the first six holes. I was getting dizzy. "So this is big league golf," I reflected. Then Frank made a few mistakes and I saw he was human, and I began to play better. At the turn I was 3 down and when we stood on the eighteenth tee I had a 4 left for a 32 coming in, and was 1 up. I was shooting some hot golf and was enjoying myself immensely.

We both hooked from this tee and one ball stopped in a fairly convenient position on top of a mound while the other was at the foot of the same mound, in a distinctly distressing situation. We were playing the same kind of ball, a Red Honor. Mine had gone on an excursion out of bounds at the second hole and was wearing a tar-stain from the roadway; I didn't change the ball every sixth hole, as I do now, figuring that the one in play may be knocked slightly off-center. I didn't stop to examine and identify the balls, but confidently whaled away at the one under the mound and missed the shot grievously, taking a 6 and losing the hole. After holing out I looked at the balls, and discovered I had

played his ball and he mine. There was nothing to do about it then—we had played out each with the wrong ball, and the score stood. We started the second round even, and I won 4-2.

By this time the golf writers were paying me a good deal of attention and some of the things they wrote made me feel extremely foolish. They wrote about my worn shoes and my dusty pants and my fresh young face and other embarrassing personal attributes. I never had considered my shoes or my pants before, so long as they held together. Golf wasn't a dress-up game, to me, and it was a new and puzzling experience to be looked at closely by so many people. I never had thought much of my face, for example, and it seemed sort of indelicate thus to expose it in print, not to mention my pants. The galleries were the largest I had ever seen, of course, and only half a dozen familiar faces, but everybody was curiously friendly. I remember thinking these Yankees must be pretty good folks, after all.

So I got through the second round and in the third round I met Robert A. Gardner, then champion, and the biggest gallery I had yet seen followed the match, which I will describe with some detail because of a certain significance it always has had, for me—it was in this match that I first got my fresh young head under the bludgeonings of chance, and, I must confess, wound up by bowing it.

Bob was playing with an infected finger, a handicap that rendered his game uncertain, and possibly cost him the championship in the end, as he lost to Chick Evans, who, however, was playing admirably in the finals.

I shot a 76 in the morning round and was 1 up. We were having a fine match, never far apart. In the afternoon we continued playing evenly and at the sixth tee we were square. When I planted my second shot on the green five yards from the pin I felt certain of going into the lead again, as Gardner's second was above the green and to the right, in a difficult place from which to approach. But he chipped stone dead and got a half.

At the next green my ball was fifteen feet below the cup and Bob's was off to the left. Again he chipped dead for a half. I wasn't discouraged. He can't keep on doing it, I told myself. I'll get him yet!

Playing the eighth hole, my second shot

was ten feet from the pin and Bob's was on the ninth tee—and this time he didn't chip dead. After his third shot he was still outside my position, and then I felt the break had come. But Gardner sank his twelve-foot putt, and I missed my ten-footer, and he had halved another. It seemed he *could* keep on doing it.

As for me, I couldn't. The break had come. But it was not my break. My fresh young head was bloody—and bowed. Frankly, I blew up. Bob won five of the next seven holes. He beat me, 5-3, holing a twenty-foot putt for a par of 4 at the fifteenth, after driving out of bounds.

They all told me it was a tough match to lose. But I've lost many a tough match since then, more than one by being clearly out-played—and more than one because I simply blew up under pressure. And I've been out-finished in more than one medal-play championship. But I never have felt quite the same way again. In after years I began to reason the business out a bit; as I said early in these memoirs, I never learned anything from a match that I won; I got my golfing education from drubbings. And very lately I have come to a sort of Presbyterian attitude toward tournament golf: I can't get away from the idea of predestination.

The professionals, you know, have a way of saying of the winner in a competition, "It was *his* tournament." And step by step, and hole by hole, and shot by shot, you may trace it back and see that he was bound to win—after it is all over. There's a tremendous lot to this game; and I fancied when I started this little story that maybe I could think a little of it out as I went along, and tell people about it. But it's a big assignment; too big for me. I may have reasoned out some of the mechanical side; perhaps just a bit of the psychological side. But behind it all, and over it all, there is something I think nobody understands.

Anyway, as they said, this was a tough match to lose, because I had played very well

up to the place where those continued recoveries of Bob's had broken my back, and next day one of the papers had a well-written account of the match which gave me a lot of credit and concluded with these lines:

Carefree and unconcerned, save with the big dish of ice cream awaiting him at the clubhouse, the Georgia schoolboy swung along from the fifteenth green in his worn shoes and dusty pants and sweat-streaked shirt, whistling an air from a recent musical comedy, as jaunty and complacent as if he had just won his first national championship instead of having just been beaten in the third round. He was thinking about the ice cream.

But I wasn't. I was puzzled, and hurt, some way. Not with Bob Gardner, who had played so pluckily when his shots were not coming off, and had kept the pressure on, when I was hitting the ball better. Bob, as I recall it, was an abstract figure: he was in the picture only as an agent for something else, something that I didn't understand. I had felt all along that I could beat Bob Gardner, but there was something besides him that was big and hard and invincible. That was what kept the pressure on me; that was what beat me. Fatality wasn't even a word to me then, and it doesn't mean now what I want it to.

But as I walked back to the clubhouse—and I got the ice cream, too—I kept wondering over and over again in a vague way what was on Bob Gardner's side that had beat me and made me blow up, when I was hitting the shots better than he was. Would it be on my side sometimes. I wondered. Or—with a queer little sinking sensation—would it always be on the other side?

You know, I never have made sure what it was, and is. I have found out this much: In the long run it seems to play no favorites—if the run is long enough. In my case it was a run of seven years.

How I Kept My Wait Down

by

WALTER HAGEN

1954 — FROM WALTER HAGEN'S FORTHCOMING AUTOBIOGRAPHY

MY TENDENCY to stay up late at night was another little bit of business that bothered a few of my fellow golfers. I usually managed to get eight hours' sleep, but there were a few times when I stepped up to tee off with an hour or less spent on my cool white pillow. Every athlete needs plenty of sleep and rest during strenuous competition. But few actually get it. This is particularly true of golfers in a championship tournament. I was able to get what I required because I knew I was going to need steady nerves and good physical coordination the next day. I never hurried. This goes for both on and off the golf course. People have written that I've no regard for time. I respect time highly and I try to make the most of it. There is just as much in saving time as there is in spending it properly. It fits the old Army gag about "Hurry up and wait." That's pretty much my idea. I don't hurry, therefore I'm not bothered with waiting.

From the minute I rose in the morning, I kept on an even keel until I reached the first tee. I got up in plenty of time to dress and breakfast leisurely and to arrive at the golf course just when I was due to play. There's a certain sort of rhythm in such a smoothed-out routine that carried over to my game . . . a rhythm that helped me avoid the jerky, gear-shifting movements which characterized the game of many easily upset or nervous golfers.

There were a few times when I stepped up to tee off with not even one hour of sleep. One such occasion has been narrated incorrectly so often that I'm going to set it straight. When I was president of the Pasadena Golf and Country Club at St. Petersburg, Florida, we made it a point to have exhibition matches over every week end and on holidays to interest the public in the home site possibilities of the place.

These exhibitions were bread-and-butter promotions for us and the main reason for building the course. This particular exhibition was scheduled for New Year's Day, at ten in the morning. My wife and I had been on a round-robin party on New Year's Eve and had ended up at the home of Gene Elliott for breakfast. Gene's place was a good half-hour drive from the club. My chauffeur, James Randall, came in and reminded me of the exhibition match.

The sun had been up so long I'd no idea of the correct time. Checking my watch I found I had slightly less than thirty minutes to motor across to Pasadena. I arrived at the first tee wearing my dinner clothes and patent leather pumps. The few hundred people in the gallery thought that was great fun. I was sliding in all directions trying to tee off in those slippery-soled shoes and after several attempts I got my drive away. I gave the gallery the impression that I intended playing the entire match in those clothes. Then, after taking my second shot, I made my excuses and explained that I'd go into the clubhouse and dress for the game. Looking over the gallery I remarked that I thought a number of them hadn't been up too long, either. They laughed and agreed I had a lot of company.

In the clubhouse I changed to regular golf clothes and spiked shoes. Even then, for the next several holes, I noticed that the fairway was much more slippery than it had ever seemed the dozens of times I'd played it. I managed to keep my footing and balance and went on to win my match with a 68.

On Diegeling

by

BERNARD DARWIN

1930 — FROM *SECOND SHOTS*

I DIEGEL, thou diegelest, he or she diegels, we all diegel or are about to diegel; and I trust that no golfer needs telling that the verb which I am conjugating signifies to try to imitate the putting methods of the hero, on the American side, of the Ryder Cup match.

Leo Diegel did not win the Championship. If he had we should all have had cricks in our backs for the rest of our lives. Even as it is, when it has been published far and wide that for one fatal round his putting forsook him, I am sure that many backs have been broken and elbows crooked to the point of agony in the attempt to get the ball into the hole as he does. Not, of course, that these thousands of sincere flatterers all over the country will admit what they are doing. They will scoff at my statement should they chance to read it, and then they will sneak away to that little corner of the lawn screened by the laurel bushes, or to that spare bedroom floor over the kitchen, knowing that the cook will not understand all that rolling and tapping over her head, or that, at any rate, she will not tell tales in the drawing room if she does.

I will not myself be guilty of any such shiftiness. I will confess that I have been evicted from room after room in the house while openly and unashamedly diegeling. So far I have met with no conspicuous success, but then the Master himself is said to have taken a year and a half to perfect his method, and I have been at it for only a few days. Moreover, I am hampered by the fact that I do not possess a square yard either of floor or garden which is reasonably true; the ball regularly misses the hole when it ought, were there any justice in the world, to have gone in, and, just as regularly, it hits the table leg when it ought to have missed it. This leaves the student in a state of painful uncertainty as to how he is getting on. I have not felt my progress sufficient to justify diegeling in a real game on a real green. The other day, in an essentially friendly match, being three up at the fourth hole I announced my intention of doing so, but my courage failed me. First of all I thought that in the approach putt I had better lay the ball dead in the ordinary manner; and I did lay it dead, but when it was dead I utterly failed to indiegel it. Still I have a year and twenty-four weeks left.

I have assumed that everyone knows in what the great man's method consists. Many writers have described it and photographers depicted it. Still there may be some whom the knowledge has passed by; so perhaps I had better give a brief recipe. You take a putter, not outrageously upright in the lie, with a reasonably long shaft. You hold it at the very top of the grip with the left hand well under. You stand square to the line of the putt, the feet spread rather wide apart. A friend of mine, an instructor of innocent boyhood who ought to know better, suggests that the stance should be called the spread-eagle stance. You next crook the elbows, particularly the left elbow, till you feel that something will break if you crook them any more. You drop the nose—not the club's but your own—lower and lower, till the top of the putter shaft lightly brushes the stomach. Then with wrists perfectly rigid you take the club back a short way: you give the ball a stiff little push, apparently with the right hand, and in it goes.

I have guarded myself by saying "apparently with the right hand" because learned persons have argued in my presence, at almost excessive length, whether the motive power comes in fact from the player's shoulders or from his feet. I am sure I don't know which is right, but I also feel sure that for the elementary student it is essential to remember that the wrists are stiff. It is so particularly because the method has been described as a pendulum method, and to many people the word pendulum conveys the swinging of the club to and fro with flexible wrists. It was in that sense that Mr. Horace Hutchinson used the word in the beloved old *Badminton,* friend of my youth, when he wrote: "The clubhead will be swinging something after the manner of a pendulum, and if the golfer gets the hanging arrangements of this pendulum correct, it cannot very well swing out of the true line." Mr. Hutchinson's putter did not swing out of the true line. With what pitiful envy, what smoldering fury have I watched him pendulum-ing the ball into the hole on those curly greens at Forest Row! But, though he crooked his elbow to some extent, he kept an insolently free wrist. To putt thus is to have genius, but it is not to diegel and I am writing about diegeling.

We all laugh at our friends and sometimes even pretend to laugh at ourselves for imitating the styles of the eminent. Yet there is this to be said, that if we are going to do it at all, the imitation of a putting style gives much the greater satisfaction. When we attempt a champion's driving swing, nobody by any chance recognizes our rendering of it. No total stranger will ever come up to us and say, "I beg your pardon, my dear sir, but I cannot help noticing that you are copying the effortless grace and free pivot of Mr. John Ball. I hope you are making good progress." On the other hand, we have only to contort ourselves for a single minute in front of the clubhouse windows and a dozen kind friends will shout "How is the diegeling getting on?" The ball may not go into the hole, but recognition is something. It encourages us to go on and, by the way, there comes to me, as I write, a most encouraging sound. It is a pleasantly purring sound as of one mowing. The gardener has been told to mow a patch for me and afterwards to roll it. Then I shall really be able to get down to it.

The Prospect for 1930

by

GRANTLAND RICE

1930 — FROM THE MAY ISSUE OF *THE AMERICAN GOLFER*

ROBERT T. JONES, JR., of Atlanta is an extremely modest young man who is willing to talk about golf whenever pressed, but who is extremely unwilling to talk much about his own game.

During the recent Southeastern Championship over Augusta's two fine courses, three or four of us, with Bobby, O. B. Keeler and Chick Ridley, had adjoining rooms at the hotel with a debating parlor at hand where every phase of every type of swing came in for lengthy discussion. During these discussions, while Bobby would not admit it openly, it was easy to see that he felt his game now was sounder and surer than it ever was before. He no longer had any fear or worry about the mashie or any type of pitch shot. And he proved later in this tournament against a strong field that no such fear need exist, since he hit the ball as perfectly as anyone could ever hope to hit with every club in the bag.

Jones, facing the 1930 season, is also facing the most tremendous undertaking of his golfing career. And he is starting better equipped in every way than he ever faced any single season before. He has had more chance to practice and he has also seasoned his spring output with two seventy-two-hole Open tests against such golfers as Horton Smith, Gene Sarazen, Johnny Farrell and others of high rank. He is going overseas better conditioned, more confident in his ability to hit the ball, no matter what the type of competition.

The Georgian's main objective in this next European invasion will be the Amateur Championship of Great Britain. This is the one major title he has yet to win where he was eligible to play. He confessed that he would rather win the British Amateur than anything else, with something to spare. He has won the British Open twice, the U. S. Open three times and the U. S. Amateur four times. But out of two starts he has yet to scrap his way through the eighteen-hole barriers which Great Britain's amateur test imposes.

I have a feeling, after a few days' visit with him, that the eighteen-hole nightmare was partially dispelled or dispersed in his defeat by Goodman at Pebble Beach. The fear of defeat in one of these shorter matches had always been upon him. Now that it has actually happened I believe most of this advance fear and worry are gone and that he will step into eighteen-hole action with much more confidence than he has ever known before.

I carried him Stewart Maiden's message— "Tell him he ought to let his opponent name the distance—eighteen holes or twelve holes or six holes or three holes. He's still the better golfer and he has a better chance to start fast than the other fellow has." Bobby grinned when the message was relayed and merely said—"Well, I'll do all I can. I've found out now I can't afford to stumble at the start."

Outside of the Walker Cup matches, which will be played over the bleak and windswept links of Sandwich, Jones will put all he has into four major championships: the British Amateur and British Open, the U. S. Open and the U. S. Amateur in the order named through May, June, July and September.

There has been no past year where he has combined as much in the way of golfing skill, experience and mental attitude as he has already for the big days on ahead. There is always the chance of course, golf being what it is, that he may not win a major crown. But there is a much better chance that he will win at least two, and he may do better than this, if he doesn't allow himself to become stale or overgolfed through the swarm of invitations to play he will receive on the other side. He must watch this carefully and store up all the nerve rest he can, for there are many times when he is too accommodating, too unwilling to hurt someone's feelings when a match is suggested.

I have never seen him hitting the ball as well with every club as he has been hitting it lately. The old tendency to slip with a mashie has been corrected. He was using his mashie as effectively at Augusta as any club in his bag. And what is more important, he had full confidence in it. And he will carry this confidence abroad.

In watching him play through the greater part of his last tournament, the one at Augusta where he faced two championship tests at the Hill course and the Forest-Ricker, I can't recall as much sureness with every club from tee to cup as he showed there. On one or two occasions he misjudged distances, but in almost every case, he hit the ball on a dead line. His tee-shots might have been fired from a rifle. There was no tendency either to hook or slice, to pull or fade. And on the longer holes he would suddenly let himself go and add at least forty yards to an already extremely long game. This was proof enough that even with the fine distance he was getting the Georgian was always playing well within himself.

Bobby's 1930 campaign, which will be his last big international bid for some time, will be one of the most interesting features in sport. If he is beaten in the British Amateur, it will be by someone shooting remarkable golf. I don't believe he will ever help to beat himself again, now that he is mentally adjusted to the hazards of the shorter journey at eighteen holes. You can sense that hereafter he will start in these matches with all the golf he can play. And at twenty-eight, with fifteen years of tournament experience back of him, with his swing better controlled than it ever was before, there is at least a first-class chance that this will be the best year he has ever had, and that will mean the best year any individual golfer ever had.

Two Niblicks

by

BERNARD DARWIN

1934 — FROM *PLAYING THE LIKE*

IT is all very well," said Mr. William Dent Pitman as he gazed at the proud waxen lady in the hairdresser's window, "it is all very well to run down the men who make these things, but there's a something——" and he walked home musing on that indefinable appeal.

Is it not thus that we often feel towards the seductive gentlemen that write advertisements? We abuse them, we mock at them, but we cannot help reading them, and in the end they very nearly seduce us. The other day I was loafing through an American magazine and came across two pages of eulogy of a certain "matched set" of iron clubs, with a picture of a long row of their shiny heads. I began, as Mrs. Malaprop recommended, "with a little aversion." When the gentleman said to me, "But, man—oh, man, what a difference in your game," my lip curled in scorn. When he urged me to "give the boys a surprise," I thought him a rather familiar and underbred person, and when he called his clubs "uncanny" I deplored his choice of epithets. Yet he was a cunning creature, for presently he hurt me in my vanity to just the right extent by telling me that I could "never hope to swap shots with the fellow that makes a business of it." Instead of agreeing with this obvious truth and having no more to do with him, I read on and began half to believe him when he insinuated that with his clubs the thing was still

possible. They would, he said, produce the shots which with other clubs could only be attained by being a "star." He explained exactly how and why this miracle could happen, and guaranteed me a long, low, quail shot, whatever that may be. I weakened; I was actually groping for my check-book in a welter of papers at my elbow, when I glanced again at my gentleman and was saved. "Oh, by the way," he remarked quite casually, "there are two niblicks."

That pulled me up short. "Two niblicks!" said I. "Oh, come now, dash it!" After that he spread his snares in vain. He was just as insinuating as ever in explaining the use of these two clubs—"the standard '8' for normal shots and the emergency '88' laid 'way back for the trick trap shots that experts get through deliberately regulating the angle of the face"— but the spell was forever broken. Love almost turned to hate as he went on in his oily way about the two mashie niblicks, "7" and "77," one, with a flat sole, for hard ground, and another, with a round sole, for ground that was soft and wet. Another glance at the picture confirmed my worst suspicions; the last of them was numbered 10, but owing to the duplication of 7's and 8's it was really No. 12. Here, then, was a whole round dozen of iron clubs, and there were four wooden ones as well, including a "No. 2" spoon—sixteen in all. Add a spare driver, a wooden or aluminum putter in case the owner went off with his two iron ones, an umbrella and a shooting-stick, and there would be quite a bagful. Indeed, there would be needed two caddies, the standard "I" and the emergency "II."

I am profoundly thankful that I was dis-illusioned in time, and that not merely because I could not or ought not to have afforded all those irons. I should have felt ashamed when I saw them bumping and banging on the back of some wretched child. Even if we are not great sinners ourselves, we do feel ashamed sometimes of the burdens that other people's caddies have to bear. Mr. Chesterton has written—not, of course, in this connection—of "that sort of impersonal but unbearable shame, with which we are filled, for instance, by the notion of physical torture, of something that humiliates humanity." In the first moment of revulsion against the man and his twelve irons this did not seem too strong language, and I am not sure that it does now. Whether or not they humiliate humanity, they humiliate golf.

Perhaps it is the near approach of Christmas —Dickens, kindliness, poor little boys, and that sort of thing—which encourages these senti-ments. Yet even if we come off our high, humane horse and forget all about the over-burdened caddie, there is surely something ridiculous as well as disgusting about these clanging armories. Those of us who played golf when it was still a strange game in a strange land can remember the gibes of the passers-by at our then modest equipment. They wanted to know what we could want with all that bag of sticks. They were irritating,

but was there, after all, some foundation for their rude, untutored mirth? At any rate, there would be now. If we cannot get round the links without sixteen clubs we are not worthy to set foot upon its turf. If we cannot lay back the face of our niblick, but have to have it laid back for us by just another degree, we are not worthy to be called golfers.

It is sometimes said that the modern golfer "buys his shot" in a shop. I am quite willing to turn nasty about him, but I do not honestly believe that to be true. You cannot buy a shot; the modern golfer is skillful enough in adapt-ing his one stroke to a number of slightly differing clubs, and I am not going to say that if he had far fewer clubs he could not learn to adapt them to his needs. No doubt he could, and he would find golf a better and more amusing though slightly more difficult game if he did. What can be said, however, is that several of the clubs that are carried round are never used and are so much dead weight and absurdity. Few of us are altogether guiltless in this regard. How often do we take a club all the way round with us on the off-chance of playing just one shot with it, and how often does it come back as clean as it started? If we did get that one shot, we either missed it or could have played it as well with something else. My own conscience is far from clear. I have several numbered irons and call them by their numbers; I have on occasions given up a coat and possess a leather jerkin; but, thank heaven, there are depths of degradation to which I have not fallen. I never have carried and I never will carry two niblicks.

The Fabulous Commodore Heard

by

GRANTLAND RICE

1934 — FROM THE AUGUST ISSUE OF *THE AMERICAN GOLFER*

TWENTY-NINE years ago a stocky Texan came from the clubhouse at Houston to the first tee. He was looking for a foursome—needed four more to make up a poker game. He was quite indignant when the four golfers refused to give up golf for a game of poker.

His name was Commodore Bryan Heard of Houston and Dallas, Texas. He was then 45 years old and he had never seen a game of golf. Twenty years later at the age of 65, he started shooting his age. That means at the age of 65 he shot a 65—at the age of 66 he shot a 66—a 67 when he was 67—a 68 when he was 68—a 69 when he was 69—and a 70 when he was 70—all over standard length courses. He is now 75 and despite cataract trouble with both eyes, with his vision badly blurred—in spite of having a leg and arm broken when a taxicab knocked him down—at the age of 75 he has turned in his 74—shooting under his age.

In many respects Commodore Bryan Heard, now of Dallas, is the most remarkable golfer in the history of the game.

In the first place you must visualize a player who started golf at 45, and who, after he was 60, has broken 70 more than a hundred times. I first heard of the stocky little Commodore in 1915. He was then 56 years old. That was the year when a famous 14-year-old phenom,

named Bobby Jones, was starting his unforgettable rampage. The kid of 14 collided with the veteran of 56 in a southern championship —and took a trimming. The Commodore stalked around in 71—too fast a pace for the 14-year-old Georgian, for almost anybody.

"How did you get started?" I once asked the Commodore.

And it developed that it all dated back to the day he tried to get up the poker game. He tried using a little derision to pry his friends away from a "sissy" pastime and was lured into showing what *he* could do in the way of hitting a little white ball. Then it was the four friends who put on the deriding act.

"I swung three times and missed," the Commodore relates, "and so I went back to town and asked at the store for a sack of sticks. 'You mean a bag of golf clubs,' the clerk said. I bought one of every kind of club he had and three dozen balls. On the way home, I saw what I think was the first Ford car that ever came to Texas—at least, it was the first I ever saw. Well, I thought while I was learning golf I would just learn to drive a car, too. So I bought the Ford. Next morning I went down and got the engineer off my boat and told him I wanted him to work the engine of the car while I steered it. With him working the levers and me steering was the way we got out to the golf course. As soon as we could get the car stopped, I got out and teed off. Then we got back in and drove off down the fairway after the ball, and ran round and round it till we could get the car stopped again. The drivin' was specially good on the greens and we would go around two or three times before I'd putt.

"And that was how I played my first game of golf. . . . We got mighty near halfway around before the greens committee came and put us off.

"Then I began practicing and playing, regular. It took me two years to get to 80 and some time longer to reach and break 70. I've always used the old fashioned two-handed grip. That's about all the grip they knew about when I started—and I still like it best. It gives my hands and wrists more power and more freedom of action—feels more natural.

"It didn't take me long," the Commodore said, "to find that it wasn't so hard to get somewhere within thirty or forty yards of the average green in two strokes. So I began working on my short game—the short pitches, the chip shots, and the putting. I kept this up until I'd bet even money that from forty yards I'd get down in two strokes."

And he'd break you at this bet. The Commodore has always had control of a low pitch-and-run or chip-and-run—also of a low cut shot where he could stop the ball within a foot of the landing spot. That shows the marvelous use he always had of his hands, getting so much backspin.

He decided the best putting method was to place the forefinger of his right hand down the shaft and then putt as if he were waving that finger on the desired line. Golf has known no better putter. Even at the age of 75 with impaired eyesight he is still deadly within ten feet of the cup. He didn't adopt his peculiar putting grip until he was 67.

By the time Commodore Heard had passed 60, he became poison to the leading amateurs and even the best professionals who came through Texas. Through past years more than one crack pro has told me of meeting a stocky Texan, giving him six or eight strokes, and taking a good beating on level terms. He took into camp such crack golfers as George Rotan and Frank Godchaux, among the best of the amateurs, and fed them 69's or 70's in various tournaments. One of the leading amateurs in Memphis once gave him eight strokes for a bet. The Commodore beat him 17 up without using a stroke in eighteen holes—breaking 70 that day—and leaving behind the most astonished golfer in the whole world.

He played Pine Valley when it was first opened—when only fourteen holes were finished. He shot every hole in par that round—and those who have played Pine Valley know what that means. He came North and they made bets against him at Lido—the old Lido. The bets were that he couldn't break 80. On his first trip around he shot a 73.

There was another remarkable exhibition of skill and stamina at Asheville, N. C. At the age of 69 he played thirty-six holes daily for thirty-one successive days, leaving that community almost bankrupt when he departed. One reason for this is the Commodore's smooth, simple, easy swing. He hits almost every shot on a straight line to the right spot. He seldom has a hook or slice. They travel like an arrow. This applies to both wood and iron.

Commodore Heard's body action is a trifle limited, but relaxed, never tightened. He gives you the impression of a great pair of hands at work swinging the head of the club. His freedom from tension is remarkable. This somewhat limited body action responds perfectly to live hands and live wrists. One of the strongest features of his game is the fine control he has of a No. 1 or No. 2 iron, even through a cross wind. This is the big test of the real golfer.

The Southwest knows all about Commodore Heard. He has been a golfing marvel for twenty years—from fifty-five to seventy-five— in addition to being one of the most popular citizens of that great commonwealth. Texas has turned out more than its share of fine golfers—but the Commodore's record still heads the parade.

Golfers with a Past

by

NOEL F. BUSCH

1937 — FROM THE JULY 17 ISSUE OF *THE NEW YORKER* MAGAZINE

UNDOUBTEDLY, the strangest golf story of the year was last week's about John Montague of Los Angeles, who, after being recognized by Grantland Rice and other golf authorities as the most proficient player in the world, was recognized by the authorities of New York State as a suspect in a holdup. The Montague epic—his mysterious appearance in California, his famous match against Bing Crosby, his ability to throw cards at the crack of a door or, when displeased, to hang his golfing competitors on the coat racks in their lockers—has been too thoroughly recited in the press for comment here. The whole affair, including Montague's shyness, which, now so explicable, was instantly and universally accepted, like Greta Garbo's, as the hallmark of a rich personality, belongs to the true Hollywood tradition. It is only regrettable that the match, about which there were rumors last spring, between Montague and a top-notch Eastern amateur for $10,000 a side, now seems most unlikely to be played.

Golf seems to have a special fascination for characters whose careers belong to a world quite different from that of country clubs. None of them have achieved Montague's inconvenient excellence, but several have been notable at least for their eccentricity. Al Capone was not a particularly able golfer, but he played honestly and with enjoyment. The same compliment cannot be paid to the late Leo Flynn, who was a member of Jack Dempsey's board of strategy when Dempsey was the world's heavyweight champion. Amiable and engaging off the golf course, Flynn, who took up the game late in life and became a fanatical devotee, was irascible when playing, and though his scores were in the low seventies, he never had enough confidence in his ability to dispense with artificial aids. The most effective of these was a Negro caddie whom Flynn once hired by the month in Florida. Friends noticed that the caddie always walked barefoot. It was his duty, when Flynn's ball went in the rough, to pick it up with his unusually long toes and, without stooping down, deposit it quietly on the fairway.

The most famous underworld golfer was, of course, Titanic Thompson, the gambler whose name was in the headlines for several weeks after the death of Arnold Rothstein. Thompson, who played left-handed, was sensationally good at golf, but even better at the side bets with which he always tried to brighten up a round. The most noteworthy example of Thompson's specialty was the thousand dollars he won when, pointing out a hound dozing on the fairway, he offered to bet his partner 5 to 1 that the dog would bark before either of them played their next shot. The instant after Thompson's friend took the bet, the dog barked —at a rabbit which Thompson, but not his companion, had seen running toward it through the long grass.

Despite Montague's glamorous reputation, the chances are that he is not the best golfer in the world. That title, if it belongs to anyone, belongs probably to Henry Cotton, who last week won the British Open Championship at Carnoustie. Not as well known in this country as some of his confrères who have played with Ryder Cup teams—which Cotton refused to join because he prefers to tour by himself—he is roughly the equivalent of a British Walter Hagen. Cotton's golf is more reliable, but a trace of the swaggering confidence that distinguished Hagen causes him to dress like a fashion plate, have a Swedish massage before important matches, and drive about in a roadster that looks as though it belonged on a speedway.

The Dr. Livingstone of Golf

by

HARRY ROBERT

1951 — FROM THE NOVEMBER ISSUE OF
USGA JOURNAL AND TURF MANAGEMENT

WHEN Ralph A. Kennedy played the Old Course at St. Andrews, Scotland, on September 17, it was an occasion to chalk up in golf records. St. Andrews was the 3,000th course Mr. Kennedy has played in a pleasantly nomadic career. It achieved an ambition he had nurtured for years, and it was to be presumed that, having established a record which is apparently unassailable, he was prepared to rest upon his laurels.

Old habits, however, are hard to break. When Mr. Kennedy visited the USGA "Golf House" a few days after his return from abroad, he had already pushed his total to 3,020 courses and was still going strong. Obviously, nobody can say where this thing may end.

Mr. Kennedy, a portly man of medium size with a jolly twinkle in his eyes, is a founder-member of the Winged Foot Golf Club, Mamaroneck, N. Y. He estimates that he has played some 8,500 rounds of golf in his life. Naturally, not all of these have been upon strange courses. If a walk around the average course covers five miles, as generally estimated, then he has tramped golf turf a distance of nearly twice around the world. He has played the game in fourteen countries. He has toured about half of the 5,000 courses in the United States, some 400 in Canada, 20 in South America, all 8 in Bermuda, and others in Cuba, Central America, and Mexico. He added 35 more to his log in his recent 24-day trip to the

British Isles: 26 in Scotland, 7 in England and 2 in Ireland.

Mr. Kennedy scheduled his trip so that historic St. Andrews would be No. 3,000. On the day he was to record that event, the ground near the starting tee was crowded with onlookers. Worried by the prospect of a gallery, he turned to Ellis Knowles, the former United States Seniors Champion, and inquired: "Who's playing here today, some champion?"

"Yes," replied Mr. Knowles. "Ralph Kennedy."

Mr. Kennedy's companions on that round were Mr. Knowles, Leonard Crawley and John Beck. The last two have been British Walker Cuppers; Beck, a former captain of the team.

"There were a lot of people watching and I was afraid I would miss my tee-shot entirely," said Mr. Kennedy. "I was in such a daze, I still don't know who hit that ball. But it was a good drive."

He scored 93 for the round and was well pleased with it. Apropos of this, he does not believe that intimate knowledge of a course and its local conditions is much of an asset in scoring. He generally plays a course better the first time he sees it than upon a return visit. "My club handicap is about ten strokes higher than I can really play," he said. "I can't play Winged Foot and it burns me up because I helped found it back in 1921."

Mr. Kennedy does not think of himself as

a celebrity but to some extent he is one. When he reached Dublin on his last trip, he arrived on a bus; as he stepped off, he approached a policeman and asked, "Where do I get a taxi around here?"

"I'll get you one, Mr. Kennedy," replied the officer, fairly dumbfounding golf's traveling representative.

"He had recognized me from a picture in one of the newspapers that morning," Mr. Kennedy explained. "But the surprising thing is that I don't think the picture was very clear and I don't see how anybody could identify me from it."

The Winged Foot man has seen almost every type of course in existence in the last half-century. "I have played desert courses in South America, courses without a blade of grass on them," he related. "The ball just falls dead where it lands and you find it in a little crater like a nest; then you're allowed to set it up on the rim for your next shot. Of course, you don't have to be alarmed about getting into sand traps there.

"The greens on some South American courses are of oiled sand and they hold a shot well. Cotton seed hull greens are not bad; they hold and they make a pretty good putting surface. You are not allowed to take a cigarette on any cotton seed green because they catch fire very easily and water won't put the fire out. They burn for days and don't stop until the seed hulls are burned out."

Mr. Kennedy has many times been asked what are his favorite courses and the worst he has seen. "I won't name the worst," he said, "but it's out in the Southwest. The grass is about two feet high, even in the fairway; in fact, they have stakes up to mark where the rough starts. You're allowed to beat the grass away with your club until you can make a swing at the ball." Among the best, Pine Valley, near Clementon, New Jersey, and Cypress Point, at Pebble Beach, California, stand high on his list, although he believes that for some reason Pine Valley plays a few strokes easier than it did about twenty years ago. "At least, it does for me," he said.

Mr. Kennedy also has a warm regard for Mid-Ocean, in Bermuda, Broadmoor, at Colorado Springs, and Capilano, in Vancouver, B. C. He considers Jasper Park, in Canada, one of the most scenic. "On eleven of the eighteen holes in Jasper Park, majestic mountain peaks are the markers for your line of play," he remarked. After he had driven at Jasper Park and came walking up to his ball, he found a small bear standing over it, sniffing curiously. "What do I do now?" he asked the pro in perplexity.

"Oh, he'll beat it as soon as you get near," the pro explained, and the prediction was borne out.

Mr. Kennedy also likes Augusta National "because it is tough and easy—tough for the good player and easy for the dub." He scored 82 there the first time he played it.

Four times Mr. Kennedy has holed tee-shots. Two were legitimate aces, one he scored as a 3 (because his first shot was in a water hazard), and one as a 4. "That last was on the ninth at the Maple Golf Club, Hope Valley, Rhode Island," he said. "There is a big maple tree in the line between the tee and the green; the hole is about 170 yards. I played a high No. 4 wood over the tree and found the ball wedged in the hole but not all below the rim of the cup.

"'It's a hole in one,' my companion said.

"'It is not,' I said. 'It's an unplayable lie and I have to take it out for a penalty of two strokes and then putt it into the hole.' We sent a description of the incident to the USGA and my ruling was upheld." Mr. Kennedy beamed, a somewhat chronic condition. "I liked that better than an ordinary hole-in-one," he said pleasedly.

Mr. Kennedy was introduced to golf in 1910 by a neighbor whose brother had been a college mate at Amherst. Against his wishes he was persuaded to go up and play Van Cortlandt Park. "I got around in 146," he said. "After that I played there quite often. It was a fine course in those days and it didn't cost you a cent to play it. I became fascinated by the game." Mr. Kennedy introduced Mrs. Kennedy to it the very next week. She has played more than six hundred courses, and was several times champion of Dunwoodie, the club at Yonkers where they used to play.

Charles Fletcher, an English music-hall actor, started Mr. Kennedy on his hobby of collecting courses. In 1919, he heard Fletcher say that he held the world record with 240. Mr. Kennedy reflected that he had played quite a few courses himself and had attested cards to show for them. He dug them up and discovered they represented 176 different layouts.

From that point, he really went in for variety. He passed Fletcher a few years later at 445. He played his 1,000th course on his fiftieth birthday in 1932; his 2,000th in 1940; his 2,500th was Pebble Beach in 1946, and in September this year he made it 3,000. Mr. Kennedy's record is completely authenticated, for he always made it a point to have his card at every course dated and attested by an official of the club. He has this collection of cards in a safe deposit box. He intends to present the St. Andrews card for his 3,000th course to the USGA.

Mr. Kennedy finds a pronounced difference in architecture between courses in the United States and Great Britain. "Over here, our courses are comparatively easy until we are within seventy-five to one hundred yards of the greens," he said. "Then they are severely trapped and it takes a well-played shot to get home. The British courses are terrific until you are within about the same distance of the green. Then they are relatively easy; you can roll the ball up to the pin."

No matter how many courses he sees, however, he remains loyal to Winged Foot. "I don't know any course less taxing for the man of advancing age," he explained. "There are no hills to climb. Yet, nobody ever murders our par."

Francis
Drives Himself In

by

S. L. McKINLAY

1951 — FROM THE SEPTEMBER 20 ISSUE OF THE GLASGOW *HERALD*

FRANCIS OUIMET, of Boston, Massachusetts, drove himself into the captaincy of the Royal and Ancient Club at eight o'clock yesterday morning, and if the youngest child among the hundred of onlookers lives to become the oldest inhabitant he may never see a better tee-shot. The drive fulfilled to the letter the club motto—"Far and sure." It was straight on the railway bridge slightly to the left of the flag, and if the caddie who eventually retrieved the ball had not beaten it down before it stopped bouncing it would have finished a good 250 yards down the green fairway.

The caddies had stationed themselves with a nice regard for the captain's ability—well beyond the road that runs across the fairway. But those who thought he would play a safe, hooky drive to the left, and those who expected an early morning slice, were equally disappointed. The drive was everything that anyone's drive ought to be, and for a captain's tee-shot it was of supreme excellence.

The captain, with a blend of caution and patriotism, used an American ball which, being larger than ours, is easier to see and hit at the hangman's hour. But the ball was not of the kind that may be bought in any professional shop; it was a special Walker Cup ball, bearing on either side of the maker's name the outline of a lion in red and of an eagle in blue, and for once the traditional sovereign was not given to the caddie who retrieved the ball. Instead he received, no doubt with the consent of the United States Secretary of the Treasury and the custodian of Fort Knox, a gold five-dollar piece encased in a plastic frame. Its nominal value is about £1 18s, but that is to put a low commercial estimate on a prize of great worth.

Long before the captain made the stroke which of itself won him two trophies of the Royal and Ancient Club—the Silver Club and the Royal Adelaide Medal—the crowds had begun to gather around the first tee. It was a perfect morning with not a drift of wind and the sun throwing the long shadow of the clubhouse across the first tee. The cannon and its attendant were in position in front of the starter's box, at the teebox a microphone had been placed to pick up the click of club meeting ball, and the crowd were lined up behind a rope barrier between the tee and the Tom Morris green. The inevitable dogs were there, but firmly leashed by cautious owners. At a few minutes before eight the past captains assembled on the tee—Viscount Simon, Lord Balfour of Burleigh, Lord Teviot, Bernard Darwin, R. H. Wethered, and C. J. H. Tolley, the last two, old opponents of their successor.

It was now nearly eight and the central figures of the ceremony came down the old steps from the clubhouse—the retiring captain, Sir George Cunningham; the captain-elect, bareheaded and bespectacled; and the professional to the R. and A., Willie Auchterlonie, at seventy-nine wrapped up against the chill morning air, but spare and erect as a man half his age. He won the Open Championship in the year the captain-elect was born, but in all his long memory of the Old Course and the great men who have played there he can never have known a more notable occasion or a central figure more worthy of being honored at the home and heart of golf. When the photographers, many Americans among them, had been accommodated, Willie Auchterlonie teed the ball, the captain-elect had the merest twitch of a practice swing, and then, with no more fuss than he has ever displayed on the course or off, he swung with a grace and ease that belied his years and struck the ball. At that precise second, by a miracle of timing, the cannon roared, full-throated and sharp enough to make even the wary jump, and the club had a new captain; another Medal Day had begun.

Footnote. Not only did the captain begin the day in the manner befitting one of his reputation, but he continued the good work in the Medal. Save for missing a shortish putt on the home green he would have equaled the best score returned up to the time of his finishing the round, but 76 was in the circumstances a noble performance and one that many competitors with half his years and less than half his skill must envy.

The Hong Kong Golf Club

by

CHRISTOPHER RAND

1952 — FROM *HONG KONG: THE ISLAND BETWEEN*

THE MAIN links of the Royal Hong Kong Golf Club are at Fanling in the New Territories, and some weeks after I had come back a friend took me to watch a tournament there. Most of Fanling was in easy mortar-range of China, a country then fighting the British in Korea, but this had not affected things much. The Fanling clubhouse is simple, like our older American ones. The inside is done largely in stained or white-painted wood, and there are modest wicker chairs in the library, along with the copies of *Country Life* and the *Illustrated London News*. Before teeing off that day the members sat at plain tables drinking coffee or tea and eating toast with marmalade. They were athletes of all ages, some getting a bit heavy, and they wore simple clothes—shirts or T-shirts, shorts, socks, golf shoes—which they changed after a shower when they came in for lunch, a meal built round steak-and-kidney pie and preceded for the most part just by beer (the day's competition was only half over). In general they were businessmen from the big Hong Kong trading firms or officers from the garrison, most of which was encamped in the New Territories. The balances of Hong Kong golf had been upset by the reinforcements of 1949; a few men of army-championship caliber had arrived then, and they had tended to dominate things.

The sun was low and dazzling as we set out, and in the shade the grass smelled dewy. Fanling is in a basin whose sides are steep dull-green ridges and whose floor is made of fairways, little knolls, and stretches of rice paddies. The knolls are planted with young pines, and some fairways are lined by screens of eucalyptus or casuarina trees. There was lots of bird song that day, lyrical in the cool morning, but rasping as the day wore on; the sun grew burdensome by noon, and gentler things gave way to harsher. There was every kind of green; the most compelling was the jade green of rice in the paddies.

The biggest piece of Chinese farm country an outsider can visit now is the New Territories. For all the golf and other things the British have put there, Chinese life goes on as it presumably does a few miles to the north, in the mysterious darkness of the Reds' country. Along the Fanling course we passed farmers in ditches, watering the paddies beside them with scoops on long handles like shovels —the kind of thing one used to see throughout South China. Humped Chinese cattle, with an occasional young buffalo, grazed here and there on the roughs. Chinese tombs, big crescent-shaped monuments with tablets, were set into knolls overlooking certain greens, places where the fengshui, the "wind-and-water" or mystic pull of nature, had been found good by Chinese geomancy.

That morning long files of Chinese peasant

124

women crossed the fairways ahead of us, going out for fuel, chattering, carrying sickles and bamboo shoulder-poles. They were dressed in dark clothing, topped by wide flat straw hats with cloth fringes hanging like curtains from their brims. In the afternoon the women crossed the other way, now loaded with bundles of dry grass at their poles' ends. They jogged along in the Chinese dogtrot, the bundles—so big they looked like haystacks on twinkling legs—journeying in time, their bearers keeping up unbroken talk in high singsong Chinese. I heard a British golfer shout "Fore!" at one group of stacks, but it did no good. The stacks kept to their pace, course and gossiping unchanged.

The golfers benefited from the low Chinese living standard. When we came to swamps or bad ditches, little Chinese boys in ragged clothes and coolie hats would be lurking there, waiting to hunt lost balls for a reward—though often, I was told, they kept from finding one till the loser had gone on; the reward for a decent one was less than the black-market resale price. The caddies earned a little over twenty American cents per round. The fee was so low, and the work so easy, by Chinese standards, that men in their prime stayed out of it. The two caddies with us were a small barefoot boy and an old man in sun helmet, steel-rimmed glasses, black pajama suit, and sandals made from tire scraps. He seemed almost blind. Caddying isn't a man's job in America either, but there a caddie can at least grow up to be a good player. This is out of the question in Hong Kong. Only the richer Chinese boys here, who would never labor for pay, can hope to have time for golf, or money to buy clubs.

Starting out in the morning we had heard the pipes of the Argyll and Sutherland Highlanders, who were encamped near by. Later,

going round, we had glimpse after glimpse of the army—a little spotter-plane field, clusters of tents and Nissen huts, groups of soldiers playing football. Once a soldier ran, at metronome pace, across a fairway and round a green before us, stripped to the waist, wearing shorts, and drenched in sweat—training for cross-country running. He was from the Argylls or Middlesex, the two regiments stationed on that piece of border. Both had just come from Korea, where they had fought for almost a year. The running soldier must have had comrades in the Chinese prison camps, puzzled about their future in the Red world whose edge was so close to us. He himself might have been there instead.

In midafternoon we came to the holes nearest the border. We weren't too close. "Even Sam Snead with the right wind," a golfer said, "couldn't hook or slice into China from here." But we weren't so far away, either. China was perhaps two miles off, beyond a sprawling, brownish-green, dry-looking ridge. The ridge was lopsided, gathered in a larger heap toward the east and then dropping off sharply to a pass. It was through this pass that the railway came down from the Chinese interior, bearing almost daily the pinched and blinking foreigners who had been sent out from there, the missionaries and others, their world fallen about them.

Westerners played golf near other Westerners dislodged by chaos, I thought as we walked back in the long shadows; soldiers killed time while their brothers were held beyond the ridge; caddies kept the imperial relationship beside a country sworn to end it; and strangers visited a little patch of Chinese landscape at will, though all the other great expanse of it was veiled as if forever. Who, I wondered, could say that such calm contrast was natural or lasting?

Watching My Wife

by

JOHN L. HULTENG

1953 — FROM AN AUGUST "IN PERSPECTIVE" EDITORIAL COLUMN
OF THE PROVIDENCE *JOURNAL-BULLETIN*

MY WIFE WAS PLAYING in a golf match the other day in the National Women's Championship, and I was in the gallery.

Fortunately, I'm never nervous on such occasions.

They teed off, and my wife's opponent dropped a magnificent putt for a birdie and won the first hole. There was a man in a yellow jacket who kept following along beside me and he turned to me:

"What are you doing?"

"I'm writing down the score," I told him.

"Hadn't you better turn the pencil around? The lead is on the other end."

"Thank you," I said, with dignity.

My wife lost the second hole, and was two down. A woman in a long peaked cap came up to me.

"Things aren't looking too bright, are they?" she said sympathetically.

"Oh," I said airily, "it's nothing to be upset about. After all, it's only a molf gatch."

She stared at me a moment. "Yes," she said. "Yes, of course."

Neither my wife nor her opponent won either of the next two holes. Then they came to a short, par three hole. My wife was about to hit her drive. The man in the yellow jacket was beside me again.

"She's about to drive," he said. "Aren't you going to watch?"

"I have to tie my shoelace," I told him.

"You've been tying that shoelace during every shot for the last three holes."

"It's an old lace," I told him. "Very slippery."

Finally the match stood all even after six holes. Then my wife hit a shot into a bad piece of rough.

"Don't be jittery now," said the man in the yellow jacket. "She can still get out of it all right."

"I'm not the slightest bit jittery and I wish you wouldn't keep talking about it," I told him, edging away.

"Hey," he said. "Watch where you re —"

Two gallery marshals helped me up out of the sand trap and brushed the sand off the back of my shirt.

"I ought to penalize your wife two strokes," one of them said darkly; "it's against the rules for a competitor to use any implement to test the consistency of a sand trap."

Around the middle of the match my wife took a one-hole lead. The tension grew. It was blazing hot on the course. I reached down for my handkerchief and mopped the perspiration off my brow.

"Do you always," said the man in the yellow jacket, "use your tie to wipe your face?"

"There are so many other matches to watch," I told him. "Why don't you go find one of them?"

My wife won another hole, and was two up with only a few holes left.

I was standing at one side of the fairway, in the shade of some trees. The woman in the peaked cap came up behind me.

"Well," she said, slapping me on the shoulder. "How do you feel now?"

"Fine," I told her from ten feet up in the tree. "Just fine."

"That's good," she said. "Don't try to get down. I'll go find a ladder."

The sun grew hotter and the tension tighter. But as it turned out my wife won the match on the sixteenth hole. Someone went up to congratulate her and asked her how she felt.

"I'm hungry," she said.

And I'm proud to say that I maintained my own icy calm right up to the final moment of the match.

In fact, I never felt more relaxed than I did as they carried me into the clubhouse.

Le Bing et le Golf

by

ART BUCHWALD

1953 — FROM THE MAY 31 ISSUE OF THE NEW YORK *HERALD TRIBUNE*

Paris, May 1953

Mr. BING CROSBY, the singer, has been in Europe for the last three months dividing his time unequally between making radio tape recordings for America and playing golf. As far as Crosby is concerned, the radio broadcasts are something to do on a rainy day, but his golf is not a joking matter and the crooner can be found on the St. Cloud golf course almost every sunny day.

Wednesday being a sunny day, that's where we found him. Crosby was in the process of selecting a woman caddie when we joined him. France is about the only country that has women caddies and it is no easy job for a golfer to choose among them. After carefully testing a half-dozen with his golf bag, which weighed close to twenty pounds, Crosby settled for a fifty-one-year-old woman named Marta. In America a caddie would give his right arm to caddy for Bing Crosby, but Marta did not seem too delighted about the arrangement. She explained her problem to us. It was a busy day at St. Cloud and if she waited she could carry two bags instead of one and get paid double for the same eighteen holes.

Crosby agreed to pay her double and she brightened up a little. On the way out to the first tee we asked Crosby if he was embarrassed to play with a woman caddie. "I was at the beginning, but now I'm not any more.

I think they're better caddies than men. They stick to their job and don't wander off like some of the boys back home. They know their golf, too. If one of these gals suggests a club and you don't use it, there's hell to pay."

Crosby has been playing golf since 1930, when he was singing with the Rhythm Boys, and is a member of ten clubs in the United States. He also sponsors his Bing Crosby National Professional-Amateur Tournament at Pebble Beach, California, a golf competition that has been awarding $12,000 annually in prizes, and will award $15,000 this year. He is considered a high-powered amateur, and has a three-stroke handicap, which is pretty low on any golf course.

As we walked around the course we asked Marta, a powerful critic, what she thought of Crosby's golf. "I think he played better when he was here two years ago," she whispered. "He doesn't hit the ball long enough but he has very good aim."

Crosby likes to play with a European golf ball because it is smaller than an American ball, you get more distance with it, and you can putt better. But the disadvantage is the European golf ball doesn't lie as well as the American golf ball. (Crosby added that there was no difference between European and American golf players, because they both lie

128

about the same.) The European ball, which is frowned on in American golfing circles because of the great distance you can clout it, has been used on occasion by Crosby and other Hollywood players without each other's knowledge. This causes consternation when the truth comes out, because the people in Crosby's league usually play for money.

The feud between Bob Hope and Bing Crosby which has been played up by motion picture press-agents really exists on the golf course, and Crosby says he'd rather play with Hope as a partner than anyone else, because he's a master at talking opponents into one-sided bets that will benefit both of them. "Nobody takes his golf as seriously as Hope, and he would rather win a golf match than an Oscar."

A short time ago, Crosby canceled his plans to go to England and play in a charity tournament. "It got too complicated. I kept getting millions of wires from other benefits in England, and if you do one you have to do them all. It's too much work. The only other benefit I'm going to do while I'm in Europe is one for Django Reinhardt, the jazz guitarist, who died last Friday. I'll be glad to do that one. He was one of the boys." We asked if the article criticizing his golf which appeared in a London paper had anything to do with his deciding to cancel his English golf plans. He said the article didn't bother him. "The only thing that steamed me up was that this one columnist said I was improperly handicapped. He said if I was a three-handicap man, then he could sing at the Palladium. I'll play with a three and take on anybody in England. I wish they'd knock me around in the States like that. I'd get a better deal on the first tee."

Since Crosby wasn't playing against anyone, he didn't keep score. (He shot a 71 at St. Cloud last fall.) Marta was tight-lipped at the end of the eighteen holes and didn't seem to approve of the careless way he played that afternoon. "You'd do better," she said, "if you concentrated on your game and talked less to this man." Marta then walked off toward the clubhouse.

"Now if I were Hope," Crosby said as he watched her go, "I'd send for a writer and have an answer to that remark."

The Golfomaniac

by

STEPHEN LEACOCK

1930 — FROM *LAUGH WITH LEACOCK*

WE RIDE in and out pretty often together, he and I, on a suburban train. That's how I came to talk to him. "Fine morning," I said as I sat down beside him yesterday and opened a newspaper.

"Great!" he answered. "The grass is drying out fast now and the greens will soon be all right to play."

"Yes," I said, "the sun is getting higher and the days are decidedly lengthening."

"For the matter of that," said my friend, "a man could begin to play at six in the morning easily. In fact, I've often wondered that there's so little golf played before breakfast. We happened to be talking about golf, a few of us last night—I don't know how it came up —and we were saying that it seems a pity that some of the best part of the day, say, from five o'clock to seven-thirty, is never used."

"That's true," I answered, and then, to shift the subject, I said, looking out of the window:

"It's a pretty bit of country just here, isn't it?"

"It is," he replied, "but it seems a shame they make no use of it—just a few market gardens and things like that. Why, I noticed along here acres and acres of just glass—some kind of houses for plants or something—and whole fields of lettuce and things like that. It's a pity they don't make something of it. I was remarking only the other day as I came along in the train with a friend of mine, that you could easily lay out an eighteen-hole course anywhere here."

"Could you?" I said.

"Oh, yes. This ground, you know, is an excellent light soil to shovel up into bunkers. You could drive some big ditches through it and make one or two deep holes—the kind they have on some of the French links. In fact, improve it to any extent."

I glanced at my morning paper. "I see," I said, "that it is again rumored that Lloyd George is at last definitely to retire."

"Funny thing about Lloyd George," answered my friend. "He never played, you know; most extraordinary thing—don't you think?—for a man in his position. Balfour, of course, was very different: I remember when I was over in Scotland last summer I had the honor of going around the course at Dumfries just after Lord Balfour. Pretty interesting experience, don't you think?"

"Were you over on business?" I asked.

"No, not exactly. I went to get a golf ball, a particular golf ball. Of course, I didn't go merely for that. I wanted to get a mashie as well. The only way, you know, to get just what you want is to go to Scotland for it."

"Did you see much of Scotland?"

"I saw it all. I was on the links at St. Andrews and I visited the Loch Lomond course and the course at Inverness. In fact, I saw everything."

"It's an interesting country, isn't it, historically?"

"It certainly is. Do you know they have played there for over five hundred years! Think of it! They showed me at Loch Lomond the place where they said Robert the Bruce played the Red Douglas (I think that was the other party—at any rate, Bruce was one of them), and I saw where Bonnie Prince Charlie disguised himself as a caddie when the Duke of Cumberland's soldiers were looking for him. Oh, it's a wonderful country historically."

After that I let a silence intervene so as to get a new start. Then I looked up again from my newspaper.

"Look at this," I said, pointing to a headline, *United States Navy Ordered Again to Nicaragua.* "Looks like more trouble, doesn't it?"

"Did you see in the paper a while back," said my companion, "that the United States Navy Department is now making golf compulsory at the training school at Annapolis? That's progressive, isn't it? I suppose it will have to mean shorter cruises at sea; in fact, probably lessen the use of the Navy for sea purposes. But it will raise the standard."

"I suppose so," I answered. "Did you read about this extraordinary murder case on Long Island?"

"No," he said. "I never read murder cases. They don't interest me. In fact, I think this whole continent is getting over-preoccupied with them —"

"Yes, but this case had such odd features —"

"Oh, they all have," he replied, with an air of weariness. "Each one is just boomed by the papers to make a sensation —"

"I know, but in this case it seems that the man was killed with a blow from a golf club."

"What's that? Eh, what's that? Killed him with a blow from a golf club!"

"Yes, some kind of club —"

"I wonder if it was an iron—let me see the paper—though, for the matter of that, I imagine that a blow with even a wooden driver, let alone one of the steel-handled drivers—where does it say it?—pshaw, it only just says 'a blow with golf club.' It's a pity the papers don't write these things up with more detail,

isn't it? But perhaps it will be better in the afternoon paper —"

"Have you played golf much?" I inquired. I saw it was no use to talk of anything else.

"No," answered my companion, "I am sorry to say I haven't. You see, I began late. I've only played twenty years, twenty-one if you count the year that's beginning in May. I don't know what I was doing. I wasted about half my life. In fact, it wasn't till I was well over thirty that I caught on to the game. I suppose a lot of us look back over our lives that way and realize what we have lost."

"And even as it is," he continued, "I don't get much chance to play. At the best I can only manage about four afternoons a week, though of course I get most of Saturday and all Sunday. I get my holiday in the summer, but it's only a month, and that's nothing. In the winter I manage to take a run south for a game once or twice and perhaps a little swack at it around Easter, but only a week at a time. I'm too busy—that's the plain truth of it." He sighed. "It's hard to leave the office before two," he said. "Something always turns up."

And after that he went on to tell me something of the technique of the game, illustrate it with a golf ball on the seat of the car, and the peculiar mental poise needed for driving, and the neat, quick action of the wrist (he showed me how it worked) that is needed to undercut a ball so that it flies straight up in the air. He explained to me how you can do practically anything with a golf ball, provided that you keep your mind absolutely poised and your eye in shape, and your body a trained machine. It appears that even Bobby Jones of Atlanta and people like that fall short very often from the high standard set up by my golfing friend in the suburban car.

So, later in the day, meeting someone in my club who was a person of authority on such things, I made inquiry about my friend. "I rode into town with Llewellyn Smith," I said. "I think he belongs to your golf club. He's a great player, isn't he?"

"A great player!" laughed the expert. "Llewellyn Smith? Why, he can hardly hit a ball! And anyway, he's only played about twenty years!"

Golfmanship

by

STEPHEN POTTER

1948 — FROM THE SEPTEMBER ISSUE OF *THE ATLANTIC MONTHLY*

ALWAYS REMEMBER that it is in golf that the skillful gamesman can bring his powers to bear most effectively. The constant companionship of golf, the cheery contact, means that *you are practically on top* of your opponent, at his elbow. The novice, therefore, will be particularly susceptible to your gambits.

Remember the basic rules. Remember the possibilities of defeat by tension. I have written elsewhere of the "Flurry," as it is called, in relation to lawn tennis. *It is an essential part of Winning Golf.* The atmosphere, of course, is worked up long before the game begins.

Your opponent is providing the car. You are a little late. You have forgotten something. Started at last, suggest that "Actually we ought to get rather a move on—otherwise we may miss our place."

"What place?" says the opponent.

"Oh, well, it's not a bad thing to be on the first tee on time." Though no time has been fixed, Opponent will soon be driving a little fast, a little tensely, and after you have provided one minor misdirection, he arrives at the clubhouse taut.

In the locker room one may call directions to an invisible steward or nonexistent timekeeper. "We ought to be off at 10.38." "Keep it going for us," and so forth.

OPPONENT.—"Who's that you're shouting to?"

GAMESMAN.—"Oh, it's only the Committee man for starting times."

Your opponent will be rattled, and be mystified too, if he comes out to find the course practically empty.

If for some reason it happens to be full, you can put into practice Crowded Coursemanship, and suggest, before every other shot Opponent plays, that "We mustn't take too long—otherwise we shall have to signal that lunatic Masterman, behind us, to come through. Then we're sunk."

Every beginner in golf gamesmanship must know when to be sympathetic to his opponent, when not. He must know the basic ways of walking, or not walking, off the tee with his opponent. If he is ignorant of that admirable little book *Bad Luck in Twenty-five Tones of Voice*, he must yet distinguish the mechanical "Bad luck!" suitable when your opponent really has had a stroke of ill fortune, from the exaggerated "What utterly filthy luck—no, really!" which increases the annoyance caused by a good honest error which hooks him into a bunker.

Here are some notes on certain general gamesmanship plays, in their relation to golf.

FRITH-MORTEROY COUNTER IN GOLF

WHAT I have described as Game Leg Play can easily be adapted to golf. The essence of the gambit is, of course, the display of the slight limp, which with set mouth you try to "disguise." Trouble in the joints is certainly more effective, against very inexperienced players, than any other complaint.

Strained or rheumatic joints are the points to play on. In the locker room, prolonged swathing of ankles and wrists in elastic bandages can be obscurely irritating to your opponent, even if he fails to sympathize.

Frith-Morteroy's counter to any kind of Crocked Ankle Play is always to sympathize and wait. When the opponent begins to limp as if in pain Frith will sympathize and wait *till the turn*. Then, after Frith's next bad shot—a topped drive, say—he suddenly stands stock-still, head down.

FRITH.—Sorry.

OPPONENT.—What's up?

FRITH.—O.K. in a second.

OPPONENT.—Indigestion?

FRITH.—No, I wish it was.

OPPONENT.—Why?

FRITH.—What? I mean it's something funny.

OPPONENT.—Funny?

FRITH.—It's called oteolitis media, or some nonsense. Uneven blood pressure. It's a tiny heart thing.

OPPONENT.—What, *heart?*

FRITH.—I'm supposed not to hit the ball too hard. I shall be all right in a second.

Thus, in the classical manner, the opponent's relatively minor affliction is made to seem ludicrously unimportant, while, if there happens to be a spectator to note it, Frith's superior sportsmanship, in concealing his dangerous condition as long as possible, will stand out in flattering contrast.

MIXED FOURSOMES

I HAVE always been an intense admirer of this phrase, "I'm supposed not to hit the ball too hard," of Frith's.

In a mixed foursome it is important in the basic foursome play (*i.e.* winning the admiration of your opponent's female partner) that your own drive should be longer than that of the opposing man, who will, of course, be playing off the same tee as yourself.

Should he possess definite superiority in length, you must either (*a*) be "dead off my drive, for some reason" all day—a difficult position to maintain throughout eighteen holes;

(*b*) say "I'm going to stick to my spoon off the tee," and drive with a Fortescue's Special Number 3—an ordinary driver disguised to look like a spoon, and named "spoon" in large letters on the surface of the head; (*c*) use the Frith-Morteroy counter.

The general play in mixed foursomes, however, differs widely from the Primary Gambits of a men's foursome. But beginners often feel the lack of a cut-and-dried guide.

In the all-male game of course, when A and B are playing against C and D, the usual thing, if all is going well, is for A and B to be on delightfully good terms with each other, a model of easy friendship and understanding. Split Play is only brought into play by the A-B partnership if C-D look like becoming 2 up. A then makes great friends with C, and is quietly sympathetic when D, C's partner, makes the suspicion of an error, until C is not very unwillingly brought to believe that he is carrying the whole burden. His dislike for D begins to show plainly. D should soon begin to play really badly.

In the mixed game, all is different. *Woo the opposing girl* is the rule. To an experienced mixed-man like Du Carte, the match is a microcosm of the whole panorama of lovers' advances.

He will start by a series of tiny services, microscopic considerations. The wooden tee picked up, her club admired, the "Is that chatter bothering you?" The whole thing done with suggestions, just discernible, that her own partner is a little insensitive to these courtlinesses, and that if only *he* were her partner, what a match they'd make of it.

Du Carte, meanwhile, would be annoying the opposing man, by saying at large, in a sickening way, that "Golf is only an excuse for getting out into the country. The average male is shy of talking about his love for birds and flowers. But isn't that . . . after all —"

Du Carte was so loathsome to his male friends at such moments that they became overanxious to win the match. Whereas the female opponent, on the contrary, was beginning to feel that golf was not perhaps so important as sympathetic understanding.

By the twelfth hole Du Carte was able to suggest, across the distance of the putting green, that he was fast falling in love. And by the crucial sixteenth, Female Opponent would have been made to feel not only that Du Carte had offered a proposal of marriage, but that she, shyly and regretfully, had refused him.

Du Carte invariably won these matches two and one. For he knew the First Law of Mixed Gamesmanship: that *No woman can refuse a man's offer of marriage and beat him in match play at the same time.*

CADDIE PLAY

REMEMBER the basic rule: *Make friends with your caddie and the game will make friends with you.* How true this is. It is easy to arrange that your guest opponent shall be deceived into undertipping his caddie at the end of the morning round, so that the news gets round among the club employees that your opponent is a no good, and the boys will gang up against him.

I myself have made a special study of Caddie Play, and would like to put forward this small suggestion for a technique of booking a caddie for your guest.

There is usually one caddie at each club who is an obvious half-wit, with mentally deficient stare and a complete ignorance of golf clubs and golf play. *Do not choose this caddie for your opponent. Take him for yourself.*

There is such a caddie in my own club. He is known as Mouldy Phillips. It is obvious from a hundred yards that this poor fellow is a congenital. While preparing for the first tee say: —

SELF.—I'm afraid my caddie isn't much to look at.

OPPONENT.—Oh, well.

SELF.—He's a bit—you know.

OPPONENT.—Is he?

SELF.—I was anxious you shouldn't get him.

OPPONENT.—But —

SELF.—It's all right. I know the course. (*Then, later, in a grave tone*) It gives him such a joy to be asked.

OPPONENT.—Why?

SELF.—Oh—I don't think they'd ever have taken him on here if I hadn't been a bit tactful about it.

It is possible to suggest that in the case of Mouldy you have saved a soul from destitution. Impossible in such circumstances for your friend to refer to, much less complain of, Mouldy's tremor of the right arm, which swings like the pendulum of a grandfather clock, to the hiccoughs or the queer throat noise he will make in the presence of strangers —habits to which you are accustomed.

Meanwhile you have succeeded in your promise to get for Opponent the best caddie on the course. A man like Formby. "He's just back from caddying in the Northern Professional," you say. So he is, and your friend soon knows it. During the first hole: —

SELF.—I suppose Formby knows this course better than anyone in the world.

FORMBY.—Ought to, sir.

Your opponent will feel bound, now, to ask advice on every shot, every club. Formby is certain to give it to him, in any case. After he has done a decent drive and a clean iron shot, Formby will probably say: "Playing here last week, Stranahan reached this point, with his brassie, *from the tee.* Yes, he can hit, that man." Here one hopes that Mouldy Phillips will say something.

MOULDY.—Aa—ooo—rer—oh.

SELF.—Jolly good, Mouldy. Yes, he's got us there, old boy.

Here Opponent should be not only distracted but mystified. Formby will redouble his advice, while in contrast Mouldy looks on with delighted admiration of everything I do.

THE LEFT HAND–RIGHT HAND PLAY

I BELIEVE it was O. Sitwell who devised this simple rule for play against left-handers. If (as so often happens) your opponent, though left-handed in games generally, yet plays golf with ordinary right-hand clubs, it is a good thing, during the first hole *after the fifth* which he plays badly, to say: —

SELF.—Do you mind if I say something?

L.H.—No. What?

SELF.—Have you ever had the feeling that you are *playing against the grain?*

L.H.—No—how do you mean?

SELF.—Well, you're really left-handed, aren't you?

L.H.—I certainly am—except for golf.

SELF.—Have you ever been tempted to make the big change?

L.H.—How do you mean?

SELF.—Play golf left-handed as well. Chuck those clubs away. Fling them into the bonfire.

Damn the expense—and get a brand-new set of left-handed clubs.

L.H.—Yes, but —

SELF.—*You know* that is your natural game. Be extravagant.

L.H.—It isn't the expense —

SELF.—Money doesn't mean anything nowadays, anyhow.

L.H.—I mean —

SELF.—Everybody's income's the same really.

The fact that your opponent has been advised to play right-handed by the best professional in the country will make him specially anxious to prove by his play that you are in the wrong. The usual results follow. If he is not only a left-hander but plays with left-handed clubs as well, the same conversation will do, substituting the word *right* for *left* where necessary.

A NOTE OF CLOTHESMANSHIP

I HAVE discussed elsewhere the importance of Clothesmanship in golf. I enlarged on Clothesman's Primary, the wearing of clothes which are absolutely correct, yet manly and gameslike, to match the gigantic golf bag, with ball cleaners, resin cases, and wooden-club mufflers dangling from its rich leather.

Then there is the tremendously effective Clothesman's Secondary, too, to counter this gambit. The baggy flannel trousers, the blue and white braces, and the boots, all made to go with the 1904 golf bag tied up with a clothesline, containing five dingy clubs very stringy round the heads. Many is the match I've seen won with this carefully planned outfit.

BEMERONDSAY TROPHY PLAY

C. BEMERONDSAY was an awkward, tricksy, inventive gamesman, full of devices, many of them too complicated for the older generation. I remember he tried to upset me once by "letting it be known" that his name "of course" was pronounced "Boundsy," or some such nonsense. Players uncertain of their position were, it is believed, actually made to feel awkward by this small gambit, and I have heard G. Carter—always conscious that his own name was a wretchedly unsuitable one for a games

player—apologize profusely for his "stupid mispronunciation."

On the other hand, Bemerondsay's Cup Trick is well worth following. I will briefly summarize it.

In play against a man like Julius Wickens, who goes in for suggesting he was once much better than he is, the dialogue runs as follows: —

BEMERONDSAY.—I have a feeling you know more about the game than you let on.

WICKENS.—Oh, I don't know.

BEMERONDSAY.—What *is* your golf history?

WICKENS.—Well, just before the war I was winning things a bit.

BEMERONDSAY.—I bet you were.

WICKENS.—Spoons—and things.

BEMERONDSAY.—Oh, you did, did you?

WICKENS.—Then in 1931 I won a half share in the July tea-tray—rather nice.

BEMERONDSAY.—Very nice indeed.

After the match, Bemerondsay asked Wickens round for a drink after the game. "I keep the stuff in my snuggery," he says, and in they go.

"Somebody must have put the drink in the cupboard," says Bemerondsay. "Why?"

He opens the cupboard door and to his "amazed surprise" out falls a small avalanche of golf cups, trophies, silver golf balls, engraved pewter mugs, symbolical groups in electroplate. "Oh hell," says Bemerondsay, slowly.

WICKENS (*really impressed*).—These all yours?

BEMERONDSAY.—Yes. This is my tin.

WICKENS.—When did you win all these?

BEMERONDSAY.—I never know where to put it.

It is of no importance in the gambit, but it is believed by most gamesmen that these "trophies" of Bemerondsay really are made of tin or silver-painted wood, or that at any rate they were bought by Bemerondsay as a job lot. It is doubtful whether he had ever entered for a club competition, as he was a shocking match player.

FAILURE OF TILE'S INTIMIDATION PLAY

AMERICANS visiting this country for a championship have sometimes created a tremendous effect by letting it be known that, on the voyage over, in order to keep in practice, they drove new golf balls from the deck of the *Queen Mary* into the Atlantic.

I believe that W. Hagen brilliantly extended this gambit by driving balls from the roof of the Savoy Hotel.

When they came to our own seaside course, to play in the Beaverbrook International Invitation Tournament, two Americans created a tremendous effect by driving new balls into the sea before the start, to limber up.

E. Tile, pleased with this, determined to create a similar impression before his match against Miss Bertha Watson, in our June handicap. He cleverly got hold of six old or nearly worthless balls, value not more than twopence each, painted them white, and teed them up to drive them into Winspit Bay. By bad luck, however, not one of his shots reached the edge of the cliff, much less the sea. So his stratagem was discovered.

G. ODOREIDA

G. ODOREIDA, I am glad to say, did not often play golf. By his sheer ruthlessness, of course, Odoreida could shock the most hardened gamesman. Woe to the man who asked him as a guest to his golf club.

He would start with some appalling and unexpected thrust. He would arrive perhaps in a motor-propelled invalid chair. Why? Or his hair would be cropped so close to the head that he seemed almost bald.

Worse still he would approach some average player of dignified and gentlemanly aspect and, for no reason, *ask for his autograph.* Again, why? One was on tenterhooks, always.

I remember one occasion on which his behavior was suspiciously orthodox. The club was Sunningdale. "Thank heaven," I thought. "Such ancient dignity pervades these precincts that even Odoreida is subdued."

I introduced him to the secretary. It was a bold move, but it seemed to work. I was anxious when I saw, however, that on that particular afternoon the secretary was inspecting the course. As he came near us Odoreida was near the hole. Without any reason, he took an iron club from his bag and took a wild practice swing on the very edge, if not on the actual surface, of the green. A huge piece of turf shot up. "Odoreida!" I said, and put the turf back with an anxious care that was perfectly genuine.

Two holes later the secretary was edging near us again. Odoreida was about to putt. He took the flag from the hole and *plunged it into the green.* "Odoreida!" I cried once more. Surely, this time, the secretary must have seen. But I remember very little of the rest of the afternoon's play. I know that Odoreida won by 7 and 5. I am glad to say that I refused to play the remaining holes.

In other words, gamesmanship can go too far. And the gamesman must never forget that his watchwords, frequently repeated to his friends, must be sportsmanship, and consideration for others.

GREAT PLAYERS, HISTORIC MOMENTS

The Triumvirate

by

BERNARD DARWIN

1932 — FROM *OUT OF THE ROUGH*

THERE IS a natural law in games by which, periodically, a genius arises and sets the standard of achievement perceptibly higher than ever before. He forces the pace; the rest have to follow as best they can, and end by squeezing out of themselves just a yard or two more than they would have believed possible.

During the last year or two we have seen this law at work in billiards. Lindrum has set up a new standard in scoring power and our players, in trying to live up to him, have excelled their old selves. The same thing has happened from time to time in golf, and those whom we call The Triumvirate undoubtedly played their part in the "speeding up" of the game.

Taylor, though by a few months the youngest of the three, was the first to take the stage, and it has always been asserted that he first made people realize what was possible in combined boldness and accuracy in playing the shots up to the pin. Anything in the nature of safety play in approaching became futile when there was a man who could play brassie shots to the flag in the manner of mashie shots. Mr. Hilton has suggested that this raising of the standard really began earlier and was due to another great Englishman, Mr. John Ball. It may well be so, for it is hard to imagine anything bolder or straighter than that great golfer's shots to the green, but

Taylor, being the younger man and coming later, burst on a much larger golfing world than had Mr. Ball. Moreover, he was a professional who played here, there and everywhere, and so was seen by a large number of golfers, whereas the great amateur, except at championship times, lay comparatively hidden at Hoylake. Time was just ripe when Taylor appeared: golf was "booming" and the hour and the man synchronized. Though in the end he failed in his first championship at Prestwick, he had done enough to show that he was going to lead golfers a dance to such a measure as they had not yet attempted. In the next year he won, and for two years after that the world struggled to keep up with him as best it could.

Then there arose somebody who could even improve on Taylor. This was Harry Vardon, who tied with him in the third year of his reign (1896) and beat him on playing off. There was an interval of one more year before the really epoch-making character of Vardon was appreciated. Then he won his second championship in 1898 and was neither to hold nor to bind. He devastated the country in a series of triumphal progresses and, as in the case of Lindrum, there was no doubt that a greater than all before him had come. To the perfect accuracy of Taylor he added a perceptible something more of power and put the standard higher by at least one peg.

139

And, it may be asked, did Braid have no effect? I hardly think he did in the same degree though he was such a tremendous player. He took longer to mature than did his two contemporaries. Of all men he seemed intended by nature to batter the unresponsive gutty to victory, and he won one championship with a gutty, but his greatest year, his real period of domination, came with the rubber core. He cannot be said to have brought in a new epoch except to this extent perhaps, that he taught people to realize that putting could be learned by hard toil. He disproved the aphorism that putting is an inspiration for, after having been not far short of an execrable putter, he made himself, during his conquering period, into as effective a putter as there was in the country. By doing so he brought new hope to many who had thought that a putter must be born, not made, and had given it up as a bad job.

Presumably everybody thinks that his own youth was spent in the golden age, and that the figures of that period were more romantic than those of any other. At any rate I can claim romance and to spare for my early years of grown-up golf, for I went up to Cambridge in 1894 and that was the year of Taylor's first win at Sandwich. Moreover, The Triumvirate were then, I am sure, far more towering figures in the public eye than are their successors of today. It was their good fortune to have no rivals from beyond the sea. They were indisputably the greatest in the world. Then, too, they had so few ups and downs. Today a professional is in the limelight one year and in almost the dreariest of shade the next, but these three, by virtue of an extraordinary consistency, always clustered round the top. Finally their zenith was the zenith of the exhibition match. They were constantly playing against one another and no matter on what mud-heap they met, the world really cared which of them won.

It is partly no doubt because I was in the most hero-worshipping stage of youth (I have never wholly emerged from it), but it is also largely due to the personalities of those great players that I can remember quite clearly the first occasion on which I saw each of them. It is a compliment my memory can pay to very few others. Taylor I first saw at Worlington (better, perhaps, known as Mildenhall) when he came almost in the first flush of his champion's honors, to play Jack White, who was then the professional there. I can see one or two shots that he played that day just as clearly as any that I have watched in the thirty-seven years since. I had seen several good Scottish professionals play before that, including my earliest hero, Willie Fernie, most graceful and dashing of golfers. I thought I knew just what a professional style was like, but here was something quite new to me. Here was a man who seemed to play his driver after the manner of a mashie. There was no tremendous swing, no glorious follow-through. Jack White, with his club, in those days, sunk well home into the palm of his right hand, was the traditional free Scottish slasher. He was driving the ball as I imagined driving. Taylor was altogether different and his style reminded me of a phrase in the Badminton book, which I knew by heart, about Jamie Anderson and his "careless little switch." One has grown used to J. H. long since, but the first view of him was intensely striking, and I am inclined to think that in his younger days he stood with his right foot more forward than he does now, so that the impression of his playing iron shots with his driver was the more marked. He was not appallingly long, but he was appallingly straight, and he won a very fine match at the thirty-fifth hole. Incidentally, the memory of that game makes me realize how much the rubber-cored ball has changed golf. The first hole at Worlington was much what it is today, except that the green was the old one on the right. Now the aspiring Cambridge undergraduate calls it a two-shot hole and is disappointed with a five there. On that day—to be sure it was against a breeze—Taylor and Jack White took three wooden club shots apiece to reach the outskirts of the green, and Taylor with a run up and a putt won it in five against six.

My first sight of Vardon came next. It was on his own course at Ganton, whither I went for the day from Whitby, and he had just won his first championship. He was playing an ordinary game and I only saw one or two shots, including his drive to the first hole. Two memories vividly remain. One was that he was wearing trousers and that from that day to this I have never seen him play except in knickerbockers, an attire which he first made fashionable amongst his brother professionals. The other is that his style seemed, as had Taylor's on a first view, entirely unique. The club appeared, contrary to all orthodox teaching, to be lifted up so very straight. Even now, when I have seen him play hundreds and hundreds of shots, I cannot quite get it out of my head that he did in those early days take up the club a little more abruptly than he did later. The ball flew away very high, with an astonishing ease, and he made the game look more magical and unattainable than anyone I had ever seen. For that matter, I think he does so still. In view of later events it is curious to recall that a good local amateur, Mr. Broadwood, who was playing with him, talked then of his putting as the most heartbreaking part of his game, and said that he holed everything. I only saw one putt and that he missed.

It must have been a year later that there came the first vision of the third member of The Triumvirate, who had hardly then attained that position. This was at Penarth, where there was a Welsh championship meeting, and Taylor and Herd were to play an exhibition match. Taylor could not come; at the last moment Braid was sent for to take his place and arrived late the night before. I remember that he did in his youthful energy what I feel sure he has not done for a long time now; he went out early after breakfast to have a look at the course and play some practice shots. His enemy, by the way, had come a whole day early and played a couple of rounds. I have almost entirely forgotten the Penarth course, and the shots I played on it myself; the one thing I can vaguely remember is the look of the first hole and of Braid hitting those shots towards it. Here was something much more in the manner that one had been brought up to believe orthodox, but with an added power; save for Mr. Edward Blackwell, with whom I had once had the honor of playing, I had never seen anyone hit so malignantly hard at the ball before. Mr. Hutchinson's phrase about his "divine fury" seemed perfectly apposite. One imagined that there was a greater chance of some error on an heroic scale than in the case of Taylor and Vardon, and so indeed there was, but I remember no noble hooks that day, nothing but a short putt or two missed when he had a winning lead so that Herd crept a little nearer to him.

From the time when I was at Cambridge till I sold my wig in 1908, my golfing education was neglected for, if I may so term it, my legal one. I played all the golf I could, which was a good deal, but watched hardly any. Therefore I never—sad to say—saw Vardon in his most dominating era, nor the great foursome match over four different courses in which he and Taylor crushed Braid and Herd, chiefly through one terrific landslide of holes at Troon. However, in the end I managed to see each of the three win two championships, Braid at Prestwick and St. Andrews in 1908 and 1910, Taylor at Deal and Hoylake, 1909 and 1913, Vardon at Sandwich and Prestwick, 1911 and 1914. I suppose the most exciting was in 1914 when Vardon and Taylor, leading the field, were drawn together on the last day, and the whole of the West of Scotland was apparently moved with a desire to watch them. Braid, too, played his part on that occasion, for had he not designed the bunker almost in the middle of the fairway at the fourth hole? And was it not fear of that bunker that drove Taylor too much to the right into the other one by the Pow Burn, so that he took a seven? No wonder J. H. said that the man who made that bunker should be buried in it with a niblick through his heart. Yes, that was a tremendous occasion, and Braid's golf in 1908—291 with an eight in it at the Cardinal—was incredibly brilliant; and Vardon's driving when he beat Massy in playing off the tie at Sandwich was, I think, the most beautiful display of wooden club hitting I ever saw; but for sheer thrilling quality give me Taylor at Hoylake in 1913. There was no great excitement since, after qualifying by the skin of his teeth, he won by strokes and strokes; but I have seen nothing else in golf which so stirred me and made me want to cry. The wind and the rain were terrific, but not so terrific as Taylor, with his cap pulled down, buffeting his way through them. There are always one or two strokes which stick faster in the memory than any others, and I noticed the other day that my friend Mr. Macfarlane recalled just the one that I should choose. It was the second shot played with a cleek to the Briars hole in the very teeth of the storm. I can still see Taylor standing on rocklike feet, glued flat on the turf, watching that ball as it whizzes over the two cross bunkers straight for the green. There never was such a cleek shot; there never will be such another as long as the world stands.

It is surely a curious fact that, though these three players dominated golf for so long, and the golfer is essentially an imitative animal, no one of them has been the founder of a school. They made people play better by having to live up to their standard, but they did not make people play like them. Here are three strongly marked and characteristic styles to choose from, and yet where are their imitators? Vardon had one, to be sure, in Mr. A. C. Lincoln, an excellent player who belonged to Totteridge; he had at any rate many of the Vardonian mannerisms and a strong superficial likeness. There is George Duncan, too, with a natural talent for mimicry; he remodeled the swing he had learned in Scotland after he first saw the master. Imagine Duncan slowed down and there is much of Vardon. Beyond those two, I can think of no one in the least like him. It is much the same with Taylor. His two sons, J. H., Jr. and Leslie, have something of the tricks of the backswing, but nobody has got the flat-footed hit and the little grunt that goes with it. Braid, with that strange combination of a portentous gravity and a sudden, furious lash, seems the most impossible model of all. I know no one who has even copied his waggle, with that little menacing shake of the clubhead in the middle of it. Each of the three was so unlike the other two that the world hesitated which model to take and ended by taking none. American players look as if they had all been cast in one admirable mold. Ours look as if they came out of innumerable different ones, and as if in nearly every mold there had been some flaw. It was part of the fascination of The Triumvirate that each was extraordinarily individual, but now it seems almost a pity for British golf. If only just one of them could have been easier to imitate! In other respects, of course, they did all three of them leave a model which could be imitated. By all the good golfing qualities of courage and sticking power and chivalry, by their modesty and dignity and self-respect, they helped to make the professional golfer a very different person from what he was when they first came on the scene. Their influence as human beings has been as remarkable as their achievements as golfers.

The First United States
Amateur Championships

by

CHARLES BLAIR MAC DONALD

1928 — FROM *SCOTLAND'S GIFT—GOLF*

IN 1894 the Newport Golf Club advertised an amateur tournament which the committee was pleased to call a championship tournament. However, there was no organization of clubs justifying any club in calling its invitation tournament a championship. Likewise, the committee of the St. Andrews Golf Club advertised an amateur championship to take place at St. Andrews. Both these meetings gave zest and impetus to the popularity of the game. Neither had any championship authority except so far as it concerned its own club.

Norman Fay, of Chicago and Newport, wired me to visit him at Newport and play in the tournament to be held the first week in September, 1894. I decided to go on from Niagara Falls where I had a country home. The tournament was two days of medal play, eighteen holes each day. The course was very crude, as it had only been laid out the year before, and we played over a pasture which had stone walls across the fairway. I failed to be the winner by one stroke, owing, as I remember it, to topping a ball under one of these stone walls.

The first day I made the lowest score for the eighteen holes, namely, 89. W. G. Lawrence, who learned his golf at Pau and won the golf cup there the year before, was 93 the first day. The second day I took 100 against Lawrence's 95, his total being 188 against my 189. In that tournament Herbert Leeds, Boston's crack player, was 217; and L. P. Stoddard, the St. Andrews crack golfer, was 102 for eighteen holes the first day, after which he withdrew.

I can recall that the tournament was extremely interesting, and the club's committee did everything to make the competitors happy.

The other eastern invitation tournament in which I played was the one at the St. Andrews Golf Club at Yonkers. It was held October 11 and 12 of the same year. There were thirty-two entries to be decided by eighteen holes (twice around nine holes) match play. In the semifinals Archie Rogers played Stoddard, and my old antagonist at Newport, Lawrence, played me.

Returning to town after the first day's play, Stanford White gave me a dinner and supper party which lasted until five o'clock in the morning. I had an engagement to breakfast with Willie Lawrence at seven o'clock. Stanford drove me home to the Waldorf, and when I told him I did not believe I would be able to keep my engagement in the morning, he said to leave it to him and he would fix me. He did. When I got up in the morning I found a note from him and a few strychnine pellets with instructions as to how to take them. This I did, and, after breakfasting with Willie Lawrence, we took the train for Yonkers. In the morning round I won from Lawrence by two and one to play. I was fast fading away. Stanford White came out to luncheon with me. Again he insisted upon pulling me together. He had evidently read Horace Hutchinson's article in *Badminton* on "Hints on Match and Medal Play," in which he described "the man to back":

"If ever you see a man who has tied with another for a medal, toying in the luncheon interval with a biscuit and a lemon-and-soda, you may go out and bet your modest half-crown against that man with a light heart. But if you see him doctoring himself with a beefsteak and a bottle of beer, or, better still, a pint of champagne, you may go forth and back that man with as stout a heart as though you had yourself partaken of his luncheon. The golfer will not do good work unless he is fed. And it is real, good, hard work that he has to do—work that will need a stout heart to do it efficiently. For it is a game of hard rubs and annoyances, a game of which the exasperations no less than the fascinations were never better summarized than in these words of the grand old golfer: 'It's aye fechtin' against ye.'"

Never was more fallacious advice given the unsuspecting golfing community, and that from one of the best golfers and best men that ever played the game. This advice has ruined many a man's game.

Stanford insisted on a bottle of champagne and a steak. I do not wish the reader to think that Stoddard would not have beaten me anyway. That I do not know; but, in any event, I played wretched golf that afternoon. We were all square and one to play. I drove my ball from the tee at the last hole into some ploughed ground. Stoddard won the hole and the match. I had an able sympathetic caddie, J. C. Ten Eyck, a prominent member of the club, who was good enough to lug my clubs around.

After the invitation tournaments of the Newport Golf Club and the St. Andrews Golf Club, there was much criticism by other clubs of their assuming to represent the golfing community in national championships. The Chicago Golf Club, having eighteen holes, held

an invitation tournament, but made no such claim. The Shinnecock Hills Golf Club, which had the best nine golfing holes in the East, made no such claim. Other clubs probably did the same. Obviously, no championship could be held and designated national without a general consensus of opinion expressed by the leading clubs of the country; consequently an association had to be organized. H. O. Tallmadge instigated the movement to form such an association. He and Laurence Curtis sent out the invitations asking the Shinnecock Hills Golf Club, The Country Club of Brookline, Mass., and the Chicago Golf Club to join the St. Andrews Golf Club and the Newport Golf Club in forming a representative body to promote the interests of the game of golf, to decide on what links the Amateur and Open Championships should be played, and to establish and enforce uniformity in the rules of the game.

Without doubt, the creation of the USGA gave fresh impetus to the formation of golf clubs throughout the country. Whereas there were only five charter members at the beginning of 1895, by the end of the year the association had enrolled ten associate members and thirteen allied members. Today, 1927, there are 943 members.

The second week in September, 1895, the Chicago Golf Club held its fall tournament and there I won both the scratch medal and the handicap cup at scratch. I was then playing better than I had since 1884 at Hoylake and was in good form to enter the first annual Amateur Championship under the auspices of the USGA to be held at Newport the first three days in October. There was no qualifying round in the first championship. It was decided by eighteen-hole matches with the final match thirty-six holes. There was an unusual incident in the Newport championship. Richard Peters put a billiard cue in his golf bag and insisted on putting out with it. Of course, the cue was disbarred by the Executive Committee. (This is the first decision the USGA made on the "form and make of golf clubs," which some fifteen years later became a burning question with the Royal and Ancient when the Schenectady putter dispute arose and disrupted unification.) There was, besides myself, only one entry in the first official Amateur Championship who had played golf abroad, namely, L. B. Stoddard, who beat me on the St. Andrews course by one up the year before. He was put out the third round by Winthrop Rutherford. All my matches I won easily, 7 and 6; 8 and 6; 5 and 3; 8 and 7; and, the final from C. E. Sands, 12 and 11. This made me the first American champion. I entered this championship in excellent form and was well taken care of, stopping with Mr. and Mrs. Henry Clews. My rounds in the Newport tournament averaged 43 to 44 for each nine holes.

How I Won the
British Amateur Championship

by

WALTER J. TRAVIS

1910 — FROM THE MARCH ISSUE OF *THE AMERICAN GOLFER*

THE HISTORY of the 1904 championship, in its personal aspects and the many side influences that had a very potent bearing on the result, has never yet been told.

A dispassionate recital of them may perhaps possess some interest for golfers generally.

I shall therefore try and tell, in a plain, unvarnished way, the many causes which led up to America's winning the event nearly six years ago.

What I have to say is not dictated in any way by any spirit of vaingloriousness; it is merely a simple, uncolored account of the affair from the standpoint of a man who won, not a man who got licked . . . which sometimes makes quite a difference, perhaps unconsciously.

I arrived in London three weeks before the meeting, my intention being to spend the last ten or twelve days at Sandwich and the interval at St. Andrews and North Berwick. I was playing so atrociously at both the latter places, however, that I left myself a week only for Sandwich, vainly hoping I might get back in form. Matters in this direction were not assisted by the acquisition of a whole lot of new clubs. When I arrived at Sandwich I was in anything but a cheerful frame of mind. Rather than run the risk of playing badly at the outset and so, unconsciously, becoming prejudiced against the course, I simply took

out a putting cleek—which I had got at North Berwick—and a few balls and walked around a few holes.

The first ball I struck I knew I was on the road to recovery. For the first time in two weeks I could "feel" the ball. The necessary "touch" and the resultant "timing" were there, in such sharp contradistinction to the entire absence of these vitally important essentials previously, that I was at once transported into the golfer's seventh heaven of delight.

I got going all right the following week in the practice rounds . . . but the putting was still the weak feature. Finally, the day before the Championship, Mr. Phillips, of the Apawamis Club, Rye, a member of our party, suggested I should try his putter, a Schenectady. It seemed to suit me in every way and I decided to stand or fall by it.

The British Championship is decided by match play throughout. Each match consists of eighteen holes excepting the final, which is at thirty-six holes.

THE FIRST ROUND

THE first round I was drawn against Mr. H. Holden of the Royal Liverpool Golf Club. I had no trouble in beating him by 4 and 3. One of the local rules at Sandwich at the time was that there was no permanent grass in a hazard. This, by the way, has since been embodied in the regular code of rules. In playing the seventh hole Mr. Holden's tee-shot found a pot bunker, the bottom of which was more or less covered with grass, his ball lying on the same.

He unwittingly soled his club. Upon his attention being drawn to the special rule referred to, he said that he had never heard of such a rule and that it was a damned silly rule anyway. And he kept talking about it so much during the round that I regretted exceedingly having said anything at all about it.

In a subsequent match against Mr. H. Hilton, the latter found the same bunker, but, mindful of my experience with Mr. Holden, I simply let him go ahead. He lost the hole anyway, as Mr. Holden would have done, quite outside the rule in question.

Each pair, during the meeting, is given a starting time. Mr. Holden and I started at twelve o'clock. It was 1:50 P.M. before we finished. The match had been played in a soaking rain.

The afternoon round, against Mr. James Robb, was scheduled to start at 2:28 P.M. Wet through, I had no time to get into dry togs. Mr. Robb, on the other hand, was quite fresh, his opponent, Mr. G. C. Whigham, having defaulted the morning's match.

We had a ding-dong match. 2 up and 3 to play, we halved the sixteenth, I lost the seventeenth and halved the eighteenth, winning the match by the narrow margin of one hole.

A POOR CADDIE

I HAD HAD, ever since I had been at Sandwich, one of the worst caddies it had ever been my misfortune to be saddled with. This young man, about twenty-six years old, was a natural-born idiot, and cross-eyed at that. He was too nervous to think of performing the customary duty of teeing a ball and rarely knew where it went.

Playing the eleventh hole, Mr. Robb and I both made the green on our seconds. I was a shade away; I laid my next up stony. My boy, who was at the flag, was asked by Mr. Robb to "tak it oot," whereupon he calmly proceeded to *lift my ball;* indeed he already had it up an inch or so before I could thunder at him to drop it. The hole was halved, Mr.

Robb, of course, making no protest, although after the match a number of players asserted he should have done so. However, in the circumstances I am satisfied his claim would not have been sustained. But I do know that I made a sorry hash of the next hole.

Now I had on several previous occasions made efforts to get another caddie, without avail. So when our match was over I asked Mr. Robb if he intended playing any more. No, he was going back that night . . . and he would be very glad to let me have his caddie, whom I had marked as a first-class one.

Well, I couldn't get him! and I couldn't get another!! No out-and-out refusal on the part of the caddie-master, but for some inscrutable reason there was perpetually "nothing doing." Then and there I made up my mind that I would stick to my poor, weak reed and do my level best to win the championship. I was assisted in coming to this determination by a conjunction of little things.

A FRIGID RECEPTION

ALL through, the atmosphere at Sandwich had been markedly frigid and in sharp contrast to that of three years before when I was over there. On both occasions I had happened to be the American amateur champion. The only explanation which suggested itself was that when we were there before we were not contestants. Then lots of attentions were showered upon us, as at all other courses we visited.

Could we now get any of the big men to play against us in practice? No! For the most part we had to flock together, inside and outside, and not a finger was lifted nor a single step taken by a soul to make us escape the uncomfortable feeling that we were pariahs.

Why, I couldn't even get a locker! My changing had to be done in a common hallway and the clubs left in the professional's shop.

What happened to Judge Russell? The Judge at that time was President of the Metropolitan Golf Association and also the Garden City Golf Club. He came over from the Continent specially to see the play for a couple of days. He was not allowed to set his foot inside the clubhouse door until he had paid a sovereign, or a half sovereign—one or the other.

When the Oxford and Cambridge team was

over here in 1903, Judge Russell paid out of his own pocket $25 per head for each member of the team for tickets to view the Yacht Race. And he had three members as guests at his summer home at Southampton during the special tournament arranged by the Shinnecock Hills Golf Club for the Oxford and Cambridge team.

During the dinner at the Bell Hotel the evening of the Judge's arrival, he asked if any members of the Oxford and Cambridge team were present. Two seated at an adjoining table were pointed out, one of whom had been staying with him at Southampton. A perfunctory wave of the hand on the part of the latter was the only response. There were other members of the O. & C. team at the Championship, but not a single thing was done by any one of them at any time in return for his many gentle courtesies. And the same remarks apply with equal force in the case of Mr. James L. Taylor, who did so much for the visiting team at Manchester, Vermont. If he should ever go across he must certainly look them up, so two or three said as they presented their cards, and they would try and do their best to reciprocate.

Mr. Taylor's cards on arrival on the other side were never acknowledged and he was practically cut dead at Sandwich.

RESOLVED TO WIN

CAN it be wondered with all these and other little things continually piling up that there should have been born in me a strong fixity of purpose to get even in the only possible way? Of course, there had been present before a determination to win but that was as nothing to the now steel-clad resolution to do so. I knew it was a big undertaking but my game was coming all the time and I believed I could do it, especially as the scoring showed I was going as well as the best of them.

THE OTHER AMERICAN CONTESTANTS

BY this time Mr. F. O. Horstmann had dropped out, being beaten in the first round by Mr. R. W. Orr, 4 and 3; Mr. John Moller had drawn a bye in the first round only to succumb in the second to Mr. Crawford Hutchison by one hole; and Mr. Devereux Emmet,

who had also drawn a bye, beat Mr. Gilbert Elliott one up in the second round but had to yield to Mr. Cairnes by 5 and 4 in the third round. Mr. W. W. Burton covered himself with glory in reaching the third round, having previously disposed of Mr. Norman Cockell by 3 and 2 and Mr. A. Cant, a very fine player from Carnoustie, by 2 and 1 in the first and second rounds, respectively, only to fall grievously by the wayside in the third round against Mr. Harold E. Reade who beat him by 9 and 8.

Mr. E. M. Byers meanwhile had beaten Mr. C. E. Dick 2 and 1 and Mr. S. A. Peto 4 and 2, but was knocked out in the third round by Mr. J. Williamson, at the nineteenth hole.

In the third round I beat Mr. A. M. Murray by 3 and 1.

A HARD MATCH

THE fourth round, against the ex-Irish champion, Mr. H. E. Reade, was the hardest match I had. I cannot do better than quote from the (London) *Times* of June 2, 1904, the following account of the match:

Mr. Travis, after a close match, qualified for the fifth round. Mr. Reade was 2 up at the 4th, and he halved the next in 2, Mr. Travis securing a 4 at "the maiden," although he had failed to carry the bunker. Putting down a 14-ft. putt at the 7th, he reduced the lead to 1. Mr. Reade became 2 up again, holing a very long putt at the 8th for a 2. Missing his next drive, Mr. Reade topped his second into the bunker. After a half in 5 at the 10th Mr. Travis squared the match at the 11th. By means of a very accurate approach, Mr. Reade won the next two holes, getting down in 4 off Mr. Travis' ball at the 13th. After a half in 5, Mr. Travis outdrove Mr. Reade at the 15th, and, reaching the green in two while Mr. Reade failed to carry the bunker, he reduced the lead to 1. Driving within four yards of the 16th hole, he squared the match with a fine 2. Winning the 17th with a safe 4, he finished the match with another good 4 at the last hole. Thus, after having been two down with 4 to play, he finished very strongly aoing the last four holes in 15, with only one putt of any length to hole.

The lengths of the holes at Sandwich were as follows:

Out—
366 312 220 420 240 160 450 180 420—2768
In—
420 357 333 431 505 433 180 350 380—3389
——
Total yards.................... 6157

The tee-shots are outstanding features of Sandwich. In a great many instances some very long carries are necessary. It is generally conceded to favor the long powerful hitter. It was remarked by J. E. Low that during the practice rounds, when the tees were much shorter than during the championship, I could just manage to nip over the hazards. When the tees were put back to the limit it was observed that I could just manage to nip over the hazards, although in a number of cases the distances were stretched twenty to thirty yards at least.

I have always enjoyed the reputation of being a short driver. So I was for several years after I commenced the game. "Give a dog a bad name," etc. With a course such as Sandwich, involving long carries, which I just managed to nip over from the forward tees, it was generally expected that I would come to a speedy end, being such a short driver, when the championship tees were used. But, with the exception of the match against Mr. Blackwell, I found that I could hold my own fairly well against all the rest of the men. The carry at the third was too much for me, however. In a direct line to the hole it meant a carry of 180 yards to clear the "Sahara," the name given to a large stretch of sand and rough intervening between the tee and the hole. Mr. Blackwell drove the green in both rounds.

AGAINST MR. HILTON

In the fifth round I met Mr. H. Hilton. The last, in fact the only time I had previously played against him was in 1901, at Hoylake. He beat me then quite easily. There is this to be said, however, that at that time I was in very poor physical shape. In fact, the trip abroad was wholly in the interests of my health. I can't recall having beaten a man of any note excepting perhaps Mr. Angus McDonald and Mr. H. W. Fowler. All the others, and there were quite a number of them, had comparatively an easy thing of it.

In the three-year interval, however, my game had not only very materially improved but my health was quite re-established, so that I looked forward to the match with Mr. Hilton with no uncertainty. He lost the first three holes. At the fourth he missed a putt of about a yard and a half and I promptly followed suit with one of about half the distance. The next three holes were halved. He lost the eighth in 4 to 3 and won the ninth in 4 to 5, which left me 3 up at the turn, scores being as follows:

Mr. Travis,
Out—4 4 3 5 4 3 5 3 5—36
Mr. Hilton,
Out—5 5 4 5 4 3 5 4 4—39

The tenth was halved. Mr. Hilton won the eleventh, reducing the lead to 2 up, but promptly lost the next three, and the match, by 5 and 4.

MR. HUTCHINSON ONE OF THE BEST

This is what the *Times* had to say concerning the match against Mr. Horace G. Hutchinson:

All doubts that may have existed as to the quality of Mr. Travis' golf were set at rest by the game in the afternoon, when he beat Mr. Hutchinson. He has played better golf each day, seeming to play well within himself, and to bring out a game just sufficient to beat each successive opponent. His short game is certainly marvelous, almost every long putt being quite dead, if not in the hole. Mr. Travis is quite imperturbable, having apparently no nerves. Playing two shots in the rough, Mr. Hutchinson lost the 1st hole to a safe 4, but the match was squared at the next, Mr. Travis missing from 6 ft. Mr. Hutchinson missed his next tee shot, hitting the ground in swinging back, and Mr. Travis put in a long putt for a 3. A magnificent second at the 4th gave Mr. Travis a safe 4, and he holed a very awkward putt from the top of the hill for a half in 3 at the 5th. A fine drive gave him a safe 3 at "the maiden," but Mr. Hutchinson got down a 5-ft. putt for a half. After a half in 5, Mr. Travis laid his second quite dead at the 8th, but his opponent holed a 3-yard putt for a half. Mr. Travis was 2 yards short with his approach putt at the 9th, but holing his 4th, he turned for home 3 up. His score was: 4 5 3 4 3 3 5 3 4—34. Mr. Hutchinson was a long way ahead from the 10th tee and he reached the green with his iron, Mr. Travis with his brassie finding an almost impossible position in the bunker, from which he took 2 to get out. He only just carried the bunker from the 11th tee, but Mr. Hutchinson missed his chance, failing at the 8-ft. putt, and the hole was halved in 5. Mr. Hutchinson reached the 12th green, using his iron for his second, while Mr. Travis had a lucky brassie shot through the bunker to within 7 yards of the hole, but a half in 4 resulted. Both lay badly off their drives at the next and Mr. Travis' second only went 30 yards, but playing on steadily he secured a 6. His opponent failed to carry the bunker with his third, and only just getting out, missed a 5-ft. putt and took 7. A half in 5 at the 14th left Mr. Travis 3 up and 4 to play. The latter at the next being bunkered off his second, Mr. Hutchinson played short with his iron, but he went too far and trickled in, so a half in 5 made Mr. Travis dormy 3, and he made the match safe by putting a perfect tee shot hole high at the 16th, while Mr. Hutchinson was short. The latter failed to use his chances at the 11th and 13th holes, but otherwise he played well, and holed several good putts in the earlier stages. Mr. Blackwell will require his very best game to win today.

The scores were:

Mr. Travis,
  Out—4 5 3 4 3 3 5 3 4—34
Mr. Hutchinson,
  Out—5 4 5 5 3 3 5 3 5—38

Mr. Travis,
  In—6 5 5 6 5 5 3
Mr. Hutchinson,
  In—5 5 5 7 5 5 4

THE FINAL ROUND

IN THE final, against Mr. Blackwell, I had the comfortable feeling all through that I would assuredly win. After some rather loose play at the first hole I managed to win in 5 to 6. At the second I holed a four-yard putt for a 3. The third was badly played and was halved in 5. I won the fourth hole in 4 to 5, also the next in 3 to 4, making me 4 up. I missed a comparatively short putt at "the maiden" which brought forth some mild hand-clapping. The seventh was halved. I won the eighth only to lose the ninth, thus leaving me 3 up at the turn. Coming in I lost the tenth, halved the eleventh and twelfth and was lucky enough to win the thirteenth, as Mr. Blackwell had all the best of the long game. Right in the teeth of the wind two magnificent wooden shots left him a comparatively easy iron to get home. This, however, he hooked badly and indifferent work on the green lost him the hole. At the fourteenth Mr. Blackwell got away a tremendous tee shot. I also, for me, got off a corker, but it was some thirty or forty yards at least back of Mr. Blackwell's. The hole is 505 yards.

I took a brassie for my second and played up about thirty yards short of the hazard guarding the green. Mr. Blackwell studied his shot for a few moments and then elected to take a cleek and play safe, short of the bunker in front of the green. He caught hold of it too clean and pitched right in. My next being laid dead I won the hole in 4. Mr. Blackwell holed a good putt at the fifteenth and won in 4 to 5. The next two were halved in 4's and I secured the last hole in 4 to 5, thus making me 4 up at the end of the morning round.

After luncheon we both again played the first hole badly, Mr. Blackwell eventually winning in 6 to 7. A poor drive by the latter on the second enabled me to win in 4 to 5, but at the third I again missed a short putt, Mr. Blackwell winning in 3 to 4. I won the fourth hole in 4 to 5, the fifth in 3 to 4 and the sixth in 3 to 4, thus making me 6 up with 12 to play. I lost the seventh in 5 to 4, halved the eighth and again lost the ninth, leaving me 4 up. The next six holes being halved, the match came to an end on the fifteenth green by 4 up and 3 to play.

Scores:
Mr. Travis,
    Out—5 3 5 4 3 4 5 3*6—38
Mr. Blackwell,
    Out—6 4 5 5 4 3 5 4 4—40
Mr. Travis,
    In—5 5 4 5 4 5 4 4 4—40—78
Mr. Blackwell,
    In—4 5 4 6 6 4 4 4 5—42—82
Mr. Travis,
    Out—7 4 4 4 3 3 6 3*5—39
Mr. Blackwell,
    Out—6 5 3 5 4 4 5 3 4—39
Mr. Travis,
    In—4 4 4 5 5 5
Mr. Blackwell,
    In—4 4 4 5 5 5
    *Approximated.

MR. BLACKWELL'S TALKATIVENESS

SOME little time after the championship, Mr. Blackwell was led to remark in a written article that I was the most remarkably silent man he had ever met, thereby proving himself an unconscious humorist of the first water. It happened in this way. Ordinarily, I do not care to talk when I am playing serious golf, but in order to be on terms of sociability, I remarked to Mr. Blackwell in the morning round, at the third tee, that his driving was wonderfully long. He merely murmured some sort of acknowledgment and that was the end of any attempt at conversation between us during the whole match.

OUTSIDE HONORS POUR IN

IF THERE had been any lukewarmness on the part of the Sandwich people, this was more than compensated for by the friendly attitude of the Cinque Ports Golf Club at Deal, right next door to Sandwich. A dinner was given to the "foreign invaders" at the invitation of Mr. James Leslie Wanklyn, M. P., captain of the Cinque Ports Golf Club, at the Union Club, adjoining the Castle at Deal, on the Saturday evening following the championship and the freedom of the course was ours. And

telegrams of congratulations poured in at the conclusion of the match from all over the United Kingdom including one from the Captain of the Royal St. George's Golf Club, the Earl of Winchelsea as well as scores from the U.S.

WHY NO DINNER WAS GIVEN

THE championship came to an end on Friday, June 3d. Playing at Sandwich on Thursday of the following week, two men approached and introduced themselves as a committee to ask if I would attend a dinner to be given at the Bell Hotel on the following Saturday evening in commemoration of my win. As I have stated, the event came to an end the week previously, and the thought instantly flashed through my mind—now the essence of these things lies in their spontaneity; had Mr. Blackwell won, a dinner would have been given at the Bell Hotel on the following evening and I would have been seated at his right hand, the guest of honor, and nothing would have been too good for me. All this flashed through my mind in about two seconds. I said, "I am extremely sorry, gentlemen, but I cannot accept your very kind invitation for the simple reason that Mrs. Travis has arranged to go up to London tomorrow morning and it was understood that before the tournament everything was to be made subservient to golf, but after the tournament I was to become her slave." And to London we went the next morning. And the cup followed (with 3/6d carriage to pay) all dented in through having been put in the wrong package.

At the conclusion of the championship when it was learned that I was going to take the cup across, Mr. Norman Hunter, one of the members of the Oxford & Cambridge Golfing Society, gratuitously remarked, "Umph! We'll never see that again." "You needn't worry," replied Mr. W. W. Burton, "we've managed to take pretty good care of the America cup for a good many years."

ON TRAINING

WHILE the feeling and general attitude of the amateurs was anything but friendly, it must be said that this was more than made up for by the encouragement extended by all the leading professionals. For some reason, they all seemed to want me to win. Benny Sayers was particularly solicitous. He wanted to know if I ever went in for rubbing. I said, "No." My only attempt at training was several years ago, back in 1897, about three weeks prior to a tournament at Lakewood. While I do not drink or smoke to excess (at all events I didn't smoke overmuch in those days) I conceived the idea that if I stopped both, my game would be improved. I did so. It was the first and only attempt at changing my regular habits and it was a dire failure. I was like a perfect baby on the putting greens. I told Benny this and he was horrified at the thought that I took such poor care of myself, and he insisted upon coming in and rubbing me down with Elliman's Embrocation. It was very good of him and I tried to wriggle out of it but he was quite insistent and I could only get rid of him by promising that I would rub myself down that night . . . and the bargain was cemented by his loaning me his favorite spoon, which proved quite invaluable.

Outside of this one rubbing, the only "training" I went in for was drinking, for me, huge quantities of stout—stuff you can drink in that cold, damp climate at that time of the year with impunity . . . and most anything else alcoholic for that matter . . . but which on this side would be almost suicidal.

That, and listening nightly to Sim Ford descant glowingly . . . yet with that characteristic gloomy sort of look at me through the corner of his eye, commingled with a grave pity that my end was so soon to come . . . on the magnificent golf which he had that day seen played by Maxwell, Ball, Laidlay, Hutchinson, Blackwell or one or the other of the big guns. All of which, as I shrewdly suspect Ford knew and accordingly kept on pumping such stuff into me, made me inwardly resolve to grit my teeth and win the next day's matches. 'Twas the best kind of training I could have had. I was never allowed to forget for a moment that I was "up against it."

These dissertations were the usual accompaniment of our regular evening's game of cribbage, played in the public room of the Bell Hotel at Sandwich, where we were staying. And it was funny to see the looks of mild surprise and commiseration on the faces of the various Englishmen, nearly all engaged in the championship, who passed us on their way to the Sandwich Club which formed part of the hotel. The doors of that same Sandwich Club which were wide open on my previous visit, were now, alas! for some reason kept as closely shut. Which was, perhaps, just as well.

As David Harum says: "A reasonable number of fleas is good for a dog; it keeps him from forgetting that he is a dog." So things of this sort helped to keep me from forgetting what I was there for.

THE CLUBS I USED

IT MAY or may not interest those players who are wedded to a particular set of clubs to learn that after every match I would go into the professional's shop and purchase one or more clubs. The result was that when I played Mr. Blackwell, of the original set with which I started, I had only two clubs, a mashie and a putter. All the rest were entirely new. As to the putter, it did excellent work during the meeting. I suppose that taking it all through my average would be slightly under two putts per green. In nearly every match I would run down two or three very long ones. As against this I would nod now and then and miss some comparatively short ones. But the putting, on the whole, was distinctly good. I have, however, on several occasions since, in competition, and also in friendly matches, putted vastly better.

The singular thing about that Schenectady which I used throughout the championship is that I have never been able to do anything with it since. I have tried it repeatedly but it seems to have lost all its virtue.

1913—The United States Open Championship

by

HENRY LEACH

1913 — FROM THE OCTOBER ISSUE OF *THE AMERICAN GOLFER*

MORE WAS DONE than the winning of the Open Championship of the United States and the defeating of two of the greatest golfers of the time—one of them the greatest of all time—when Mr. Francis Ouimet played round the course of The Country Club, at Brookline, in seventy-two strokes on the morning of the twentieth of September. That new era of international rivalry which we have been talking about and considering for the last year or two, when it has indeed been a real thing, was brought suddenly to a close. Instead of it there was begun at once yet another era which will be one of the fiercest and sternest competitions between the golfers of the two greatest golfing countries—and none the less friendly for all the fierceness and intensity. We have been dallying with our international rivalry so far. Britain has been complacent and America has been—if I dare say it—a little timid. There will be no more of this sort of thing.

If Americans think that British competitive golf will remain quiet and undisturbed under the tremendous blow that it has received, they are certainly mistaken. Nothing can dim the merit and the glory of Mr. Ouimet's victory; no British golfer would ever wish for an instant to injure the imperishability of the honor that was achieved on that dripping day in Massachusetts. To the victor the spoils, and well were they won and magnificently deserved. But British golfers must take another view of this question of international rivalry now, and you may assume it as absolutely certain that efforts will be made, greater and more thorough than they have ever been made before, to gain not one but several victories on American soil to balance this one amazing defeat—if anything can ever balance it. I am absolutely sure that next year you will have a stronger British fighting force sent against you than you have had this—not that I am suggesting that there are better golfers to be sent over than Vardon and Ray. There are other considerations. Whether they succeed or fail, the attempt will be made again and again, and no doubt America will retaliate. That is what I mean when I say that a new era has begun since the twentieth of September. America has indeed graduated now as a first-class golfing power. I am glad of it; it is all for the good of the game, and Francis Ouimet, besides having achieved immortal fame among golfers, has done something splendid for the good of that game. Any regrets that I, as an Englishman, may have concerning that British defeat are tempered by this consideration and again by the other one that no victory was better or more thoroughly and decisively gained than that of Mr. Ouimet, so that I almost come to feel indeed that I have no regrets at all. America has a champion now of whom she may well be proud.

It was indeed a wonderful conquest that was accomplished at the end of an exciting meeting, the like of which I do not remember. If the weather for the last two days was very wet and unpleasant it was hardly noticed in the prevailing excitement, and it did vastly less injury to the course than one might have expected; indeed Brookline played very well indeed from start to finish. I was over this course last season and liked it very much at that time; but somehow it impressed me far more this time and it must now be placed in the very highest class of American courses. The quality and the strong character of most of its holes are splendid and it was in superb condition at the opening of the meeting, fairway and putting greens and everything. To this it is to be added that the arrangements made by The Country Club for dealing with the greatest championship meeting ever held on the American continent or anywhere else outside Great Britain were perfect, and an immense amount of credit is due to Messrs. G. Herbert Windeler and Herbert Jaques for the success that they achieved and for the manner in which they pleased and delighted all who were concerned. And then on the other side the administration by President Robert Watson and Secretary John Reid, of the USGA, was flawless.

The big crowd that assembled to watch the play, especially in the closing stages, was well managed and splendidly behaved, though I do wish these American golfing congregations would restrain themselves more in the matter of their applause, which becomes very wearisome and trying in its frequency. There is more applause during the playing of one round by one couple in America than there is in a whole championship at home, and I am bound to think that our quiet way is the better one. Some time it will be the same in America; and in the meantime I wish that officials and people with flags would do something to discourage this constant clapping of hands and cheering at strokes which are often nothing much out of the ordinary, for after all a golf course is not a circus, and the other man who is not cheered has to be remembered. But the meeting, which was attended by some hundred and seventy competitors, including a very fair show of amateurs, from all over the States and elsewhere, was in every sense a great sporting event and one which those who attended it will surely never forget.

Big history was made at Brookline in the third week of September.

And now to the main point. It is given to few men at twenty years of age to achieve such immense distinction in any branch of sport as Mr. Francis Ouimet on this occasion. It is given to still fewer to deserve the distinction so utterly and completely as he does. To still fewer is the opportunity afforded of proving their right to it on two successive days and accepting the opportunity, as he did. If he had won the championship on Friday, as he nearly did, that would have been magnificent; to tie indeed was in the circumstances practically to win. But to repeat it the next day in the very severest form of contest, with his two great rivals alongside him all the time doing their best, with all their ripe judgment and splendid skill, to defeat him—that was an accomplishment which for its thoroughness and for its supreme merit can hardly ever be equaled again. There was no fluke about the victory; it was thoroughly well earned, and America in general and Mr. Ouimet in particular are entitled to their pride. But even yet I can hardly realize it, so amazing are the facts. There is this boy—for born on May 8, 1893, he is nothing more—beating our Harry Vardon and Edward Ray when they are at the prime of their golfing lives and at something uncommonly like their best. Then, too, he is an amateur, and when before did an amateur stand up like this against the very best professionals and beat them at their own game? Not in the present generation. I was greatly impressed by his methods and his temperament at Garden City and knew that he would do something big in time, but none of us were prepared for such an early and magnificent conquest. He has the golf, he has the mind, he has the temperament and he has something even better, the fine sporting character that enables him to conduct himself modestly in the manner of a splendid little gentleman at a time of enormous and magnificent achievement, and for every reason America has an Open champion of whom she may be intensely proud. Mr. Ouimet intends to remain an amateur, he tells me, despite the enormous temptations that must now be held before him. I hope that he will come to Sandwich to our amateur championship next year; indeed how can he fail to come there? He will be given a hearty welcome and he will be the biggest attraction we have ever had on our links—the boy amateur who has beaten Vardon and Ray for a championship, indeed I should think so!

In dealing with the play, especially in its preliminary stages, I shall confine myself to impressions and general features, for it would be futile and impossible to consider the holes that were played, stroke by stroke, by even the foremost competitors. At the beginning, however, the lengths of these holes should be stated for the understanding of the figures that follow by those who are not very familiar with the Brookline course. The official measurements are as follows:

Out—
430 300 435 300 420 275 185 380 520—3245
In—
140 390 415 320 470 370 125 360 410—3000
Total yards 6245

The large number of entrants made it necessary for the first time to hold a qualifying competition on the British system, and consequently the meeting, which was at first planned for two days, was extended to four, and, through the tie that took place at the finish of the competition proper, to five. The field was divided into two sections, half the entrants playing two rounds on Tuesday, September 16, and the other half on the following day, the top thirty-two, with all who tied for the thirty-second place in each case, going forward to the competition proper, which was decided on the Thursday and Friday.

FIRST DAY

TUESDAY, SEPTEMBER 16

THERE were many good players in this section of the qualifying competition, but it was natural that chief interst should be centered on Harry Vardon, Francis Ouimet, Tom Mac-Namara and Louis Tellier. Ouimet struck the key of all that was to follow by taking the lead in the first round. He played a beautiful 74 which was practically flawless, and when all the returns had been made it was found that he was leading Vardon by a stroke, while Alec Ross, of Brae-Burn, and J. M. Barnes, of Tacoma, Washington, were next with 76. Vardon on the whole was playing a fine game;

but there was some unsteadiness in his putting, and this was noticeable again in the afternoon. Ouimet was playing only a little way behind him and there was a time in the afternoon when he had a lead of two strokes on the British player. He became aware of the fact, I believe, somewhere round about the thirteenth hole and whether it was the knowledge that upset him or not (this was suggested, but in the light of subsequent events, the coolness he displayed, and the utter indifference to what his opponents did, I cannot believe it), the fact remains that the only bad hole he played all day was the fourteenth. He found more than one bunker on his way from the tee to the green, and he wound up by taking three putts and doing the hole in seven. Even at that he looked certain to be level with the British player at the finish, but Vardon ran down a ten-yard putt for a 3 at the home hole and Ouimet got a 5 at the seventeenth—the hole that did so much to give him the championship afterwards by the 3's that he obtained at it. The upshot was that Vardon just came out on top. A splendid show was made by the youngest member of the Smith family, MacDonald, brother of Alec and Willie. He has a nice, easy style, is full of shots, and is undoubtedly a player of great promise. He made himself a considerable force in the championship up to its closing stages. Tellier was a comfortable qualifier. The other scores must be left to speak for themselves, as follows:

PLAYER AND CLUB	1st	2nd	Ttl.
Harry Vardon, South Herts G. C., Eng.	75	76	151
Mr. Francis Ouimet, Woodland G. C.	74	78	152
MacDonald Smith, Wykagyl C. C.	77	77	154
Alec Ross, Brae-Burn	76	81	157
Tom MacNamara, Boston	78	80	158
J. M. Barnes, Tacoma, Wash...	82	76	158
H. Hampton, N'th Andover C. C.	79	81	160
Louis Tellier, France	80	81	161
Alec Campbell, The Country..	84	77	161
C. R. Murray, R'l Montreal G. C.	86	76	162
T. Kerrigan, Dedham	79	83	162
E. W. Laving, Arcola C. C. ...	83	79	162
J. A. Croke, Calumet C. C. ...	78	85	163

PLAYER AND CLUB	1st	2nd	Ttl.
Jack Hutchinson, Allegheny C. C.	80	84	164
J. A. Donaldson, Glen View C. C.	84	81	165
Fred Ryall, Waumbek G. C.	83	82	165
Peter Robertson, Fall River	83	82	165
C. D. Thom, Shinnecock Hills.	84	81	165
Fred McLeod, Columbia G. C.	81	84	165
Herbert Strong, Inwood	81	85	166
C. H. Anderson, Winthrop	83	83	166
F. H. Bellwood, Garden City	83	83	166
David Ogilvie, Morris City G. C.	83	83	166
A. H. Murray, Kanawaki G. C.	84	82	166
Mr. A. G. Lockwood, Belmont Springs	84	83	167
Mr. Fred Herreshoff, Nat'l Golf Links	85	82	167
H. H. Barker, Roe Buck C. C.	79	88	167
Tom Vardon, Onwentsia	85	82	167
Mr. W. C. Fownes, Jr., Oakmont	81	87	168
J. R. Thomson, Phila. C. C.	84	84	168
Otto Hackbarth, Hinsdale G. C.	85	83	168
Norman Clark, Westmoreland C. C.	82	88	170
T. M. Anderson, Commonwealth	82	88	170

Did not qualify:

PLAYER AND CLUB	1st	2nd	Ttl.
Jack Jolly, Newark N. J.	83	88	171
G. F. Sparling, Brooklawn C. C.	91	80	171
H. J. Harris, Inverness G. C.	82	89	171
F. McNamara, Siaconset G. C.	86	85	171
Alfred Campbell, Oak Hill C. C.	81	90	171
R. D. Thomson, Portchester C. C.	90	81	171
Fred Brand, Clinton	84	88	172
W. Byrne, Overbrook G. C.	85	87	172
James Milligan, Wyoming V. C. C.	87	85	172
W. J. Bell, Scarboro G. & C. C.	80	92	172
A. T. Chisholm, Portland C. C.	86	87	173
J. G. Campbell, Mt. Tom G. C.	88	85	173
Charles Burgess, Woodland	87	86	173
Mr. G. A. Ormiston, Oakmont C. C.	93	80	173
C. G. Adams, Pittsfield C. C.	84	89	173
C. H. Rowe, Beaver Valley C. C.	84	89	173
H. H. Beckett, Washington C. C.	83	91	174
A. H. Fenn, Poland Spring	88	86	174

PLAYER AND CLUB	1st	2nd	Ttl.
G. O. Simpson, Omaha C. C.	92	83	175
J. J. Whittingham, M'stown G. C.	82	93	175
C. W. Singleton, Sacandaga G. C.	89	87	176
Mr. John Reid, Jr., St. And'ws G. C.	86	91	177
Jack Gordon, Rhode I. C. C.	88	89	177
Dave Stevens, Mohawk C. C.	91	86	177
L. B. Paton, unattached	91	87	178
W. H. Murphy, Alpine G. C.	88	90	178
D. E. Miner, Kenilworth C. C.	87	92	179
Mr. J. B. Hylan, Vesper	82	99	181
Ralph Thomas, Framingham	89	92	181
Herbert Martin, Quogue G. C.	92	90	182
J. Doeberl, Greenwich C. C.	93	90	183
Mr. H. MacDonald, Rochester.	99	90	189
Mr. J. D. Foot, Apawamis G. C.	89	103	192
R. Fitzjohn, Adelphia C. C.	99	94	193
E. H. Anderson, Winthrop	103	100	203
H. C. Lagerblade, Youngstown	81	no card	
James Spencer, Highland C. C.	86	no card	
Mr. P. W. Whittemore, The Country	86	no card	
N. De Mane, unattached	87	no card	
Ernest Killick, Wee Burn G. C.	88	no card	
J. M. Connors, Rangely G. C.	88	no card	
Tom Young, Westport G. C.	90	no card	
Mr. Charles McKenna, Rochester	93	no card	
Mr. R. C. Watson, Westbrook, G. C.	91	no card	
Mr. V. S. Lawrence, Woodland	94	no card	
C. J. MacGrath, Tatnuck	no card		

SECOND DAY

WEDNESDAY, SEPTEMBER 17

THERE was more strength in the field on the second qualifying day, even if it was without Vardon and Ouimet, and for this reason and also because there was a general feeling that it would be dangerous to do such scores as some of those who qualified the previous day, there was a general disposition to brace up. Ray, McDermott, Wilfrid Reid, Alec Smith, Jerome Travers and a number of others of excellent quality were in the list. Ray had Jack Hobens for his partner and Hobens made the pace very nicely for him in the matter of length from the tee if Ray wanted any pacemaking; often the two balls were practically level if indeed the British ball was not a shade to the rear. In the two rounds he made returns of two even 74's and they were the result of sound careful play in every part of the game. Ray was putting well, but it struck me that he could have driven a little farther if he had wanted to do so. When he lets out, however, the rough has a great attraction for him and at Brookline he had developed a holy horror of the trees that line the fairway and told me that his greatest fear in regard to the championship was the dire trouble that he might get into through crooked driving. However he kept out of difficulties on this occasion. His 148 became course record for two rounds. But the best golf of the day was played by little Wilfrid Reid who belongs to the Banstead Downs Club which is near to Walton Heath, Braid's place, some twenty miles out of London. From the time when he came out here Reid, who is an English international player of several years standing and certainly deserved more attention for his capacity than was given to him at first, played exceedingly fine golf and it would not have surprised me if he had come nearer to winning the championship than any other of the British invaders. Whether it was an advantage to him or something quite the other way that the limelight was not on him all the time as it was on his compatriots, and he was more or less ignored, while they were being prematurely glorified, is a point I cannot judge upon. But it is to be remembered to Reid's credit that he came out for this championship entirely on his own account and at his own expense, and I believe that if there had been no other Englishmen here he would have pressed young Ouimet desperately close at the finish. On the occasion of this qualifying competition he produced just the same form as he had displayed several times in practice, driving a good clean ball and putting beautifully, and it was good enough to give him a 72 for his morning round and to put him at the top for the time being along with R. G. MacDonald, once of Dornoch, who played perfect golf from start to finish. In the afternoon Reid and MacDonald fell away a little and curiously enough each did the same score as the other again, but Ray was first in the reckoning by three clear strokes. McDermott, Brady and Alec Smith qualified comfortably and that is nearly all that need be said about

them. McDermott was playing steadily but not putting very well. At the fourteenth hole in the morning he came by a curious incident. He hooked his tee-shot in the direction of a big tree a long way from the tee, and the ball came down in very thick grass. When it was found it was discovered to be resting on top of another ball—one that had been lost and not found again. The question arose as to what could or should be done in the circumstances and Mr. Watson, the U. S. G. A. president, was appealed to and properly declared that the ball should be played just as it was. McDermott considered the case and determined that the only thing to do was to play at the stray ball, the one that did not belong to him, which he did accordingly, his own shooting off at an angle into more rough grass and the hole costing him six.

The amateurs did well, and it was interesting to see Mr. John Anderson, the finalist in the Amateur Championship at Garden City coming out at the head of the list, and above his conqueror, Mr. Travers, who was led to express the opinion at the close of his performance that he was the "worst putter in America"—which is very far from being true. Ben Nicholls failed to qualify, and sad to say, there also failed the player who is joint holder of the record of the old course of St. Andrews, Willie Smith, of Mexico. The day's scores and the details of the leaders are as follows:

Edward Ray, Oxhey, England:
  Out—5 4 4 3 5 4 3 4 6—38
  In —4 4 4 3 4 5 4 4 4—36—74
  Out—3 4 4 5 4 4 3 5 5—37
  In —3 5 5 4 4 4 3 5 4—37—74—148

Wilfrid Reid, Banstead Downs, England:
  Out—3 3 4 4 4 6 4 4 5—37
  In —3 4 6 4 4 3 2 4 5—35—72
  Out—5 4 7 4 4 4 4 5 5—42
  In —4 4 5 4 4 4 3 5 4—37—79—151

R. Macdonald, Hyde Park, Cinn. O.:
  Out—4 4 4 4 4 4 4 5 5—38
  In —3 4 4 5 3 4 3 4 4—34—72
  Out—5 3 5 4 5 3 3 5 8—41
  In —2 4 5 5 5 4 3 6 4—38—79—151

PLAYER AND CLUB	1st	2nd	Ttl.
George Sargent, Chevy Chase .	79	75	154
Walter Hagen, Rochester	78	79	157
Joseph Sylvester, Van Cortlandt	78	79	157

PLAYER AND CLUB	1st	2nd	Ttl.
J. Hobens, Englewood	75	84	159
J. Dingwall, Stanton Heights	77	82	159
E. Towns, Hartford	83	76	159
M. Campbell, Country Club	79	81	160
Robert Andrew, New Haven	77	83	160
George W. Cummings, Toronto	80	80	160
Mr. J. G. Anderson, Brae-Burn	81	79	160
Mr. H. Schmidt, Worcester	81	80	161
J. H. Taylor, Lakeside	80	81	161
J. J. McDermott, Atlantic City	81	80	161
G. L. Bowden, Tedesco	80	81	161
M. J. Brady, Wollaston	80	81	161
T. Bonner, Mecklenburg	83	79	162
J. Dowling, Scarsdale	77	85	162
T. Mulgrew, Cooperstown	80	82	162
Karl Keffer, Ottawa	82	81	163
Alec Smith, Wykagyl	84	79	163
R. M. Thompson, Glen Ridge	83	80	163
J. J. O'Brien, Westbrook	84	80	164
Mr. J. D. Travers, Upper Montclair	82	83	165
T. Anderson, Jr., Oakmont	79	86	165
J. M. Shippen, Maidstone	84	81	165
George Low, Baltusrol	81	84	165
D. S. Black, Rivermeade	83	82	165
W. McFarlane, Saegkill	84	81	165
Patrick Doyle, Myopia	83	83	166
Mr. Brice S. Evans, Belmont	86	80	166
W. G. Fovargue, Skokie	79	87	166
W. Maguire, Houston	81	85	166
Gilbert Nicholls, Wilmington	85	81	166

THIRD DAY

Thursday, September 18

THE play on the first day of the competition proper for the championship was of a very remarkable character, both morning and afternoon, and it resulted in a state of things which was very disquieting to the Americans, for when the two rounds were done the Englishmen, Reid and Vardon, were at the head of affairs with aggregates of 147, and Ray was third with 149. Nothing seemed more certain then than that the championship title would go abroad. Vardon and Reid did sound 75's in the morning, in which there was no special feature. Two or three did better. Two practically unknown men, Barnes of Tacoma, Washington, a very long driver, and Hagen of Rochester, who made 74 and 73, respec-

tively, began to make themselves a force in the tournament straight away and continued to do so almost to the end. Two of the homebreds, MacNamara and McDermott, played at something very nearly like the top of their game in the first round and raised the hopes of the Americans for the little lead they gained on the Englishmen, and a happy feature of the round was the fine show made by Mr. Fred Herreshoff, who not only equaled Vardon and Ray but, if he had had any luck, would have beaten them. Mr. Travers was now using wood from the tee. But the best rounds were done by Alex Ross and MacDonald Smith, who each put in cards of 71, which were the result of superb golf. Ray was disappointing to himself and others in this round and he ran up a total of 79, which placed him in a rather anxious position. He seemed a little nervous at the beginning and said that he feared he had played too much good golf on the previous day. His play was rather unsteady in more departments than one, especially going out—judged on the highest championship standard, of course—and when his round was done he uttered a declaration that he would do a 70 in the afternoon to make up for it. And he did it! That second round of his was one of the best he has played for a very long time, and he had actually a yard putt for a 69 on the home green at the finish but missed it after taking extreme pains to make a success of the task. This round became competition record of the course. Among those in the high places the scoring nearly all round was lower in the afternoon than in the morning, and Vardon and Reid with 72's took foremost positions. Ouimet had made a bad beginning in the morning with 6's at the first and second holes, but he turned in 41 and came home in a fine 36. In the afternoon he clipped no fewer than five strokes off his morning round for the first nine holes. Although his 74 was a very fine performance it would have been a much better one but for one or two blemishes coming in, particularly a 5 at the short sixteenth, where he played his tee-shot too heavily and was bunkered.

Cards, and a few details, were as follows:

W. E. Reid, England:
Out—5 4 4 4 5 4 3 5 4—38
In —3 5 5 4 5 4 3 4 4—37—75

Out—4 4 4 4 4 3 4 4 5—36
In —2 5 5 4 4 4 3 5 5—36—72—147
Harry Vardon, England:
Out—4 4 4 4 5 5 4 4 5—39
In —3 4 5 4 5 4 3 5 3—36—75
Out—5 4 4 3 4 4 4 4 5—37
In —3 4 5 4 4 4 3 4 4—35—72—147
Edward Ray, England:
Out—4 5 5 4 5 4 3 4 6—40
In —3 5 5 5 5 4 4 4 4—39—79
Out—4 3 5 4 4 3 3 4 5—35
In —3 4 3 4 5 5 3 4 4—35—70—149
Herbert Strong, Inwood C. C.:
Out—5 4 6 3 4 4 3 4 5—38
In —3 5 4 5 5 5 3 5 4—37—75
Out—5 3 3 4 5 4 2 4 5—35
In —3 4 4 5 5 5 4 4 5—39—74—149
MacDonald Smith, Wykagyl:
Out—4 4 4 4 5 3 3 4 5—36
In —3 4 4 5 5 4 3 3 4—35—71
Out—6 4 4 4 4 6 6 5 5—44
In —3 5 4 4 4 4 3 4 4—35—79—150
J. M. Barnes, Tacoma, Wash.:
Out—5 4 5 4 5 4 4 4 5—40
In —3 4 3 3 5 4 3 5 4—34—74
Out—5 4 5 4 5 3 3 4 6—39
In —3 4 3 5 4 4 4 4 6—37—76—150
Mr. Francis Ouimet, Woodland:
Out—6 6 5 4 4 4 3 4 5—41
In —3 4 5 4 4 4 4 4 4—36—77
Out—4 4 4 3 4 4 4 5 4—36
In —3 4 4 4 6 4 5 4 4—38—74—151
Alec Ross, Brae-Burn:
Out—4 4 6 4 4 4 3 5 5—39
In —2 4 3 3 5 4 3 4 4—32—71
Out—4 5 6 4 8 4 4 4 6—45
In —3 4 4 4 5 4 3 3 5—35—80—151
George Sargent, Chevy Chase:
Out—5 4 5 4 3 4 4 5 5—39
In —4 4 4 4 5 4 3 4 4—36—75
Out—4 4 5 4 5 5 3 4 6—40
In —3 5 5 4 4 4 3 4 4—36—76—151
W. Hagen, Rochester:
Out—4 4 4 4 4 4 3 5 5—37
In —3 3 4 5 4 5 3 5 4—36—73
Out—5 4 3 4 4 4 4 4 6—38
In —4 4 5 5 5 4 3 5 5—40—78—151

PLAYER AND CLUB	1st	2nd	Ttl.
C. D. Thom, Shinnecock Hills .	76	76	152
Louis Tellier, France	76	76	152
Mr. Fred Herreshoff, National Golf Links	75	78	153
J. J. McDermott, Atlantic City .	74	79	153
Jack Hutchinson, Allegheny ..	77	76	153
W. C. Fownes, Jr., Oakmont .	79	75	154
John Dowling, Scarsdale	77	77	154
J. M. Shippen, Maidstone	81	73	154
J. A. Croke, Calumet	72	83	155
J. A. Donaldson, Glen View ...	79	76	155
R. Andrews, New Haven	73	83	156
E. W. Loving, Arcola	76	80	156
Mr. J. D. Travers, Upper Montclair	78	78	156
Alec Campbell, The Country ..	77	80	157
M. J. Brady, Wollaston	83	74	157
Jack Hobens, Englewood	78	79	157
Alec Smith, Wykagyl	77	80	157
Tom Anderson, Jr., Oakmont .	82	75	157
P. Doyle, Myopia	78	80	158
H. Hampton, North Andover ..	78	80	158
David Ogilvie, Morris County .	81	77	158
A. H. Murray, Kanawaki	76	82	158
R. G. MacDonald, Cincinnati .	80	79	159
Tom MacNamara, Boston ...	73	86	159
Peter Robertson, Fall River ...	79	80	159
H. H. Barker, Roe Buck	80	79	159
J. R. Thomson, Philadelphia .	80	79	159
C. R. Murray, Royal Montreal	80	80	160
G. W. Cummings, Toronto ...	81	79	160
J. H. Taylor, Lakeside	81	80	161
George Low, Baltusrol	80	81	161
Joseph Sylvester, New York ..	81	81	162
F. H. Belwood, Garden City ..	79	83	162
W. G. Fovargue, Skokie	79	83	162
Karl Keffer, Royal Ottawa ..	79	84	163
R. M. Thomson, Glen View ..	84	79	163
Matt Campell, The Country .	84	79	163
Tom Vardon, Onwentsia	85	78	163
Mr. B. S. Evans, Belmont Spr'g	89	75	164
J. M. Anderson, Com'onw'th .	86	78	164
Fred. McLeod, Columbia	80	85	165
Willie Maguire, Houston, Tex. .	85	80	165
J. J. O'Brien, Westbrook	83	82	165
Tom Bonnar, Mecklenburg ...	86	79	165
W. MacFarlane, Saegkill	81	84	165
The following were eliminated:			
D. L. Black, Rivermede	83	83	166
Tom Mulgrew, Cooperstown .	82	84	166
Mr. H. Schmidt, Worcester ..	83	83	166
Fred. Ryall, Waumbek	90	76	166
Norman Clark, Westmoreland .	81	86	167
Jack Dingwall, Stanton Hts. ..	88	79	167
Tom Kerrigan, Dedham	83	85	168
Mr. A. G. Lockwood, Belmont Spring	86	83	169

PLAYER AND CLUB	1st	2nd	Ttl.
G. L. Bowden, Tedesco	91	79	170
Otto Hackbarth, Hinsdale	82	88	170
C. H. Anderson, Winthrop ...	83	87	170
Edwin Town, Hartford	92	88	180

FOURTH DAY

FRIDAY, SEPTEMBER 19

THIS was a strange day's championship golf, with a big thrill at the finish. It began to rain heavily at two o'clock in the morning and it kept up throughout the day. The Englishmen were by no means at their best in the circumstances. Wilfrid Reid dropped clean out of it, doing so many 6's that he soon ceased to be a factor in the championship. But I will not say he cracked, for there was some considerable excuse for what happened. Vardon and Ray labored heavily to the turn, which each reached in 41, the former's putting again causing him much anxiety and loss. They both came back much steadier, especially Ray, who said that the last nine holes agreed with him so much better than the first that he would like to "carry them round with him and use them instead of the first nine." Ouimet, playing beautiful golf for his 74, did better than either of them, and Hagen and Barnes closed up on the leaders also, the chief result of the round being that Vardon, Ray and Ouimet were now level for first place with aggregates of 225 each. Again in the afternoon Vardon and Ray were very weak in the first half, Vardon's putting and Ray's short game in general being mainly responsible. Vardon very rarely smokes when playing in public, though he is as fond of his pipe as any man alive. It was an indication of his anxiety, therefore, when he lighted up at the fourteenth hole and he played better afterwards. He told me that he wished he had begun to smoke earlier! When these two Englishmen had finished with aggregates of 304 they were both very despondent and neither of them thought they had a chance of winning. It seemed to them that their expedition had failed. "There are three or four still out who will beat us," said Vardon to me. "I am very sorry, but it is my putting that has let me down again. I feared it would." "I played rotten," said Ray, "and to make matters worse Harry went and did the same thing."

But the British outlook improved surprisingly as time went on, and this pessimism soon gave way to a great hope. One after another the most dangerous Americans failed to equal them. Hagen, Barnes and McDermott were beaten. There were reports that Louis Tellier, the plucky little Frenchman, was doing great things, and he was, but he slipped on the tee at the twelfth and made a bad hole there which put him out of the running. Then there was only Ouimet left, and Vardon and Ray went out to the fourteenth to watch him finish, and a great finish they saw, which impressed them enormously even if in the circumstances it did not exactly delight them. Ouimet had gone to the turn rather badly with two 6's and a total of 43, but he picked up splendidly afterwards, and going to the fifteenth he was left to get two 3's and two 4's to tie with the Englishmen. The task seemed too much for him or anyone else, for the par of those last four holes is 4, 3, 4, 4, respectively, and so he had to gain a stroke on it somewhere. He nearly lost a stroke instead at the fifteenth, where he pushed his second too much away to the right, but he pitched almost to the very edge of the hole and had nothing to do but tap his ball in for the 4. The 3 came all right at the short hole and then at the seventeenth he gained the stroke he wanted by holing a twelve-yard putt for a 3. That was a great putt for America and a great 3. But for it there would have been no championship for a homebred player this time. He had now only to do a steady 4 at the home hole to tie, and he played it with a fine confidence, holing a yard putt at the finish with no more hesitation than if he were practicing. So he tied, and what happened in the way of cheering immediately afterwards may be imagined. Scores and details:

Mr. Francis Ouimet, Woodland G. C.:
Third Round 38
  36-74
Fourth Round:
Out—5 4 5 4 6 5 3 6 5—43
In —5 4 5 3 5 4 3 3 4—36—79—153
Previous score, 151; total, 72 holes, 304.
Harry Vardon, England:

Third Round 41
Fourth Round .... 37—78
Out—5 5 6 5 5 4 3 4 5—42
In —3 5 4 5 5 4 3 4 4—37—79—157
Previous score, 147; total, 72 holes, 304.
Edward Ray, England:
Third Round 41
Fourth Round .... 35—76
Out—5 5 4 6 3 4 5 5 6—43
In —4 3 5 3 5 4 4 4 4—36—79—155
Previous score, 149; total, 72 holes, 304.
Other scores:

	1st & 2d rds.	3d & 4th rds.	Ttl.
Macdonald Smith, Wykagyl .	150	157	307
Louis Tellier, France	151	156	307
Walter Hagen, Rochester ...	151	156	307
J. M. Barnes, Tacoma	150	157	307
J. J. McDermott, Atlantic C.	153	155	308
Herbert Strong, Inwood ..	149	161	310
P. Doyle, Myopia	158	153	311
Mr. W. C. Fownes, Oakmont	154	158	312
E. W. Loving, Arcola	156	156	312
Alec Campbell, The Country	157	156	313
M. J. Brady, Wollaston ...	157	158	315
Matt Campbell, The Country	162	154	316
Mr. Fred Herreshoff, Nat'l .	153	165	318
W. E. Reid, England	147	171	318
Alec Smith, Wykagyl	157	161	318
Tom MacNamara, Boston .	159	159	318
J. A. Croke, Calumet	155	164	319
R. Andrews, New Haven ..	156	163	319
Geo. Sargent, Chevy Chase .	151	168	319
C. Thom, Shinnecock	152	169	321
Jack Dowling, Scarsdale ...	154	167	321
Mr. J. D. Travers, Up. Mont.	156	166	322
F. Belwood, Garden City ..	162	161	323
J. Taylor, Lakeside	161	162	323
J. Donaldson, Glen View ...	155	168	323
C. H. Murray, Montreal	160	164	324
D. Ogilvie, Morris County ..	162	162	324
J. Hobens, Englewood	157	167	324
H. H. Barker, Roebuck	159	167	326
Tom Anderson, Oakmont ..	157	169	326
Alex Ross, Brae-Burn	151	175	325
Fred McLeod, Columbia ...	165	162	327
Tom Vardon, Onwentsia ...	163	164	327
J. Shippen, Maidstone	154	174	328
W. Maguire, Houston	165	164	329
W. C. Fovargue, Skokie ...	162	168	330
K. Keffer, Ottawa	163	169	332
G. Cummings, Toronto	160	174	334
T. Bonnar, Mecklenburg ..	165	173	338

THE LAST DAY

SATURDAY, SEPTEMBER 20

THE weather for this very fateful day in golf history was still bad. It had been raining continuously for over thirty hours when ten o'clock came and the three men who had qualified for the ordeal went to the teeing ground. The course was heavy in parts; but on the whole it bore the soaking wonderfully well. Perhaps in the circumstances the pace of the green was difficult to judge sometimes; and the authorities found it advisable to make a local rule for the day to the effect that a ball that came down heavily on the green and got stuck might be loosened by the referee. Despite the discouraging conditions the interest of the people round about in the great events that were happening was thoroughly aroused, and there was a very large attendance of spectators, which by the time the play had proceeded to the turn had amounted to several thousands.

Of course the great question at the beginning was whether Ouimet, with his wonderful exhibition of nerve before, could stand the strain any longer. Perhaps most people imagined that he would break down at last. It was announced that Vardon and Ray would not falter and, being two to one against the Massachusetts boy, I think that the very general feeling was that it would be a day of British victory.

But those who watched things most closely and with most discernment at the start must have decided very quickly that Mr. Ouimet's nerves were all right. At the first hole Vardon drove the straightest ball, right down the middle of the course, Ray and Ouimet being away to the right. But Vardon had to play first afterwards, and as he could not reach the green he decided to take an iron and remain short of the racetrack, which was in a very sticky state. But Ouimet went for it with a brassie and just cleared it, though he was given a bad hanging lie on the bank afterwards. Ray got farthest with his second, but was away in the rough to the right of the green. Both Vardon and Ouimet were nicely on with their thirds and close together, but Ray made rather a mess of his and had then to struggle hard to get close to the hole. However, it turned out that all got 5's, and the only excuse for these details is that in a certain measure they were an indication of what was to follow. Ray was struggling hard for the greater part of the round.

At the second hole each man had a putt for a 3 from about seven yards range. Both Vardon and Ray gave the hole every chance and went past it; Ouimet was a trifle short, and if there was the semblance of a fault with his tactics during the round it was that two or three times he was thus short with his putts, and if ever there was a round played when a man should not be short it was this one. All were fours. Playing the third hole Ray got out a trifle too far to the right with his tee-shot and had to make his second from a stance far below the ball. He hooked it round to the near left-hand corner of the green and had a very long and difficult run up. He went some way beyond the hole and failing to sink the next one, took 5. The others were each down with comfortable 4's, and so Ray dropped a point behind them. Ouimet had to hole a four-foot putt at the fourth to get the 4 that each of the others did; but he again showed that his nerves were sound and steady.

There was more incident at the long fifth. Ray went to the rough with his drive and Ouimet sliced out of bounds on his second, but with his next he reached the right-hand side of the green but just off it, near to the place where Vardon was with his second. In the play of the short game he gained the stroke that he had lost and was down in five like the others. The American had to play his pitch to the uphill sixth before the other two, and laid his ball about six yards beyond the hole, Ray placing his a yard further back, while Vardon got nearest and was only about three yards from the pin, and from this position holed for a 3, the others taking 4 each, but being within an inch of getting their 3's. At this stage, therefore, Vardon led Ouimet by a stroke and Ouimet was still one in front of Ray. The last named gained a stroke on both of his rivals at the seventh by running so close to the hole from just off the edge of the green as to get down with his third, which neither Vardon nor Ouimet was able to do. Then at the eighth there was a touch of

sensation, for Ouimet pitched dead, not more than eighteen inches from the hole, and got his 3, while Ray equaled him by running down a twelve-yard putt. These achievements enabled them both to gain a stroke on Vardon, so that at this stage all were level again with scores of 33. Vardon was off the line and in the rough on the edge of the woods to the left with his tee-shot to the long ninth, but all got fives, and so at the turn the scoring was level—38 each.

Ouimet took the lead immediately afterwards, and never lost it later. At the short tenth both Ray and Vardon missed their putts for 3's, the former being six feet from the hole with his second. In a very confident sort of way the young American holed a yard putt for the par figure and I felt then that he had gone a very long way toward making himself the victor. All this time he was driving a clean, straight ball, his seconds were as good as seconds need be, and his putting was sound. Once he got the lead I was very much afraid for our British representatives, and I think they were a little afraid too. No man ever looked less like cracking than young Ouimet. All were 4's at the eleventh, Ray and Vardon both making good bids for 3's; but at the twelfth Ouimet scored with his approach, keeping to the straight line, while Vardon was just off the green to the left and Ray just off it on the right. Neither got his 4, and Ouimet had a chance to gain two strokes at once with a twelve-foot putt, and, I think, should have gone for it for all he was worth. But he ran very carefully up to the hole for his very sure 4, and was a trifle short. Perhaps after all he was wise; he was taking no risks.

At the thirteenth Vardon and Ouimet each approached to within three yards of the pin, and Vardon holed while Ouimet missed by an inch, and as Ray was 4 also, Vardon gained a point on each of the other two. Each man had a faulty shot in going to the fourteenth. Vardon was away towards the woods with his drive, Ray was in the rough with his second and Ouimet topped his brassie, this and the slice out of bounds at the fifth being really his only bad shots in the round. The hole ended in 5's all round. I did not like the look of things from the English point of view at this stage. Ouimet was still leading Vardon by one stroke and Ray by two and both our men were evincing signs of anxiety.

Disaster fell heavily and quickly upon the invaders from this point and the title was settled very decisively in the next three holes. Ray was the first to go; the fifteenth did for him. Up to here no man of the three had been once bunkered, but at the fifteenth the long driver was trapped with his second on the right near side of the green. He was close up to the face of the hazard and when he failed to get out in one his chance of being American champion had gone. With his second bunker shot he sent his ball beyond the green on the other side. Vardon, who had been a trifle too strong with his approach, had to struggle for his 4 but got it; so did Ouimet, who had to putt from the corner of the green. Ray took 6, and so now the fight was between Vardon and Ouimet. Both of them got their 3's at the short hole that followed, but Ray, apparently a little downhearted now, was careless in his putting and took 4.

From the seventeenth tee Ouimet drove safely to the right and had the hole nicely opened up for him. The hole is slightly dog-legged, and Vardon in attempting to pinch the corner too closely got bunkered. Ray hurled himself wildly at his ball and drove it a tremendous length on the straight line, where there was no possible chance of safety, and of course had to play his next from the rough, though, as he realized, nothing mattered now. Ouimet played a straight approach about six yards beyond the pin, but Vardon had to make his bunker shot out sideways and was three on the green. He and Ray both got 5's, and then the young American jumped to his great opportunity and, playing it with very little hesitation, made a beautiful putt which was a holer all the way, the ball dropping in for a lovely 3, just as it did the night before. Ouimet will remember forever with the greatest kindness this seventeenth hole at Brookline. He had now a lead of three clean strokes over Vardon and seven over Ray, and the championship was surely his. The playing of the last hole in the circumstances was a mere formality. Ray got a 3 at it, Ouimet a safe and steady 4, while Vardon who was off the line with his tee-shot, on the racetrack with his second and missed a little putt at the finish, took 6. So with the final scores,

Ouimet 72, Vardon 77 and Ray 78, the American was a splendid and most deserving winner.

The cards of the three for this historic round were as follows:

Ouimet:
Out—5 4 4 4 5 4 4 3 5—38
In —3 4 4 4 5 4 3 3 4—34—72
Vardon:
Out—5 4 4 4 5 3 4 4 5—38
In —4 4 5 3 5 4 3 5 6—39—77
Ray:
Out—5 4 5 4 5 4 3 3 5—38
In —4 4 5 4 5 6 4 5 3—40—78

As soon as the putting had been done a wild burst of cheering broke out from the delighted crowd and Ouimet was hoisted high on American shoulders. A few minutes later the prizes were presented in front of the clubhouse by Mr. John Reid, Jr., the secretary of the USGA, Mr. Watson, the president, not being able to be present. "It is customary," said Mr. Reid, in handing the cup to Ouimet, "to receive security for this trophy, but in this case the only security which the United States Golf Association will demand is that the Woodland Golf Club shall see that Francis keeps up his game." In his reply the champion made a neat little speech, saying, "I am as much surprised and as pleased as anyone here. Naturally it was always my hope to win out. I simply tried my best to keep this cup from going to our friends across the water. I am very glad to have been the agency for keeping the cup in America."

Both Vardon and Ray gave unstinted and unqualified praise to the winner. A collection was made among the assembled people for Edwin Laurie, Ouimet's little ten-year-old caddie, and more than a hundred dollars was obtained. So ended a meeting that will forever hold a great place in golfing history.

And let my last word be one of sincerest congratulations to Ouimet. I have seen many championships played for in different lands during many years, but I have never seen one better or more thoroughly won than this one. It was a splendid victory most richly deserved, and again I say that the United States has now a young Open champion of whom the country may very well be proud.

Walter Hagen—
My Hero, My Rival

by

GENE SARAZEN

1950—FROM *THIRTY YEARS OF CHAMPIONSHIP GOLF*

AFTER I had beaten Barnes and Hutchison in man-against-man matches, I was eager to prove to the golfing world that I was a better man than the remaining third of the old triumvirate, Walter Hagen. Hagen, who had won the PGA the year before, had passed up that tournament in 1922. My supporters claimed that he was ducking me. Hagen's army of followers said nothing could have been more remote from the truth. Walter, they pointed out, had decided that his match against Abe Mitchell should take precedence over everything else. (Walter, incidentally, had pulled the Mitchell match out of the fire when it appeared that he was hopelessly beaten. He had stood 4 down with 9 to play when he uncorked one of those whirlwind finishes with which his name was synonymous.) The two rival camps, egged on by the sportswriters, finally got together, and it was arranged that Walter and I would meet in a seventy-two-hole match for "The World's Golf Championship," the first thirty-six to be played October 6 at Oakmont, the second thirty-six on the following day at the Westchester-Biltmore in Rye, New York. The winner would receive two-thirds of the $3,000 guarantee. There have been tens of matches since this one that have been advertised as deciding the world's championship in golf, but ours, I believe, was the only one that ever deserved that extravagant billing. Hagen was the British Open Champion, and in Mitchell he had defeated the best of the British match players. I held the American Open and PGA Championship and had privately accounted for Barnes.

I was eager to get at Hagen for a personal reason. Walter had been consistently pleasant to me—there wasn't a mean streak in the guy—but I didn't like the way he kept calling me "kid" and treating me as a young upstart. I wasn't any young upstart, I was a champion, and I wanted Hagen to respect me as a champion and his equal. When I heard that Walter had ordered, especially for our match, two pairs of golf hose with his name knitted around the cuff, I made up my mind that I would outdress him. I ordered two new golf suits and announced that I would wear one suit at Oakmont, the other at the Westchester-Biltmore. When I look back now at how seriously I took such shenanigans, I shake my head in amused disbelief, but these were the early twenties and all America behaved something like Hollywood.

Walter emerged from the first half of our match with a 2-up lead. I had been 4 down at one stage and I had missed five putts of under five feet, but Walter had outplayed me in every department except distance off the tees, and I was fortunate not to be more holes down than I was. That night we traveled together by train from Pittsburgh to New York.

We passed part of the evening shooting dice, another game that Hagen played expertly. At one point, after he had reeled off a run of passes, Walter looked up from the carpet and grinned bitter-sweetly. "Kid, I can beat you at anything." I had a hard time sleeping that night, and nervousness had nothing to do with it. I felt queasy. It seemed that every tie in the tracks had a point on it, my stomach was that jarred by the ride. Two winters before, my stomach had acted up at Miami Beach, and returning via train to Titusville after the 1921 PGA, I had developed cramps. I tossed these things over in my mind as I lay in my berth, and concluded that I would have to watch my diet more closely in the future. I fell asleep around four in the morning.

I was feeling better when our train pulled into New York. A motorcycle escort sped us under lowering skies to the Westchester-Biltmore Club. The course was soaked. It had been raining in the New York area for several days. It began to come down again before we teed off, and it showered on and off during the match. By noon, all the orange in the orange-and-white tie I was wearing had washed off onto my shirt. I kept the tie on, though. It had arrived at the club that morning in a box with the following card: "You probably don't remember me but I'm the blonde from the Follies you met. Don't look for me in the gallery. I don't want you to take your mind off Hagen. I want you to wear this tie for good luck."

Two thousand hardy fanatics followed Hagen and me down the first fairway when we strode off on the second leg of our marathon. On the second hole, a 138-yarder, I put my mashie-niblick ten inches from the cup, and my birdie won the hole. Hagen retaliated with a birdie 4 on the long third and was 2 up again. Then I began to move. I squared the match by taking the fourth with a par and the fifth with a birdie, halved the sixth and the seventh, and drove out in front for the first time in the entire match by winning the eighth and the ninth. Walter rallied with three fine birdies on the in-nine but I came up with two of my own, and went to lunch protecting a one-hole lead.

Hagen ate a hearty meal. I didn't feel like eating. I walked fretfully up and down the committee room, anxious to get on with the match. Walter saw me pacing and called me over to his table. "Say, kid," he said with a mischievous twinkle in his eyes, as if he had already briefed the others at the table on what he was going to say, "that's a handsome tie you've got on. Where'd you get it?" I told him that a friend had given it to me. "Just a *friend*?" Hagen said. "Why, I thought I had written in that note that your mysterious admirer was a Follies girl who wanted you to pay strict attention to beating Hagen." I should have suspected a notorious practical joker like Walter from the beginning. I had been looking for that blonde all morning.

I felt nauseated when play was resumed, but under the circumstances I couldn't very well ask for a postponement. A claim of sudden sickness would have looked like an alibi concocted by a man fearing defeat. I tried to focus all my concentration on the task at hand —beating Hagen. When we finished the sixty-third, I was 2 up. Recalling Hagen's rush down the stretch against Mitchell and numerous other victims, the spectators were buzzing to each other to keep their eyes on Hagen and watch how golf's Garrison did it. Hagen did open up with a barrage of great golf— and so did I. I played the last seven holes in two under 4's, including an eagle 3 on the twelfth or sixty-fifth. I holed the putt I needed on the seventieth green for a 3-and-2 victory.

George Sparling, who had caddied for me, and other friends walked me back to the clubhouse. I napped for a few hours, and though my right side was hurting me, thought I felt well enough to keep my dinner date with the Bill Danforths. The sight of food upset me, however, and I asked Bill and Mrs. Danforth if they would excuse me. I went back to my room. A friend summoned two doctors who were at the club. They probed my stomach, and proclaimed blandly that I just had a touch of nervous indigestion, brought on by the tension of competition.

"I don't get nervous when I play a match like this," I told the Park Avenue scientists. "It has nothing to do with my digestive organs."

They winked knowingly and prescribed a good night's rest. At four in the morning when my pain had deepened acutely, I asked a friend to call Dr. Frank Landolfe, a fellow I had grown up with in Harrison who was then practicing in Port Chester. Frank drove over immediately. Within an hour after his arrival, I was on the table at St. Luke's Riverside Hospital in Yonkers, undergoing an emergency appendectomy.

The following spring, after I had been back in the curing climate of golf for a few months, I sailed for Britain aboard the *Aquitania*, along with Walter Hagen, Johnny Farrell, Mac Smith, and Gil Nicholls. Hagen was going over to defend his British crown at Troon, and the rest of us had our eye on succeeding him. In later years, after I had failed a number of times in the British Open, I developed such a complex about this championship that my subsequent attempts to win it took on the overcharged emotional proportions of a crusade. But in 1923 I thought of the British Open as just another tournament, and I saw no reason why I couldn't annex it in stride.

Win? I didn't even qualify! I was one of the contestants assigned to the municipal course in Troon for the qualifying rounds. My first eighteen was a 75, a comfortable score. I wasn't trying to break any course records. I had drawn the first starting time for the day of the second qualifying round. On that morning a cold, driving storm was sweeping off the ocean with such fury that the fishermen in the town were not allowed to go out, and the waves were hurdling the sea-wall and washing up to the edge of the championship course. On the first tee I warmed my hands in my pockets, and after being blown off my stance once or twice, managed to stand up to the ball and knock it a short distance down the fairway. I picked up my umbrella, and the force of the wind ripped it inside out the moment I opened it. I think I got out of the first hole with a 5, but on the second I buried my drive in the face of the bunker in front of the tee. I wasted two shots before I dislodged my ball, and wallowed away nine strokes in all on that hole. I knew I was in trouble. By the fifth hole I had got a grip on myself, and considering the ferocity of the elements, was not playing too badly. At the rate I was going I would finish in the middle eighties, but I thought that the other players would have just as bad a time standing up in the storm as I did. I posted my 85 and was not too uneasy about my chances of qualifying, until the wind began to die down at

noon and the sun came out. Then I really began to worry. The later starters, playing under relatively ideal conditions, began to bring in scores in the seventies, and I learned in the evening that I had failed to qualify by a stroke. That was the most crushing blow my self-esteem had ever received. I felt ashamed to face anyone, and decided not to stay around and watch the championship as a humiliated also-failed-to-qualify. I returned to London immediately.

Arthur Havers won that Open with Hagen a stroke behind. Walter had all but carried the day with another of his spectacular eleventh-hour rallies. His courageous play down the stretch had whittled away all but one stroke of Havers' lead when Walter came to the seventy-second. He needed a birdie on the home hole to tie. Walter drove well here but cut his approach shot a shade too much, and it slipped over the green and into a bunker. He didn't bat an eyelash. He lined up his trap-shot as if it were an ordinary hole-able putt, and he just did fail to sink it. You had to hand it to that guy. Three years later in the 1926 British Open, which Jones won, "The Haig" made a finish rather reminiscent of his rush at Troon. On the seventy-second, a good par 4, he was told that he needed an eagle 2 to equal Jones's total. Hagen had no use for second place. It was first or nothing. He slapped out a long tee-shot. Before playing second, he walked the rest of the way to the green—about 155 yards—theatrically surveyed the position of the cup, and asked the referee to have the pin removed from the hole. He walked calmly back to the approach he had to hole to tie, and played a really lovely shot that hit the green only two feet from the flagless hole. Had anyone but Hagen requested the flag to be removed in such a spot, it would have been laughable. Coming from Walter, it was Hagen.

The English understood how seriously I had been shaken by failing to qualify. Bernard Darwin's sympathy was typical. When I met that greatest of all golf writers after the Open, he told me that the samples he had seen of my shots had given him the very definite conviction that I would be a force in international golf for many years to come. He hoped I wouldn't let my disappointment at Troon deter me from trying the British Open again.

"I'll be back," I told Mr. Darwin. "I'll be back even if I have to swim across."

The attitude of the American sportswriters when I returned from my inglorious expedition was, to put it mildly, less kindly than Darwin's. Grantland Rice wrote that his faith in my ability remained as steadfast as ever, but the other columnists and golf reporters said that I was all washed up, just a flash-in-the-pan whose luck had run out. Had I made a spirited defense of my American Open title that July at Inwood, I could have squelched the dirge they were chanting, I know, but on three of my rounds I was all over the course and I finished fourteen strokes behind Bob Jones. My showings in the other summer tournaments did nothing to stabilize my skid. When I arrived at Pelham in the autumn to defend the last of my titles, the PGA, I was almost willing to admit that my critics had pegged me correctly. I wouldn't have entered the PGA, the way I was playing, had I not been the defending champion.

I won my first two matches at Pelham easily, but my opponents had not played professional golf. Old Nipper Campbell almost knocked me out on the third round, and my 3-and-2 margin was not the result of my good play but the Nipper's addiction to three-putting the greens. I had to face Barnes next. If there was one man in the field I preferred not to lose to, it was Barnes. I thought to myself: "Well, here it comes, Genie. Jim's on his own course and he'll be tougher than ever. Do your damnedest but be prepared to take it like a man." Against Barnes I came onto my game a little. After we had played thirty-five holes, we were tired, grim, and all even. The last hole at Pelham is an unusal finishing hole. A par-4 measuring only 285 yards, over a hill and bending slightly to the left, the entrance to its green was tightly patrolled by traps in order to add some headaches to a hole which a long hitter could drive. I had this particular tee-shot down cold, and against Barnes I really tied into one. My drive bounced down the middle of the alley to the green and finished about eighteen feet from the cup. Barnes couldn't match that drive or my birdie 3, and I had edged him out 1 up. Beating Barnes on his home course gave me a good shot in the arm. I took care of Bobby Cruikshank in the semifinals, and scarcely believing that I had come that far, found myself in the final. The other finalist was Walter Hagen.

There has never been a golfer who could outthink and outmaneuver a match-player opponent as Walter Hagen could. You couldn't rattle Hagen, whatever you did. Throw a string of birdies in his face, and he'd smile that disturbingly undisturbed smile of his, and then hurl some birds of his own back at you, when it counted. But Hagen could rattle *you*. He was a master of psychological warfare. One of his most successful strategies was to kill an opponent with kindness, a bonhomie you knew was bogus but impenetrable. When a youngster got hot against him, Hagen would charm him into submission by raving to the newcomer about the remarkable quality of his shots. "After you win this championship," Hagen would tell him, "we'll go on a tour together." Before the youngster knew what had happened, Hagen had slipped away from him, and then there was no more talk of a tour. Walter always had Jim Barnes licked before their matches began by ribbing him about the super-seriousness, the tension with which Barnes was taking "just another round."

I was edgy before my match with Hagen because I viewed it as the one and only opportunity I had to redeem my reputation. Hagen also meant business. He never liked to be without a title to place beneath his name, and in 1923 he had been stripped of the British and had nothing to wear in its stead. For another thing, I had incurred his ill will by ridiculing his stunt of making easy shots in exhibition matches look like Greek drama. For instance, Walter would have a lie in the wooded rough, with a nice opening to the green between two trees. He knew the moment he saw how his ball was lying that he would play it between those two trees, and eventually he did, ten minutes later, after his caddie had excavated every rock in the area and Walter had explored the wilderness for openings he hadn't the slightest intention of using. The gallery would go wild when he finally played a run-of-the-mill recovery through the obvious opening. These phony dramatics irritated me. As Hagen dawdled before his recovery I would chirp up impatiently, "That's a simple shot, Walter. I'll walk ahead and meet you at the green." We had another score to settle—this was our rubber match. I had beaten Walter over seventy-two holes in 1922. He had evened the score in Florida the next winter in a weird match arranged by Bob Harlow, his manager, in which we played over three different courses, eighteen holes at Sanford, eighteen at Miami-Biltmore, and the final thirty-six at Walter's winter affiliation, the Pasadena course.

For all these points of conflict, the final of the PGA between Walter and myself might not have taken on the proportions of a grudge match, which it did, if our supporters hadn't been clawing at each other. Hagen's camp followers were an arrogant bunch. They made it very clear that they thought it an indignity for their hero to have to put up with a roughneck like Sarazen who had never dined with royalty and who had been seen fumbling for the correct fork and the right words. The chill of expressed animosity was in the air that October day when Walter and I went out to see which of us would be champion.

Just before we were called to the first tee, Jim Barnes came over to give me the benefit of his knowledge of the course. I listened politely but not attentively. I didn't think Barnes's friendliness had been brought on as much by his desire to call off our feud as by his even greater pique over his defeats by Hagen. Perhaps I did him an injustice. I must add, however, that at an earlier time Barnes had tipped me off to a trick Hagen used to resort to in tight corners. One winter when Hagen and Barnes had been playing an important match in New Orleans, they battled on even terms over thirty-six holes. On the thirty-seventh, as the match went into extra holes, Barnes held the honor as they prepared to play that tricky, 135-yard par 3. Uncertain as to how much club he needed on the shot, Barnes glanced over to see what club Walter was going to play. Walter was holding his No. 6 iron. Jim, accordingly, took a No. 7 for the shot and sent the ball over the back of the steeply banked green. Hagen grinned a little, and then replaced the No. 6 with the No. 8 iron he had intended to use all along. He plunked the ball on the green and sewed up the match. Walter worked this trick entirely by pantomime. He never misled an opponent by *saying* he planned to use such-and-such a club, but it worked out as neatly as if he had. Early in the final of the PGA, I nettled Walter

by letting him have a taste of his own medicine. On one hole where there was little if any distance between our drives, I pulled my mid-iron from my bag. Walter was away, and remarking my selection, played a mid-iron himself. He hit a fine shot on line all the way, and glowered unhappily when it fell a full twenty yards short of the green. I took my brassie, which I knew was the club from the beginning, put my ball on the carpet, and picked up that hole.

Neither of us was able to gain more than a one-hole lead at any time during the morning eighteen. I was 1 down going to the eighteenth but my drive again caught the alley to the green perfectly, and my birdie 3 squared the match.

Hagen was not his usual effervescent self during the interval between rounds, nor had he been since the sixth hole when we had flared up at each other over a technical point that would have been settled smoothly in a match less bitterly waged. My second shot on the sixth had come to rest on a patch of leaf-strewn earth between two green-high bunkers. Before playing my third, I asked the referee, Warren Wood, for a ruling: Was the area in which my ball lay considered part of the hazard? Wood ruled that it wasn't, and added that ordinarily the patch was grassy but that the week's trampling by spectators had given it the appearance of a path. After receiving this information, I was free to lift the leaves from around my ball. I was preparing to play my shot when Hagen walked over. He wasn't smiling. "You can't do that, kid—remove leaves from a hazard and ground your club," he barked at me. "You've been around long enough to know the rules." I referred him to the referee who repeated his ruling for Walter's benefit. I was still seething inside over Walter's uncalled-for insinuations, and played a very poor run-up fifteen feet short of the cup. I missed my putt and Walter took the hole with his par 4. "I'm glad you won that hole, Walter," I said sharply on the next tee. "I don't want to hear any squawking from you tonight."

I played offensive golf on the first nine of the last eighteen—I was out in 35—and with nine to go, I stood 3 up. Walter got one of these holes back with a great niblick on the twenty-ninth, but I held my ground after that and reached the thirty-fourth tee two holes to the good. Walter won the thirty-fourth. On the thirty-fifth, a par 5 that was neither exceptionally difficult nor exceptionally easy, both our drives were adequate. I played first and socked a brassie into the trap to the right of the green. I was sauntering down the fairway, watching Hagen over my shoulder, when I saw his second shot hook sharply and crash out-of-bounds. "That does it!" I said happily to myself. "He'll never be able to halve the sure 5 I've got." Hagen coolly accepted the penalty and dropped a ball over his shoulder. He decided to stay with his brassie. This time he drilled a long, low, unwavering screamer that ran all the way to the green, twenty feet from the pin. I elected to play conservatively from the trap, blasting out cautiously and leaving myself a thirty-footer. My approach putt slid three feet past the cup. And then Hagen—he had it in the clutch, all right— rolled his twenty-footer into the very center of the cup. He had got down in 2 from 250 yards off the green. I stepped up to my three-footer. I needed it for a half now. It looked a lot longer than three feet, doubling its length the way all crucial putts do for the man who has to make them. I stroked the ball, stroked it well, but it twisted off the rim of the cup and hung on the lip. I had permitted Hagen to win a hole that I had expected to win. More than that, I had allowed him to erase the two-hole advantage I had held on the thirty-fourth tee. We were all square as we came to the home hole, both of us dour and determined.

Hagen's drive rolled into a trap guarding the green. Once again, mine found the corridor between the traps and finished on the apron. Hagen's recovery left him fifteen feet short of the cup. My chip trickled five feet past. Hagen putted for his birdie. Not a good putt. Off to the right. The relief I felt when I saw his ball veer off the line vanished immediately. Hagen's ball lay me a full stymie. I had no chance to go for the cup on my five-footer. Walter had sneaked off with a half.

Extra holes. No blood on the thirty-seventh. I dropped a three-and-a-half-footer for my half in 4. On to the thirty-eighth. Walter, still up, took the safe route on his tee-shot, placing it just beyond the sharp break to the left on this tree-lined dog-leg par 4. This set him up for an easy pitch to the green and a probable birdie. I decided to take my chance here. Boldly, perhaps foolishly, I went all out in an attempt to carry the trees in the V of the dog-leg. I hit the ball with a little more hook than I wanted and then heard a sickening crash. The ball had struck either the roof of the cottage in the trees or the trees themselves. A bad ricochet and I would be out-of-bounds. The best I could hope for was a playable lie in the wooded rough. This was the opening Walter had been waiting for. He walked briskly down the fairway.

My caddie uncovered my ball, safely in bounds. I had been lucky in one respect. The ball had caromed past the thickest cluster of trees in the angle of the dog-leg, and I had a fair opening to the green. On the other hand, my ball lay heavily matted by the tall, spiky growths in the rough, almost hidden from view. I braced myself with the firmest stance I could manage under the circumstances, and flailed my niblick through the rough and into the ball; I felt the blade catch the ball solidly and saw it fly out of the rough and kick onto the green, run for the pin, slow down and die out just two feet away. The shoe was on the other foot now. I looked over to see what dent that recovery had made in Walter's armor. He was visibly shaken. I had never seen Hagen lose his poise before and I doubt if any man in the gallery had. When he finally played his wee pitch he floofed it, like a duffer, into the trap between him and the green. His fighting instinct surged back then. He made a brave effort to hole his shot from the trap. When he failed by inches, he had lost the PGA Championship.

The hour after that match was the first and only time I have seen Hagen depressed. Usually the only sign by which you could tell when disappointment or dismay lay concealed behind Walter's oriental mask was the speed with which he gobbled his drinks when he hit the locker room. That afternoon concealment was beyond Walter's power. He was disconsolate and he was angry. "Uh-h," he groaned in disgust when we met in the locker room, "you're the luckiest golfer who ever lived. I've seen a lot of lucky shots in my time, but today—I give up."

"Whaddya mean, lucky?" I asked pugnaciously.

"I could name a million shots. That one on the thirty-eighth."

"Look, Walter. You were pretty darn lucky yourself," I came back. "Don't think you halved the thirty-sixth through any great playing on your part. Without that stymie you'd have been a dead duck right there."

I left him sitting on a locker room bench and telling his crestfallen court to leave him alone for a while.

A golfer of Walter Hagen's class and fortitude didn't go very long without a championship. The very next spring he recaptured the British Open and was back in full stride again. We forgot the ill-feeling that had been brewed at Pelham, though Hagen to this day believes that my drive on the thirty-eighth went out-of-bounds and that the family living in the house in the woods threw the ball back onto the course. "There are an awful lot of Italians living in that neighborhood, Gene," he would say in complete seriousness. During the decade and more that we battled on two continents, Walter and I fought each other furiously on the golf course and had our occasional disagreements off the course, but I thought of Walter as a fine, reliable friend and I believe my feelings were reciprocated. We spent a great many pleasant hours in each other's company, growing closer as we grew older. Whenever Hagen was out of the running in a tournament, he rooted for me to win.

Golf has never had a showman like him. All the professionals who have a chance to go after the big money today should say a silent thanks to Walter each time they stretch a check between their fingers. It was Walter who made professional golf what it is. Before Hagen broke down the walls of prejudice, a professional golfer had no standing whatever. In England, which set the example for our country club conduct, professionals were not allowed to enter the clubhouse by the front door. Walter believed that he was just as good as anybody else, and defied the snobs to pigeonhole him as a low-caste nuisance. He made his point on his first trip across in 1920. He traveled in high style with a secretary-manager. He made the Ritz his London headquarters. When he was not allowed to enter the dining room of the clubs where he was playing, he had a picnic lunch served to him with conspicuous ceremony by the foot-

man who rode in his rented Rolls Royce. When such unheard-of deportment came to the attention of Lord Northcliffe, the owner of the *Times,* he sent a reporter to interview Hagen, with instructions to put that American pro in his place. Hagen met the reporter in his suite at the Ritz, glowing like a maharajah in his expensive purple dressing-gown. He made sense and he was charming. The interviewer reported back to Northcliffe that any story he wrote about Hagen would have to be a complimentary one. That was the opening wedge in the new respect Hagen compelled the public to have for the men in his profession.

Hagen was at home with all classes of society, far more so than Dempsey or Ruth, the other great champions of the twenties whom he resembled in the blackness of his hair, his amazing personal magnetism, his love of admiring crowds, and his rise from humble beginnings. He was a product of Rochester, New York. Before his golf carried him to the attention of George Eastman, Hagen had once worked in a flour mill lugging hundred-pound sacks. He had natural good taste and unfailing *savoir-faire.* "Call every woman 'Sugar' and you can't go wrong," was one of his favorite maxims. He met his first wife when he went crazy over a handsome hunting dog he saw at a country club. He asked the woman who owned the dog if he could buy it, and she yielded to his persistence. The ex-owner wanted to make certain that her pet was receiving the proper attention, and made frequent trips to Hagen's house to check. After a while she found that, while she wasn't exactly bored with the dog's adjustment, she was more interested in its owner, in fact, much more interested in him than in another Hagen named Roscoe who was giving her the big rush. She and Walter were married quite soon afterwards.

Hagen loved the high life and hated to see money pile up drably in a bank account. I shared a liquor bill with him on one Atlantic crossing, and was staggered when my half came to three hundred dollars. "The Haig" was a Scotch drinker, and I could never understand why there wasn't an advertising tie-up between him and Haig and Haig. It would have been a natural. Walter was renowned for the tremendous quantities of the stuff he could find a good home for. I used to wonder how he could absorb so much and play so well until I noticed that the drinks he took before a match were very light ones. After a match, there was liquor in them there glasses. After Walter won his fourth and final British Open in 1929, he invited his Ryder Cup teammates to celebrate with him at Gleneagles, and chaperone him. His Scotch, his hotel bills, his regal wardrobe, his rented Rolls Royces, his philanthropy toward his sundry parasites, and his paper-money tips all added up, of course, and there were times when Walter had little to live on except his bravado. Returning to New York one summer after a trip to England with Walter, Jr., he was flat broke. He borrowed the thirty dollars his son had left, and told the taxi driver to take them to the Delmonico Hotel. There he asked for and got the best suite, ordered a case of Scotch and five hundred dollars to be sent up, and refused to let the slightest worry interfere with his relaxation. A couple of tournaments and he was back in the black.

On the winter circuit Walter stayed at the fashionable hotels and dressed for dinner nightly, because he liked those things. But his extravagant ways served a secondary unplanned purpose. It gave his rival pros, who camped out in cabins and ate in cafeterias, an acute inferiority complex. They went to pieces when they were confronted by the legend in the flesh. Hagen had a glib tongue. Tommy Armour, I would say, was the only other pro who could hold his own in banter or oratory with Hagen. He was an incurable kidder. When we crossed to Britain for the Ryder matches, for example, Walter would

have the dining-room steward deliver the flowers from the empty tables to the other members of the team—"Compliments of Mr. Hagen and Mr. Sarazen." He outdressed the millionaire set with which he traveled and reveled in the attention his flamboyant combinations attracted. I remember one sartorial incident that burned him up. One winter a Miami newspaper devoted a half-page to a photo story of Hagen and his wardrobe. He loved it. We were playing together a day or two later when two very social and very handsome girls galloped down the bridle path adjoining the fairway. They dismounted and watched us play our shots. "That must be Sarazen," one of the girls said in a carrying voice, as she pointed to Hagen. "The smaller one must be Hagen, he's dressed so beautifully."

Walter's record as a golfer speaks for itself —four British Opens, two United States Opens, five PGA Championships, and as many minor titles as any golfer has ever collected. He was the finest short-iron player the game has ever known. He was a magnificent putter. He had courage, and unquestioning faith in himself. He won the 1924 British Open after a first qualifying round of 83 that would have crushed a less gallant spirit. After breakfast the next day, a group of us discovered that a large crowd had gathered outside the Adelphia Hotel. They were waiting for a glimpse of the Lord Mayor togged out in his colorful robes of office, but Hagen assumed that they had congregated to see Walter Hagen. He mounted a small platform and waved appreciatively at the gathering—this, after an 83. But who won that tournament? Walter Hagen.

Hagen at Hoylake

by

BERNARD DARWIN

1928 — FROM *GREEN MEMORIES*

DUNCAN's pursuit of Hagen at Sandwich in 1922 was a tremendous affair, and by good luck I was one of the few people who saw at least some of it. Hagen had finished in 72. Barnes, who had had a rather cruel piece of luck at the Sahara, had just failed to catch him; so had Hutchison, equally unlucky at the fourth hole. Duncan was out somewhere in the dim distance with a 68 to tie and a 67 to win. It was all over and Hagen was very naturally allowing himself a peaceful cigar. Whether it was extreme conscientiousness or some gift of second sight that took my weary legs out again to look for Duncan, I do not know, but at any rate out I went, all alone, and found him with not more than a dozen onlookers somewhere about the twelfth hole. Those few onlookers were almost beside themselves: they were at once frantic with joy over his amazing play up to the green and in despair because he was not holing the putts that would rob America of the championship. Never was a golfer more clearly inspired than Duncan on that evening. No matter what the length of the shot from a brassie to a mashie-niblick, once he was within range of the hole, it seemed certain that he would have a good chance of holing out with his next shot. While I watched him he was not actually missing putts, but he did not hole nor look like holing those eminently possible putts, any one of which would probably have

meant victory. Perhaps it was too much to hope for and putting is so easy to the looker-on, but there was the exasperating, heart-breaking fact. Even so he fought on so gallantly that he had a four to tie and then took five. His run-up at the last hole was indeed a sad effort. There is no more to be said about that, but I have always thought that his second shot, played with a spoon as I remember it, was rather unlucky. Perhaps that is not really the right word, but it is the word we should all of us have applied to it, if we could have played such a shot ourselves. It was played so clearly with the intention that the ball should drift in towards the hole from the left and it was struck just too well, so that it held on its course and did not turn enough. Well, well—it was a wonderful round, but—allowing ever so little for "ifs and ands," it might have been the most wonderful round ever played.

Two years later at Hoylake the position was reversed in that it was Hagen who had to make the spurt, though it was not Duncan who set the pace. At the beginning of the last round Hagen and Ernest Whitcombe were leading, dead level. Three strokes behind them came Duncan, Ball, and Macdonald Smith, and one stroke behind them came Taylor, tired out but full of such magnificent golf and such an indomitable spirit that he still seemed almost capable of achieving the impossible. What befell those other four does not matter now, though it mattered very much then to the wretched spectator who had to be in six places at once. I must simplify the story and stick to Whitcombe and Hagen.

Duncan, who was, so we heard, out of the hunt, Macdonald Smith, and Ball were all somewhere in the distance, when Whitcombe, Britain's chief hope, was starting. A five at the first hole was not serious, but a six at the second was dreadful: the long grass behind some of the Hoylake greens was terribly cruel that year. Two steadily played holes revived our hopes, but then, at the Telegraph, came an unlucky kick into a bunker and another five. There were four strokes dropped in five holes, and with a sick heart I turned back to look for Hagen. Instead, however, I watched Ball and Macdonald Smith for a while. They tied —England and America—with 304 for the four rounds, and now we knew what Whitcombe and Hagen—England and America—had got to do.

By this time Hagen, like Whitcombe, had disappeared into the unknown, but there were lots of excited people to tell me what had happened. "He began with a six," cried one. "He was bunkered and —" "He took another six at the third," gasped another. This sounded cheerful, and then a third and gloomy patriot dashed our hopes. "What's the good of two sixes?" said he. "Whitcombe's taken 43 to the turn and broken down utterly." Just then up rushed a fourth man, in time to hear the last four words. "Broken down, has he?" he snapped. "He's started home 4, 3, 4, 3. He's playing like an angel now. He's only four over fours going to the Lake." We looked away to the fifteenth green in the distance and there, sure enough, was a big crowd. "They would not be sticking to Whitcombe if he wasn't doing well," said one skilled in omens and portents, and then, as a faint burst of cheering was borne to us on the breeze, "By gad! I bet that's a four; he's done a four at the Lake."

What was to be done next? It was difficult to decide. I finally hardened my heart, resolved not to wait for Whitcombe's finish, but to see Hagen's last nine holes. I reached the tenth green just as Hagen was playing his second shot up to it. The ball was making for the green, but with a little cut upon it. "Look out!" came an agonized screech. "Let it go."

The crowd tumbled out of the way and down the bank just in time, and over the edge of the green rolled the ball. Hagen's next shot was too strong and ran well past, and there was Hagen very seriously studying that six-yard putt for his four.

While he was looking at it, the all-important news flashed like wildfire through the waiting crowd. First of all Whitcombe had finished in 78—a wonderful effort in the circumstances —and had a total of 302. Secondly, Hagen had gone out in 41. Therefore he had to come home in 36 to win and 37 to tie; he looked likely to begin with a five, and 37 home at Hoylake, at full stretch, with those tremendous four holes from the Field to the Royal, means tremendous work. He could hardly do it—England might yet be saved.

All that takes some time to write down, but it did not take long to think. We knew the best and the worst; we had done our calculations and there was Hagen still brooding. And then he hit that ball right into the middle of the hole and we all clapped, though we did not want him to win. It was a gallant putt, and if there was one shot more than another that made victory possible, this was it.

With that putt began as fine a stern chase as could be imagined. It divides itself in my mind into two distinct periods: the first a brave scramble, the second a triumphant march. He had made a mistake at the Dee and recovered from it; he made a mistake at the Alps, at the Hilbre, at the Rushes, yet his net loss from those four errors was just one shot, so indomitable were his recoveries. At the Rushes he seemed a beaten man when he pitched a feeble tee-shot slap into a bunker in front of the green. "That's done it," said a famous golfer standing near to me. "He can never do it now." But Hagen took a good long look, pitched beautifully out of the bunker and ran down a five-foot putt. And then suddenly it seemed certain that he would do it. There was no holding a man who could recover and keep on recovering like that. True, he still wanted four fours and a five to win—perfect play and that over the severest finishing holes in all golf. Still, it was borne in on us that he would do it, and Hagen looked as if he thought so too. He cast away that recovering mood. He looked no longer grave but radiant, and he played faultlessly.

173

Bang, bang, went his long wooden club shots, as straight as arrows, to the Field, the Lake and the Dun. Now he wanted two fours to win, and who that saw it will forget that wholehearted long iron shot smashed right up to the Royal green, with the road on one side and the bunker creeping in on the other? That finally did it. Hagen played the home hole with the very palpable intention of making sure of his five and so at least tying with Whitcombe. His second was a bold one and over the green. What happened after that I could not see. I could only hear, "He's played a good run-up, but he isn't dead," and then, after an infinite wait, "He's holed it." If ever there were a case for our old friends "the ranks of Tuscany" who could "scare forbear to cheer," this was the one.

That spurt was one for all the golfing ages. Whitcombe's spurt was as fine a one, but there is this difference between the two, as there is so often between Hagen and the other man. Hagen just won and the other man just didn't.

Two Matches with Glenna

by

JOYCE WETHERED

1933 — FROM *GOLFING MEMORIES AND METHODS*

ONE OF THE most agreeable things about championship golf is the yearly alternation of the links on which it is played. If it were not for the "rota," which is a little of a mystery to me, and the variety of scene which the system encourages, a great deal of the charm of these meetings would be lost.

With me there were never any reservations as to which country I looked forward to most. Scotland has something about her golf finer and more characteristic than any other country, as is only fitting and natural for the land of its birth. I have the feeling, too, that the fiercest battles I have ever been engaged in which happened at Troon and St. Andrews could never have happened anywhere else. The air, the enthusiasm and the play itself, seem sharper and keener in the north. Or is this only imagination?

It was my privilege to meet Glenna Collett in both these championships and my matches with her remain amongst the pleasantest of memories in championship golf. As an opponent she was unequaled in the generous-minded and sporting attitude that was natural to her. She has never been a player quick to protest against the misfortunes of a round. On the contrary, she has taken her defeats as well as her victories with a calm philosophy that nothing can move. There is no doubt that fortune has not treated her too kindly in her visits

to this country; I believe there have been five up to now. Something has always just gone wrong on each of these occasions and an English golfer has seized the opportunity, when the moment arrived, to snatch a victory from her.

Of all the great players I have known, Glenna presents the most detached of attitudes in playing a match. She intrudes her presence to the smallest degree upon her opponents. I would even say that she appears to withdraw herself almost entirely from everything except the game, and her shots alone remind one of the brilliant adversary one is up against. If she is finding her true form then there is little hope, except by a miracle, of surviving—at any rate in an eighteen-hole match. But there are also some vague days in between, when her interest and concentration seem to be elsewhere. Her charm, however, to my mind as a golfer and a companion lies in a freedom of spirit which does not make her feel that success is everything in the world. Those who are so generous in defeat are the people most to be envied.

At Troon the match anticipated between her and myself was worked up to such a pitch beforehand that, when the day came, one of two things was almost bound to happen. Either we should rise to the occasion or one of us would fail under the strain of it. As events happily turned out for me, I played the best golf that I have ever succeeded in producing. With the exception of two poorish putts I know that I have never played the rest of the game so accurately or so well before or since. I have never strung so many good shots together (or so faultlessly for me) even if I have been able to produce similar figures (that is, fours for the match) by other and less correct means. But because I was hitting the ball so surely I was able to avoid what might easily have occurred under the stress of the moment—the slipping of one or two important shots and perhaps the loss of the match as well. I think this probably explains the reason why Glenna topped two drives at the sixth and ninth holes, strokes which as genuinely surprised herself, I remember, as they surprised everyone else. Unexpected as they were, they undoubtedly turned the tide in my favor, the second slip coming at a very crucial moment to make me one up after I had lost the lead at the short eighth by a weak putt. Up till that moment there had been nothing in it between us. Glenna had drawn first blood at the third, holing a very good putt for a three; I had drawn level at the fifth and taken the lead at the sixth only to lose it again, as I have mentioned, at the short "Postage Stamp."

On turning for home one up I won the tenth owing to a loose third by Glenna, and the eleventh by holing a long putt. It was at this point that I again lived up to my curious reputation for not noticing trains. As was remarked in *The Times*: "Miss Wethered holed a long curly putt for a three characteristically enough with an engine snorting on the line behind her." But this time I was more fully aware of the reality of the train in question. It was puffing smoke in clouds behind the green in a way that could not very well be ignored. However, I was too well acquainted with the ways of a Scotch engine driver not to know that he was determined to wait to see the hole played to a finish before he continued with his goods to Ayr. Knowing this, there was little to be gained by my waiting. Besides, it was just possible that a train was not an unlucky portent. Whatever may be the truth of that supposition the putt made me three up and almost decided, I think, the result of the game. We halved the next two; at the fourteenth Glenna missed a short one and so

gave me another hole; and a half at the fifteenth brought the game to a conclusion, four and three.

The next time we met was four years later at St. Andrews, and this was the championship that I certainly enjoyed the most. Perhaps one of the reasons was that I was able to enter after an interval with much less expected of me than usual. There could be no justification for such remarks as, "Of course you will do well," which in a game like golf spell ruin if they are believed for one moment. I was prepared for anything or everything to happen, however disastrous or extraordinary. It created an enchanting sense of freedom to feel that the well-meaning friends who come up after a bad shot and say, "That really wasn't like you!" would not this time allow themselves to be so easily shocked.

It has often been attributed to me that I entered for this event in a purely patriotic spirit, with the expressed intention of preventing any of the American invaders from winning our championship. I must really protest against this rather pretentious statement. The fact that Glenna Collett and I actually met in the final lent some color to the rumor, but I feel I should never be justified in entering for the sole purpose of hoping to prevent some other particular player from winning. A championship in my opinion is an event originally instituted solely for private enterprise and for the best player to win and it seems to me a pity that it need necessarily be converted into an international match on a larger scale.

At St. Andrews I did not, as a matter of fact, feel I need be weighed down by any responsibilities that might be thrust upon me. I was no longer a regular player in competitions. The moment had merely arrived when I could take part in an event to which I had looked forward for years.

The first round started perhaps somewhat appropriately in a very happy-go-lucky state of confusion. Phyllis Lobbett and I were timed to start between the awkward hours of one and two o'clock, and although a crowd had collected there was scarcely a flag-wagger to be seen on the links. The first few holes were played with everyone running and rushing about in any direction he pleased. No one, not even the players and the caddies, knew where the balls lay. That they must be somewhere on the fairway amongst the feet of the crowd was all that was positively known, and this produced a bewildering state of affairs which made progress distinctly difficult. Eventually the arrival of more flags about the fourth hole helped to straighten out the mêlée, and soon after some of those whose luncheon hour had been disturbed drifted homewards.

In the next five rounds I played one Irish, one Scotch and three English ladies. Against Molly Gourlay I certainly played the best golf I had hitherto produced and was two under fours when the match finished.

In spite of a succession of good rounds, however, St. Andrews is not exactly a course where one can ever feel very safe. The greens are never sympathetic if one's putting is uncertain, and it is easy enough to lapse into a habit of taking three putts too frequently.

Glenna, I believe, was experiencing the same difficulty; she never struck the top of her form until the final round. I remember that she dined with us at Rusack's on the Wednesday night, and I watched her as she walked over from the Grand Hotel, a charming and striking picture in blue and gold against the gray buildings. She was not particularly happy that evening, a little dispirited with the course, and rather depressed and dissatisfied with her golf; up till then only flashes of her true form had been visible in the matches she had played.

The next day she cheered up very considerably after appearing in something like her true colors against Mrs. Watson and Doris Park. She showed such convincing form in both these matches that I ruefully, and truthfully, prophesied that evening that there was trouble brewing for me on the morrow. To keep one's place successfully in a championship and yet reserve one's best game for the two or three last rounds is the most comforting mode of progress—much better than seeing one's game show signs of petering out the other way.

The final round was a match of the most extraordinary vicissitudes. Never has a close game swung in such a pendulum fashion. Glenna's first nine holes of the match, which she did in 34, was the finest sequence of holes I have ever seen a lady play. By the ninth green I was faced with a deficit of five holes.

It was not that I had played badly through the green, but the putts would not go down and I frittered away my chances round the hole. If the touch of the putter leaves you at St. Andrews on those fast and immense greens, then heaven help you! You are indeed lost until you recover it.

I have always had the tendency to be nervous and rather jumpy round the hole in the early stages of a match and the only remedy that can cure me is to hole a good firm one. On the tenth green I did make a good putt of about three yards, but it just came out again, and that is no use from the remedial point of view! We halved the eleventh. The twelfth, to my mind, was the crux of the whole game. I believe that Glenna missed her chance there of making the match almost a certainty. We were both on the green in two and my first putt was woefully short. Finally, after I had missed the next, Glenna was left a putt of from three to four feet to win the hole. If she had become six up at this point of the game, due to my criminally taking three putts again, I do not think the result would ever have been a close one. But she let me off, missed her first putt of the match and left me a ray of hope.

There is almost always a quick reaction when an important chance is missed. Nothing can be so heartening to the player who is behind, and the mistake encourages a feeling of strain and uncertainty in the leader, however strongly he or she may be going at the time. On the next green I holed my first putt —a good one of four yards—and from that moment began to be able to get down the important ones. Glenna did not keep up her relentless attack and relaxed the pressure sufficiently to allow me to win back three of the five holes before luncheon.

Even then the position was none too good. My St. Andrews supporters had been through a black morning and the period during which I had been five down, I am afraid, had tried them almost as sorely as myself. A stranger, quite indifferent to golf, who was walking in the streets of St. Andrews bent on seeing the Cathedral and the University was surprised to find himself addressed by a postman in a depressed tone of voice as he passed gloomily on his rounds with the remark, "She's five doon." What the stranger thought of this unsolicited piece of information I cannot imagine.

The fluctuations and figures of the match continued to be amazing. Our best-ball score in the morning was seventy-one. Glenna's deluge of par figures and under up to the twelfth hole consisted of nine fours, one three and a two. Then my turn of good luck began. From the ninth I took 73 for the next eighteen holes and in the afternoon actually stood four up at the ninth, a difference of nine holes from the position at the same point in the morning round. One might imagine from the psychology of the game that the excitement of the match was now probably over, and that all would perhaps end quietly on a green four or five holes from home. From any likelihood of such a peaceful ending I was rudely awakened by Glenna doing the next two holes in three apiece and winning them both. To lose two holes so abruptly altered the whole complexion of the game, and I must confess that I found the playing of the remaining holes a very trying experience. I had also the memory of throwing away a lead at Troon in a previous year which did not tend to make the position any more comforting. At the fifteenth the state of the match was still two up. I had in the meantime won another hole, but lost the Long Hole In, taking a number of strokes which still make me blush when I think of them.

The fifteenth finally decided the result. I had sliced my drive and was unable to reach the green in two. A poor run up left me still six yards from the hole with Glenna lying practically dead in three. It looked very like being only one up, and in such a crisis, with still three holes to go, anything might have happened. But the most opportune putt I have ever made came to my rescue. I holed

the six-yarder for a half and kept my lead of two, which I was able to hold on to till the seventeenth green. I did not feel in the least like holing the putt, and even when it was on its way I scarcely realized that it was going in. Generally there is an instinct about a putt which tells you what is probably going to happen. This time I had no such warning. I only remember feeling distinctly desperate and hitting the ball rather hard as the putt was uphill; and then the hole gobbled it up. Thank heavens there are still such happy surprises in the world!

The next hole we halved to make me dormy two. Then at the seventeenth, a very exacting hole in any circumstances, I was relieved of the responsibility of playing it really well, as Glenna took four to reach the plateau. All the same I shall not easily forget the anxiety of keeping the ball safely in play on nearing the dreaded green. It is the most trying of all experiences to keep cool just on the brink of winning; so easy to lose control and spoil it all. It was also impossible to ignore the pent-up excitement of the crowd which was ready to break out as soon as the last putt was struck. When the moment finally came it threatened very nearly to destroy us. Glenna and I were torn apart and became the center of a squeezing, swaying, and almost hysterical mob, shouting and cheering themselves hoarse.

Thrilling as was the wild enthusiasm around us I was gratefully relieved to find struggling at my side two stalwart officers of the law. After what seemed an eternity we were able to force our way, yard by yard, through the crowd to the road by the side of the green, and from there gradually to the steps of the hotel. How Glenna fared in the meantime I never quite discovered; evidently she escaped by another route.

The Immortal Bobby

by

BERNARD DARWIN

1944 — FROM *GOLF BETWEEN TWO WARS*

As far as the United States is concerned the Bobby Jones era began, I suppose, in 1916 when at the age of fourteen-and-a-half he reached the third round of the American National Championship at Merion and went down after a hard match before an ex-champion, Robert Gardner. From this time onward till he retired full of honors if not of years, he was a great figure in American golf. For us, however, his era began somewhat later, since he came here first in 1922 and did not show us his full powers till 1926 when he had reached the immense age of twenty-four. He then won our Open Championship for the first time and perhaps this is the best place to set out his record in the barest and briefest outline. In his own country he won the Open Championship four times (he also tied for it twice and lost the play-off) and the Amateur Championship five times. Here he won one Amateur and three Open Championships. In 1930 he established what has been pictur-esquely called "the impregnable quadrilateral" by winning the Open and Amateur Champion-ships of both countries in a single summer. He played against Britain in six International Matches, five of them for the Walker Cup; he won his single every time, sometimes by immense margins, and he won his foursome five times and lost once by a single hole.

Bobby's first appearance here was in the International Match preceding the Amateur Championship at Hoylake in 1921. He won both his single and his foursome handsomely and impressed everybody, as he could not fail to do. Then came anticlimax. His career in the Amateur Championship was short and rather checkered. He began well enough against a good Scottish player, Mr. Manford, and there followed that rather farcical encounter with Mr. Hamlet of Wrexham. Whatever he might be at Wrexham it is pardonable to say that Mr. Hamlet was not of the stature to face Hoylake, even though it was made less formi-dably long than usual by the hard ground. Yet with the match all square going to the Royal, which is the seventeenth, it really seemed as if he were going to beat Bobby, which, as Euclid might remark, would have been absurd. This was not due to any great golf of his but to a sort of general futility and paralysis on the greens on Bobby's part. How-ever, the crisis passed, Bobby scrambled through with a score nearer ninety than eighty and proceeded to play devastatingly well in his next match against Mr. Robert Harris. He had got his bad round over, he was going to win—and then he relapsed again and was beaten by many holes by Mr. Allan Graham. There was a chance of redeeming himself in the Open at St. Andrews but all went ill; he felt a puzzled hatred for the links which he came afterwards to love and at the eleventh hole in the third round he picked up his ball.

Legend declares that he relieved his feelings by teeing it up and driving it far out into the Eden. If he did it was a gesture deserving of sympathy, and if he did not I am very sure he wanted to.

In 1921, at the age of nineteen, Bobby was already a magnificent golfer, as great a hitter of the ball though not as great a player of matches or medal rounds as he ever was. Several years before Mr. Walter Travis had said he could never improve his strokes, and that was true enough; there was, humanly speaking, no room for improvement; it was simply a matter of stringing them together more successfully. There could be no more fascinating player to watch not only for the free and rhythmic character of his swing but for the swiftness with which he played. He had as brief a preliminary address as Duncan himself, but there was nothing hurried or slapdash about it and the swing itself, if not positively slow, had a certain drowsy beauty which gave the feeling of slowness. There was nothing that could conceivably be called a weak spot. The utmost that could be said— and this may be a purely personal impression— was that he did not seem quite so supremely happy with a mashie-niblick as when playing approaches with longer irons.

People liked Bobby at once, and that not only for his natural pleasantness of manner; they discerned in him a very human quality; he was no cold machine but took his game very much to heart as did humbler people. In his almost infantile days he had been inclined to throw his clubs about. This we were told since the American press had once emphasized it rather unkindly; otherwise we should never have guessed it, for he had already tamed his naturally fiery temperament into betraying no outward signs. Those indeed who knew him well professed to know the symptoms which showed the flames leaping up within. I remember once watching him at an Open Championship, it may have been at St. Anne's, in company with that fine American golfer, the late Mr. J. G. Anderson; Bobby missed a shortish putt and "Now, he's mad," said my companion. I could detect nothing, but doubtless Mr. Anderson knew his man and Bobby did hate missing a shot. Perhaps that was why he missed so few, for in the end that highly-strung nervous temperament, if it had never been his master, became his invaluable servant. In his most youthful and tempestuous days he had never been angry with his opponent and not often, I think, with Fate, but he had been furiously angry with himself. He set himself an almost impossibly high standard; he thought it an act of incredible folly if not a positive crime to make a stroke that was not exactly as it ought to be made and as he knew he could make it. If he ever derogated from that standard he may even in his most mature days have been "mad" in the recesses of his heart, but he became outwardly a man of ice, with the very best of golfing manners.

How much other people have suffered over their golf we do not always know; the light of fame has not beaten on them so fiercely and they have not possessed such a friend and *vates sacer* combined as Bobby had in Mr. O. B. Keeler. Of Bobby we do know that he suffered greatly. How he could scarcely eat anything till the day's play was over; how on occasion he felt that he could not even button his shirt collar for fear of the direst consequences; how he could lose a stone in weight during a championship; how he was capable of breaking down to the point of tears not from any distress but from pure emotional overstrain—these things are now well known and may be found in Mr. Keeler's admirable and Boswellian pages. No doubt his capacity for an emotional outlet was at that time a relief and a help to him, but there must be a limit. I was in his company soon after he had finished his fourth round when he won the last of his three Open Championships here in 1930, and seeing him nearly past speech I thought that the time had come for him to call a halt and that this game could not much longer be worth such an agonizing candle. He had great courage and great ambition, and these not only pulled him through but probably made him a more successful player than he would have been had he been gifted with a more placid temperament. There is much to be said for the stolid, phlegmatic player, but the great golfers have never had what I once heard Jack White call a dead nerve. It is worth remembering that James Braid, most rocklike and apparently impassive of men, has said that he "liked to be a wee bit nervous" before a big game. The steady-going and unimaginative will often beat the more eager champion and they will get very near the top, but there, I think, they will stop. The prose laborer must yield to the poet and Bobby as a golfer had a strain of poetry in him. He stands forever as the greatest encourager of the highly-strung player who is bent on conquering himself.

In 1926 we saw Bobby on his second visit. Four years had passed since he had been here before and he had now, as the Americans called it, "broken through"; the lean years were over. In 1923 he had won the American Open after a tie with Cruikshank, thus emulating Mr. Hilton here in winning the Open before the Amateur. In the following year he had put this to rights by winning the Amateur with triumphant ease and had been runner-up in the Open. In 1925 he had won the Amateur again and had tied in the Open, to lose rather surprisingly after a protracted play-off with Willie Macfarlane. He was in the plenitude of his powers and who should stand before him? And yet there was a moment when it seemed as if his second visit, like his first, would end in disappointment. All went swimmingly in the Amateur Championship at Muirfield till he reached the fifth round and then out he went and that with a resounding crash, for he was well and truly beaten by Mr. Andrew Jamieson who was then hardly known outside Scotland. I believe that Bobby woke with a stiff neck that morning though he was most anxious to conceal it. Certainly he seemed to lack something of his usual ease, but Jamieson, a very neat, unobtrusive, efficient golfer, did play uncommonly well, well enough to beat anybody if anybody gave him, as Bobby did, the very slightest opening. What was more, having got away with a lead he never grew frightened of it but played with victorious confidence. I saw only odd holes of the match but I remember one vividly. This was the short thirteenth called "The Postage Stamp," though whether it or the hole at Troon has the prior right to the title I do not know. The hole as it then was had a long narrow green with a drop to perdition on the right, and on the left a high rough bank. Jamieson, with victory firmly in his grasp, if he could keep steady, had the honor and he made a slip; he hooked his tee-shot and the ball lighted on the top of the left-hand bank. Would it stay

there? It hovered for a moment and then, audibly encouraged by the crowd, began to topple downward by stages, almost coming to rest and then moving on again till at last it ended its rather nefarious career on the green. That was the final blow and Jamieson, having had his little bit of luck, went on to win calmly and easily by 4 and 3.

Mrs. Gamp has remarked how little we know "what lays before us." If Bobby had won that championship he has said that he would have sailed straight for home after the Walker Cup match. As it was he decided to give himself another chance in the Open at St. Anne's. So, after duly doing his deadly stuff at St. Andrews in the Walker Cup—he beat Cyril Tolley by 12 and 11—he went to Sunningdale for the qualifying rounds of the Open and proceeded to play there what was by common consent as nearly flawless a round as ever had been played. He went round in 66 and he may be said to have holed only one putt worthy of mention, one of eight yards or so for a three on the fifth. Otherwise if he missed nothing short—and there were one or two putts missed to be called shortish—he holed nothing that could conceivably be called long. He simply went on and on with exact perfection. There was indeed one slip, an iron shot pushed out into a bunker at the short thirteenth, but it cost the player nothing since he chipped the ball out dead. It probably brought relief to him as it did to the spectators, who had been feeling that they must scream if perfection endured much longer. It was Mr. Keeler, I think, who once wrote, "They wound up the mechanical man of golf yesterday and set him clicking round the East Lake course." All great golfers at their best are more or less mechanical, for they do the same thing over and over again, but I doubt if any of them save perhaps one has given quite such an impression of well-oiled, impeccable machinery as Bobby did from tee to green. The notions of beauty and machinery do not go well together; the word "clicking" may suggest something done "by numbers" and so far it is inappropriate; but Mr. Keeler's was nevertheless an apt and memorable phrase. Harry Vardon and Bobby Jones combined exquisiteness of art with utterly relentless precision in a way not quite given to any other golfers.

Few joys in this world are unalloyed, and

though Bobby was naturally and humanly pleased with that 66 he was a trifle worried because he had "reached the peak" rather too soon before going to St. Anne's. His second round of 68, with, if I remember, one innocuous misunderstanding with a tree, did nothing to reassure him on this point and he was so far right that, though he won at St. Anne's, his play there was not quite of the same unrippled smoothness as at Sunningdale. The game was by contrast "aye fechtin'" against him and he had to work hard for his scores. That was as exciting a championship as any between wars, save only for this, that from the very start it seemed that no Briton was likely to win it. Mitchell ended fifth but he only accomplished so much by two very fine rounds on the last day; as far as winning was concerned he had put himself out of court by beginning with two 78's. So to the narrowly patriotic this championship was merely a brilliant, alien exhibition contest.

The invaders went off with a bang: Hagen had a 68 and the powerful, broad-backed, rough-hewn Mehlhorn, said to have graduated as hod-carrier to the champion bricklayer of America, had a 70. Then came M'Leod, an expatriated Scot, and Al Watrous with 71 and then Bobby in the position he liked, lying well up but not prematurely leading, with a 72. It was a good round but he had to fight for it, since at each one of the last four holes he made some sort of a slip and had, in Mr. Laidlay's phrase, to "trust to a pitch and a putt" to get his four. In the second round Hagen had a compensating and disastrous 77 and at the end of it Mehlhorn with 70 and 74 and Bobby with two 72's led the field. Watrous, 71 and 75, was two shots behind them.

On the last day Bobby and Watrous were drawn together, and as it turned out this chance involved just such a strain on them and just such a terrific duel for first place as Vardon and Taylor had endured at Prestwick ten years earlier. Watrous was a very good player who has left no very distinct image on my mind; he had no tremendous power, but he had all the American virtue of smoothness and rhythm and he was a very fine putter, bang on his putting. Bobby was two strokes ahead when they set out and he had a 73 in a good fresh wind, but Watrous playing perfectly had a 69 and so—again this brought back

memories of Vardon and Taylor—turned the deficit of two into a lead of two. Hagen took 74 and Mehlhorn began to fade. So the battle was to be fought out between these two and they were fully conscious of it as they went back to their hotel together, lunched together and even lay down to rest in the same room— a pleasant picture of friendly rivalry.

When it was all over and Mr. Topping, who had been in charge of this couple, gave away the prizes he declared that Bobby had made but one remark to him in the course of the last round, "My golf is terrible." In fact it was terribly good except in one important respect; he was taking too many putts. By his own account he took thirty-nine of them and what he gained on Watrous in length he certainly threw away on the greens. The short ninth which had consistently bothered him beat him again and he was still two down with five to play; in what was in effect a match the language of match play may be used. Then at last the strokes came back one at a time and the pair were all square with three to play. At the seventeenth came Bobby's historic second, which I must presently describe yet again, but before that on the sixteenth came an incident of which a friend has lately reminded me; it gives force to the ruthless doctrine that someone ought to murder a photographer *pour encourager les autres*. Watrous had played his second to the green and Bobby had got halfway up with some pitching club when a fiend with a camera stepped out and tried to snap him. Bobby stopped and began again, and again the photographer tried. This time he was metaphorically lynched; he was shooed out of the way, and Bobby, by a considerable display of control, pitched safely to the green and the hole was halved in four.

Now for the seventeenth, a hole a little over 400 yards in length. The course of the hole bends to the left and the line is well out to the right, in order to get a clear view of the hole and avoid the sandhills guarding the left-hand side of the green. Nor is that the only reason for keeping to the right, for on the left of the fairway is a wilderness of sandy, scrubby country dotted here and there with bunkers. Bobby with the honor, drew his tee-shot, not badly but badly enough to be obviously in some form of trouble; Watrous went straight and playing the odd reached the green; he was some way from the hole but he was on the green and that looked good enough. Bobby's ball lay in a shallow bunker and it lay clean, but he was 170 yards or more from the flag and between him and it were the sandhills. He took what I think he called his mashie-iron (it now reposes a sacred relic in the St. Anne's Club) and hit the ball perfectly clean, playing it somewhat out into the wind so that it came in to finish on the green and nearer the hole than his opponent. Admittedly the ball lay as clean as clean could be and this was the kind of shot that he might very well have played in a practice game, but in the circumstances, when a teaspoonful too much sand might have meant irretrievable ruin, it was a staggering shot, and it staggered poor Al Watrous. He took three putts, Bobby got down in two and everybody felt that that shot had settled it. Watrous was bunkered at the home hole, Bobby nearly bunkered but not quite; he got a four against a five and finished in 74 against 78, 291 against 293.

There still remained Hagen and George Von Elm, both of whom were rumored to be doing well. Hagen arrived on the last tee wanting a four for 74 and a two to tie. He could doubtless have tied for second place with Watrous but Hagen was never interested in second prizes. After a fine drive, he walked some way forward and then with a characteristic gesture had the flag taken out. His ball very nearly pitched into the hole and ran on into the bunker behind the green. *Aut Caesar,* etc. His effort had failed and he took four more to get down, so that Von Elm, coming with a wet sheet and a 72, tied with him for third place. Let me add as a postscript that the Council of the Royal Lytham and St. Anne's Club have now decided to mark, as far as it can exactly be done, the spot at the seventeenth from which Bobby played his shot. This is a precedent that could not often be followed, but here the geographical conditions are favorable and if now and then someone has to lift a drop from behind the monument he will do so in a reverent rather than an exasperated spirit.

I have written at perhaps excessive length about the St. Anne's Championship both because it was Bobby's first and because it was so dramatic. When he came back next year to

defend his title at St. Andrews, having in the meanwhile won the American Open at Scioto, he played unquestionably better; he enjoyed the greatest single triumph he ever had here, but there seems much less to say about it, for the reason that it was "his" championship, he was winning all the while. By this time St. Andrews had taken a thorough hold on him. He was amused by its problems; he knew whereabouts were its hidden bunkers and was not annoyed by them, as some people never cease to be, because they are hidden; he had devised some three different ways of playing the Long Hole In according to the wind; he had realized that for a player of his parts the Road Hole need hold no excessive terrors, unless he is overambitious. In short he had proved the truth of Mrs. Malaprop's saying that "'Tis safest in matrimony to begin with a little aversion," for he was now thoroughly in love with the Old Course and played it as if he loved it.

Bobby's four rounds were 68, 72, 73 and 72 and he led from the start. I do not know that he played any better for his 68 than in any of the other three rounds; it was simply that everything came off for him, as for example a putt holed for three at the Hole o' Cross going out. It is by far the biggest green in the world and if this was not the longest putt ever holed it must have been very nearly so. Mr. Keeler's brow was a little knitted, for he was not sure how his man would like to be "in the lead" straight away instead of lying a stroke or two behind, but the general impression was that there would be no holding Bobby. After two rounds he only led Hodson by two strokes, but good player as Hodson was he could scarcely hope to give the leader two strokes; in fact the third round destroyed him as far as winning was concerned and those who were more likely to hold on were several shots further behind. At the end of the third round Bobby led Fred Robson, who had just done a splendid 69, by four shots and Aubrey Boomer by six, and it was for him to set the pace.

Only at the beginning of the last round was there a moment's doubt, for Bobby frittered away a couple of shots in the first four holes, and so with an orthodox five at the fifth his score was three over fours—a definitely vulnerable star. At that point I left him to look at other people, meaning to pick him up again at the thirteenth on the way home. Some bursts of clapping from the neighborhood of the "loop" suggested that he was doing well, but how well no one of us waiting on the big double green knew. The advance guard of his crowd came towards us, in the van one who trotted briskly, as if big with news to impart. I have a well-grounded distrust of spectators' tales but this one looked a man of good counsel, sober and unimaginative; so I button-holed him and asked his tidings. When he said that Bobby was now two under fours I thought he was only the usual liar, but what he said was true, for Bobby had done the holes from the sixth to the twelfth in twenty-four shots. After that the round was a tri-umphal procession. His second to the last hole was a little cautious and ended in the Valley of Sin. Thence he ran it up dead and as he scaled the bank the crowd stormed up after him and lined the edge of the green, barely restraining themselves. He holed his short one and the next instant there was no green visible, only a dark seething mass, in the midst of which was Bobby hoisted on fervent shoulders and holding his putter, "Calamity Jane," at arm's length over his head lest she be crushed to death. Calamity Jane had two pieces of whipping bound round her shaft where she had been broken, not we may trust in anger but by some mischance. When some years later the market was flooded with exact models of her, each of them duly bore two superfluous black bands. Did ever imita-tion pay sincerer flattery than that?

Only once more, in 1930, were we destined to see Bobby here in battle array, though he has returned once since his retirement and in playing a friendly round of the Old Course took the major part of St. Andrews round with him. It was at St. Andrews in 1930, the year of the "impregnable quadrilateral," that he realized almost his last unachieved ambition and won our Amateur Championship. He did not win it without his bad moments, for he had never concealed his dislike of eighteen-hole matches. In the American Championship the first two rounds, which were of eighteen holes only, had at least once brought him to grief and he had had, in the words of old Beldham the cricketer, "many an all but." Once safely through them and in the haven

of thirty-six holes, where he felt that he had space to maneuver, he had crushed his men one after the other by murderous margins. Thus in our championship he could never feel really at ease until in the final and he had never yet reached the final. He set out on the enterprise strung up to a high pitch and no one who saw the beginning of his match against a good Nottinghamshire golfer, Mr. Roper, will forget it. On the first green he holed a long putt for a three, the ball going in with an almost suspicious rattle against the back of the tin. Bobby looked a little apologetic and made several little practice movements of his club. I remember Mr. Hilton whisper-ing to me that he was trying to get the swing of his putter smooth; that first putt, success-ful as it was, had shown signs of tension. After a four at the second he holed another and shorter putt for a three at the Cartgate and then at the fourth hit a very long tee-shot rather to the left into the Cottage bunker. Thence, a culminating atrocity, he holed out, a full shot of 150 yards or so, with some sort of iron, for a two.

After this astonishing display Bobby be-came comparatively quiescent and had to struggle as hard to get through as many less gifted players have done. Two of his most close-run things were against compatriots, Mr. Harrison Johnston and Mr. George Voigt. Mr. Johnston, after being several holes down, chased him to the last gasp and Mr. Voigt, if I may permit myself an "if," ought to have beaten him. Bobby was obviously struggling and when Mr. Voigt, very cool and steady and putting beautifully, stood two up with five to go, he looked like a winner. And then he committed what the onlooker, who has nothing to do but criticize, felt inclined to call a gratuitous folly. With the broad space of the Elysian Fields to drive into he cut his tee-shot over the wall and out of bounds. It was a heaven-sent reprieve; Bobby took it and fought his way home to win by a hole.

Yet even this paled before his battle with Cyril Tolley. Every man, woman and child in St. Andrews went out to watch it, and Mr. Gerard Fairlie was quite right to set the scene of the murder in one of his stories on the afternoon of that match. There would have been ample opportunity to commit several murders and escape undetected through the lonely streets, though stained with the marks of crime. Never was there more perceptible the silence of expectation, that lull before the storm in which men speak instinctively in whispers, and Cyril gave it if possible a more thrilling emphasis, since he began with a full-blooded top from the first tee. It was ominous but it was no presage of disaster for he played finely afterwards and a dog-fight on a magnificent scale ensued, which delighted everyone save other poor wretches who were trying to play their own insignificant matches. Each man seeing the mighty flood approach him must needs crouch over his ball guarding it as best he might and pick himself up again when the torrent has swept over him. The most discussed shot in the match was Bobby's second to the Road Hole, as to which hundreds are prepared to take their oath that the ball would have been on the road if it had not hit a spectator and an equal number of witnesses are quite certain that it would not. I was there but was running for my life with my head well down at the moment and can offer no opinion. The hole was halved; so was the last and Bobby won at the nineteenth, where his adversary played a rather loose second and was punished by a stymie. Exactly how good the golf was I cannot now remember for there are occasions when that is of secondary importance. It was the devil of a match.

At last Bobby was in the final—against Mr. Wethered; his chance had come and he did not mean to waste it; he was on his favorite long trail of thirty-six holes. At the very first hole a shudder of surprise went through the crowd as he entirely missed his pitch and stayed short of the burn, but from there he chipped dead and got his four; nor did he ever exceed that figure till he put his second into the Road bunker at the seventeenth. I can see him very clearly now, as the stewards are moving away the crowd at the back of the green. He is gently smiling a protest to the effect that he does not mean to go on to the road. In fact his explosion shot gave him quite a good chance of a four but the putt did not drop; there was to be no fiveless round for him. His opponent fought manfully but without avail and Bobby won by 7 and 6.

Now for the last lap, the Open at Hoylake, which was won in the end as had been that at St. Anne's by sheer, hard fighting. As at St.

Andrews Bobby jumped away with the lead with a 70 which was equaled by MacDonald Smith. He added a 72 while Mac Smith took 77 and his nearest pursuer was now Fred Robson with 143. The third round was sound enough, 74, but meanwhile another British hope had arisen. Compston, who had begun with 74 and 73, added to these a tremendous 68 and led Bobby by a stroke. Diegel was not far behind with a 71, giving him a total of 228; but Diegel, though having an astonishing game in him, has been in championships one of those unfortunates who can never quite do it. He has said bitterly himself that however hard the other fellows try to give it to him he will not take it. This may be partly due to his highly artificial method of putting, "contorted almost to anguish," as was written of a fine putter of a much older generation. Such styles are always apt to break down under strain, and apart from this Diegel was cursed with a temperament the most highly strung possible. Walter Hagen, once sitting up cheerfully late before a final against Diegel, was told in a tone of mild reproach that his adversary had been in bed for hours. "Ah," said Hagen, "but he's not asleep." I have seen Diegel, as "crazy" as ever was Duncan, and as brilliant as anyone I ever did see, but somehow he did not quite seem the man to stop Bobby, and in any case it was with Compston that were all British hearts.

I went out to see him play the first hole in the last round. His drive was perfect; his iron shot adequate, to the edge of the green, and he took three putts. One five meant nothing to be sure but there came other fives and the final 82 was heartbreaking. So out again in search of Bobby. All went if not perfectly according to plan at least reasonably well until he came to the eighth or Far Hole, which measures according to the books 527 yards, two shots and a pitch for Bobby in ordinary conditions with the ground fairly fast. The two shots were entirely satisfactory but the pitch was weak and the ball rolled back from the plateau; the next was nothing to boast of and at the last he missed a shortish putt; result, a horrid seven without touching a bunker. As Ben Sayers might have said, "It was no possible but it was a fact." The news of that seven quickly spread all over the links bringing consternation or encouragement. To Bobby himself it must have been a cruel blow but he pulled himself together and fought his way home, much, I imagine, in the frame of mind of a runner running himself blind, not seeing the tape but determined to get there. He was round in 75 and now we knew what had to be done. Compston was dead and buried; Diegel did a 75, good but not quite good enough for he had started two strokes behind. Those of us who were with him in one of the smaller rooms of the clubhouse united in assuring Bobby that all was well, as he wandered restlessly about holding a glass in two hands. And then there came a suggestion that all might not be well since Mac Smith was doing great things. To be sure he had to do a 69 to tie and that to an impartial judgment seemed very unlikely, but at such moments judgments can scarcely be impartial.

I remember very well going out to meet him. I could not go far for I had to broadcast and time was getting hideously short, but I *must* know. He holed out at the Dun taking to my jaundiced eye a very long time over it, and then we knew; two threes to tie. It was almost but not quite impossible. I saw him

play the Royal—I was to broadcast from a house not far off—and his putt for three did not go in. Two to tie and that was surely impossible, but with an obstinate fidelity to duty I waited till his second had pitched on the home green and had palpably not holed out. Then I ran and ran and arrived just in time to announce in breathless tones to an expectant world that Bobby had won again.

I will not follow him home to America. He won the Open at Interlaken and the Amateur at Merion where he had played in his first championship at fourteen and won his first Amateur Championship at twenty-two. But as far as this country is concerned he departed in a blaze of glory from Hoylake.

He retired at the right time and could say with Charles Lamb, "I have worked task work and have the rest of the day to myself." After Tom Cribb had beaten Molineaux for the second time in the great battle of Thistleton Gap it was decided that he need never fight again but should bear the title of Champion to the end of his days. I think that most golfers in their hearts grant the same privilege to Bobby Jones.

28 Holes

in 100 Strokes

by

GENE SARAZEN

1950 — FROM *THIRTY YEARS OF CHAMPIONSHIP GOLF*

LIKE MOST athletes I know, I have always played hunches and cultivated my superstitions, consciously and unconsciously. I entered 1932, for example, certain from the first day of January on that I would enjoy a banner year. After my rapid climb to the top in 1922, I had adopted 2 as my lucky number. It also did nicely for me at the roulette tables. On the golf course I came to interpret a birdie 2 as an omen of a hot streak, luckier than a birdie 3 or a birdie 4. A 2 on the sixty-ninth ignited my sub-par dash at Agua Caliente, and 2's appeared in numerous other tournaments when I was looking for some sign that Sarazen was supposed to win. The year 1932, I had a hunch, might be another 1922.

I was right on the stick that winter, as Daniels would say. Through patience and practice I had mastered my grip and grooved a swing that I knew was compact, correct, and natural. I knew myself a bit better. I felt that I had a tighter rein on my impetuousness. In the twenties I had repeatedly made the mistake of trying to redeem a bad hole by forcing foolhardy miracle shots on the next, which only dug my grave deeper. I also had the sand-iron now and could stand up confidently to any trap shot, clean, half-buried, or buried. I had the game, I thought, to win

the National Open at Fresh Meadow and the additional advantage of knowing every yard of that course. I'd been the pro at Fresh Meadow for six seasons, from 1925 through 1930.

One of my reasons for leaving Fresh Meadow was the old golf superstition that a pro can never win a tournament held on his own course. I had come face to face with that superstition and found that apparently it held true in my case. Fresh Meadow had been host to the 1930 PGA. With my club members cheering me on I had made my way to the final, where I met Tommy Armour. I must have been inside of Tommy on four out of every five holes, and yet I couldn't shake him off. He finally squared the match on the thirty-fifth when he played an incredible No. 4 iron from a knee-deep lie in a Chinese vegetable garden. On the thirty-sixth tee, however, Tommy hit a bad smothered hook. A straight tee-shot and I had him. I missed my opening, my drive following Tommy's into the large trap at the left. We were both on in three, Tommy thirty-five feet away, myself ten feet inside him. Before he even took his line on the cup, I knew Tommy would sink that putt. He tapped it in. I missed mine, as I knew I would. I was the home pro. Weak golf had as much to do with my defeat as strong superstition, I realized, but when I learned that the 1932 Open was scheduled for Fresh Meadow, I decided that I ought to get myself another job and give myself a fair chance to win that Open. I became the home pro at Lakeville.

In the winter of 1932, as I gave my hunch about the Open every chance to grow, I began to think about the New Orleans Open. In 1922, previous to winning the National Open, I had led the field in that earlier version of the New Orleans Open, the Southern Open. Might not be a bad idea, I reflected, to nourish the parallel between 1922 and 1932 by winning at New Orleans. I crossed it out. That was pushing things too far. Two days before the New Orleans Open was set to begin, I was lounging around my home in New Port Richey, Florida, discussing possible itineraries for a hunting trip with my old friend Lester Rice of the *New York Journal-American*. All of a sudden I was seized by an indefinable restlessness. I paced up and down the living room, trying to figure out what was bothering me. I cornered it. "Lester, pack your bag," I said, snapping my fingers. "We're going to New Orleans. I've got a hunch that if I can win that tournament, I'll win the National Open again this year." Inside of a half-hour, we were on our way. We drove the eight hundred miles to New Orleans nonstop, taking time out only to feed ourselves at roadside diners.

I won at New Orleans. On the last hole I snagged the 4 I needed by playing my second shot onto the green with my driver. I play a driver off the fairway very rarely, but I had used that club on my second shot on the last hole at Skokie in 1922 to set up my winning 4. Replaying my last round as I drove home from New Orleans, I wondered whether I had purposely played the driver on the eighteenth because I had remembered Skokie, or if the odd similarity between the two finishes had popped into my mind only after I had made the shot. It wasn't worth quibbling about, I decided. Either way, I liked it.

In June something went wrong. I won the British Open. That made it confusing. I hadn't won that championship in 1922, and so it hadn't entered into my plans for 1932. It was obvious that I had slipped up somewhere, misinterpreted some augury from which I should have been able to divine that it was the *British* Open and not the *United States* Open I was meant to win. If that was the way it was supposed to be, okay, I had no kick coming. I am not a choosy man. I'll settle for either of the two Opens any year.

All supersition aside, I did not think I had much of a chance to win our Open when I returned from England about a week before the field was due to tee off at Fresh Meadow. The British Open had left me worn out and nervously tired. The last thing I wanted to do was subject myself to the strain of another championship. I discovered, however, at the wonderful victory dinners my friends gave me, that I was expected to duplicate what Jones had done in 1930—win both the Opens in the same year. I dragged myself out to Fresh Meadow, feeling like a businessman who had slaved for weeks so that he could take off on a short vacation and then had been called back to his office from the Maine woods. My game was listless. A week was too short a period, anyhow, for it to regain the sharp edge it had in England.

Fresh Meadow was not a great course, but it was a tough one to score on. Like nearly all the courses designed by A. W. Tillinghast, it featured bottleneck greens guarded on both the right and the left by unusually deep bunkers. Unless my will to win was suddenly rekindled in the fire of competition, which I very much doubted it would be, my best chance in the Open, I thought, was to follow safety-first tactics. I decided that I would play for the pin only when the position of my tee-shot gave me the true opening to the pin. If it didn't, then I would play my approach cautiously to the front edge of the narrow opening to the green and take my chances on getting down in two putts once I was on. Sand-iron or no sand-iron, I didn't want to tangle with those brutal traps any more than I had to. The greens, I knew from six years of practicing on them, presented no such headache. Uniformly flat and unsubtle, you could get down in two on them regardless of the length of your approach putt.

I adhered faithfully to this calculated plan of attack, or nonattack, on my first two rounds. I was puzzled when it rewarded me with two mediocre scores, a 74 and a 76, which left me five shots behind the pacemaking total of 145 posted by Phil Perkins, the ex-English ex-amateur. Moreover, I had played shabbier golf than my scores indicated. I could have been three or four shots higher on each round if I hadn't been putting like a Hagen. I made up my mind, nevertheless, to stick with my conservative tactics on the third and fourth rounds. There was an awful lot of trouble on Fresh Meadow, as the high scores testified. Only two men, Perkins and Olin Dutra, had broken par, 70, on either of the first two rounds.

On the morning of the final day, as I was leaving our house to drive to the club, I stopped in the front hallway, sensing that I had forgotten something I might need. I ran through the list of possible omissions: Car keys? Wallet? Fresh underwear and socks? Cigars? No, I had them all. Oh, I knew what it was! I tiptoed back into the bedroom, where my wife, Mary, lay sleeping, and withdrew from the clothes closet the gabardine jacket I had worn for the presentation ceremonies at Prince's.

I fell farther behind the leaders on the third round, losing a stroke to par on four of the first eight holes. The one club in the bag I was playing with decisiveness was my putter, a Calamity Jane model that I had sawed off at the neck and rewelded to gain a shade more loft. For the rest, my game had degenerated from cagey conservatism to downright timidity. I was amazed to learn from Jack Doyle, the betting commissioner, that even when I stood seven strokes off the pace after the first eight holes of the third round, my old club members at Fresh Meadow and other old friends were still placing bets that I would win, without bothering to inquire what the odds were. That was blind faith, if ever I saw it. When I stood on the ninth tee, I had a 3 for a 39.

On the ninth tee I made a couple of impulsive decisions. I asked the two motorcycle policemen, who had appointed themselves my private bodyguard, to hit the road. "I don't care where you go, boys," I told them. "Go to the races at Belmont. Go to the beach. Go any place. You fellows are a jinx." And there and then I made up my mind to chuck my dainty safety tactics. Maybe they paid dividends for other golfers, but I'd given them a fair trial and they suited me like a cage does a robin. I smashed a No. 7 iron twelve feet from the pin on the short ninth and ran my

putt down for a birdie 2. That was more like it. From that hole on, I threw caution to the winds. I belted my drives harder. The harder I hit them, the straighter they went. I rifled my irons right for the flag—to blazes with the bunkers. I began hitting the greens, and close enough to the hole to have a good crack for my birdies.

I started back with four straight pars, the easiest kind of pars. On the fourteenth I dropped a putt for a 2, gathering precision with every hole, and made it three birdies in a row with a 3 on the fifteenth and a 4 on the 587-yard sixteenth. Two clean-cut pars on the seventeenth and eighteenth rounded out a 32 back and a 70. I walked over to the score board to see what good, if any, my comeback had done. Well, I had picked up four strokes on Phil Perkins and five on Dutra. Perkins was still in front with 219 for his three rounds, but I was breathing down his neck now with 220. Diegel was also at 220, and Dutra and Bobby Cruickshank were a stroke behind. Bobby had played a 69. There was a fighter to admire. Bobby's home club had folded just a few weeks before the Open, and he really had to win prize money. His valiant 69 followed a 79 and a 74.

When I am battling for an Open crown I want to concentrate, and I have no patience with the golf pests who slap you on the back and ask if you don't remember how they bought you a Moxie at Worcester in '25, or the time they acted as marshal at an exhibition in '27 at the Old Rough and Ready Country Club. I can't help being short with these intruders. There are times for social conversation and there are times when you ought to have enough sense to leave a man alone. I wouldn't barge in on a businessman in the middle of an important deal, and it beats me how some galleryites cannot realize that a golfer is a man at work when the chips are down in an important championship. Other athletes are luckier than golfers. I can think of no other sport in which a spectator is permitted on the playing field where he can touch the hand and bend the ear of a player who is in the throes of competition.

I know who my true friends are by the consideration they show me when I am under that all-encompassing pressure, as I was with eighteen to go at Fresh Meadow. Tom and Frances Meighan and my other friends from Lakeville and Fresh Meadow just said hello and wished me luck when we passed each other, understanding my preoccupation. Al Ciuci had a guard posted at the locker room entrance to keep out the autograph collectors and the advertising agents scurrying around to sign up anyone who looked as if he could win. This locker room guard was stumped when an elderly person who looked neither like an ad man nor an autograph hound requested permission to speak to me. "He's an old gent in a black suit and a stiff collar," the guard reported. "Oh, that's Mr. Wheeler," I said, smiling through my seriousness. "That's one man I always want to see." Archie walked in and shook my hand warmly. "I'll only stay a minute, Gene," he said. "I wouldn't have intruded now except that I don't want to bother you when you're playing. Here," he said, removing a small package from his pocket, "is a little token of the tremendous pleasure you gave me by winning the British Open. That was an excellent performance, Gene." I had scarcely thanked Mr. Wheeler for his gift, a set of platinum-and-sapphire cuff links, when he was shuffling his way out of the locker room.

I enjoyed a relaxing lunch with Bob Jones and a friend of his, Reg Newton, although we were interrupted from time to time by human radar sets bursting in with reports on the front runners. As I told Bob, I was stumped by the way everyone seemed so eager to tell me that my rivals were burning up the course. I remember that I toasted Perkins as I started draining my second bottle of beer. It was the first time I had ever toasted an opponent while the battle still raged, and I didn't know exactly why I had done it. Long before I learned for a fact that Perkins had turned in 35 and Cruickshank 33, I sensed that I would have to be 68 or better to beat their marks. I was the last contender to go out.

The wind was blowing slightly with the players on the first hole. That was a good sign. It meant that the wind would be with me on the sixth and the eighth and the other rough holes. I started with a par on the 1st, 437 yards long, playing my second on with a No. 2

iron. I missed my par 4 on the second hole—395 yards, a sharp dog-leg to the left—when I shoved my drive into trouble on the right and dumped my recovery into a trap. I got that stroke right back with a birdie 3 on the third, and then went below par by adding a birdie 2 on the fourth. I hit a very satisfying No. 2 iron there, nine feet from the cup on a hole that played longer than its 188 yards because of the gusty cross wind. I slapped two straight woods up the fifth, a 578-yard par 5, pitched on about fifteen feet away, missed my putt, and took a 5.

In my books, the most dangerous hole at Fresh Meadow was the sixth. It was 428 yards long and menaced from tee to green along the left by a stout line of trees. This tight left side placed a heavy premium on straightness off the tee, but that was only half the battle. To carry the pond that nosed well into the fairway on the right, you had to bang a tee-shot that carried 220 yards. Because of the frequent high scores I had blown myself to on this hole, I used to rate it a par 5, a psychological dodge that did me as much harm as good. I must have played that hole well over a thousand times, but I never played it better than I did on the afternoon of June 25, 1932: a solid tee-shot well over the pond, a No. 2 iron that split the pin all the way and sat down four feet from the cup, and a firm putt that hit the back of the cup and dropped for a birdie 3.

As I walked to the seventh tee, for the first time during the tournament, I was struck by the feeling that I *could* win. The front nine, in my opinion, held far more terror than the second, and I was past the danger zone on that first nine, alive and kicking and two under par. If I could strike a happy medium between brazen boldness and overcaution, hit my shots hard and crisp but only after I had thought each shot out clearly, there was no reason why I couldn't keep pace with par the rest of the round.

To finish 4-4-3 on the first nine was not hard for a player who knew the course as well as I did. Placement of the tee-shot was the key to the seventh, a slight dog-leg to the left, 412 yards into the wind. Birdie-hungry players always tried to cut off a little of the corner, but I couldn't see the percentage in fooling around with the tall trees and the trap at the break. I played down the right-hand side of the fairway and had a No. 6 iron for my second. The pin was on the left side of the green, but I didn't go for it, although the opening was inviting. I aimed for the center of the green, playing the percentages. If I missed my approach shot to the right, I figured I would wind up in a trap, but there would be a reasonable amount of room between that trap and the pin in which to control my explosion shot. However, if I erred to the left and found the trap on that side, I would leave myself a much smaller area of the green, and consequently a much more difficult explosion shot. I played my No. 6 iron twenty feet to the right of the flag and got down in two comfortable putts for my par 4. On this approach putt and my others I didn't gun for the hole. I tried to roll the ball up nice and gently so that it would die about a foot past the cup. If it caught a corner, chances were that it would drop. If it went by, I wouldn't be left with a sizable putt back. Those three-footers back knock the stuffings out of you in a tournament, even if you get them.

The wind was with me on the eighth and that helped. It changed that 425-yard 4 from a drive and a long iron or spoon into a drive and a pitch. The trouble off the tee was on the right here, rough grass and young maples. Plenty of room on the left. I played a right-to-left tee-shot, aiming for the center of the fairway, knowing I would have a shot to the green regardless of how much I hooked my drive. It got out there a very long way, about 300 yards, I would guess, and in any event, just a moderate No. 6 iron from the pin. Once again the pin had been tucked on the left side of the pear-shaped green to bring the long trap on the left into play. I lofted a pitch with adequate backspin to the center of the green, putted up close and made my 4.

The ninth was a short short-hole, 143 yards. The green was typically Tillinghast, bounded along the left by one long trap, built up at the back, and with a circle of traps fringing the right. I punched a No. 7 iron fifteen feet past the pin, in the center of the green. On this hole I deviated from the roll-'em-close putting strategy I had adopted for this crucial round. I went boldly for the cup with my putt, and knocked it in. The reason why I could afford to gamble on that green was that I knew

every inch of it cold. It was right next to the pro shop, and during my years at Fresh Meadow it had served as my practice green. I must have spent two hundred hours all told on it, and what I didn't know about that green, Churchill doesn't know about oratory.

As a man whose lucky number was 2, I took full cognizance of the fact that my second 2 of the day on the ninth gave me a 32 for the first nine. I was confident and assured as I started the long voyage home. My guess was that a 68 would be good enough to win, and I felt that I had a 36, one over par, in my system. I was concentrating well. I know that as my gallery swelled by the thousand I was not conscious of their number, their movements, their cheers or their groans. I set my sights on starting back with a 4 on the tenth (385 yards), a 4 on the eleventh (413 yards), and a 3 on the twelfth (155 yards).

Looking down the tenth was like greeting an old friend. I had laid out the fairway traps. The trap on the left was 220 yards out, the one on the right 240 out, so the sensible thing to do was to stay away from the right. I deliberately aimed for the trap on the left, as I was sure I could carry it and had no qualms about playing my second out of the rough. My drive sailed over the right-hand corner of the trap, fading perfectly to suit the contour of the fairway. I was fifteen feet below the hole with my approach, a No. 7 iron. Down in two for my par 4.

The eleventh was not a difficult hole. It demanded nothing more than a straightaway drive and a straightaway second to a punch-bowl green. My tee-shot traveled on a line a shade to the right of the center of the fairway. I was playing my drives on definite fairway points, allowing for a slight draw. If the draw didn't take, as it didn't on this drive, I had nothing to worry about. If the draw did come off, there would be ample room on the left to handle it. I was playing those right-to-left tee-shots with ease, really moving into the ball. The pin on the eleventh was well to the back of the green. I could have used the mashie for my approach but I settled on my No. 6. I didn't want to go over that green or even be past the pin and have a down-hiller coming back. I made the center of the green my target area once again, and hit it. My approach putt from eighteen feet died a few inches beyond the hole, and I got my regulation 4.

On the twelfth I met my first shock. I elected to play a right-to-left iron to that green, 155 yards away. I half-missed my mashie, it fell short of the trap on the right-hand side of the entrance to the green, and I was confronted with a shot that gave me the shakes. I lay forty feet from the pin, positioned on the slippery right deck of the green barely ten feet beyond the far edge of the trap. I couldn't afford not to play for the pin and sacrifice my par, I wanted a 3 desperately. If I could drop the ball delicately over the edge of the trap, I'd have a holeable putt for my 3 —but I'd have a possible 5 if I choked the faintest fraction. It was a gamble I had to take. I asked my caddie for the sand-iron and prayed that my many hours of practice with that club would enable my reflexes to function perfectly under the enormous pressure I felt. I did nip the ball just right. It cleared the sand trap by three scant feet, backspin slowed it down abruptly, and the ball spun itself dead two feet from the hole. I sank my two-footer for my par. Whew!

The thirteenth, fourteenth, and fifteenth—I found I was planning my play three holes at a time——were rugged, testing holes. The thirteenth fairway, 448 yards from the tee to a staunchly trapped green, was hemmed in by woods on both sides. If you hooked or sliced, all you could do was to play safely, almost at right angles, back onto the fairway and be prepared to accept a 5. I didn't even think of the trees, I was that confident on the tee. I took the route down the right side of the fairway to open up the shot to the green. The approach called for was a long iron and it had to be straight. It might have been a No. 3 iron, but discretion prompted a No. 4. My ball hit and stuck twenty feet below the pin. Again down in two for my par, my fourth consecutive par coming back.

I matched par once again on the fourteenth, a stiff short-hole measuring 219 yards. I took a spoon and played as fine a shot as I did during the entire tournament. It buzzed on a beeline for the pin, landed on the front edge of the green, and rolled to within sixteen feet of the cup. I putted up and got my 3. I was feeling very, very confident at this point. Wild Bill Cushing, my old Florida caddie who was acting as my spotter, brought in a final report on Perkins and Cruickshank. They hadn't slowed down. Phil had taken a 70, which gave him a total of 289. Bobby had tied that total with a 68. I did a little figuring before stepping onto the fifteenth or the sixty-ninth tee. I would need a 69 to tie, a 68 to win—I was three under par, and par was 70—I could drop one stroke to par on the last four holes and still edge out Perkins and Cruickshank. Well, I wasn't going to think in those negative terms. I was going to keep right on marching, hitting my shots full, thinking out each hole and each shot intelligently.

The fifteenth, which bent a bit to the left, was purely a tee-shot hole. Deep traps banked the green on this 424-yard 4 and there were traps about thirty yards in front of the green, but as long as you hit a sturdy tee-shot down the middle, you didn't have to worry too much about those green hazards. The place to miss your tee-shot, if you were going to miss it, was down the right. There was trouble on that side, trees, but nothing compared with what you had on the left—out-of-bounds and a cyclone fence. If you got up against this fence, you could use up a lot of strokes. Dutra had the day before. I cracked my drive down the right-hand edge of the fairway, and here I got a break. Had my ball carried ten feet farther, it could have ended up in the rough behind a tree. It landed on soft ground and stuck, a foot inside the fairway. As I studied my approach, for the first time memories began to spin around in my mind. Here was the hole where I had let Armour get off the hook in the PGA two years earlier. I had played my second rashly and had taken an unnecessary 5. Armour had got down in two from a trap, and had pulled out a hole I had counted on winning. I studied my approach carefully. I wanted nothing to do with that heavy-lipped trap on the left. I was going to be short, if anything. I played a No. 7 iron for the apron. My ball landed shorter than I had wanted it to, but it got a fast bounce off the worn-out turf and skipped up the green ten feet from the cup. I holed it for a birdie, a very lucky birdie. I had gained an insurance stroke I hadn't deserved. Luck may be the residue of careful planning, as the wise men say, or it can be just plain luck.

The course was playing very short on this last round but getting home in two on the 587-yard sixteenth was out of the question. I split the fairway with a right-to-left tee-shot and its overspin gave it a long roll. I decided I would use my driver instead of a brassie or spoon for my second. It wasn't so much a desire for distance as my concern about the shallow trap on the right-hand side of the fairway about one hundred yards from the green. If I happened to push the shot to the right, the low trajectory I would get with the driver would give my ball a better chance of running through that trap. I really tagged that second. It landed just before the trap, shot over on one big bounce, and rolled to within forty yards of the green. The pin was on the right, too close to a bunker to be tempting. I made no attempt to get a 4. A sand-iron shot took me to the center of the green on my third, and I holed in two from fifteen feet. That was another helpful par. I needed only two more of them now.

The seventeenth at Fresh Meadow was only 373 yards long, a drive and pitch if you kept away from the heavy rough, the stone wall, and the out-of-bounds on the left. I played my drive over the trees on the right—there was lots of room—and had a simple sand-iron shot to the plateau green. I dropped it on, hole-high and ten feet to the right. I rolled my first putt to the lip and tapped in the two-incher I had for my par.

The eighteenth, 404 undulating yards, was a robust finishing hole. I was glad the wind was with me. As I was teeing up, my thoughts suddenly darted back to the Armour match again. I had hooked my drive off the thirty-sixth sharply into the trap on the left. I was determined not to repeat that error. A good drive and I couldn't lose. I had a 7 to tie Perkins and Cruickshank.

I waited until the marshals had herded the swarming gallery away from the right-hand side, the safe side of the fairway. I aimed down the right and brought my tee-shot in from right to left. I had been concentrating on direction but I must have hit that ball. I had just a No. 7 iron left to the green and I couldn't remember ever having played that hole with a No. 7 iron before. And then, with victory in the palm of my hand, I had to go and push my approach into the treacherous

trap on the right. How I played that shot into the trap is something I still don't know today. One point I can clear up, though: I did not purposely play my ball into that trap, a fable that has gained considerable circulation. I had great confidence in my sand-iron, yes, but it would have been stupid to have deliberately played into trouble. I could have landed in a footprint or buried myself in the wall of the trap. Actually, I was disgusted with myself for hitting such a brainless, careless shot.

I was all set to march into the trap with my sand-iron when I heard Paul Gallico, the sportswriter, shouting anxiously to me, "Gene, Gene! Wait a moment! Wait until they get that crowd back! For Pete's sake, don't play that shot until that green is cleared!" I felt very cool and capable. I couldn't understand how Paul could be so upset. "Don't worry, Paul," I called back to him. "I'm not playing this shot. My sand-iron is. It'll take care of me." The spectators were still shushing each other and milling on the fringe of the green when I took a peek at the hole from the trap and flipped the ball with my sand-iron eight feet from the cup. Then the marshals lost complete control of the gallery, which spilled onto the green and formed a tight twenty-foot circle around my ball and the hole. I didn't need the putt. I just tried to get it up close and was pleasantly surprised when it went in —66. My 286 was three strokes lower than Perkins and Cruickshank.

The gallery, which had been rooting hard for me on every shot, broke loose with such a demonstration of joy and affection that I got very excited. I was finally rescued by the two motorcycle cops whom I had sent away on the ninth tee in the morning. They had been checking the heavy beach traffic when they heard over the radio that I had come back and was on my way to victory. They had jumped on their bikes and had arrived at the course as I was coming up the eighteenth. That accounted for the sirens I had been hearing. The boys escorted me to the locker room. I had a drink there with Tom Meighan while I changed into my presentation jacket—now I knew why I had brought it along—and knotted the green tie with the white question mark I had also worn at Prince's. And then I remember Hagen approaching and throwing his arms in the air. "Gene, you've broken every record that I know of!" He placed his arm around my shoulder. "Gene, I don't think you know what you did. You played the last 28 holes in 100 strokes." It was the first time I had realized it.

Mary—I remember she was all in white—was at my side during the presentation ceremonies.

Bob Jones, a regular contributor to *The American Golfer,* commented on the 1932 Open in the next issue of that magazine. I was thrilled, genuinely thrilled, when I read Bob's more than generous observations: "From the beginning of his career at Inverness in 1920—Sarazen has ever been the impatient, headlong player who went for everything in the hope of feeling the timely touch of inspiration. When the wand touches him, he is likely to win in a great finish as he did at Fresh Meadow and Skokie, or in a parade as he did at Prince's, but if it touch him not throughout the four rounds, the boldness of his play leaves no middle ground. When he is in the right mood, he is probably the greatest scorer in the game, possibly, that the game has ever seen."

I should like to print my card for the last 28 holes of the 1932 Open, what Bob called "the finest competitive exhibition on record."

HOLE	LENGTH	PAR	SARAZEN
45th	143	3	2
46th	385	4	4
47th	413	4	4
48th	155	3	3
49th	448	4	4
50th	219	3	2
51st	424	4	3
52nd	587	5	4
53rd	373	4	4
54th	404	4	4
55th	437	4	4
56th	395	4	5
57th	391	4	3
58th	188	3	2
59th	578	5	5
60th	428	4	3
61st	412	4	4
62nd	435	4	4
63rd	143	3	2
64th	385	4	4
65th	413	4	4
66th	155	3	3
67th	448	4	4
68th	219	3	3
69th	424	4	3
70th	587	5	5
71st	373	4	4
72nd	404	4	4

strokes for 28 holes: 100

Little,
at Prestwick and St. Anne's

by

PETER LAWLESS

1934, 1935 — FROM ACCOUNTS IN THE LONDON *MORNING POST*

THE 1934 FINAL AT PRESTWICK

THOSE who do not study the causes of the victory will say immediately that Jimmy Wallace failed to make a fight of it, and that the final came as an anticlimax to a week of golf unequaled in the championship series. But Lawson Little was ten under fours and six under par for the twenty-three holes it took him to win. That at the age of twenty-three he is a student of economics adds irony to such a score. In the first eighteen holes he was round in sixty-six, three shots better than the record established by MacDonald Smith in the Open Championship of 1925, the year in which Robert Harris beat K. F. Fradgley in the Amateur by thirteen and twelve. "But," said Harris this evening, "I did not play golf like Little." For a full round in a championship final there has been nothing to compare with it.

An early start was made to enable Little to catch the boat back to America, and there were few people present when the game started in sunshine and the mildest of breezes shortly after nine o'clock—a game that was to end at ten minutes past two. It started ominously for those hoping for Wallace's success. When he had finished his brilliant victory the day before, he had been putting with an accurate confidence that was inspiring to watch. Now, beaten by the slowness of the green, he took three to get down from the left-hand edge on the first hole. Little got a safe four, and took the lead, which he was never to lose, rapidly to swell. Wallace ran a grand approach putt up dead at the short second for a half, Little's tee-shot being dead on the flag all the way and finishing on the back of the green. Length won Little the next, for he banged a great brassie over the "Cardinal" bunker and five yards past the pin (500 yards). Wallace played quite a good approach to be on in three. Little responded by sinking his putt for a three to become two up.

Even so, optimism still ran high. Many have started thus in a thirty-six-hole match. But Wallace sent his tee-shot at the fourth into a yawning bunker beside the burn, whence only the most brilliant of recoveries can get the delinquent a half. The brilliant recovery was not forthcoming—three down. A cut-tee shot to the short fifth over the "Himalayas"—four down. Then at the sixth Little holed from twelve yards to win in three—five down—or up, according to sympathy.

The crowd was growing every minute now, but a crowd that was beginning to understand that they were onlookers at a procession. One cannot be in the gallery and join in the procession, though there were still some who had not realized that Wallace was fighting gamely against such golf as man rarely sees, and were inclined to blame him. Little was bunkered from the tee at the seventh, and Wallace missed a great chance of stemming the tide, and striking back, for he missed a putt of six feet and had to be content with a half in five. Then, after a half in four, he took three putts from the back of the ninth green to become six down, with Little out in thirty-three.

Little played a really great shot to the long tenth, to be pin high just off the green with an iron. Wallace failed to hole from seven feet, and his opponent, who had put his third three feet past the hole, became seven up. Still, Wallace was fighting, and it was greatly to his credit that, at the short eleventh, he went boldly for the hole to get his two. Had he holed that one or the return from seven feet he might still have stopped the avalanche. He failed, and from then onwards it became a question of the margin by which he would lose. Little was bunkered with his second at the next, but got his five with Wallace struggling all the way. The American played a grand iron shot twelve yards past the pin at the thirteenth. Wallace was short, and short again, to become ten down.

But this category of subjection is better replaced perhaps by one of Little's prowess. However, I will have it that Wallace never stopped fighting, fighting against golf that no player living—amateur or professional—could have checked, and certainly not overcome. Little hit the pin at the fourteenth with his second and got a three; there was a half in four with Wallace playing a fine approach, but, with his putting touch all gone, missing from three feet; Little almost driving the green at the sixteenth, chipping up and winning in three; a half in four; then Little banging his drive home to the eighteenth green (283 yards), and conceding his opponent a four-foot putt for a half in three. And so twelve up and lunch!

Little had been astounding in the morning. He left us speechless now. A putt of ten yards went down at the first for a win in three, and the end came at the short fifth, where Little was well inside with Wallace away to the left. Little's figures were:

MORNING: 4 3 3 4 3 3 5 4 4 — 33 out
           4 3 5 4 3 4 3 4 3 — 33 home — 66
AFTERNOON: 3 3 4 3 3

* * *

THE 1935 FINAL AT LYTHAM AND ST. ANNE'S

LITTLE started in his most confident, intimidating fashion, putting a chip shot at the first hole on the lip and crashing a really great iron shot home to the middle of the second green to be two up, so that from the very start Tweddell was struggling. But his were not the struggles of a drowning man. With the utmost resource, tenacity, and composure, Tweddell exercised all his golfing ability. The occasion, his opponent's lead, the jostling crowd appeared to mean nothing to him. Before he played any shot he applied his whole mind to shrewd calculation, holding his palms to test the wind, sending a caddie forward to point the line before any blind shot, leaving nothing to chance. A clever, cold-brained, dangerous opponent, ever ready to strike back at the glint of an opportunity.

Tweddell was consistently outdriven, twenty to thirty yards as a rule, eighty at times, forced to match his woods against Little's iron, yet never once did he lapse from his cold, leisurely normality and hurry his swing in hazardous pursuit of extra length. When the excited crowd applauded his shots through the green, where almost unfailingly he was playing the odd, he silenced them that Little should play undisturbed. He was greater in defeat than he could ever have been in victory—victory that he touched with his fingertips in the afternoon, to thrill us far more than is good for us.

That period of intense excitement started at the eighth in the afternoon. Tweddell holed a six-foot putt to win the ninth in two, and reduced a three-hole deficit. He halved the tenth in four, then hit the most glorious shot out of short rough to the left of the eleventh, about five feet from the pin, and holed the putt for a winning three. A roar of approbation from the crowd, pell-mell to the next teeing-ground, Tweddell the imperturbable wiping his hands on a handkerchief, the sudden hush as he took his stance, then another roar as his spoon shot soared against the blue sky to finish on the green. Little pulled his iron shot badly and followed with one of the few weak chips he had played all the week. Tweddell ran his putt up stone dead, and each man deafened his neighbor with a spontaneous bellow—"Square"—before breaking into a gallop towards the thirteenth, with the blue flags of the stewards bobbing overhead.

Order at last—by courtesy out of mulish obstinacy—Tweddell down the middle, Little pushed well out. Little played the odd over the bunkered sandhill, and then the cheering broke out again as Tweddell's second finished nine feet from the pin. But his putt was never quite firm enough, never quite on the line, and a great chance went sighing into the trees. Tweddell played a rather lucky iron shot which had enough draw and topspin to run on and on to reach the edge of the fourteenth green. Little pulled his a bit, and it was a pretty question, and, I think, the biggest of the day, as to who should play first. Little actually played, but I think out of turn, though I did not actually pace out the distances. He made a champion's thrust, running a little approach up dead—what a man! Tweddell's long approach putt ran away and finished five feet to the right of the hole; his putt hit the right lip and stayed out—one down again.

Little hit two good ones home to the fifteenth, but Tweddell's second trickled with agonizing procrastination into a bunker to the right of the green. Tweddell deliberated between two clubs, took the mashie, and, hitting the sand, only just got out. He made a gallant attempt to hole the long putt, but it slipped by—two down. At the sixteenth Little again showed what a grand fighter he is. He was bunkered with a slightly pulled second just off the green. Tweddell chipped his home six yards from the flag. Little exploded out and was just inside him. Tweddell then putted dead. Little replied by hitting his putt firmly into the hole for a half to become dormy.

It was a devastating thrust, but it did not break Tweddell. He played a shot at the seventeenth which must stamp him forever as a player of indomitable courage. He was bunkered to the right of the dog-legged seventeenth in two. At the fifteenth he had failed to chip out cleanly. Now—at the thirty-fifth hole of the match, mark you—he again took his mashie and played a delicate flick off the sand. To a thousand "Oo's!" the ball rolled straight over the hole, to stop four feet past. Little, who had cut his second, too, was twelve feet past with his approach and missed the putt. Dormy one.

All the windows of the clubhouse and the balconies were packed with spectators, a crowd ten deep was packed round the back of the eighteenth green, and now the moving gallery looped the whole fairway. Both had good drives, Tweddell was about ten yards short of the pin with his second, and Little about the same distance past. He putted first, and any hopes of three putts faded as his ball rolled to rest near the hole. Tweddell made his last great bid. The ball was firmly struck, but gradually slipped off the line to finish a few inches to the right. So the cup will cross the Atlantic again.

FIRST ROUND

LITTLE	Out:	3 4 5 4 4 5 5 3 4 — 37	
	Home:	4 3 4 4 4 4 5 4 4 — 36 — 73	
TWEDDELL	Out:	4 5 5 5 4 5 5 4 3 — 40	
	Home:	4 4 4 3 4 5 5 4 3 — 36 — 76	

SECOND ROUND

LITTLE	Out:	4 6 6 4 4 4 6 4 3 — 41	
	Home:	4 4 4 4 3 4 4 5 4 — 36 — 77	
TWEDDELL	Out:	3 5 6 4 5 5 5 5 2 — 40	
	Home:	4 3 3 4 4 5 4 4 4 — 35 — 75	

Failure of a Mission

by

HENRY LONGHURST

1941 — FROM *IT WAS GOOD WHILE IT LASTED*

THERE is only one way to travel, believe me, and that is first class at the expense of Lord Beaverbrook. That is how I went to the United States for the second time.

Being in pretty good form at the time (with the pen, I mean; journalists have their on and off periods just like anyone else), I was invited to record for the *Evening Standard* the activities of the 1936 Walker Cup team, who were to play the Americans at Pine Valley early in September, and at the same time given a roving commission to cover anything else that might appear to be of interest.

No journalist ever had a more welcome assignment. To be sent at all was a compliment that had been paid, I believe, only to one golf correspondent before—naturally Mr. Bernard Darwin. Incidentally, a member of the team fell ill, Mr. Darwin took the last place—and won his match. I suspect that the same thing very nearly happened to me, but we needn't go into that.

Of a million golfers in Britain it falls to a tiny percentage to make the Walker Cup pilgrimage to America. Some of the best would give a year's income for the experience. I was getting it for nothing. Couldn't be better.

We set out in an atmosphere of bitter controversy. We were to travel on the *Transylvania* which, if it docked to schedule, would still leave the team less than a week for prac-

tice. The *Queen Mary*, recently put into service, was sailing at exactly the convenient time. Why not the *Queen Mary?*

However, last-minute intrigues failed to get the team transferred to the *Queen Mary*, and so one dark night we converged one by one upon an unprepossessing Glasgow quay and groped our way on board the good ship *Transylvania*. (Three or four months ago I shed a nostalgic tear over the news that she had been sunk while serving as an auxiliary cruiser.)

We were an odd assortment. Whether the team were the ten best golfers in Great Britain I'm not prepared to say, but geographically representative they certainly were—and for that reason I had my doubts as to whether they would not very soon be falling out among themselves.

Harmony on these outings depends largely, as you'll agree if you've taken part in one, on the captain. Our captain—I say "our," for although I was not officially attached to the team I was at once invited to consider myself as such, despite the last-minute assurance of the secretary of the R. and A. that it was "against all precedent" to have a Walker Cup team contaminated by journalists—our captain was a thirty-nine-year-old Midland practitioner, Dr. William Tweddell.

A reserved, amiable fellow was Tweddell, all for a quiet life. I doubted his ability to hold his miscellaneous crew together without friction. After all, he had nothing closer than a nodding acquaintance with any of them, and their ages, their interests and outlook on life, their incomes, even their accents, were as divergent as could be. I could see them, as the half-empty *Transylvania* bored its leisurely way across the Atlantic with a load of Middle West sightseers, getting on each other's nerves, or worse, breaking up into cliques.

We were, as I say, a motley crew—four Scotsmen, an Irishman, a Lancastrian, a Midlander, three Londoners (stockbroker, undergraduate, and schoolboy), and the official scribe. Of the Scots, Hector Thomson, by virtue of his amateur championship, was reckoned our leading golfer, with Jack McLean a close second. Golf was their abiding interest. Gordon Peters was another fine Glasgow player, though more catholic in his tastes, while the irrepressible Morton Dykes, who had played Rugby football for Scotland, was by that time a purely week-end golfer. He earned his place on his play in the championship a few weeks before, yet he confessed that he had really had no intention of playing in it. He only entered, he said, because it was at St. Andrews—and he always enjoyed a week at St. Andrews.

The Irishman was Cecil Ewing, a bespectacled giant from Sligo with a mighty drive and strong political principles. Harry Bentley, with his typically Lancastrian shrewdness and gay philosophical wit, was the "character" of the party.

Alec Hill, Laddie Lucas, and John Langley represented the pampered south—and the old school tie. When the selectors had left a couple of places open till the championship results were known, Hill, a semifinalist, got one of them. He, too, was the purest week-end golfer (a compliment, this), and had gone to St. Andrews for no better reason than that a friend of his canceled his room in the hotel at the last moment, and so left it available for Hill. Rather "thin on the top," this pillar of the London Stock Exchange looked the oldest member of the party. He was, in fact, twenty-eight. We found that we had much in common.

Lucas at the time of his selection was in his second year at Cambridge and was to be captain the following year. He had the physique of an athlete, had been captain of cricket and

football at Stowe, and was probably the best left-hander in the world at that time.

If Lucas, chosen while still an undergraduate, was *rara avis*, Langley was *rarissima*. He was chosen during his last holiday from Stowe, before ever he went as a freshman to Cambridge. Indeed, he was the youngest player ever chosen by either side.

Well, for two days we felt our way cautiously, each on his best behavior, especially in the presence of the head master, Bill Tweddell. A comparatively insignificant incident broke the ice on the second night out. The head master had a second glass of kümmel with his dinner.

Golfing excellence, unlike excellence in most other games, goes hand in hand with alcohol, as many an Open and Amateur champion has shown. Incidentally, Harry Vardon had the last word on this subject. When, during the last war, a woman asked him to join the temperance movement, he replied: "Moderation is essential in all things, madam, *but never in my life have I failed to beat a teetotaler.*"

We arrived in New York and berthed insignificantly beside the *Queen Mary*. She had come in on the previous day, having left six days after us, and had broken the record. It was all rather galling.

Every one who plays golf has heard of Pine Valley, few have had the luck to play there. I look on it as the greatest of all inland courses, the perfect "examination" of the golfer's physical and psychological powers. It was cut at spectacular expense from some virgin forest slopes fifteen miles below Philadelphia, and such is Pine Valley's challenge to the conceit of American golfers, such is the legend of its defiance to mere man, that the club has two thousand country members, some of them living three thousand miles away.

The singular difficulty of Pine Valley is easily described. It has no rough, in the accepted sense of the term, and no semirough. Your ball is either on the fairway, in which case it sits invitingly on a flawless carpet of turf, or it is not. If it is not, you play out sideways till it is. In a week's golf, including the Walker Cup match, I saw no single recovery shot, as we use the expression. You don't make "recoveries" at Pine Valley, except of course from the sand traps—you merely push your way into the undergrowth and endeavor to knock your ball out through the bushes to where it ought to have been in the first place.

The sand bunkers are desert wastes left bare and unraked round the greens. Small bushes grow in them, and no one is expected to smooth out his footprints. The greens, like the fairways, are perfect—once you get there. Par is seventy—with two long holes that no man has ever reached in two, and four short holes.

One of these, the fifth, may be the greatest golf hole in the world. Green and tee are on a level, two hundred and twenty-five yards apart, but between the two lies a vast depression, with a lake full of turtles and other unlikely creatures. The green itself, long and narrow, slopes sheer away on the right, and a ball that misses the green bobbles merrily down until stopped by a tree trunk. On the left a gravel pit gnaws its way into the green. To ensure a satisfactory level of casualties the club committee are in the habit of placing the flag far back in the left-hand corner.

I never forgot this fifth hole after our 1930 visit to Pine Valley. On the voyage across I enlarged upon its terrors to the team, none of whom had seen it before. The time came at last to play it once again. "I've waited six years for this shot," I observed—and nothing shall stop me from telling the rest of the story. The drive flew straight for the flag—just enough "draw" to keep it from slipping down into the forest on the right, not enough to take it into the gravel pit. It finished, amid murmurs of applause, my own perhaps the most audible, nine feet from the hole; and the putt ran gently in for a two. Nothing much mattered after that. I was out, very cocksure, in thirty-four—but let no man rejoice at Pine Valley till the last putt is safely bottled in the hole. It took me forty-one to get home.

They'll lay odds of anything up to ten to one against the ordinary scratch golfer breaking eighty in his first round at Pine Valley, and they are rarely known to lose. There's a tradition at the club—I know of no parallel—that the cup of misfortune must be drained to the dregs, and no man shall pick up his ball midway to save the ultimate ignominy of revealing his score. Each hole carries its legend of tragedy to some victim or other. Roger Wethered's name, for instance, will always be linked with the eighth, a mere drive and a pitch—though what a pitch! The plateau green is microscopically small and pretty well surrounded by sand. Poor Roger, going strongly at the time, pitched in the sand. Thence he went to and fro, from sand unto sand, and holed out in eleven.

One partner of mine completed the shortest hole on the course in twenty-three. Laddie Lucas was another who fell. Like so many left-handed players he was liable to spells of inaccuracy. He started "spraying" his tee-shots, as the Americans say—and Pine Valley is no place for the sprayer. In three rounds that I played with him before the match his lowest total was ninety-four—a score which in England, even at the age of twenty, he probably had not taken once in the past six years.

It was in one of these rounds that his caddie made an observation that will cling to Lucas to the end of his days. He and the caddie had already spent most of their time in the woods when at the seventh hole Lucas hit another wild, curving slice that soared away over the forest. "Watch it," he cried. "Watch it!"

"You don't have to watch 'em," said the caddie, "you gotta listen for 'em."

Incidentally, while we are talking of caddies—here is an "It couldn't happen here" story. I was standing one evening at the bar of the roadhouse a mile or two from Pine Valley in which I stayed for the match, when I fell into conversation with a good-looking young American, attired in "faultless evening dress" and accompanied by an equally elegant young woman with corn-colored hair. After the inevitable comparisons of conditions in Great Britain and the United States, we fell to talking of the prospects for the Walker Cup match and the performances of the various players in practice. He had been there during the day, it seemed, and was thoroughly familiar with the contestants on both sides. He criticized their style with an obvious knowledge of the game, and later events bore out his judgment in picking Gordon Peters as one of the best of our team.

Next day I saw him again on the course. He was Morton Dykes's caddie.

Both the Walker Cup teams were lodged in the Pine Valley clubhouse, and it wasn't long, if the truth be told, before the suspense, the solitude, and the pine-scented stuffiness of the atmosphere began to get on the nerves of the British side.

Tweddell in these circumstances made an ideal captain. He combined firmness with his natural amiability, and his reward was the life-long friendship and respect of ten fellows from all walks of life whom he scarcely knew before. The loyalty of the team (not always, I may add, a feature of such outings) broke down Tweddell's innate reserve, and he made a great hit with the Americans. One night at a roadhouse, when the team's identity became known, Tweddell was dragged to a spotlighted microphone and made a speech that had two or three hundred people standing on chairs to applaud. I fancy he'd never have backed himself to do such a thing when he left Glasgow.

The American team turned up at Pine Valley soon after ourselves and it was amusing to hear that two of them, Scotty Campbell and Harry Givan, had traveled farther to reach the club than we had. They had come from Seattle.

It didn't take long to realize that all these young full-time American golfers were not only a cut above our own full-timers in the shape of Thomson and McLean, but could give fifty yards in a hundred to week-end amateurs like Tweddell, Hill, Dykes, and Ewing, who played golf largely for their own amusement. They were suitably impressed, but not the least frightened, by the course. Its tightness only accentuated their superiority. To ask some of our team to play round Pine Valley was like sending a boy for a scholarship when he could not pass a common entrance exam.

The Americans were captained by Francis Ouimet (pronounced "We met"), one of the gentlest and most respected personalities in the game, who had earned immortality twenty-three years previously when, as an ex-caddie of nineteen, he beat Harry Vardon and Ted Ray in the play-off for the United States Open championship at The Country Club, Brookline.

I suppose their best player was Johnny Goodman, a tough, ruthless little fellow from Omaha with an astonishing facial resemblance to Lord Mandeville—well aware of his own ability and with no hesitation about rubbing it in.

"Good shot!" cried a spectator ecstatically.

"I'll say!" said Goodman. Three years before, at the age of twenty-four, he had won the United States Open, starting with a sixty-six and finishing with a string of fours and threes.

Four of their side hailed from the South, and wickedly good players they were too: Ed White, from Texas, slim and dark with humorous film-star eyes; Walter Emery, of Oklahoma City, a big, happy-go-lucky fellow of infinite jest; Reynolds Smith, from Dallas, stocky, dark, and determined; and Charles Yates, a wise-cracking, happy-go-lucky young protégé of Bobby Jones down in Atlanta. So infectious, incidentally, were Yates's high spirits that two years later he accomplished the unprecedented feat of standing on the steps of the Royal and Ancient clubhouse at St. Andrews after the Walker Cup match and inducing the crowd to accompany him in *A Wee Doch and Doris*.

The voices of this quartet intrigued their British visitors, who had not heard the like except in the movies and had hardly believed it then. Their average age was twenty-three, which in golfing maturity is equivalent perhaps to thirty over here. They chewed stubs of black cigars and let forth a barrage of wise-cracking good humor. Emery had a broad-brimmed hat and needed only a lasso hanging from his golf bag to complete the picture.

The remaining Americans were George Voigt, an old campaigner at thirty-nine; Johnny Fischer, of Cincinnati, long-legged, shock-headed, and nervously reticent, a truly magnificent golfer; and amiable George Dunlap, New York "socialite" and an old friend of mine, who was already beginning to suspect that sixty-nines round golf courses were not the end-all and be-all of life.

When the great day arrived, it was seen that the two captains, though each had had a seventy in practice, had left themselves out of the teams, Ouimet remarking characteristically: "Waal, I've been at this game a long enough time to give these young boys a chance to get some of the nice things of golf." Lucas was dropped, inevitably, from our team, Dunlap from theirs.

We had a lovely day for the match, warm and easy, and the remoteness of Pine Valley kept the crowd down to people genuinely anxious to see the golf. No sightseers; no peanuts.

I am afraid I had come to the conclusion before the start that if the match were to be played under identical conditions ten times we should be lucky to win it once. I think most of the team knew it too. We buoyed ourselves up with the hope that this might be the tenth time—but it wasn't long before we saw that it was going to be one of the other nine. I don't think that collectively a better team than these ten young Americans ever played in a Walker Cup match.

Tweddell, on the principle of not putting his two best eggs in one basket, split up the Thomson-McLean partnership, putting Bentley to play top with Thomson and Langley second with McLean. Peters and Dykes were third, Hill and Ewing fourth.

Incidentally, it was simple enough for the spectators to tell the teams apart. Every one of our side except Bentley wore the "national costume" of white shirt and gray flannel trousers. Bentley wore a pair of trousers that had already been "written up" by every American correspondent. A spectator had come up to him and remarked with a knowing air: "It's easy enough to tell you're English by the cut of your trousers." Harry's reply was: "Yes, they're good, aren't they? I bought them in Clementon the other day for a dollar sixty-nine!" It was quite true.

By lunch time our four pairs were five down, one down, one up, and four down, respectively. By half-past three in the afternoon I knew I was going to have to cable home a score card of four noughts out of four.

Thomson and Bentley had been one up on Goodman and Campbell after ten holes in the morning—and then the deluge. They lost six holes out of the remaining eight and were five down. McLean and Langley, temperamentally ill-fitted to each other as it turned out, held on well enough to be only one down to Reynolds and White. Our third pair played some magnificent golf and were round in seventy-three against seventy-five by Yates and Emery, which gave them the only hole on the credit side of the balance. Hill and Ewing, bringing up the rear, lost the last two holes to Givan and Voigt and finished four down, seemingly outclassed.

Luncheon and mint juleps revived our spirits—I can still hear the old colored servants offering their inevitable first course of "cante-

lupe, rassp-*berries*, or snapper soup"—and we consoled ourselves with much wishful thinking, to use the current cliché, regarding the second and third pairs.

For thirteen holes in the afternoon Thomson and Bentley were only two over fours, but there was no arguing with Goodman and Campbell. They won two more holes and the match by seven and five. Worse was to come. Langley and McLean, full of hope, lost the first four holes and were scuttled almost before they were launched. Poor McLean, he lived for golf. I recall his saying: "I have been playing serious golf for eleven years and I have been a good many down without losing heart. This is the first time I have had my spirit really broken." They lost by eight and seven.

So it seemed that if we were to save anything from the wreck, enough at any rate to preserve any interest in the morrow's play, Peters and Dykes had to win at number three. What a match that was! And what a hero was Peters! They began, unpromisingly enough, with three fives, and were lucky not to lose more than the single hole by which they had led. It was Peters who turned the scale by slamming an iron shot to within a couple of feet at the fourth. At the sixth he holed a twelve-footer. When I said that I saw no "recovery" shot played at Pine Valley, I was wrong. I saw one. It was played by Peters at the seventh and I remember it well. The hole is, I suppose, one of the most architecturally perfect long holes in the world. The drive has to be placed on the left-hand side of an island of turf between the woods. The second has to carry one hundred and twenty yards of sand and scrub to a second island. The third has to pitch on a green which is itself an island surrounded by sand. The hole is about five hundred and eighty yards long.

Dykes hooked their second shot, thus to all intents declaring a minimum of six, but Peters, up to his knees in grass among the poplar trees, hacked their ball onto the green and followed it up by lofting it into the hole from seven feet over a stymie.

Some more wild shots by Dykes lost them the eighth and tenth and at the eleventh the Americans had such luck as I never did see. Emery hooked his drive round his neck into the forest and we heard it clattering about among the trees, when suddenly it was seen to ricochet high into the air and fall on the fairway. Yates hit a glorious spoon shot to within seven feet of the flag, when by rights he should have been crawling about on all fours in the undergrowth, and Emery, of course, holed the putt for a three. They went on with another three at the twelfth and suddenly, instead of three down, found themselves one up.

Peters banged another long iron shot to the pin at the fifteenth and they won it with a four —the hole is six hundred and five yards long, over a lake and then uphill all the way; so far as I know, no man has ever reached it in two— and Dykes came in with a fine second from an awkward place at the seventeenth, and an equally awkward putt for a half. All square with one to play.

I trembled for poor Dykes, for the last drive is played from a considerable height down to a fairway sloping from left to right and bounded by every kind of horror, but he came up trumps and the ball was seen, amid gasps of British relief, to finish in play. It never entered anyone's head that the Americans would take more than four, and so Peters was left with his last iron shot, over the lake and up to the plateau green between the trees. It had to be high—not easy from a downhill lie— and it had to be long. I stood beside him as he played it, and can certify that it was both. "Marvelous," said I. "Aye—trembling with bravery!" he said.

So Peters and Dykes halved their match, and their half point, it seemed, was to be the extent of our ration from the four matches. Hill and Ewing had lost three of the first six holes to be seven down, and frankly neither I nor anyone else paid much further attention to them. It did not seem to matter very much whether they lost by twelve and eleven, or thirteen and twelve.

When Hill holed a four-yarder with his old aluminum putter to win the long seventh in four, he can scarcely have dreamed that he was starting one of the most astonishing "comebacks" in Walker Cup history. But so it proved. He holed another good one on the ninth, and Ewing ran down a ten-yarder for a two on the tenth. Back to four down.

The Americans exploded from a bunker to within one inch of the hole on the eleventh, but Hill kept things going with a seven-footer. He had another for a "birdie" three at the twelfth and the next they won easily. Only two down now, and the Americans clearly shaken. Such treatment was unusual from English golfers. At this critical moment Hill played an excellent stroke to the island green at the fourteenth. To see the British ball sitting serenely on the green below would have made Voigt distinctly uneasy—but, alas, Hill had taken the wrong club and his ball sailed over the green and fell with a splash into the lake beyond. Three down with four to play.

Young Givan, showing distinct signs of strain, went into the trees at the long fifteenth, though in the end Hill had to hole from four yards to win it. Ewing in turn found the forest at the next, but Givan obliged by doing likewise and Britain won the hole. We had a perfect four at the seventeenth and, thanks to a slice by Givan, won it. All square with one to play.

Givan with the brilliance so often born of despair hit a beauty to within ten feet of the eighteenth, while Ewing's was every inch of fifteen yards away. Could he and Hill get this ball down in two between them, and could Voigt fail with his ten-footer?

The answer was yes. Hill judged the long one to a nicety, and Voigt, going boldly for the hole, overran by three feet. Not for a hundred dollars would I have changed places with Harry Givan as he tried to sink that putt. In deathly silence he pushed it nervously towards the hole. It toppled in at its last gasp.

So two halves left us something to play for in the singles after all, and after the gloom of mid-afternoon there was something approaching jubilation in the camp. Alas, it took no time at all on the following morning to see that these Americans, if some of them were fallible in foursome play, to which they were unaccustomed, were quite unbeatable once they were on their own. I won't go into details. Suffice to say that at luncheon the British positions in the eight matches were two down, all square, two down, eight down, three down, four down, two down, five down. A melancholy catalogue. Yet our first three performers, Thomson, McLean, and Ewing, had had scores of seventy-four, seventy-three, and seventy-five.

In the afternoon there was no holding the

Americans. Goodman polished off Thomson by nonchalantly rolling in a five-yard putt at the thirty-fourth. Campbell put paid to McLean with the three threes in a row. Fischer, three under fours for eleven holes, saw Ewing off the course to the tune of eight and seven. Yates, most devastating of the lot, beat Dykes by as much. His afternoon figures are worth quoting, bearing in mind the course on which they were played. They were: 4, 4, 4, 3, 3, 4, 4, 4, 4, 3, 3.

Langley could do nothing at all with White, though his swing remained polished and smooth to the end. Only Bentley and Peters made any sort of impression. Peters went gallantly round in seventy-two which, jointly with Goodman's morning round, was the lowest score of the day, but he only won two holes back from Emery and that was just one too few. And so it was left to Bentley to hole a putt of one yard before the assembled multitude to credit Britain with a solitary half out of eight matches. He was round in seventy-six.

The British side of the scoreboard looked like a daisy chain, with twelve noughts one beneath the other. I settled down to cable the mournful tale and felt more than ever convinced that I should never live to see the Walker Cup won by Great Britain.

For the sake of the record here are the scores:

FOURSOMES

Great Britain		United States	
H. Thomson		J. Goodman	
H. Bentley	0	A. E. Campbell (7 and 5)	1
J. McLean		Reynolds Smith	
J. D. A. Langley	0	E. White (8 and 7)	1
G. Peters		C. Yates	
J. M. Dykes	0	W. Emery	0
G. A. Hill		J. L. Givan	
C. Ewing	0	G. J. Voigt	0

SINGLES

H. Thomson	0	J. Goodman (3 and 2)	1
J. McLean	0	A. E. Campbell (5 and 4)	1
C. Ewing	0	J. Fischer (8 and 7)	1
G. A. Hill	0	Reynolds Smith (11 and 9)	1
G. Peters	0	W. Emery (1 hole)	1
J. M. Dykes	0	C. Yates (8 and 7)	1
H. G. Bentley	0	G. Dunlap	0
J. D. A. Langley	0	E. White (6 and 5)	1

Guldahl Wins
the Masters

by

WILLIAM D. RICHARDSON

1939 — FROM THE MAY ISSUE OF *GOLF*

To THE accompaniment of something new —a real hailstorm that spattered off players' domes like machine-gun bullets at a gangsters' lawn party—another Masters tournament has passed into history, leaving behind another epochal performance, namely, Ralph Guldahl's great finish.

Almost every Masters tourney since the very beginning has left something to posterity, such as Gene Sarazen's "double-eagle" on the fifteenth hole which enabled him to tie Craig Wood whom he then beat in a play-off, back in '35, or Guldahl's misfortune at the twelfth hole two years ago when he lost three strokes to Byron Nelson who went on to win a title that only a few moments before seemed irretrievably lost. This one had everything that goes to make up a sensational, nerve-racking tournament and sustained interest right up to the very last shot. First of all there was the great 69 by Billy Burke, Cleveland veteran, in the opening round when he led the pack of hand-picked stars. That was followed by Sarazen's 66 which must go down in history as one of the great rounds of all time, even surpassing the 66 he made in the last round of the U. S. Open Championship at Fresh Meadow in '32 when he played the last twenty-eight holes of the championship in precisely 100 strokes to squeeze Bobby Cruickshank and Phil Perkins into second place.

And then came the final act with Guldahl, fully cognizant of what he had to do on the last nine holes if he wanted to beat Sam Snead, actually doing it and gaining the coveted title with a record score of 279.

The story of the '39 Masters, sixth in the series of tournaments played over the Augusta National course in commemoration of Bobby Jones's great achievements before he retired with the first and only "Grand Slam" to his credit, deals chiefly with Guldahl's final nine which represented perhaps the greatest "pressure" golf ever played.

As the big, droop-shouldered Open champion came off the ninth green on that final swing, he heard the announcer on the eighteenth, which is adjacent, call out: "Sam Snead, 68. Total, 280." That meant that he (Guldahl) had to finish in thirty-three strokes in order to win. Which is precisely what he did!

On the tenth hole, which architect Perry D. Maxwell had made into one of the finest two-shotters to be found anywhere in the world (he also did a fine job on the seventh, making it a fine drive and pitch hole), Guldahl got a birdie 3 which must have been encouraging, for Snead had missed a three-foot putt there and taken a 5. Guldahl could have had a birdie 3 on the eleventh for his ball landed only a club's length from the hole and skidded across the green. Even then he almost sank his putt, the ball stopping dead in line, only four inches short.

Now he faced the hole that ruined his chances two years before when his ball landed on the bank and rolled back into the water from where he had to drop out and finally take a 5 which was followed by a 6 at the next while Nelson, coming along later, made a 2 and a 3, a birdie and eagle, to pick up six shots!

Nothing like that happened this year, however, for Guldahl went straight for the pin and stopped his ball within five feet of the cup for another crack at a birdie—which he missed.

So here he was, with six holes left to play in two under par in order to win—and most of them treacherous ones where strokes can vanish with amazing rapidity. Then came the shot that almost matched Sarazen's famous brassie second that went into the hole for a "deuce," three under par. This one was made, not on the fifteenth where Sarazen's was, but on the thirteenth—a dog's-leg to the left with a ravine skirting the left-hand edge of the fairway most of the way up to the green where it veers to the right, protecting the front and the right-hand side of the putting surface. Guldahl's tee-shot was none too long. In fact it was "skied" a bit and on the short side. From even farther along both Sarazen and Picard, the defending title-holder, had refused to gamble, taking irons and playing safe. Not Guldahl! Despite the distance to be carried in order to clear the creek—at least 230 yards—and a side-hill lie, big Ralph jerked out a No. 3 wood and tore into the ball, sending it on a low trajectory and in a dead line for the pin which was cut dangerously close to the right-hand edge—less than thirty feet from the creek.

No sooner had the ball left the clubhead than the crowd, greatest in Masters history—more than 8,000, it was estimated—let up a roar, for it was plain to see that it would wind up somewhere on the green which would have been an achievement in itself. But it did better than that. It ran almost up to the pin, topping less than six feet away from where he putted it in for an eagle 3!

And there the title was won, for all he had to do now was to watch his step from there in which is what he did, getting a "hard" 4 on the fourteenth, a great 4 (almost an eagle 3) on the fifteenth where Sarazen made his "double-eagle," a par on the short sixteenth, and a par 4 on the eighteenth, after wasting a stroke on the seventeenth where his second shot went over the green, causing him to take a 5.

A word about his 4 on the home hole. Having just lost his "insurance" when he took the 5 at the seventeenth, Guldahl was in a rather ticklish position playing the last hole on which a 5 is not very hard to take since the tee-shot must be perfectly placed in order to be able to get into the green from the right angle.

Guldahl's drive was almost as perfect as if he had carried the ball and placed it in the most favorable spot he could find—dead for the green's opening. He started out to use a No. 4 iron, but changed to a No. 3 and sent the ball on a bee-line for the back edge of the green from where he had only to dribble it down and tap it into the hole for his 4. And that was that.

Nelson at His Peak

by

ARTHUR MANN

1945 — FROM AN AUGUST ISSUE OF *COLLIER'S*

SIX YEARS AGO, after six years of professional golf, John Byron Nelson ironed out his difficulties, so to speak, with an amazing string of successes, topped by a triple tie with Craig Wood and Denny Shute in the United States Open and a victory in the three-cornered play-off. At the end of the year, he surveyed a batch of cups and prizes and a cushion of cash in the bank.

"Well, honey," he said to his pretty wife, "Ah sure can't play any better than that."

His wife, the former Louise Shofner, smiled and attended to her knitting, which consists chiefly of Argyll socks, those varicolored plaid things that require eighty-nine needles, as many balls of yarn and a slide rule to keep track of stitches. Of course, she knocks off a cable-stitch pullover now and then, but her specialty, as she travels with her husband, is those dazzling hose, which rival golfers envy almost as much as Nelson's magic with the short irons. She disagreed with his silly notion six years ago about reaching the saturation point of golf skill, but withheld comment, because she knew that deep down he probably didn't believe it either.

And it wasn't true, as Nelson proved by knocking off Sam Snead for his first PGA Championship at Hershey, Pennsylvania, the next year. Nelson's old Texas caddie rival, little

Ben Hogan, was top money winner for the campaign, but Nelson had improved his financial position no end. Still, as the year closed, he said, "Well, honey, Ah sure can't play any better than *that.*"

"Try this on for size, dear," the little woman replied. "The heel seems a little full."

If you have been amazed by the phenomenal rise of Byron Nelson, consider his personal astonishment after each annual confession about not playing any better. Sectional titles and big-money specials have gone his way. At Christmastime last year, his winnings in War Bonds totaled $47,600, a nice amount in any business, and more so in golf, with most championship tournaments frozen by war. But Nelson managed to make all stops, between appearances in Red Cross and hospital benefits (he played one hundred such exhibitions in 1943). With a 1944 "take" of close to $50,000, the old refrain about not getting any better was understandable. Even rival golfers called his game the closest ever to perfection.

"Sure Ah said it again last year," he confesses. "An' Ah meant it more'n Ah ever did." Yet before the echo of his gloomy and repetitious prophecy had died down, he was making a shambles of the 1945 golfing situation. Just look at his pickings for the first five months:

January	$4,600.00
February	2,685.00
March	4,312.50
April	1,687.50
May	9,330.00
	$22,615.00

Very warm for May. However, except for the weather, Nelson found June an ideal month, with $5,333.33 won in the first two weeks. He shot a 268 in the Canadian PGA Championship at Montreal, starting with a round of 63, and finished twenty strokes under par and ten under McSpaden. In the PGA Rehabilitation Fund tournament on the Llanerch Club course in Philadelphia a week later, he trailed McSpaden, Jimmy Hines and Johnny Bulla for three rounds. Nelson didn't even make a headline until the final round, when he turned in a record-breaking 64 that knocked three strokes off the course record and flattened poor McSpaden, who had equaled the course mark with a 66 to total 271. Nelson had shot 269. The Mechanical Master was two under par through the first dozen holes of that final round. At the twelfth, they told him that McSpaden, who had started with a one-stroke lead, had shot an eagle on the seventh hole. Nelson pulled his pitching wedge from the bag. It's a deep-faced niblick, devised in 1929 and actually the only new club introduced in more than a quarter-century. It's called a dynamiter and a sand wedge, but the current wizard calls it "my half-Nelson, because I can always strangle the opposition with it." Finishing under pressure from his best friend, Nelson towroped the Philadelphia field, and the pitching wedge did the trick. On the thirteenth he blasted from the sand within an inch of the cup for a birdie. He pitched to within four inches of the cup on the fifteenth for a birdie, and two inches from the cup for another on the eighteenth. Five birdies on the last six holes for a 30!

"It was the hottest stretch of golf Ah ever played," Nelson declared. "Ah don't guess Ah'll ever beat that." It was undoubtedly some of the hottest golf anybody has ever played, but that business about never doing any better—well, he should start wondering about the rest of the golfing world. No player in the game's history has ever stood so supreme above the opposition.

The war is on, you might bear in mind. Otherwise, Nelson's position might be a little less secure. Perhaps, but statistics and experts argue to the contrary. No one in service (and Nelson would be uniformed were he not 4F) could match his current par-shattering steadiness or his nerveless competitive spirit without a year or more of practice and preparation. The victory in Philadelphia was Nelson's sixth straight tournament triumph for a PGA record. He had won at Charlotte, Greensboro, Durham, Atlanta and Montreal. He has the financial distinction of being a money winner in eighty-seven consecutive tournaments. From January 1 through June 17 he played twenty-four rounds of competitive golf to average 67.45 strokes for each eighteen holes, or 3.75 strokes per hole.

The wonder of this mild-mannered and humble Texan is that he can be topped by specialists in practically all phases of the game. He appears to do no single thing better than someone else you might name, yet none of the specialists can be called a better golfer. There is nothing freakish about his personality and less about his game. You cannot single out any phase of it as better than another. Nelson is deadly serious about life and golf, but wholly without delusions of grandeur or his own importance. He expects V-J Day to let loose a batch of repressed golf addicts who will topple the existing champions within a year. His humility is the backbone of his game, and therein you will find the answer to the man himself and to his mechanical technique.

For years, Nelson's driving was a major problem. He couldn't even use a driver. Some would say that the ball wouldn't rise. But Nelson admits that *he* couldn't raise the trajectory. He gripped the club wrong for years. In trying to loft the ball with a driver, which has an almost vertical face, he'd hook. He escaped financial ruin by the simple expedient of using a brassie off the tee. The slanted face gave him the desired height. With the brassie he worked to correct the faulty grip, perfected his swing by making it normal to eliminate the hook, and eventually mastered the use of a driver. He learned exactly what he could do with this club, and he charges his success to the fact that he is always conscious of his limitations.

This early regimentation became his forte.

His self-analysis amounted to introspection, but in it Nelson found the answer to his mistakes. Today he is a study in humility that stands as an indictment of anyone who labors under the silly delusion that he can play golf, for Nelson has never played a "satisfactory" round. How far below 63 is satisfactory, he wouldn't say, but conveys the general idea this way:

"There's always a mistake in the best round. An honest golfer takes eagles and birdies for granted. He profits by remembering what he did wrong, and never by gloating over what he may have managed to do right." Nelson believes that the average golfer could lower his score and perhaps live longer by injecting a maximum of humility into his habit of self-analysis. Golf addicts are necessarily introverts, constantly studying themselves with all the intensity of a woman before a mirror, but they seldom get around to recognizing their specific limitations until too late. He has seen a lot of tempers lost and has watched the game become a psychological millstone. He is startled by the fact that more than a few doctors in prewar days were toying with the idea of discarding golf as a medium of relaxation for patients because it was too often the opposite. And it wasn't golf's fault; it was because the average human likes to think himself capable of doing more than he ever will.

"If the playing foundation is right, which it seldom is," Nelson adds, "habit and ego fortify the beginner. He buys a set of clubs, or receives a set as a gift. Some are too heavy or too light for his physique. He goes to a strange golf course with no knowledge of its distances or subtleties for a hit-or-miss afternoon, with fewer hits than misses. When the game's complexities finally conquer him, he decides to 'take a few lessons.' The poor pro at the club faces a horrible mess. He wants to tell the guy to burn his clubs, that his faults have become habits and too fixed for correction. But the pro can't chase away business, so he tackles it as honestly as possible. He advises the lift of a heel, the twist of a wrist, foot-movement, weight-shifting. All are undoubtedly good suggestions, but it's like adding a few shingles to a roof that leaks all over. It needs a completely new surface."

A teacher cannot do it alone, Nelson contends. It's up to the golfer himself, but the victim quickly becomes a golfing hypochondriac through substituting alibis and excuses for simple admission of limitations. "A golfer, good or bad, must face reality and shortcomings like a pro," Nelson insists, "and practice with honesty and patience, not to eliminate faults, but to find out what his body can do, and build his game around those shots. If a player's best drive is 225 yards, the length of the hole shouldn't make him try for 300. But no, he wants a 300-yard drive and an easy mid-iron shot that will put him on the green for a one-putt and an eagle that he can talk about for a week at the office. So he winds up in the woods, takes an eight on the hole and spends a miserable afternoon."

This is not advice from a born golfer, but from a former caddie of Fort Worth, Texas, who has spent fifteen years at hard labor trying to correct his own mistakes. His early zeal and interest captivated members of the Glen Garden Club, and they sponsored his career with a junior membership. Only sixteen, Nelson showed his gratitude by winning the club's junior title. He quit high school to clerk for the Fort Worth & Denver City R.R. and had more time for golf. He first played professionally in late November of 1932 in the Texarkana $500 Open, placing third behind Ted Longworth and Ky Laffoon to win $75. Backed by the Glen Garden members, the situation looked very rosy, but he won only $12.50 more during that winter.

Two years later, he won $924 and the pretty Louise Shofner, also a Texan. With a wife to support, Nelson threw away his driver and used a brassie off the tee. The next year, 1935, he took down $2,708, and followed that with a victory in the Metropolitan Open, his first plum. He's been picking them steadily ever since.

Nelson ridicules the frequent suggestion that golf courses of today are easier than a generation ago, and that Bobby Jones's scores of 280-290 wouldn't get him very far in today's sub-270's. "If Jones or Hagen or any of the past masters had needed a 270 to win," Nelson says, "they'd have shot it. Neither the courses, ball nor clubs have changed. Bigger prizes, more tournaments, and more competition force players to keep in shape and practice at all times. They can't afford to risk a single week of idleness, because they know that a dozen others are hard at work. They know that one bad shot—one shot, mind you—may cost them a thousand bucks.

"Ah don't kid myself for a minute about my own position, because Ah expect to get knocked off by the kids coming up or coming out of the service. Ah've seen a couple already in Army camps that made me blink. If the PGA can put up all the golf courses we'd like to right next to those hospitals, you'll see the hottest golf the game has ever known—much better than Ah expect to play. . . ."

The Affluent Hillbilly

by

BOB HARLOW

1949 — FROM THE NOVEMBER ISSUE OF *GOLF WORLD*

IT WAS A NIPPY fall afternoon, Wednesday, November the ninth, as the parade moved slowly along that portion of U.S. Highway 60 which is the main street of White Sulphur Springs, West Virginia. Samuel Jackson Snead sat beside the Negro driver on top of the elegant old stagecoach of 1870, pulled by two mountain mules, Jack and Jim. The mules followed a brass band and four companies of cadets from the Greenbrier Military School in nearby Lewisburg. Main Street was crowded, for White Sulphur Springs. Everybody in the mountain village knew that the New Greenbrier Hotel was celebrating Sam Snead Day to honor the resort's popular professional, The Golfer of the Year. Children rattled noisemakers, and grown-ups along the route applauded and shouted compliments as Sam passed in review atop the coach which for many years was used to ferry guests from the Chesapeake & Ohio railroad station to and from the Old Greenbrier. The coach is the only old thing the management of the New Greenbrier tolerates.

The parade was the opening number of Sam Snead Day which reached its peak that evening when the golfing clan of the mountains gathered with a number of city slickers in the Old White Clubroom of the New Greenbrier. The cocktail party and the dinner which followed were a real homecoming for the Sneads and their friends. Sam was happy his broth-

ers and their wives and his sister and her husband and most of his nephews and nieces were able to be present for the ceremonies— Lyle and his wife Virginia; Homer and his wife Alice and their four children; Janet and her husband, C. W. Stinespring, and their six children; Jesse and his wife Sylvia and their four children; Pete and his wife Lucy and their four children. Sam and his wife Audrey, with one child, Samuel Jackson, Jr., are a bit under par for the Sneads on the population score card. Sam's parents, who were both natives of Virginia, are dead. Pete, who is the pro at The Cascades Golf Club in Hot Springs, Virginia, the Sneads' hometown, is the only other pro in the family.

Sam's wife, Audrey, was a grade- and high-school classmate of his. Harold Bell, former principal of the Valley High School in Hot Springs and coach of its athletic teams, was a guest at dinner and confirmed the stories that Sam was a great schoolboy athlete. Mr. Bell stated that Sam was a first-class football back, fast and shifty and, behind proper blocking, would have been a standout. He was a good pitcher, wild during his first two seasons, but in his third year he had control and could throw an effective drop and an assortment of curves. Basketball was one of Sam's best games. He had an uncanny eye for the basket, and in many games he personally scored more points than the entire opposing team. It was

Bell who took Sam to his first golf tournament, a Virginia Interscholastic Championship held at the Woodberry Forest School. Sam arrived just as his name was being called, changed his shoes in the car, ran to the tee and served notice on the golfing world—"Here comes Snead." He won the driving contest but not the tournament. When a number of colleges sought Snead because of his athletic prowess, Schoolmaster Bell advised him to devote his efforts to golf. That was in 1933, the year Sam graduated from high school. In regard to his studies, Bell said Sam had "aptitude" but was not a bookworm. He was well behaved.

At dinner Sam made an excellent talk. He reminisced about his start as a golf professional and his reaction to various experiences. "My first job was working in a restaurant from 8 A.M. until 12 P.M. for $20 a month," he said. "Then I got a job repairing clubs at The Cascades Club in Hot Springs." He had moved up to the position of assistant professional at that club when, in September, 1935, a number of big name pros came down for The Cascades Open. "I was so nervous I had to use both hands to tee my ball but I got around in 63 and was leading the field. During the tournament I couldn't eat or sleep. I finally took an 80 on the last round but finished in a tie for third with Bobby Cruickshank with 295, and won $275." Sam remembered that he looked over the return of his first big competitive attempt, noticed he had finished ahead of a number of proved stars, and said to himself, "Sammy boy, you're a golfer."

It was not until 1937 that Sam went on the winter circuit. His pal was Johnny "Boo Boo" Bulla. They traveled together in a rattletrap car to California. "Boo Boo was winning dollar Nassaus from me regularly until I got a new driver and putter, the two most important clubs. Then I began to get even with him. But when I suggested we divide our winnings on the tour, he refused and told me, 'You can't hit a lick.' A few days later I won the California Open and Boo Boo was out of the money."

Since that winter, Samuel Jackson Snead has done very well. He owns a seven-room stucco house in Hot Springs and for the past few years has hit such a high income bracket that an offer of expenses plus a guarantee of

$2,500 could not lure him to the $17,500 Philippines Open to be played next month in Manila. He does not care for the thirty-hour flight. His present plans are to play the Miami Open, the Havana Amateur-Pro, to return home for Christmas, and then pick up the tour at the Los Angeles Open. He will play in most of the tournaments but perhaps not in all of them—"The grind is too tough and you run into a lot of nasty weather." Sam's most recent victory was scored only last week in the North and South Championship at Pinehurst. He tapered off by playing an exhibition match with Chandler Harper in Portsmouth, Virginia, and scored a 62. The day before Sam Snead Day, he played a 62 on the No. 3 course at the Greenbrier. He holds the record for this course with a 61 and for the No. 1 course with a 62.

A short time ago, when I visited Sam in his pro shop, he pulled out his lesson appointment book, showing he had been booked up solid between tournaments giving lessons at $14 an hour. Last October he got so tired he thought he was ill. His back ached. Then he realized that he had been bending over from 700 to 1,000 times each morning teeing up the balls for his pupils. He never teaches on the practice tee in the afternoon, reserving what the West Virginians call "the evening" for playing-lessons. Sam gets $20 and his caddie's fee for one of these lessons, but plans to raise the price to $25.

Following the dinner on Sam Snead Day, Sam held an informal conference with the newspapermen who had gathered for the event. As was inevitable, he was asked about the eight he took on the final hole of the 1939 U. S. Open Championship played on the Spring Mills Course of the Philadelphia Country Club. It was the most tragic of Sam's several all-buts in this event: he would have won with a five, and a six would have enabled him to have participated in the play-off with Byron Nelson, Craig Wood and Denny Shute. Sam defended his action in playing a wooden club from the rough on his second shot on that fatal last hole, a par five. He didn't know what score he needed to win and knew if he got away with a second shot, he would be within a short pitch of the hole and have a chance for a birdie. The ball just failed to get up high enough and cracked into a bunker 100 yards farther down the fairway. The top of the bunker had been sodded with loose squares and when he missed his first stroke there, the ball became lodged between two sods and he could do nothing but hack it out. As Sam says, "That is water over the dam." He revealed that in 1940, when he returned to the Spring Mills course for an exhibition, he played it in sixty-four strokes. On the eighteenth he exploded out of a bunker and holed his putt for a four.

"They remember when you blow a championship," Sam said with a sigh, "but they forget about some of the times you finish as hot as a firecracker. In one Los Angeles Open, I needed a four on the last hole to win. I banged an iron second up within a few feet and sank the putt. This hole is at the foot of a hill and the entire hill was covered with people. When my putt dropped, some spectators became so excited they lost their balance and came tumbling down on the green by the dozen. It was the greatest ovation I ever received."

He told the one about the spectator who was watching him practice at a major tournament and asked him, "When do the pros start playing?" Sam replied that he didn't know—"I was just sent out to break in the course." This testimony does not jibe with the stories told by the Honorable William Campbell of the West Virginia House of Representatives. Campbell says that whenever Sam plays on a practice tee at any tournament, a crowd is sure to follow and the crowd will include a number of Sam's foremost rivals. They want to see that "flowing power" and try to duplicate it.

The All-Britisher
at the All-American

by

HENRY LONGHURST

1952 — FROM *GOLF MIXTURE*

OF HIS many glittering exploits, none save the winning of the British Open can have given Bobby Locke more satisfaction than his recent victory in the Tam O'Shanter All-American professional golf tournament at Chicago.

It is, I hope, no breach of confidence to reveal that Locke flew off to America with the comfortable sensation of a man who has been promised several thousand dollars merely to appear in the tournament irrespective of his fortunes. His check as the winner was $2,500. More was at stake than this, however, as it was his first appearance in the States since he was banned from this happy hunting ground a year and a half ago.

The Tam O'Shanter tournament, run by a colorful character called George S. May, who enlivens the proceedings by changing into a series of multi-hued shirts during the course of the day, is not only the most lucrative event of its kind, but also a public jamboree, complete with side-shows and the rest of it, on a scale mercifully unknown over here. [Mr. May is also one of golf's luckiest entrepreneurs. At Tam O'Shanter in 1953, with a national television audience looking on, Lew Worsham holed a wedge shot on the seventy-second hole worth $25,000, the most sensational shot since Gene Sarazen's double-eagle 2 at the Augusta National in the 1935 Masters.]

One has the impression of Locke that, the longer a tournament lasts, the more certain he is to win it. To capture this prize in Chicago, he rode, as one might say, a Harry Wragg race, but over the last furlong even he must have been resigned to having left it too late. After two rounds he lay eleventh, five shots behind the leaders, and equal with Ossie Pickworth of Australia, who, incidentally, made a most successful debut in America. The third round saw him fifth, four shots behind.

In the final round Lloyd Mangrum, the par of the course being 36-36—72, went out in 31. Regulation figures on the homeward half gave him a 67 and a total of 282. He and Locke had started level, so, when Locke later took 36 to the turn, Mangrum, who according to my informant had "won $20,000 and all but the doorknobs" here in 1948, may have spent an hour of pleasing anticipation.

Locke started home by holing a putt for a three and followed this with three par figures. Each of the next four holes is a par four and Locke was on each green in two. One may imagine so well the scene on these greens. The slow weighing-up of the putting surface, the two little practice swings, the swift decisive putt with the audible click of club and ball, the pause, the cheers, the solemn touching of the white cap in acknowledgment. All four putts went in—from 32, 12, 22 and 15 feet. A four at the last gave him his 31 and a tie, his homeward half being 3, 4, 4, 4, 3, 3, 3, 3, 4.

As for the play-off on the following day (which may have recalled to Locke's mind a similar occasion on a fine Saturady at Walton Heath, to which the prospect of free admission lures multitudes whose knowledge of golf is inclined to be rudimentary):—"A swarm of 12,000 persons, all admitted free, romped after them. Some carried radios to get baseball broadcasts and thus keep up on sports to the minute. In the unwieldy throng were several new fathers hauling their offspring around in baby carriages. It was a poor man's show, and quite a picnic."

How long the play-off took is not revealed. My own guess would be in the neighborhood of five hours. At any rate Locke took the lead with one of his putts on the second and never lost it. He was round in 69 against Mangrum's 74, and observed, understandably enough, as he pocketed his reward, "I just can't say how nice it is to be back in the States."

Nice work, indeed, if you can get it!

Pinehurst
and a Ryder Cup Match

by

HENRY LONGHURST

1953 — FROM *ROUND IN SIXTY-EIGHT*

UNLIKE the orthodox oasis, which consists of a few trees in a sea of sand, Pinehurst is an oasis of sixty-three rectangular grass strips, plus a certain amount of sand, in a sea of trees. The grass strips are, of course, the fairways of the three and a half golf courses which its protagonists like to call the St. Andrews of America—a fair enough claim, no doubt, though challengeable I thought from later experience, by the Monterey Peninsula in California.

Other more elongated strips indicate the roads by which nonaviators can wriggle their way into and out of Pinehurst by car. In clearings off these roads, each protected from the prying eye of the populace by a fringe of pines, are specimens of those lovely, white, Colonial-style American homes familiar to the British film-goer. General Marshall rents one. Dick Chapman, the 1951 British Amateur champion, and his conversational wife, Eloise, have another, and so has the hospitable Earl of Carrick.

As to the others, what with Singer Sewing Machines, Heinz's 57 Varieties (surely more by now?), Somebody's Ball Bearings and Somebody Else's Motors, the guide on my privately conducted tour might have been reciting from a handbook of the industrial nobility.

With all this, and bearing in mind its resounding reputation, it was a surprise to find Pinehurst a village of some 998 inhabitants. They are, of course, outnumbered all the year round by visitors and it must be many a long day since less than 1,000 souls were in Pinehurst at any one moment. In the summer they come up to escape the sweltering heat of the south; in the winter they descend from freezing New York, Detroit, and Chicago. Pinehurst, in fact, has it all ways.

Nevertheless it remains, curiously yet completely, a village, and a model village at that, law-abiding, of good behavior, and, as Pepys put it, "all things civil, no rudeness anywhere." I cannot imagine there to exist a Pinehurst policeman.

And now it really is time to make our way down to the club, either by a pleasant stroll through the pine trees or by the ancient bus which long since came of age and lingers on as a symbol of an unhurried way of life that lures people back to Pinehurst year by year as an antidote to city life. The bus has been driven since birth by an elderly bespectacled character called "Happy," and you feel that the two of them, despite their savage arguments over the gears, are now part and parcel of each other. "Happy" drives back and forth, waving at all and sundry, stopping dead at each little crossing to peer right and left over his spectacles, and, in contrast with others of his kind, cheerfully stopping to encourage those on foot to jump in and join the party. His lounge and locker room cry of "Bus to the Ho-tale . . . Bus to the Ho-tale" must be an almost universal Pinehurst memory.

The clubhouse, by comparison with the little converted farmhouse at Mildenhall or the tin-shed architecture of Rye or Westward Ho! so beloved of all who know them, might seem positively Ritzian, but by American country club standards it is by no means ostentatious and reflects the fact that the Pinehurst visitor, while liking to do himself well, has come mainly to play golf. I had not been there long when the Ryder Cup team arrived, fresh—or, rather, far from fresh and for the most part, alas, unshaven—from a night in the train, little suspecting that they were to be driven straight to the club and lined up for pictorial purposes for a ceremonial unfurling of the flag.

"They have come," I recorded, "to a land of soft accents, smiling faces, and unfailing courtesy. Dozens of times daily someone seems to be saying, 'You're welcome!' and all appear to mean it. And if this does not remind them of home, there are in the clubhouse those universal pictures of golf—the foursome on Leith Links in 1682 and the rest, and Harry Vardon playing here in 1900—to say nothing of the Quorn in full cry over the reception desk."

Golf is the Esperanto of sport. All over the world golfers talk the same language—much of it nonsense and much unprintable—endure the same frustrations, discover the same infallible secrets of putting, share the same illusory joys. And nothing, it has seemed to me in my travels, so symbolizes this common language as the pictures they hang on their walls. I have seen the same pictures in St. Andrews, Shanghai, Singapore, Ceylon, Rochester N. Y., Pinehurst, Atlanta, California, Christchurch, Melbourne, and Sydney. Perhaps the most familiar, after the long-faced gentleman in the red coat and three-cornered hat carrying over his shoulder an equally long-faced wooden putter, with an uncouth caddie and the Blackheath windmill in the background, is the St. Andrews scene entitled simply "The Golfers." This is the one showing a distinguished body of spectators clustered round four players in the foreground, the latter peering down in great animation at what might have been a stymie. Irreverent Americans, not appreciating the hallowed nature of the scene, have been heard, I fear, to call it "The Crap Game."

As for Harry Vardon, what a fantastic ball he set rolling in those tours of his at the beginning of the century! All over the States he set the golfing flame alight. North, south, and on the Pacific coast you see the same, fading sepia-toned photographs of "Vardon here in nineteen-o-something"—the elementary, barren-looking terrain, the thin line of bewhiskered, bowler-hatted onlookers with here and there, greatly daring, one or two lady spectators attired as though for motoring, and in the foreground the familiar figure in his tight knickerbockers, with coat tails flying as he swings. What a flawless swing, too, for all your present-day bashers!

The Pinehurst courses—Nos. 1, 2, and 3, they call them, in a manner strangely prosaic in a country so given to romantic nomenclature—radiate fanwise from the clubhouse. The left edge of the fan is the first hole on the No. 2, or championship course. Beside it is the eighteenth, then a practice ground, then the eighteenth and first holes of No. 1, and finally, away on the right, the first and last holes of No. 3. In front of the club are two enormous practice greens, of which my last memory is of Hogan lining up six balls from perhaps fifteen feet. "You watch!" said a man beside me. "He'll hole the lot." I watched, and he did.

All three courses, and the odd nine holes which is squeezed in somewhere between No. 2 and No. 1—I never did quite discover its whereabouts—were designed by a Scot, Donald Ross, who left his mark all over the American golfing scene at the turn of the century. Whether his architectural ideas seemed advanced then, I do not know, but his Pinehurst courses, little altered, I believe, from the day of conception, stand up to the most modern ideas of strategic and "intelligent" golf architecture, in distinction to those of his contemporaries in England and Scotland, notably Willie Park, whose formula in those days was the pure frontal attack, a kind of Grand National Steeplechase, with a great crossbunker to carry with your drive and another to jump with your second. As I played round the No. 3 course with N. C. Selway—the Cambridge golfer of the twenties, whose accounts of this Ryder Cup match for the *Times,* his first venture in this sphere, proved that all you require, in order to write first-class descriptions of golf, is to know the game and then write home and tell your friends what happened—we found ourselves constantly brought up short with the feeling, "Surely, somewhere, we have played this hole before?" There was indeed, on this course and on the No. 1, a remarkable similarity with others we both knew well. At home, Swinley Forest, Woking, the Blue course at the Berkshire, and New Zealand, that little frequented but delightful course near Byfleet, all came to mind, but none was the one we were searching for. I do not know who thought of it in the end but the answer was Morfontaine, the delightful heather, fir, and silver birch course outside Paris—where incidentally, and damn it to this day, I once lost the French Amateur Championship final by a putt on the last green.

The No. 2 course, the scene of the Ryder Cup match, is Pinehurst's pride and joy. When we were there, it had been closed for some three months, specially nursed for the occasion, and by a kindly dispensation, to enable me to comment for the *Sunday Times,* I believe I had the honor of playing the first round on it. I asked them if they could manage to fix me up with a partner.

In 1930, when, as I have mentioned, ten of us set forth from Cambridge to tour the United States, we had played a match against Harvard. Of our opponents, I remembered through the years the name only of Jim Baldwin, whose mighty slugging of the ball was then notorious in undergraduate golfing circles. Walking back to christen the No. 2 course at Pinehurst, I found waiting to partner me none other than Baldwin, now a prosperous New York businessman. Baldwin is one of those golfers, like P. B. Lucas at home, who in practice or out, seem unable to hit the ball at all without hitting it a long way, a secret which those of us who become more and more puny as the years go by may envy but no longer hope to fathom. If ever there was a course on which length was everything, it was Pinehurst at this time. Hogan, they said, had once done it in 65 and had had 271 for seventy-two holes, or

seventeen under fours, and Tommy Armour claimed to have done eighteen consecutive rounds of 68 or better. With the grass about three inches thick on the fairways and the ground untrodden for three months, they could hardly have done such things to it then. For minor fry, at 7,007 yards on the card and playing more like 9,000, it was murder—brassies, brassies all the way, as the poet might have said—and it was not long before my partner and I agreed upon it as an admirable battlefield for the Sneads and Mangrums of this world but no fit stamping ground for aging investment brokers and golf correspondents.

Still, we established one record which, unless some radical change comes over American golf, is likely to stand for years. We did it in two hours and twenty-five minutes.

Even after the fairways had been "played in" by the practice rounds and later had been mowed, the course was still gigantic. And it was good in these days, when so many people will go to absurd lengths to prevent low scores, thus ruining the designs of the architect, to see that for the match itself many of the farthest tees were not used.

What a farce is this business of length! Golf is surely the only game, either in the United States or Britain, whose whole character has been changed solely by so-called "improvements" in the instruments with which it is played. None of these changes have been solicited by, or had the approval of, the ruling body. Year by year we have altered 36,000 tees, and the Americans, I suppose, have altered 90,000, to accommodate Messrs. ——'s confounded new ball. Year by year we walk farther and farther and year by year get fewer shots in the process. No one, so far as I can see, benefits and many lose. X drives farther than Harry Vardon did, but only the dumbest of clucks would derive much satisfaction from that, since Y and Z and even your humble servant do the same. What with all this and the creeping paralysis that has come over the game in that country, innumerable Americans now play nine holes in two hours in the morning and another nine in another two hours in the afternoon—and then call it a day's golf. Vardon's golf comes by no means within the category of "ancient." The problems he faced were the same in principle as today; his style and methods were recognizable in

Bobby Jones and are certainly recognizable in the classical style of Jackie Burke, perhaps the most promising young player in the world at the moment of writing. Yet when Vardon played Pinehurst at the turn of the century he had only to walk 5,400 yards. He averaged 73 and his best score was 71. In the Ryder Cup match, Dai Rees, who was twice round in 71, had in each case to walk almost a mile further. I cannot believe that the parties concerned would alter the stands at Wimbledon, Forest Hills, Wembley and the Yankee Stadium simply to accommodate a new ball, which when struck in the same manner, happened to go farther. I rather fancy they would tell the manufacturers what to do with their new ball.

The Americans, however, as befits the now senior partner, have taken some sort of lead in this matter. They have an apparatus consisting of a fifteen-foot trough, behind which is a rotating wheel with "club" attached. You insert the ball; it flies up the trough; an "electric eye" measures its speed; and if this exceeds 255 feet per second, the ball is illegal. They take balls at random from professionals' shops and even from players on the course in tournaments.

The above impressive technicalities were described to me by Mr. Richard S. Tufts, a slight, earnestly genial figure whose name is as synonymous with that of Pinehurst as the late C. B. Macdonald's was with the National. His father founded it and he has now ascended the throne as uncrowned king of "Pinehurst Inc." This benevolent and, I believe, non-profit making institution is the complete Lord of the Manor. It owns all the ground, the club, the golf courses, and the stately homes. As a member of the U. S. Golf Association Mr. Tufts has done much not only for the game over there but indirectly for us all, since he was a member of the "negotiating body" who came to consult with St. Andrews over the rules. Their deliberations, which resulted in the present universal code, were conducted in a spirit calculated to give poor Molotov a heart attack. Opening in the cloistered calm of a committee room in the House of Lords, as guests of Lord Brabazon, they settled down not to be two negotiating bodies from rival establishments but a single body of grown-up people with a common affection for golf and a common desire that we should all play to the same rules. As presiding genius of Pinehurst Inc., Mr. Tufts was organizer-in-chief for the Ryder Cup matches. He did the job so well that, even with a blank first day, they took, in this remote hamlet, some 23,000 dollars. What it cost them over and above this is anybody's guess.

I had not intended to go into golfing technicalities but, in view of Hogan's eminence, will risk one exception. After watching my puny efforts on the practice ground he asked why it was that British players brought the club up so abruptly after impact. When I demurred that, fat and forty, I was "hardly representative . . . etc.," he said, "No, no. All your team do it. I have often noticed. Why? We reckon," he went on, "to keep the left arm straight on the way back and the right arm straight on the way through, right to the end—like this." It was here that he seized me and performed the armed combat demonstration.

To the original question I replied with some confidence that it was because we habitually wore more clothes for our all-the-year-round golf. Hogan and those who follow the tournament trail also "follow the sun," as the title of his film confirmed. They play in shirtsleeves. For much of the year we play with a pullover, surmounted by a thick sweater or jacket, in which this right-arm elongation is impossible save to the ultra-lissom. Dai Rees, on the other hand, thought the British method of following through resulted from "trying to get the ball up off hard ground"—but this, with due respect, is simply not true for at least half the year, and I must prefer my own explanation.

At any rate, unimpeded by spectators, I watched Hogan closely in a practice round with Burke, Demaret and Claude Harmon. Each of these three was driving a colossal sort of ball which, when it should have been descending, would bore onwards towards the hole, and it seemed impossible that a man the size of Hogan, who happened to be driving last, could reach them. Time and again, however, he lashed the ball along thirty feet from the ground, or "quail high" as they say in Texas. It ran perhaps thirty yards where theirs had stopped almost dead on the soft fairways, and finished five yards past the lot.

Since then I have been consulting his book, *Power Golf,* to see whether, unlike so many golfers who write books, he practices what he preaches. The answer is "Yes, he does." I never saw anything quite like it. By taking his club far away from him on the backswing, and then almost as far back round his neck as our own James Adams, and then thrusting it even farther away in front after impact (by which time he is already on the outside of his left foot, with the right heel high in the air) he attains, in fact, the swing of at least a six-footer. His right arm never bends after impact and it finishes in a position with which the middle-aged reader may care at his own risk to experiment, namely dead straight and pointing, almost horizontally, behind his head. "The speed and momentum," says the caption, "have carried me to a full finish." They would carry most of us to the infirmary.

The Ryder Cup match itself is ancient history, though I will later append the results, but the play, as Sherlock Holmes would have said, "presented certain points of interest."

Wise before the event, for once—and prepared to produce written testimony to this effect in the shape of newspaper cuttings—I reckoned the British team's "par" to be one foursome and two singles (out of four foursomes and eight singles). In fact they won one foursome and one and a half singles.

Perhaps the most extraordinary feature of the proceedings was the weather on the first morning. With the impression still fresh in the mind I find that I cabled back that evening:

"This really has been one of the most extraordinary days of golf I can remember. We have been sweltering for days, sometimes in almost tropical heat, and now we wake up to what might be a December morning at Gleneagles or the Berkshire, with an authentic Scotch mist limiting visibility to a drive and a brassie, shivering spectators, and players blowing on their fingers to keep them warm.

"Among the gallery in the fourth match, bearing no outward and visible sign connecting him with the proceedings, is a small dark man with gray raincoat, gray cap, gray trousers and inscrutable expression, looking somewhat like a Pinkerton detective on unobtrusive watch for pickpockets. This is the world's greatest golfer, Ben Hogan, participating in the Ryder Cup match. His partner, the nor-

mally flamboyant Jimmy Demaret, is concealed in a flowing check ulster with a distinctly Sherlock Holmes air. From time to time they step forward, undress, give the ball a resounding slam, and return to anonymity.

"As if this is not enough, the afternoon turns to rain, pouring relentlessly down on the avenues of silent pines. Sodden spectators, strangely woebegone in their bizarre headgear, trickle back to the clubhouse, the refreshment tent runs out of 'hot dogs,' and what has so long been a sunny, colorful scene turns to something approaching a wet Sunday afternoon in Wigan."

In the course of a previous expedition across the Atlantic, Gerald Micklem used casually an expression, new to the company, which was fastened upon by some of us and incorporated into common usage as expressing much in a graphically brief way. I forget the context but he remarked of someone who had done something praiseworthy, "March that man in for credit!" This, it appears, is a term used in Her Majesty's Brigade of Guards, in which Micklem served in the war. Men who have earned official approval are detailed for the orderly room parade, and marched in for credit in rather the same way as the common defaulter is marched in for discredit.

Though the British team lost the Ryder Cup match easily enough, several of them might justifiably have been marched in for credit on the morning after. And none for greater credit than the oldest member of the party, Arthur Lees, of Sunningdale, who had become the first British player in the history of the contest to win both foursome and single in the United States. In partnership with Charles Ward he beat Ed Oliver and Harry Ransom by 2 and 1 and in the singles beat Oliver by 2 up. In the rain and mist of the first day nothing finer was seen in the State of Carolina than Ward and Lees' homeward half of 33, the lowest for either nine holes on either side, and they were round in 69 to be 3 up. In the afternoon they were still 3 up after nine and it was by this time clear that, barring miracles, we must win this match to avoid that all too frequent spectacle in America, the British side of the scoreboard resembling a daisy chain of noughts. At this point Ward nearly gave us a heart attack, and a 6 and a 5 saw two precious holes go west. These moments of crisis are the true test of the golfer. At one minute every-thing in the garden is lovely. At the next there comes over one the familiar feeling that close behind some fearful fiend doth tread. How-ever, a half at the twelfth gave them breathing space and they cruised home with 3, 4, 4, 4, 3 against a par of 4, 4, 3, 5, 3. As it turned out, almost precisely the same thing happened to Lees in the singles and he again kept his head. Indeed, at both these periods, stumping steadily along in his deliberate Yorkshire sort of way, he delivered the kind of golf that he is liable to turn out in a summer evening four-ball at Sunningdale. His iron shots flew to the target as though on a piece of elastic attached to the flag.

Faulkner and Rees did well, too, but al-though their 71 would have been level with one American pair and 2 or 3 up on the other two, they were "exposed to a 69," as the Amer-icans say, by Heafner and Burke and this saw them a couple down. As to Panton and Adams, one can hardly envisage waking up on a chilly morning with a more intimidating prospect than playing Snead and Mangrum in a Ryder Cup foursome in America. Our Scottish pair, who had done well in practice—Panton espe-cially impressing the critics and drawing from the sage, Armour, the compliment that he was the best player sent over from Britain in twenty years—never looked like chipping the granite surface of these hardened competitors. A 76 left them 5 down and it was not until the twenty-sixth that they won a hole.

In the remaining match Daly and Bousfield did what I must now have seen dozens of Brit-ish players do in these matches—professionals, amateurs, and women. They got off to a bad start and hung a millstone around their necks in the first half-hour. Out in 41 they were 5 down and against a pair like Hogan and De-maret had reluctantly to be written off.

At the end of the singles, having handed the bouquet to Lees, we were still able to march in for credit one or two of the losers, to say nothing of Daly, who, delayed in the early stages by an unruly putter, rode too much of a waiting race against Heafner, left his effort too late, and might have won with another furlong to go. The diminutive Ward for instance—what a show he put up against Hogan! The answer to Hogan is, I fancy, that if Hogan means to win, you lose. To take him to the

thirty-fourth green entitles any man to a pat on the back.

One cannot see everything in these matches, but one part of this encounter which I did see lingers in the memory. After seven holes in the afternoon Ward was still only 2 down. The eighth is a hole of some 488 yards, with a nar-row opening to the green, and the only man I saw reach it in 2 was the equally diminutive Hogan. Ward pitched his third gallantly up within holing distance, whereupon Hogan, in the silent, steely-eyed, remorseless way that hypnotizes his opponents, rolled in his ten-yarder for a 3.

The ninth is a short one, with the pin on a plateau to the left. Ward's ball did its best but eventually slithered down to the right, leaving a putt long enough and awkward enough to arouse suspicions of three more to come. He struck it beautifully. It breasted the slope, pushed along towards the hole, and fell in for a 2. This brought them to the longest hole on the course, declared by the card to be 593 yards but only, I rather suspect, be-cause Pinehurst Inc. are a little shy of admit-ting it to be more than 600. Some estimates put it as high as 630. At any rate after two shots as hard as they could hit them, the longest hitters on either side were still debat-ing between a No. 4 iron and a No. 5 for their third. Here Ward, only 2 down again now, played three good orthodox shots and his ball lay safely on the green, some distance from the hole. The great man on the other hand had driven into the forest.

Here he manufactured some sort of shot which moved him along down the fairway but still far enough away to need one of his biggest to reach the edge of the green. This he duly delivered, but it left him still every bit of twenty-five yards from the flag. He surveyed it from end to end, tight-lipped and inscruta-ble, and you could have heard a pin drop as at last he hit the ball. Up and up it came to-wards the hole. As it dropped in, the whole population must have heard the roar. Golf may be the slowest game in the world but, my word, there are times when it can be ex-citing!

Who else deserves a retrospective pat on the back? Dai Rees, certainly. For a combination of good golf, good spirit and a photo-finish I remember few things better than his match with the cheerful Jimmy Demaret. All the morning and half the afternoon he was 1 up, 2 up, 1 up. Then in five holes Demaret had four "birdies," turned the deficit into a lead of one, and held it to the end. Still, Rees had one consolation. He was described by a Washington paper as "the sort of charming kid that women like to make a fuss of!"

Faulkner, too, deserves a consolation prize. The Americans like to have a strong man to bring up the rear, and in the singles Snead, the American captain, had put himself at the tail. On the same principle Arthur Lacey put Faulkner, the Open champion, last. It is true that at no point did Faulkner look like beating the redoubtable Samuel Jackson Snead, but many would have been murdered and Faulkner, beaten by 4 and 3, assuredly was not. Snead completed the first round in 67, by two strokes the lowest on either day. Looking back, I still rate this with the conjuror's final trick—"not only difficult, ladies and gentlemen, but actually impossible." The Americans, I think, took to Faulkner and I saw some kindly things written about him after the match. Though he has been criticized in Britain on buffoonery and on other grounds, he is essentially a likeable, friendly fellow and, if he has his faults, then at least they are all on the surface, which is more than most of us can say. He tried for a while to emulate Demaret, who in America has made a "corner" in bizarre clothing—not, as the latter will cheerfully admit, because he particularly likes appearing in fancy dress but because the ensuing public attention pays him to do so. We are a little more staid on this side of the Atlantic and do not take readily to primrose col-ored trousers—and in any case the common man, whose century this unhappily is, does not like people to be "different."

Before closing the Ryder Cup episode let me lift my hat to that mighty minnow, Ben Hogan. Hogan is a fascinating study, almost as fascinating, in an opposite way, as Hagen, with whose name his own used so often to be confused. Hagen was colorful, eccentric, theatrical, gregarious. He loved wine and women and his fellow men, from caddies to Princes of Wales, and saw no reason why life should not permanently be standing him a bottle of champagne. Hogan is the reverse of the coin—steel-hard, wiry, self-disciplined, austere. Hagen was a gift to golf writers. Of Hogan, till his motor smash and subsequent recovery made him an idol of sporting America, they could find little to say except that he had again gone round in 68.

Nowadays, after physical and mental suffering on the grand scale, the genuine admiration of a whole nation, and the comforting feeling that he has no more golfing or financial worlds to conquer, Hogan has mellowed a good deal—on the surface, that is. Perhaps, underneath, he was mellow all the time. At any rate I must record that I find his company highly stimulating. I am not by nature a celebrity hunter—if anything the reverse—but, if you have seen so much of golf and golfers, you can hardly fail to be intrigued by a man who plays it rather better than does anyone else in the world.

Here, for the record, are the Ryder Cup results:

FOURSOMES

U.S.A.		BRITAIN	
Clayton Heafner and Jack Burke (5 and 4)	1	Max Faulkner and Dai Rees	0
Ed Oliver and Henry Ranson	0	Charles Ward and Arthur Lees (2 and 1)	1
Lloyd Mangrum and Sam Snead (5 and 4)	1	James Adams and John Panton	0
Ben Hogan and Jimmy Demaret (5 and 4)	1	Fred Daly and Ken Bousfield	0
Foursomes Totals	3		1

Singles

J. Burke (4 and 3)	1	J. Adams	0
J. Demaret (2 up)	1	D. Rees	0
C. Heafner	½	F. Daly	½
L. Mangrum (6 and 5)	1	H. Weetman	0
E. Oliver	0	A. Lees (2 up)	1
B. Hogan (3 and 2)	1	C. Ward	0
S. Alexander (8 and 7)	1	J. Panton	0
S. Snead (4 and 3)	1	M. Faulkner	0
Singles Totals	6½		1½

Perfection at Oakmont

by

PHILIP W. WRENN, JR.

1953 — FROM THE JUNE 20 ISSUE OF *THE NEW YORKER* MAGAZINE

A S FAR AS the galleries were concerned, the 1953 Open Championship of the United States Golf Association, played last week at the Oakmont Country Club, near Pittsburgh, can be put down as the perfect tournament. The weather and the course were both beyond any possible criticism, and Ben Hogan's winning 283, which broke a nineteen-year-old course record by eleven strokes, was as near to perfection as anything anyone is ever likely to see. In my opinion, Hogan hit only three shots during the seventy-two holes that were open to reasonable question, and all of them were made on the horrendous fifteenth, perhaps the most difficult par 4 hole on one of the most difficult courses in the world. The hole is four hundred and fifty-eight yards, the drive is uphill, the green is heavily trapped and invisible from the tee, and the second largest trap on the course is just over the hill crest, to the right of the narrow fairway. On the third round, Hogan faded his drive into that trap, chipped to the fairway, and then sliced a No. 3 iron shot into another trap, to the right of the green. He came out nicely but took two putts from twelve feet for a 6. In the final round, his drive was long and straight, but, as he admitted afterward, he misjudged the distance and played a No. 2 iron when he should have used a No. 3, with the result that he went into a trap beyond the green and needed three more strokes from

there. Otherwise, I can recall nothing really egregious. He three-putted a few times, but on the lightning-fast Oakmont greens, some of which are fifty yards long, an occasional three-putter can scarcely be considered a lapse.

Sam Snead, the second-best player in the starting field of three hundred, making his thirteenth try for the one major professional title he has never won, was the only serious opposition Hogan faced after the third round on Saturday morning. At the end of forty-five holes, Snead actually led by a stroke, and when he went to lunch, he was only one stroke behind Hogan's 212. Obviously as taut as a zither string as he started his afternoon bout, Sam missed four putts of three feet or under, and an equal number of possible birdie putts, to finish in second place with 289. He has, it seems to me, an even smoother swing than Hogan, but he lacks Hogan's calm, dispassionate judgment. A good example of this difference occurred at the seventeenth hole in the third round. It's a two-hundred-and-ninety-two-yard, uphill affair, and Snead, one of the longest hitters of all, put his drive on the green, about forty feet from the cup. Instead of playing safe for a birdie 3, he went for the eagle, slid eight or nine feet past the cup, and missed again coming back. Hogan can hit as long a ball as Snead when he thinks it advisable, and he thought it advisable on the same hole in the final round. He also drove the

224

green, but he played it safe a foot or so short of the hole and got a 3.

For those who have an idea that the placing of pins on the greens during a national tournament is pretty much a hit-or-miss proposition, I can report that such a notion is without foundation. At five o'clock Thursday morning, I accompanied two representatives of the USGA, John Fischer and Richard Garlington, as they went about the business. They carried topographical maps of the various greens, on which Richard Tufts, the vice-president of the association, after making a round of the course a couple of days before the tournament, had marked the approximate locations of the pins for each day's play. The USGA insists that the area within three feet of the pin be completely flat, and it was up to Fischer and Garlington to find the precise spot nearest the one indicated by Tufts that met that specification. Sometimes they spent as much as fifteen minutes on a green, and it was almost two and a half hours before the whole job had been completed to their satisfaction. Back in the clubhouse, Garlington sighed and said, "In about an hour the chorus will start: 'Now, what simple-minded clown put that *there*?'"

The Greatest Year
of My Life

by

BEN HOGAN
as told to GENE GREGSTON

1953 — FROM THE OCTOBER 17 ISSUE OF *THE SATURDAY EVENING POST*

CHIPPING OUT of sand is the hardest shot in the world for me to make. But such a shot proved to be the turning point this year in my first bid for the British Open Championship. It came on the fifth hole of the final round at Carnoustie, Scotland, on Friday, July tenth. I was tied for the lead with Roberto De Vicenzo, of Argentina. Tony Cerda, also of Argentina, and Great Britain's Dai Rees were deadlocked at second, just a stroke back.

I had played the first four holes even par when Cerda, playing behind me, birdied the third hole. That made him one under fours. I knew he'd caught me. And I realized then that I had to get a couple of birdies some place and shoot a 70, or right around 70, to win.

At the fifth, a slight dog-leg to the right, my second shot hit the green, backed off and stopped in the fringe of a sand trap to the left and about thirty-five or forty feet from the pin. It hung on the edge of the bunker, held by two blades of grass. It kept moving, barely. Then it stopped, still on the edge.

I didn't know how much sand was under the ball or if it could have been blasted out. But I couldn't take a chance on that, for fear the ball might go over the green and leave me in real trouble coming back downhill to the pin. So I chipped with a No. 9 iron, something I ordinarily would never do. I've never been able to chip out of sand successfully—usually I either leave the ball there or hit it too far.

This time, as luck would have it, I hit it just right. It was nipped just enough for backspin. The ball pitched against the bank of the green, skidded uphill to the pin, banged the back of the cup, bounced three or four inches into the air—then fell into the hole.

It was a birdie three, my first birdie on the final round. De Vicenzo had played nine holes one over par, so I felt I was in the lead by a stroke, the first time I had been able to get in front of the tournament. It had been a long, tiring road to that lead, and every step of the way reaffirmed my belief that no one does anything unless the Lord's with him. I think it was fate, and supposed to be, that I won this tournament. Otherwise, I wouldn't have won it or four other titles this year.

In a golfing sense this has been the greatest of my forty-one years, in that I have been fortunate enough to win five out of six tournaments. And personally it's been a tremendously satisfying year, if for no other reason than the homecoming celebrations given my wife, Valerie, and me in New York City and in our home town of Fort Worth on our return from Scotland.

Victory in the British Open was the climax of my 1953 tournament activity, and some have termed it the crowning achievement of my career to date. Yet the decision to undertake the trip had been difficult to make.

I told Valerie after the Masters Tournament in April that I thought I would enter the British Open—"if I win the U. S. Open." She wasn't excited at the prospect. She gets travel-sick regardless of the mode of transportation, and she knew what hardship the overseas trip would involve because we had made a similar journey with the Ryder Cup team in 1949.

But all she said was, "I should think you'd want to play in the British Open if you didn't win the U. S. Open."

That's Valerie, a wonderful wife, partner, companion, trainer and adviser who deserves more credit than I can possibly give her for any success I've had. Her answer more or less settled the question between us, but it still was far from definite, and no one else was told of my intention until some time later.

"If I win the U. S. Open"—that was a mighty big "If." But it ultimately did not rest on that. My entry for the British Open was mailed before the U. S. Open was played, and I knew then that I'd go to Scotland whether I won my fourth U. S. Open or not.

I went to the British Open for several reasons. First of all, the trip was not undertaken merely to bring their cup home. Naturally, any tournament I enter I try as hard as possible to win, but the main reason for my going was to satisfy so many people's wishes that I play. I felt that if they had that much faith in me and wanted me to represent the United States in the British Open, I should reciprocate.

The second reason was that it was a challenge. I'd always heard about Carnoustie—pronounced "Car-NOOSE-tee"—being one of the finest courses in the world and one of the toughest on which to score. Then everyone told me the weather posed a problem we don't have over here. I wanted to try my hand at it. Also, I wanted to see how I'd fare with the smaller-sized British ball. I'd heard it said several times that I could not play the small ball with my deep-faced clubs.

Many comments to the effect that people didn't believe I could win under those conditions came to me secondhand, and I was somewhat determined to prove that I could. I think that's been one of my driving forces all my life, because over a period of years people have said I couldn't do this or that.

Even at Colonial, my home course in Fort Worth, several said this year that I couldn't win because I wasn't a very good wind player.

The third reason for the trip was that the United States Golf Association and the Royal and Ancient Golf Club of St. Andrews had made their rules identical, for the good of world golf, except the rule concerning size of the ball. The example of this standardization which most affected me was that the British agreed to permit use of the center-shafted putter after having banned it for many years. My putter, which has a brass-blade head made from an old doorknob while World War II was in progress and brass couldn't be obtained, is classed as center-shafted.

For another thing, the British Open this year came at a time when it didn't conflict with any of my commitments in this country. It seems silly to have that many reasons for going to a golf tournament, doesn't it? After all, I am a professional golfer and playing tournaments is my business.

But we've done a lot of traveling in nineteen years—more than those years show, perhaps. We knew this trip would be tough. In fact, I don't think Valerie believed me at first when I told her I might go. And I kept delaying sending my entry until the deadline of June sixth neared. Then, after mailing it, I began to feel a pressure that I've never experienced before about a tournament.

It wasn't that I felt I might lose a lot by going, yet I believed that if I didn't win, everyone would say, "I told you so." And I think if I hadn't won, the people over there would have thought, *Well, American players aren't so good as they're supposed to be, especially under British conditions.*

You know, a great many people have built up in their minds a mythical Hogan who wins whenever he wants to win. Well, it does not work out that way. That's just not true. If you win 1 per cent of the tournaments you play, you're very lucky.

Some have asked me if I set out to make this a banner year because of a comparatively poor 1952 showing and comments implying that I was "through." Well, that comes within the "driving forces" I mentioned previously. When I went to Augusta, Georgia, for the Masters in April, I felt that I was hitting the ball better than ever before. I'd practiced every day of the winter. This is no plug for Palm Springs, California, but the turf there is ideal for development of your swing. It's firm, and the sand underneath gives it a good cushion. I think my four rounds of 70-69-66-69 for 274 in the Masters were the best I've ever shot in the course of one tournament.

All this time Valerie and I had been making preparations for the trip to Scotland. My mother, remembering 1949, when I became ill in Great Britain and had to return home, didn't think we should go, for fear of repetition of that sickness. I did get a touch of influenza this time, but it wasn't serious.

It's true my mother tried to get me to give up golf when I was a boy, but there's nothing to the story that at sixteen years of age I told her that some day I was going to be the greatest golfer in the world. She never did approve of my playing golf, however, and I'm still not sure she approves of it.

When we arrived at Carnoustie I had my first look at the course. It was quite a contrast to the beautiful farms and fields of the countryside. It was extremely drab looking. The color was a mixture between brown and green. There were no trees. It was land that's never been developed since the Year One, I suppose.

We stayed at the Tay Park House at Dundee, about eleven miles from Carnoustie. This is the National Cash Register Company's guest house for use of executives and business people who come to Dundee, where the company has a factory. We had been offered accommodations there before we left the United States. We rented a car, a British Humber, and hired a chauffeur for our stay there.

A professional caddie named Cecil Timms, or Timmy, about thirty-three or thirty-four years old, who had worked for Harvie Ward and Dick Chapman, two of our top amateurs, in previous British events, asked me for a trial. He proved to be satisfactory, if a bit too nervous.

Naturally I was eager to begin practice with the smaller ball and get acquainted with the Carnoustie championship course, where the tournament was to be played, and the shorter Burnside course, where one qualifying round was to be played.

The practice area at Carnoustie is about a mile out on the course from the first tee. But it also is an army firing range. So help me, it is. About 200 yards away they'd be shooting machine guns, rifles and pistols, and you'd be trying to practice. The noise was terrific, so I moved to the more private Barry course between Carnoustie and Dundee.

My daily routine started with a breakfast of bacon and eggs. Then I'd drive to Barry for an hour or an hour and a half of practice, have lunch, then drive over to Carnoustie for a round of golf in the afternoon. After dinner, there wasn't much time left in the evenings, but Valerie and I did attend two movies while we were there.

I played two or three balls on every hole of my practice rounds. You can hit the small ball a mile! I'd say, conservatively, that it goes twenty-five yards farther than the American ball, and against the wind there is more difference than that. My biggest troubles were getting accustomed to the distance I could hit the smaller ball and learning to judge distances on the course.

I kept finding myself taking about two clubs less than we would with our ball, and, I suppose just subconsciously, I'd then hit it harder than I should. Since I never was able to trust myself to look and judge what club should be used, I memorized what it should take from various places on the fairway, taking the weather and other factors into consideration, and I played the tournament from that memory.

Their wind isn't any stronger than it is at some places in the United States, but it's a lot heavier and has a lot more moisture as it comes in off the sea. For instance, in my practice rounds I never hit more than a light No. 8 iron on my second shot on the first hole. But on the first round of the tournament I hit a driver and a No. 2 iron just as hard as I could nail them because of the high wind in my face. That's how much difference it can make over there.

And par changes with the wind. If you play a hole in the morning and you're going downwind, it's a par four. But in the afternoon, if the wind has changed and you're facing it, the same hole is a par five. They don't go by par, as we know it, however. They judge play on "level fours," a total of 72 for eighteen holes.

In the United States we play what I term "target golf." Our courses have boundaries, or borders, of trees, fences and hedges, and our fairways are well defined, easily distinguishable from the rough. Sometimes at Carnoustie it was almost impossible to determine from the tee where the fairway ended and the rough began because fairway and rough were identical in color.

When they build a course they just go out

and seed a tee, seed a green, mow a fairway between them, and leave the rough the same way it's been for a thousand years and will be for two thousand more. They put sand traps everywhere. Traps on six of the holes were strategically placed in the middle of the fairway at the perfect driving distance required for those holes. You had to find your way around those traps because if you played short of them you could not reach the green on the second shot.

Normally, they mow the fairways about once a month and mow the greens about once a week. Since this type of course is easy to build and easy to maintain, golf is very inexpensive and everyone plays. The fee for a round at Carnoustie is forty-nine cents. It's unfortunate that we do not have a larger number of courses with similar fees, so more people could play golf over here.

Heather and gorse are abundant in the rough. Heather, something like a fern, grows in clumps about eight inches to a foot high and is as thick as it can be. If you get in it, you have to hit the ball about ten times as hard as you would otherwise, and then most times it won't go more than ten yards or so. I was in it only once, thank goodness, and that was on a qualifying round. It was up close to a green and fortunately I came out of it all right.

Gorse is taller, sometimes waist- to head-high, and is a brambly bush. I don't know what you do if you get into it, and I never wanted to find out. I didn't practice getting out of the gorse or heather because I figured anyone who got into it frequently wouldn't have a chance anyway.

Every fairway is rolling and full of mounds, and you hardly ever have a level lie. It was bounce golf. I'd hit a shot and never know which way it might bounce when it landed. I do know that in seventy-two holes of the tournament I never bounced an approach shot "stiff" to the pin. By that, I mean close enough for what we'd consider a cinch putt. You'd think in seventy-two holes anyone would "luck" one up there that close, but I never did.

It was what I'd call a "burn-happy" layout too. There are two burns, or creeks—the bigger Barry Burn and Jockie's Burn—that play a large part in making the course difficult. In addition, there are several long ditches, or

trenches, in the roughs. I suppose they're drainage ditches, but I don't know. In practice I tried to find all of them, not only because it was a certain one-stroke penalty if you hit a ball into one but because if I ever walked out into the rough I didn't want to fall into one and break my leg. They're about three feet deep, and I'm surprised there aren't a lot more one-legged golfers over there because of those ditches.

Their championship tees are called "tiger" tees. I thought this was because they were so far back in the heather and gorse that only tigers would be there. I didn't learn differently until my return to New York, when Bobby Jones told me where the name originated. The people call a golfer who plays from the back tees a "tiger," and the golfer who plays from the much shorter, front tees a "rabbit." I played several rounds at Carnoustie before I realized I was being a rabbit part of the time. You can't find some of those tiger tees unless you have a caddie or partner who knows the course well.

While practicing, I formulated my plans for the tournament. My degree of sharpness at the time governs my attack and expectations for a particular tournament. A lot of things enter into this plan—the type of course, the weather, places where there's a possible need for sacrifice, and places where chances may be taken. I believed after two weeks of practice that the tee shot would be the most important because of the course and the weather, and thought that a score of 283 would win it.

You have to hit an extremely long tee shot at Carnoustie—the course measures more than 7200 yards from the tiger tees—and you have to keep your drive out of the heather, gorse and sand traps. Therefore, I did a lot of practicing with wood clubs, more than I normally do for tournaments.

In qualifying rounds I shot a 70 at Burnside and a 75 at Carnoustie, the 145 total qualifying easily. Many have asked if I coast along in qualifying rounds. Let's put it this way: I try, all right, but I just can't work up to as high a competitive pitch as in a tournament.

When I walked up to the first tee at Burnside for my first qualifying round and first official shot in a British Open, I didn't see anyone in charge, no one announcing players as we do in America. There was a little house off to the side and a woman sitting in it by herself. The twosome in front had teed off and played their second shots; still no one, not even my partner, Bill Branch, of England, who was a very quiet fellow, said anything to me about teeing off. So, when I thought it was about time, I walked onto the tee and put my ball down. Some people shook their heads negatively.

While I was waiting for some word, a train came up the tracks that run alongside the first fairway. The engineer gave me three short blasts on his whistle, stopped the train and waved. I didn't shoo him away, as the news stories reported. I merely waved back to him. Then I heard this horn go "beep-beep." The woman in the little house had blown the horn, and that was the signal to tee off. All the people lining the fairway on both sides nodded their heads, indicating it was now all right for me to drive. Valerie said later that she could see I was about to burst with laughter, and I was. It was all new and funny to me, but, I guess, perfectly normal to them.

On that first qualifying round I also learned that my caddie, Timmy, is a very nervous fellow. He was a good caddie. He treated my clubs as if they were the crown jewels and kept them clean and shining all the time. He took my shoes home with him every night to polish them. But when things got tight on the course, he'd get extremely upset. And the more nervous he became, the more he'd talk. Each time, I'd stop and quiet him. Many times when I'd have a long putt he'd hold his head down between his arms and wouldn't look, indicating his lack of confidence in my putting. And most of the time I didn't want to look either. I putted poorly over there. I knew the greens were hard and I kept expecting them to be fast, but they never were.

Timmy was never wrong. I don't ask a caddie what club to use, but if I picked a No. 5 iron, for example, and the shot was short, I might comment that I should have taken more club. Every time I did this, Timmy would say, "Yes, I had me hand on the four-iron." He always knew—after the shot was made.

On the first day of the tournament the wind was blowing very hard. About five minutes before Ugo Grappasonni, of Italy, my playing partner for the first two rounds, and I were to tee off, Bobby Locke, of South Africa, finished his first round with a 72, and I had

an opportunity to congratulate him.

I thought he'd shot a wonderful round in those weather conditions, and I thought he surely would be leading, or not more than one stroke back, after the first round. That proved to be wrong, however, because Frank Stranahan, our fine amateur, shot a 70 and took the lead.

I shot a 73. My play that day was satisfactory, except for my putting. Leaving the course afterward, I was somewhat tired, as I usually am after the first round. It seems as though the first is always the most tiring round for me in a tournament. And as I had lost some twenty pounds since February, my weight was down pretty fine, as low as I wanted it to get.

The diet was restricted, of course, since they were still on rations, trying to recover from the war. Fruit was plentiful, though, and it helped me retain my strength. I also carried some candy fruit drops in my bag and ate them frequently for energy. At the start I gave Timmy a share of this candy, but on two rounds he ate all of his and mine too. Finally, after two or three warnings, he was convinced he'd better leave my candy alone.

I felt I played well in the second round, but again couldn't get my putts to drop, and scored a 71 that left me two strokes back of Britain's Dai Rees and Scotland's Eric Brown, who were tied for the lead at 142.

Rees, Brown and the other golfers from the British Isles played with much more confidence in their own surroundings and with their own ball. The transition was amazing, they play so much better over there than they do here. But just the reverse is true with our players, too, so I suppose it's like being more comfortable in your own home.

It seemed to me, however, that British golfers have a more leisurely approach to the game. Technically, their game is about the same as ours in so far as swing, stroke and method are concerned and most of them use American-made clubs.

The field was cut for the final thirty-six holes. I had learned on the first two rounds, and, in fact, all the while I was over there, that the Scottish galleries, composed of people who came from all over the British Isles, are very respectful and know their golf well. They treated Valerie and me wonderfully.

I gained a tie for the lead in the third

round of the tournament Friday morning by shooting a 70 for a total of 214, same as that of De Vicenzo. My partner for the last two rounds was Hector Thompson, of Scotland. Like Ugo Grappasonni, who could speak broken English, and Bill Branch, Thompson was a very quiet fellow.

It rained intermittently during the last three rounds of the tournament, but the wind wasn't as fierce as it had been on the first day. While eating my lunch before the last round, I kept thinking of the job at hand. I felt that my original plan had to be changed somewhat. As the tournament progressed, the pressure kept building up, and although I didn't feel well physically, having taken the flu the night before, the excitement of being tied for the lead with one round to go was offsetting my physical discomfort, and I actually felt stronger moving into the afternoon's final round.

I always do. My blood stream seems to get an extra shot of adrenalin from my body. Knowing that I hit the ball farther in the final round than I ever do in previous rounds because of this added strength, I purposely underclub each shot. For instance, where I normally use a No. 5 iron in the first to third rounds, a No. 6 iron would be used in the final round.

I might add right here that the only time I alter my original plan for a tournament is on the last round, as I was doing this time, when I'm in a corner and have to fight my way out. If you're in front, you can let the other fellow make the mistakes. This time I was tied with De Vicenzo, and Rees and Cerda were only one stroke back.

The husky De Vicenzo was the strongest man over there and a very long driver. He could carry over at least three of those sand traps in the fairways, and was always using two or three clubs less on his second shots than anyone else. I thought before it started that he'd run away with the tournament with any sort of luck on the greens, and he might have had he not knocked a ball out of bounds on the ninth hole of the third round.

Rees is a little fellow, but a fine player. Cerda is about my size, five feet, ten inches tall and 160 pounds or so. He's not so strong as De Vicenzo, naturally, but he has a fine swing and a well-rounded game.

De Vicenzo was about six to eight holes ahead of Thompson and me when we started

the final round. Rees was in front of De Vicenzo, and Cerda was behind me. I had played the fourth hole in even fours when I heard about Cerda's birdie on the third. That's when I was fortunate enough to chip in from the sand trap for the birdie three on the fifth hole.

When I made that shot and heard that De Vicenzo was one over at the turn, I felt as the jockey must feel when he's finally poked his horse's nose out front of the pack in a Kentucky Derby.

I went through the first nine holes in 34. By then, I'd heard that Stranahan was in with 286 after shooting a great 69, and Rees had shot a 71 to tie Frank. De Vicenzo was playing the sixteenth or seventeenth and was still one over. The only thing I had to worry about was holding what I had and keeping track of Cerda right behind me.

But misfortune almost struck on the tenth hole. As I was taking my stance on the tee, out of the corner of my eye I saw this big black dog walk across the tee about ten yards in front of me. I thought I saw him walk in to the crowd, but as I hit a full driver the dog walked across. My ball didn't miss him two inches. If it had hit him, it probably would have killed the dog, could have messed up my score pretty badly and there might have been a different ending to this story.

I got my four on the tenth, though, and fours on the eleventh and twelfth. On the thirteenth I hit a No. 5 iron to the green and sank a twelve-foot putt for a birdie deuce, and that put me four under fours. De Vicenzo had finished one over for a 73 and a total of 287. I also learned that Cerda, who had stayed within one stroke of me through the eleventh hole, was now one over fours after his ball hit a spectator on the twelfth. I felt for the first time that I had the championship if I didn't do anything foolish.

Fortunately, I didn't. My good luck held and I finished four under fours for a 68, a total of 282 and victory in my first British Open. Someone informed me that the 68 was a new competitive eighteen-hole record for the Carnoustie course. I never had any thought of a record during the round, however, and I do not play to break records.

I play to win, and I think the Lord has let me win for a purpose. I hope that purpose is to give courage to those people who are sick or injured and broken in body.

Walker Cup Matches— the Full Parade

by

JOHN P. ENGLISH

1953 — FROM THE SEPTEMBER ISSUE OF
USGA JOURNAL AND TURF MANAGEMENT

THE Walker Cup competition was begun in the wake of the First World War with a view to stimulating golf interest on both sides of the Atlantic.

It was born in an era of dawning internationalism and grew, at least in part, out of two international matches between Canada and the United States. In 1919, the Royal Canadian Golf Association invited the USGA to send an amateur team to Canada. The invitation was accepted, and William C. Fownes, Jr., was appointed captain. His ten-man team consisted of John G. Anderson, Eben M. Byers, Charles Evans, Jr., Robert A. Gardner, Robert T. Jones, Jr., Oswald Kirkby, Max Marston, Francis D. Ouimet, George Ormiston and Jerome D. Travers. Playing foursomes in the morning and singles in the afternoon, it defeated the Canadians, 12 to 3, at the Hamilton (Ont.) Golf Club on July 25, 1919. The USGA Team won a return match the following year, in September, at the Engineers Country Club, Roslyn, N. Y., 10 to 4.

Simultaneously, British and Americans were seriously seeking each other's championships. In the spring of 1920, Bob Gardner had gone to the final of the British Amateur at Muirfield, losing to Cyril Tolley on the thirty-seventh hole. The USGA Amateur that fall also had an international aspect. In addition to members of the Canadian team, Tolley, Roger, Wethered, Lord Charles Hope and Tommy Armour came from Great Britain. Most of these failed to qualify, and the last foreign contender, Armour, was beaten by Ouimet in the third round.

The Executive Committee of the USGA, meanwhile, was invited abroad to confer with the Royal and Ancient Golf Club's Rules Committee regarding the advisability of amending or modifying various rules. The invitation was accepted and the USGA representatives sailed in the spring of 1920. The conferees met frequently in England and Scotland and played many of the well-known links.

Among the participants was George Herbert Walker, of the National Golf Links of America, Southampton, N. Y., President of the USGA in 1920, who passed away last June. Mr. Walker had been a low-handicap player in St. Louis and was a keen advocate of the game.

Upon the Executive Committee's return to the United States, the possibility of international team matches was discussed. The idea so appealed to Mr. Walker that, at a meeting of the Committee at the Links Club, in Manhattan, on the afternoon of December 21, 1920, he presented a plan for an international golf championship and offered to donate an International Challenge Trophy. When the newspapers printed the news, they called it, to Mr. Walker's chagrin, the "Walker Cup," and the name has stuck.

Early in 1921, the USGA invited all countries interested in golf to send teams to compete for the Trophy, but no country was able to accept that year. The American urge for international competition was rampant, however, and Fownes, who had twice assembled the amateur teams which played against Canada, rounded up a third team in the spring of 1921 and took it to Hoylake, England, where in an informal match it defeated a British team, 9 to 3, on the day before the British Amateur.

If there had been any sentiment that the Americans could not provide adequate competition, this must have dispelled it. The members of that informal United States team were: Charles Evans, Jr., William C. Fownes, Jr., Jesse P. Guilford, Paul Hunter, Robert T. Jones, Jr., Francis D. Ouimet, J. Wood Platt and Frederick J. Wright, Jr. They won all four of the morning foursomes and five of the eight afternoon singles.

Although the Americans were not successful in the British Amateur, Wright did go to the quarter-finals and Jock Hutchison later that year won the British Open, after a play-off with Roger Wethered.

The following spring, the Royal and Ancient Golf Club of St. Andrews, Scotland, announced that it would send a team to compete for the Walker Cup in the United States that year, 1922. Howard F. Whitney, who had succeeded Mr. Walker as president of the USGA in 1921, made the arrangements for the match, selecting as the site Mr. Walker's home club, the National Golf Links of America. The dates were Monday and Tuesday, August 28 and 29. The plan was for each side to select eight players and to play foursomes the first day and singles the second day.

The team selected to represent the United States was again captained by Fownes. The other members were Charles Evans, Jr., Robert A. Gardner, Jesse P. Guilford, Robert T. Jones, Jr., Max R. Marston, Francis D. Ouimet and Jess W. Sweetser. Guilford held the Amateur Championship. Robert Harris was nominated to captain the British team. His side consisted of Cyril J. H. Tolley, Roger H. Wethered, Colin C. Aylmer, C. V. L. Hooman,

W. B. Torrance, John Caven and W. Willis Mackenzie. A notable absentee was Ernest W. E. Holderness, the British Champion, who was unable to make the trip.

Bernard Darwin, the golf writer of the *Times* of London, came with the team as a correspondent. When Harris fell ill before the match, Darwin was invited to compete in his stead and serve as playing captain. He defeated Fownes, 3 and 1, in an interesting singles match after losing the first three holes. In the final singles match, Hooman defeated Sweetser on the first extra hole. It was the only extra hole match ever played in Walker Cup competitions. Since that time, matches which finish even have not been played out, and no points are awarded to either side.

Although many of the matches in that first meeting were close, the United States won three of the four foursomes and the first five of the eight singles to score an 8 to 4 victory in the first official match for the Walker Cup.

The members of the British team went from the National to Brookline, Mass., for the USGA Amateur and only Tolley went as far as the quarter-finals in quest of the title which Sweetser won so impressively.

An invitation to send a team to St. Andrews, Scotland, to defend the cup was quickly accepted the following winter, and the Americans nearly received their come-uppance in May, 1923. There had been many changes in personnel. Robert A. Gardner succeeded William C. Fownes, Jr., as captain, and ten players were selected so that alternates would be available on the scene. In addition to Gardner, Francis Ouimet, Jess Sweetser and Max Marston continued as members. S. Davidson Herron, Harrison R. Johnston, J. F. Neville, George V. Rotan, Dr. O. F. Willing and Frederick J. Wright, Jr., replaced Evans, Fownes, Guilford and Jones, who was studying at Harvard.

In the British Amateur at Deal, which preceded the match, Ouimet, who had won the Gold Vase, went to the semifinals, along with Douglas Grant, a fellow-American who was living abroad. Roger Wethered defeated Robert Harris, 7 and 6, in the final, and he remains the only Briton who has won a British Amateur in a year when a United States Walker Cup Team was playing abroad.

On the first day of the match at St. Andrews, with Cyril Tolley and Roger Wethered leading off, the British won three of the four foursomes, so that the Americans went into the eight singles needing five victories to tie and six to win. The prospect became even more gloomy when most of the Americans were trailing in their singles matches at noon. At one point the team, collectively, had been 24 holes down. Then their competitive fire was kindled. Ouimet, 2 down with three to play, made 3's on the thirty-fourth and thirty-sixth holes, the latter by holing an eighteen-foot putt around a partial stymie, to halve with Wethered and equal the course record of 70. Rotan, who had been 6 down after fourteen holes, rallied to win eleven of the next twelve holes and defeat Mackenzie, 6 and 4. Marston, who had been 1 down at noon, came back to beat W. L. Hope, 5 and 4. Wright, 2 down with three to play, won the last three holes, the final one with a seven-foot putt for a birdie 3, to defeat Holderness.

These comebacks, coupled with Gardner's 1-up victory over Harris, the British Captain, tied the match, and the decision rode on the contest between Dr. Willing and William A. Murray. They were the last on the course, and with three holes to play, they were even. But Dr. Willing won the thirty-fourth and thirty-fifth to give the United States a 6-to-5 victory and retain the Cup.

In his report to the Executive Committee, Howard F. Whitney, chairman of the International Matches and Relations Committee, wrote: "Your committee is of the opinion that international competition in golf has done as much for the development of the game as any other factor."

Another match was scheduled for September, 1924, at the Garden City Golf Club. Captain Gardner's American team was particularly strong that year, every member having been a veteran Cup player. It won, 9 to 3, over Captain Cyril Tolley's side, although not one of the Americans clinched a victory earlier than the thirty-third green. This match was the last to be played on an annual basis. It was felt that the financial strain of annual matches was too severe and that interest might drop if the matches were played too frequently. A decision was made to meet in alternate years thereafter.

In 1926, the Americans, again captained by Gardner, went first to Muirfield, Scotland, for the British Amateur. Jess Sweetser, suffering severely from near-pneumonia, became the first American-born winner of that Championship. Then the team, comprising a nucleus of veterans, with George Von Elm and the two youngsters, Roland MacKenzie, who was only seventeen, and Watts Gunn, returned to St. Andrews for the match and defended the Cup by the narrowest of margins.

Bob Jones, who later that year was to win his first British Open, started his series of one-sided victories in singles play by defeating Cyril Tolley, 12 and 11. Jones never was defeated in five singles matches. But the Americans won only six contests against Captain Harris's side, and their 6 to 5 victory traced to Von Elm's tie with Major Charles O. Hezlet in a grim singles contest on the final day.

After that match, Jones assumed the captaincy of the team and, in 1928 at the Chicago Golf Club and in 1930 at Sandwich, inaugurated a period of ascendancy which saw the Americans winning, 11 to 1 and 10 to 2. Jones set the pace in 1928 when he defeated T. Philip Perkins, 13 and 12, in the first singles match. It was the widest margin in the history of the series.

George J. Voigt and Donald K. Moe joined the team in 1930, and Moe won one of the great matches of the series from James A. (Bill) Stout. Stout played the course in 68 in the morning and stood 4 up. He started the afternoon round 3-3-3 and went 7 up, and he was still 7 up with 13 to play. Moe then took back every one of the seven holes and won the match with a birdie 3 on the last hole. His score for the round was 67. After the match, Stout remarked reverently: "That was not golf; that was a visitation from the Lord!"

Upon Jones's retirement after his Grand Slam in 1930, Francis Ouimet, who had participated in every international match, took over the captaincy in 1932 and retained it for six matches, through 1949. His personal record reveals four victories and two defeats in eight singles matches and five wins and three losses in eight foursomes. He last played in 1934 at St. Andrews but continued as a nonplaying captain.

The personnel of the teams changed rapidly,

too, after the Jones era, as Charles H. Seaver, Gus T. Moreland, George T. Dunlap, Jr., William Howell, Jack Westland, a player in 1932 and 1934 and again in 1953, Maurice J. McCarthy, Jr., W. Lawson Little, Jr., John Goodman, the veteran H. Chandler Egan, who played in 1934 at the age of 50, John W. Fischer, Albert E. Campbell, Reynolds Smith, Charles R. Yates, Walter Emery, Harry L. Givan, Ed White, Charles R. Kocsis, Marvin H. Ward, Raymond E. Billows and Fred Haas, Jr., successively entered the scene in the pre-war years.

At The Country Club in 1932, when the match was played during a total eclipse of the sun, the biggest dent the British made in the Cup was by Leonard G. Crawley. He not only won the only point for Captain T. A. Torrance's side, defeating George J. Voigt by a hole, but his errant iron shot to the eighteenth green at noon hit the Cup on the fly. The Americans won the dented Cup, 8 to 1. The British side that year included two brothers, Rex W. and W. Lister Hartley, and they were paired together in the first foursome.

Playing at St. Andrews in 1934 and then at the Pine Valley Golf Club in 1936, the Americans won their eighth and ninth successive victories, by 9 to 2 and then, in the only shutout of the series, by 9 to 0. The British side in 1934 was captained by the Hon. Michael Scott, who had won the 1933 British Amateur at the age of fifty-five and the following year became the oldest competitor in the Walker Cup series. Again the American invasion included a victory in the British Amateur, Lawson Little winning at Prestwick.

The British went down fighting, however, in 1936. In the foursome play at Pine Valley, Alec Hill and Cecil Ewing were 7 down to George Voigt and Harry Givan with 11 to play. They squared the match on the thirty-fifth hole and halved the last to gain a tie. And Jock McLean, of the British Team, nearly carried away our Amateur Championship; Johnny Fischer had to play the last three holes in birdies to beat him on the thirty-seventh green in the final.

The succession of nine victories, the last four decisive, set the stage for the comeuppance which had been so narrowly averted in 1923. There was every reason for the Americans to be confident again when they went to Scotland in 1938, and Charles R. Yates, the captain this year, won the British Amateur at Troon, prior to the Walker Cup play, to increase this confidence.

The British, however, were most serious about the match. Captain John B. Beck conducted trials for a squad of players in an effort to end the American string of nine successive victories. When the teams met at St. Andrews, the British won two and halved another of the four foursomes to take a lead they never relinquished. An indication of their excellence was the fact that James Bruen, Jr., and Harry G. Bentley, 3 down at noon, came back with an approximate 68 to halve Fischer and Kocsis.

The Americans needed five victories in singles to insure defense of the Cup. Ward played the Old Course in 67 in the first round and beat Frank Pennink, 12 and 11. Fischer, 4 down at noon, was 6 under 4's for sixteen holes in the afternoon to beat Leonard Crawley. Yates also won. But their victories were not enough. Great Britain finally took possession of the Cup, 7 to 4, in its tenth challenge.

It took a decade for the United States to regain the Cup. The war intervened and no match was played until the USGA sent a team to St. Andrews in 1947. Under normal circumstances, the match would have been played in this country, but postwar conditions would have made the trip difficult for the British.

The match was another close one, closer than the score indicated. Captain Ouimet's side won two foursomes, and Captain Beck's side won two. After eighteen holes of singles play, four British players were ahead and four Americans were leading. It was anyone's match, but the Americans were equal to the occasion. Bud Ward, 3 down at noon, played fifteen holes in three under 4's to beat Leonard Crawley, 5 and 3, in the No. 1 contest. Frank Stranahan, 2 down at noon, went to the turn in 34 and defeated Charles Stowe, 2 and 1. The four Americans who had been ahead at noon held their advantages, and the United States regained the Cup, 8 to 4. The team stayed abroad for the British Amateur, at Carnoustie, and Willie Turnesa won.

Only one member of this 1947 team had played in 1938—Bud Ward. In the war decade, Ted Bishop, Dick Chapman, Fred Kammer,

Smiley Quick, Skee Riegel, Stranahan and Turnesa achieved Cup status and took over from the veterans. In 1951 Turnesa replaced Ouimet as captain. These players were joined in the following two Cup Matches by Billy Campbell, Charley Coe, John Dawson, Bobby Knowles, Bruce McCormick, Harold Paddock and Sam Urzetta.

When the match was next held in the United States, in 1949 at the Winged Foot Golf Club, Mamaroneck, N. Y., it was not so close. Laddie Lucas, a left-handed golfer, provided outstanding leadership as a nonplaying captain, but United States skill with the sand wedge and putter could not be overcome. Ronnie White, the British lead-off player, won his singles and his foursome, the latter with Joe Carr, but these were the only points the British took. The United States won, 10 to 2.

This superiority was maintained at Birkdale in 1951, although on English soil the margin of this twelfth United States victory was a less emphatic 6 to 3. As a matter of fact, after eighteen holes of first-day foursomes, the British led in three matches and the fourth was even, but Captain Turnesa's men rallied to win two of the foursomes and halve the other two. The next day they won four and halved one of the eight singles. Paddock saved the half after being 3 down with four to play and 2 down with two to play, finishing 3-4-3-4. White again was the mainstay of the British side, playing thirty-five holes in three under fours to edge Coe in singles after pairing with Carr to halve his foursome. White has never been defeated in Cup play.

Following the match, Dick Chapman won the British Amateur, defeating Coe in an all-American final. It marked the seventh successive occasion on which a member of a visiting United States Walker Cup Team had won.

During this visit, representatives of the Royal and Ancient Golf Club and of the USGA met in London and St. Andrews, with representatives of Australia and Canada, and drafted a uniform code of Rules. Thus the series which had developed in part from the 1920 conference on Rules itself spawned another and more successful conference on Rules. Every match until 1949 had been played under a purely verbal, informal agreement. Early that year, however, the Royal and Ancient Golf Club and the USGA finally wrote a cover-

ing agreement which was signed by Commander J. A. S. Carson for the R. and A. and by Isaac B. Grainger for the USGA.

When weather is normal along the Massachusetts coast, a southwest breeze whips up white caps on Buzzards Bay and blows briskly across the Kittansett Club's golf course. The weather was by no means normal, however, during the fourteenth international match for the Walker Cup, held at Kittansett in September, 1953. It was calm and hot most of the time. Thus the seaside course which had seemed likely to provide cooling winds favorable to the British offered conditions which differed little from those at many an inland course on the hot days of Labor Day weekend.

There is no way of estimating how this freak of weather affected the result. It may be that the United States side, which exhibited remarkable control of the ball, would have been able to find its targets through the wind just as well as the British. However, it was clearly American weather, not British weather. In this native sultry heat, the United States proved clearly superior in depth and won the Cup for the thirteenth time, 9 to 3.

The United States won the first three of the four foursomes on the first day, and although the British played bravely and stubbornly, it seemed throughout the day that they were fated to trail. The most spectacular play came in the third foursome, where James G. Jackson and Gene A. Littler played alternate strokes in par over thirty-two holes to defeat the two Scotsmen, Roy C. MacGregor and James C. Wilson, 3 and 2.

This was a whirlaway sort of a victory, for Jackson and Littler were 3 down playing from the fourth tee. Wilson chipped in for a birdie 3 to win the first hole and then Jackson discovered and reported while walking up the second fairway that he had sixteen clubs in his bag, two more than Rule 3 allows. He had neglected to remove his brassie and an extra wedge. The penalty is, of course, disqualification, and the first reaction of the Executive Committee was to invoke it. However, the British immediately asserted their desire to win their points on their play of the game. The Committee then yielded and modified the penalty to two holes, the number which Jackson had played in inadvertent violation, as it was empowered to do by Rule 36-5. Since the British already had won the first hole, the United States pair was penalized the second and third holes and was sent to the fourth tee 3 down. They were still 3 down at the turn, but a homecoming 33 gained them five holes and a lead they never relinquished.

The next best performance was displayed by the British team of Gerald H. Micklem and John L. Morgan, who were only three over par for thirty-three holes in besting William C. Campbell and Charles R. Coe, 4 and 3, to win the only foursome point for their side.

It was in the singles play on the second day, however, that the heroic match occurred. The United States won six of the eight singles, and certainly incurred no embarrassment over the second engagement, in which Ronald J. White, of Great Britain, defeated Richard D. Chapman, who is a member of the Kittansett Club, 1 up.

After thirty holes, Chapman was 3 up. It looked very much as if White, who had gone unbeaten in both foursomes and singles in three previous matches but had lost his foursome the day before, had come altogether to the end of his string. But not so. White played the last six holes in three birdies and three pars, three 3's and three 4's, to win four of them and his fourth successive Walker Cup singles. Chapman survived the first two birdies and was still 1 up with two to play, but White hit a superb half shot from the rough with a No. 4 iron on the thirty-fifth and ran in a ten-foot putt for a birdie 3 to square the match. The last hole is a 455-yarder into a quartering breeze which had sprung up at the end of the day, and White was handsomely on with his second while Chapman was bunkered near the green. The match turned when Chapman did not explode quite close enough to match White's par 4. White's score was 77-70 —147 and Chapman, even with 7's on the fifteenth hole in each round, did two 74's.

The best scoring in singles was turned in by E. Harvie Ward, Jr., and Gene Littler, of the United States. Both were one under par for thirty-three holes and they needed it, Ward to defeat Joseph B. Carr, the British Amateur Champion, 4 and 3, in the first match and Littler to beat Gerald Micklem, the English Amateur Champion, 5 and 3, in the third match. The depth of the United States strength was apparent, however, in the achievements of Sam Urzetta and Kenneth P. Venturi, who were only one over par, and of Donald R. Cherry, the Canadian Champion, and Congressman Jack Westland, the USGA Amateur Champion, who were only three over in wrapping up four more victories.

John Morgan won the third and last British point when he beat Charles R. Coe, 3 and 2, and he was the only Briton to score in both foursomes and singles. He and Gerald Micklem had gotten the better of Coe and William C. Campbell on the previous day.

Generally speaking, the United States side played the larger American ball and the British played the smaller British ball. Play with either ball in an international team match is permitted by Rule 2-3a. Discussions of the relative merits of the two balls were inconclusive, however.

Most of the United States players carried a few of the smaller balls against the possibility of high winds, but the winds never really came. Chapman started his singles match with the smaller ball but switched to the larger ball after seven holes. A few of the others put the smaller ball into play for a particular hole only. The consensus was that the balls act differently in coming off the clubface around and on the greens, and each side seemed reluctant to abandon the ball it understood best around the greens.

As is customary with Walker Cup matches, however, the play was by no means the whole show. The Kittansett Club carried out like a veteran its traditional role as host, and provided not only a most testing course but also an enjoyable week of golf and festivities which enabled the two teams to get to know one another intimately and to compete on the friendliest basis.

There seems no doubt that this match, like its predecessors, served the purposes which the late George Herbert Walker had in mind when he established the competition: to set an example in good golf and good sportsmanship and to tighten the bonds of international friendship. The worth of these purposes was acknowledged by the highest office in the land during the dinner for the two teams, when the following letter addressed to Senator Prescott S. Bush, a former President of the USGA, was read:

Denver, Colorado
September 3, 1953

Dear Pres:

Some time ago I sent Mr. Reece a formal message of welcome and greeting to the members of the British and American teams participating in the Walker Cup Matches at the Kittansett Club on September 4th and 5th. Now, however, I would like to join with the friends and relatives of George Herbert Walker in saluting his memory on this occasion. He was a distinguished citizen and sportsman, and I am proud to have known and admired him.

Good luck to all who are participating in the Walker Cup Matches at Kittansett!

With warm personal regards to you and Mrs. Bush,

Sincerely,

DWIGHT D. EISENHOWER

INTERNATIONAL MATCH FOR THE WALKER CUP
Held at the Kittansett Club, Marion, Mass.
September 4 and 5, 1953

FOURSOMES

GREAT BRITAIN		UNITED STATES	
Joseph B. Carr and Ronald J. White	0	Sam Urzetta and Kenneth P. Venturi (6 and 4)	1
John D. A. Langley and Arthur H. Perowne	0	E. Harvie Ward, Jr., and Jack Westland (9 and 8)	1
James C. Wilson and Roy C. MacGregor..	0	James G. Jackson and Gene A. Littler (3 and 2)	1
Gerald H. Micklem and John L. Morgan (4 and 3)	1	William C. Campbell and Charles R. Coe	0
Foursomes Totals	1		3

SINGLES

GREAT BRITAIN		UNITED STATES	
Joseph B. Carr	0	E. Harvie Ward, Jr. (4 and 3)	1
Ronald J. White (1 up)	1	Richard D. Chapman	0
Gerald H. Micklem	0	Gene A. Littler (5 and 3)	1
Roy C. MacGregor	0	Jack Westland (7 and 5)	1
Norman V. Drew	0	Donald R. Cherry (9 and 7)	1
James C. Wilson	0	Kenneth P. Venturi (9 and 8)	1
John L. Morgan (3 and 2)	1	Charles R. Coe	0
John D. A. Langley	0	Sam Urzetta (3 and 2)	1
Singles totals	2		6
Grand totals	3		9
Captain: Lt. Col. A. A. Duncan		Captain: Charles R. Yates	

The Babe Comes Back

by

AL LANEY

1954 — FROM THE JULY 4 ISSUE OF THE NEW YORK *HERALD TRIBUNE*

Peabody, Mass., July 3

MILDRED ZAHARIAS, she who is known to all as The Babe, won the second women's National Open golf championship at the Salem Country Club today by the overwhelming margin of twelve strokes and with the very fine seventy-two-hole score of 291.

Mrs. Zaharias, leading by seven strokes as the final day began, played two closing rounds in 73 and 75 and the mere figures of her four rounds—72—71—73—75—speak eloquently of her quality as golfer, athlete and competitor. The total is three strokes above a really difficult course par and all three were dropped on the final few holes when she was very tired and so far ahead as to be practically out of sight.

The positions of those who were behind her in a field which included all of the best professional girls and many of the fine amateurs of the country, does not really matter, but here is the order in which they finished.

Betty Hicks, a former amateur champion, was second with a total of 303 and Louise Suggs was third at 307. Tied at 308 with Mary Wright, the low amateur, was Betsy Rawls, defending champion, and then came Jacqueline Pung who lost a play-off to Miss Rawls last year, at 309. The remainder of the forty who qualified for the last two rounds then were strung out, some with well-known names but very high scores.

It is impossible to praise too highly the play of the new champion for what we saw here probably was the finest consecutive four rounds of golf on a championship course under championship conditions ever played by a woman.

Mrs. Zaharias was the only one of all the girls here who understood how the difficult Salem course should be played and had the shots to do it. She alone negotiated the strenuous three-day journey without once faltering until near the end when she was very tired and had many strokes in hand, playing the same fine brand of golf in every round, never once yielding to the pressure and tension that an Open championship, under the banner of the U. S. G. A. must always bring.

She was tied with Claire Doran, the Cleveland amateur, at the end of the first round for a 2-stroke lead and she moved to a 7-stroke lead at the halfway mark which would have enabled her to coast home today. But by noon it had increased to 10 strokes.

Other girls had fine single rounds though none so fine as her best and none could put two such together. Four such as she achieved seemed wholly out of the reach of any other. It is a score which any male golfer in the land could be happy to have on his card.

So now The Babe's name will be engraved on the new U. S. G. A. Open Trophy where it belongs, just below that of Miss Rawls, who won the first Open at Rochester last year. The Babe did not play in that one. Everyone will remember that she was then just recovering from a cancer operation and the fact that she has come back in so short a time to play such wonderful golf makes her victory the more remarkable.

There is no doubt that The Babe's excellence took something from the tournament in the way of tension and excitement but it stands alone as a performance to be admired by all. After she had fired her 71 on Friday, the tournament was over so far as the winner was concerned, leaving only the battle for second money by way of a contest.

But the struggle for second place in a big golf tournament is not really very interesting and nobody bothered much about what the other girls were doing on the last day. They were, in fact, having a nice quiet little scramble for position which, if The Babe's score had been removed from the top, could have developed into an exciting event.

The champion's play, however, was most interesting from several points of view. With so big a lead to start the third round this morning she was in a position to play it safely and conservatively for a moderately good score. Even a 75 or a 76 would have made her position practically impregnable at lunch time.

She did play it this way for the most part but with the caution dictated by circumstances she mingled great boldness at times. First she made sure that on no hole would her score get out of control but she was forever seeking opportunities to save a stroke. Many times she went straight for the pin when everyone expected her to play safely to the middle of the green for par.

Sometimes this cost her strokes but at other points she got them back by the same methods. Going out this morning she was over par twice and under once and coming home she was over once and under once. She was in the happy position of being able to lose a stroke without the slightest worry, knowing she could probably get it back somewhere along the line and not caring much if she did or didn't.

This made every hole a little adventure for her and the crowd. The Babe thoroughly enjoyed the day and so did all of us who went with her. We all knew that we were seeing the best there is, a real champion giving an outstanding performance.

She acted the part of a champion to perfection and her progress twice around the course was a queenly procession with her nearest pursuers, already dimly seen in the far distance at the start, fading more and more out of the picture as the day wore on.

At the very end the champion's quality stood out most strongly. Over the last four or five holes The Babe had begun to fly the first faint distress signals. Her tee shots, which had been wonderfully accurate for three days, began to fade and hook badly, a sure sign of fatigue.

At the final hole, with all the people lining the course and waiting to escort her home, she sliced her drive badly into a wicked place among trees. She could have used as many strokes as she pleased to finish and the sensible thing to do was to sacrifice a stroke and play back to the fairway. But The Babe took the position that this was no way to finish. She found a tiny opening and she took a long iron and went through it toward the distant green. A champion's shot and a great roar greeted it. It gave her a chance for a par-4. She missed it by an inch but she had finished in a champion's way.

For The Babe has now completely outclassed all her challengers. She has set the pattern by which a champion should act on the course and off it and in the future all women golfers must be judged as they measure up to the standard or fail to do so.

The scores:

Mrs. M. Zaharias, Niles, Ill.	72-71-73-76—291
Betty Hicks, Durham, N.C.	76-76-75-77—303
Louise Suggs, Atlanta	76-77-78-76—307
*Mary K. Wright, La Jolla, Calif.	74-79-79-76—308
B. Rawls, Spartanburg, S.C.	77-73-78-80—308
Mrs. Jacqueline Pung, Glasgow, Ky.	81-77-78-73—309
*P. Ann Lesser, Seattle ...	79-73-78-80—310
Beverly Hanson, Fargo, N.D.	77-80-78-75—310
Fay Crocker, Montevideo, Uruguay	77-82-79-73—311
*Claire Doran, Cleveland	72-79-80-80—311
*Mrs. Mae Murray Jones, Rutland, Vt.	79-81-74-78—312
Patty Berg, St. Andrews, Ill.	78-76-78-81—313
Betty Dodd, Louisville ...	77-77-78-82—314
B. Jameson, San Antonio, Tex.	78-78-80-80—316
Bonnie Randolph, Linworth, Ohio	82-81-74-79—316
Mrs. Betty Bush, Hammond, Ind.	79-79-83-75—316
*Mary Lena Faulk, Thomasville, Ga.	77-76-84-79—316
P. O'Sullivan, Orange, Conn.	76-79-81-82—318
*J. Ziske, Waterford, Wis.	78-82-78-80—318
Marilyn Smith, Wichita...	83-75-79-82—319
Betty MacKinnon, Savannah	78-80-82-80—320
*Mrs. Helen Siegel Wilson, Bala, Pa.	80-82-84-76—322
*Jean Hopkins, Cleveland.	78-79-83-86—326
*Mrs. Edward J. McAuliffe, Newton, Mass. .	82-83-81-84—330

* Amateur.

THE
MASTERS' VOICES

Their Views on Theory,
Technique, Learning and Playing

The Importance of Style

by

WILLIE PARK

1896 — FROM *THE GAME OF GOLF*

IT IS of the first importance that a golfer should have a good style of play, these words being here used as including grip of club, stance, and swing. One frequently hears it said, "What does my style signify provided I can play a good game?" To this I would reply, "In the majority of cases it is hardly possible to play a good game unless you have a good style." It is also said that if the best golfers be closely watched no two of them have the same style, and which among all these styles is the correct one? My answer to this is that there are few crack players who have not a good style, and that although there may be, and undoubtedly are, many whose styles are different in detail, they are fundamentally the same—they are all modeled on the recognized lines. There are, however, among the followers of every game men whose play can hardly be excelled, and who yet violate the canons of style. Such players have been termed geniuses, and a few are to be found among the ranks of golfers; but I would further say that these are the exceptions that prove the rule. The imitators of geniuses seldom attain to any perfection, and generally find it difficult to reach mediocrity. For geniuses no rules can be laid down—their success justifies their play, but only their success. Failure would heap on their heads deserved ridicule.

I would recommend all golfers to model their styles upon the recognized lines that have stood the test of decades of play at the hands of the best amateurs and professionals. If anyone finds himself to be a genius, he can easily carve out his own particular style, and will be none the worse, but probably much the better, for having begun upon the orthodox lines.

Styles and Methods, Then and Now

by

HENRY COTTON

1952 — FROM *THE HISTORY OF GOLF IN BRITAIN*

SINCE Sir Walter Simpson wrote *The Art of Golf* in 1887, golf has gone a long way. His book may not have been the first book on the game, but it is one of the earliest which attempted to give golf readers some theory of the game.

To show that there is really little new in golf except the equipment itself, I will quote a few words from the chapter "Of Driving in General": "Do I maintain, then, the reader may ask, that everyone ought to have the same style? By no means; on the contrary for you or me to model ourselves on a champion is about as profitless as to copy out *Hamlet* in the hope of becoming Shakespeare. There is no more fruitful source of bad golf than to suppose there is some best style for each individual which must be searched out by him if he is to get the best results out of himself. In a broad and general way, each player ought to have, and has, a style which is the reflection of himself, his build, his mind, the age at which he began, and his previous habits."

Here we have written in 1887 truths which are still true today, yet many famous golfers still contribute golf books in which they pursue one theory and ignore such words of wisdom. I can only assume that they *believe* there is one system, or alternatively are catering to public demand or satisfying their publishers' request.

In the days of the hickory shaft and the stony gutty—it seems pointless to go back to the feather ball days, for there I am sure it was essential to "nurse" the ball to stop it bursting—players began to play more as balls were plentiful and cheap and to hit the ball as hard as they could. With hard hitting came the necessity to insulate the shock, and that is one reason for the thick grips then used generally. The thick grips, leather-faced clubs (so faced to absorb shock and to protect the soft beechwood heads), I feel, made gripping of the club a job for the palms and not for the fingers and hands as today.

Whilst gripping the club was not ignored in teaching golf, one has only to look at the photos of old golfers taken playing some fifty years ago to realize that the shaft slid about in the hands freely.

I am astounded that with such loose grips Harold Hilton, John Ball, Jr., H. G. Hutchinson, J. L. Low and Edward Blackwell—to name but a few top players of the end of the nineteenth century—could win fame. For they held the club in the palms of both hands, left thumbs outside, and then allowed the hands to slide on the shaft during the swing—an action which we condemn strongly today. J. H. Taylor, Harry Vardon, James Braid, L. Balfour Melville, R. Maxwell, John Graham, Jr., were amongst players of the same era who had grips that would be accepted as sound today. This is really an understatement, for the

244

modern overlapping grip is accredited to Harry Vardon—although there is evidence that Leslie Balfour Melville used it first, and J. H. Taylor, using the overlapping grip, was also winning before Harry Vardon scored major successes.

"Keep your eye on the ball" is by no means a new slogan. It has been an essential part of the game of golf ever since the game started, and the fact that you could stare at the ball too much has also not escaped notice. In the 1880's, before the overlapping grip was recognized as a help to getting the hands working together, players were advised to keep their hands as near to one another as possible. To show the importance of this, Sir Walter Simpson warns players that every inch the hands are apart knocks ten yards off the length of the shot. I have never thought of such positions in terms of inches and yards, but I imagine he must have got the information from somewhere.

Style as such seems to be given a smaller and smaller place in the game, for today no one really cares if certain players look elegant when they play—only results talk. It does so happen fortunately that most of the great players today look grand when they play, but we have had winners also who appear quite unorthodox with methods which confound many accepted theories.

Years ago, style was admired, I suppose, more in life in general; now utility and efficacy have outdone sheer beauty. Style was looked upon as an essential part of the make-up of a golfer. Today, unless it justifies the end, it can be ignored.

With the exception of J. H. Taylor, who was a short sturdy player of exceptional strength for his size, all the great golfers of years ago had long free swings, and seemed to throw themselves about more as they hit. I am sure that the ball itself had much to do with this, for unless you have played a gutty ball you cannot imagine what an unresponsive object it is and what an effort it takes to drive it 200 yards. As I write this I am looking at an impact photograph (Beldam's *Great Golfers,* p. 148) of J. H. Taylor taken in 1903 at a speed of one-thousandth of a second, in which he is seen hitting the ball with a driving mashie, which fitted in his set between the cleek and the mashie iron. By today's stand-

ards the cleek would be a strong No. 2 iron and the mashie iron a strong No. 4 iron, so the driving mashie would be a No. 3 or thereabouts with a medium deep face. Taylor hit that particular shot 150 yards—a very good shot for those days. Beneath the photo of a drive taken at the same period it mentioned the shot as being 200 yards in length.

The surprising thing when getting down to make a study of styles and methods of today and yesterday is that they are fundamentally so nearly similar that the hints of yesterday can apply today and tomorrow. Here is a series of "Do's and Don't's of the Day" written nearly fifty years ago (with my comments after them) which remain as enlightening to today's reader as they did no doubt to the reader in knickerbockers, cap, and Norfolk jacket—the golfer's dress of those days.

Don't take the club back too quickly. This advice can surely never change.

Don't hurry downward swing but allow the club naturally to increase speed. This can be the old way of saying "swing the clubhead," a slogan of today which brings in countless dollars to a few instructors in the U.S.A.

Don't think of the circle described in the swing as being vertically up and down the line of flight of the ball, as in cricket. Golfers claimed most of their successful adherents from the cricket field, but already in these days the path of the clubhead was seen as being not a circle but a looping movement. This shows that all the astonishment expressed by the golfing world on discovering Bobby Jones's perfect flowing swing was looping as it was flowing was a display of ignorance, for it was already known years earlier that a golf clubhead did not follow a perfect circular route.

Don't swing any club so far back as to lose control of it. Today we might say, do not overswing: or, as I wrote in my first golf book when talking of the three-quarter swing, that it was preferable to hold on to the club all the time, and be restricted by the flexibility of the left wrist to a less than full backswing, if to swing to the horizontal meant letting go.

Don't forget the clubhead should be

traveling at its greatest velocity when it reaches the ball, having gradually increased in speed, with no perceptible pause on the top of the swing. This would to-day be written as "hit late," get the maximum speed at impact, but the "no perceptible pause on the top of the swing" seems hard to explain.

Don't hit at the ball; the rhythm of the swing must not be destroyed. "Slow back" means that time must be given to allow the clubhead to gradually gain speed until the highest momentum is reached at the point of impact. This is to some extent a repetition of previous advice but "wait for the hit" might apply. The softer, more whippy hickory shafts needed a different timing from our modern steel shafts.

Don't, in swinging back, take the clubhead so far out that the right elbow has to leave the side. Do not swing too upright.

Don't bend the left knee too soon with wood clubs in the upward swing. Keep the left heel down as long as possible in the backswing might be more in line with to-day's parlance.

Don't swing so much with iron clubs, but take them back rather more upright than in driving. Here the word upright comes in, which is self-explanatory, but a simpler expression would be use a shorter swing with the iron clubs. Iron clubs can be swung on the same arc, more or less, as the woods—they need only be more upright because the ball is nearer to the player.

Don't, in wrist mashie shot, allow the wrists to go too far through after striking the ball. A wrist stroke generally contains a little forearm. There is no such thing as a pure wrist stroke in golf, except for very short shots. Here is a distinction between the flick and the push. The wrist mashie shot is the flick, the push would be the forerunner of what today is the wedge shot. How true it is that most shots, except the little delicate chips, are forearm and wrist, not wrist alone.

*Do let the wrists take the clubhead back first; let the arms follow, then let the body turn from the hips; in the down-*ward swing the body turns immediately, the wrists take the club through, pulling the arms after them, then the body turns again and faces the hole. To-day we say let the arms and hands take the club back together, let the body follow, begin to unwind the body, the club follows, the body unwind checks momentarily for the clubhead to pass the body, then continues after impact.

Do keep the head steady throughout the swing; there should be no jumping up, either at the top of the swing or at the moment of impact. Play under the head would be a simple way of telling the golfer not to permit his head to move all over the place.

Don't look up too soon after the ball has been struck. Cricketers are apt to do this. Why only cricketers every modern reader must ask, for it is a general international complaint for which there is no certain trick cure. The only way to overcome this fault is simply not to do it.

Do look at the part of the ball to be struck, not at the ball in an absent-minded abstract kind of way. Focus on the back of the ball not just on the ball in general. Concentrate on where you are to make impact.

It might seem that I am trying to make out that there is "nothing new under the sun" by making these comparisons which amount to very little, for the advice offered fifty years ago stands today.

I think that, as the game has grown and more people have studied it, one can put the study which has been made—and the players of the day have inspired that study—into periods. The balls and the implements as much as the players have been responsible for the trends, and the improvement in the courses has also had an effect on the technique during these periods.

It is correct to say that with the hickory shaft a bigger variety of strokes could be played willingly and unwillingly. Now the almost torsionless steel shaft of recent times has simplified stroke production. The average "dub" or "duffer" will refute the suggestions that his counterpart of pre-steel shaft days could "spray" the ball in a greater variety of ways than he can, but this was true because he had the torsion of the shaft to contend with.

With hickory shafts and golf balls of varying weights and sizes—a state of affairs which existed up to May 1, 1921, when a standard ball was made to Royal and Ancient specifications—players molded their styles to suit their strength, as now, but also included in their calculations the type of ball being used. A small heavy ball suited certain methods and was difficult to get in the air, so, apart from requiring great strength to send it on its way, it was usually cut up through the green. The time from the first rubber-cored ball, the Haskell, in 1902, to the adoption of the standard ball, 1.62 in. in diameter and 1.62 oz. in weight, and still unchanged to-day, could be one period. From 1921-29 when the steel shaft came in, another period. From 1929 onwards to today, a further period, during which time the American influence on style and method could be more felt, for in 1932 with the breaking away from our ball (on the grounds that it made golf too easy) and the adoption of the 1.68 in. and 1.62 oz. ball (a bigger size which they still use today), a slightly different system was necessary to keep this naturally higher-flying ball under the same control.

Jones, Hagen and Sarazen, brought up on hickory and the small ball, reigned supreme in world golf in the twenties and their reign overlapped into the thirties.

The methods of Braid, Vardon and Taylor which were the patterns of the day have stood the test of time, for they—and I might humbly add myself to this list as a further example of a wrist golfer—have been able to keep a reasonable standard of play for long years and devote time to other things in life, whereas it seems to me that since the end of World War II, the top golfers have required to hit golf balls all day long and nearly every day in order to make their play sound enough. Walter Hagen said to me during a recent meeting we had that if he had needed to slog at the game like the present-day golfers in order to reach his form he would have chosen another profession.

Joyce Wethered was another example of the wrist-under-the-shaft golfer, getting into form with the minimum of effort. These cases might be attributed to inborn ability, but I cannot help but feel that method has something to do with it.

The very strong hitters, and there are many in postwar golf, will always need to flight the ball more than the weaker players in order to stop the ball climbing so high that it is too long at the mercy of the wind, and that is one reason for a veering towards a more closed clubface, for there is a limit to the "straight-facedness" of a driver and to the depth of face.

GUTTY BALL PERIOD

There is not much left in golf today, outside old clubs in show cases in clubhouse lounges, which can remind us of the golf game as it was in the gutty ball era when the game really began to develop. The game grew but slowly with the gutty, although this ball came into golf as long ago as in 1848, and in 1896 there were only sixty-one courses in Scotland and forty-six in England. Wooden-headed clubs for approaching were gradually superseded by the long-headed iron ones; and then J. H. Taylor, the first English-born player to show the Scots that golfing well was not a Scotsman's prerogative, launched the mashie—a short-faced lofted iron used for pitching.

Golfers began to score better as the gutty improved in its composition and markings, and I suppose also because players could get balls to stand up to the practicing required to acquire a good swing. The unresilient gutty was a difficult ball to propel and it really wanted a terrific sweeping stroke to get it on its way; the more sweep the better, for the shock of impact then seemed less. Admittedly its stony "deadness" made play around the green a more simple matter. Scores in the old days were ridiculously high by our standards today and any attempt at making comparisons with a period almost a hundred years later must be even sillier, but a golfer whose span of life took him from the days of Young Tom Morris's Championship Belt win at Prestwick in 1870, when the course used was only twelve holes long, said that his score of 149 for thirty-six holes, three times round, was but two over par, as par by our standards was forty-nine for the twelve holes. There were stylists no doubt before Harry Vardon, but he—because his swing seemed to give as good or better results

247

than any contemporary with less apparent effort—was known as "the stylist." Controlled shots have no doubt always been played and recognized as such, for shots of this type only came to be considered obsolete when batteries of iron clubs appeared, numbered even in half numbers—2½, 3½, etc.—whereby it was assumed that one swing was good enough for the whole game.

The wooden putter died with the gutty ball. This club, one of the original and most used clubs amongst the few carried loose under the arm, was employed for any sort of approach shot, at times from as far as 100 yards from the hole, particularly on such hard-baked bare fairways as were to be found in certain periods of the year on links like St. Andrews.

A few older golfers prize these handmade treasures of bygone days, but as no top-grade golfer has used one for years, it can be concluded that for modern golf they are completely obsolete.

RUBBER-CORED BALL DAYS

IT is obviously just a coincidence that, with the advent of the Haskell, the first satisfactory rubber-cored ball, when golf took a big leap forward in popularity, the camera became a sufficiently improved apparatus to "freeze" the swings of the leading players and so open up the study of what took place during a golf swing.

Later the slow-motion cinematograph "burst open" positively a number of theories, particularly the one that a perfect swing was a true circular movement, whereas in fact the swing was found to be a looping action (Sir Walter Simpson's book of 1887 had already stated this, as I have quoted). Since the rubber-cored ball turned an ordinary clumsy golfer overnight into a moderate performer (for mis-hits often gave as much as a 75 per cent result), the long hitters were obliged to learn control, and so came the controlled backswings for play to the pin and the use of more lofted clubs which give greater backspin and ball control.

From 1902 to 1921 players had all the scope they wanted to get the most out of themselves, for there was no limit to the size and weight of the ball which could be used and, of course, extremes were tested. Small heavy balls and big floaters all appeared, and appealed to various people; but naturally they complicated the game, for during a single round the golfer was inclined to use the small heavy ball against the wind and the larger ball downwind, seeking to get the maximum out of himself—or, if he did not do so, regretted that he had not tried.

These conditions, and the fact that artificial watering to keep the greens holding was not encouraged (the Open Championship was held as usual in midsummer and the putting greens were often shiny brown "skating rinks"), caused the player to learn to play all the shots, and in his never-ending search there is no doubt that the hickory shaft was a help. With the torsion of the hickory shaft and the fine adjustment of the feel of any club by filing it down the shaft, golfers could make experiments which are impossible today.

In these 1902-21 days it does appear that a successful golfer had to be a smart person, for he had to think up the exact shot he was wanting, and he had a big variety from which to pick. The hands, always very important for the part they play in the swing, took on an even more important role—a peep at George Beldam's excellent book *Great Golfers, Their Methods at a Glance*, published in 1904, will show how golfers of that day had time, with the flexible "torsionful" hickory shaft, to *make* the shots with their hands. A pitch and run shot was played with a most pronounced turnover of the wrists, forearms and shoulders, and a cut-up pitch was played with a definite slicing-across-the-ball action, left elbow riding high. These exaggerated actions almost seem to be caricatures today and seem as dated as the acting in the first silent films. Yet little has changed fundamentally in the methods, for a golf ball, of necessity following the laws of ballistics, responds to the same spins.

Players in this era began to practice more because competition was fiercer and it became more necessary than ever to specialize; yet prior to World War I players in both professional and amateur ranks would often begin to polish up their game not more than one week before the championships. Braid, Vardon and Taylor dominated golf in this period. They had varying styles because they were of distinctly different builds. Braid, tall and wiry, when at his best, very flexible, was 6 ft. 1½ in.

tall and weighed 12 st. 6 lb.; Vardon, 5 ft. 9½ in. and weight 11 st., was very wiry; Taylor, 5 ft. 8½ in. and 11 st. 7 lb., short and sturdy. They all played with their left wrists under the shaft at the top of the swing and this became *the* position to copy. It was not that other players did not keep the left wrist in line with the left forearm (now spoken of as the latest American method), but I think that the different equipment in use at the time, and also the type and weight of ball used, had a great varying influence on the methods of the different players. Balls would fly at all sort of trajectories, for little was known in those days of the effects of the various markings on flight and steadiness. John Ball, Jr., who had an exceptional record as an amateur in gutty and immediate post-gutty days, although he had a curious double-handed palm grip (right hand so far under that the fingers of the hand faced the sky) used "the latest American method" then. I refer to the method by this name ironically, because I find many of our young players today breaking their backs (almost in fact) practicing it, believing that it is the secret of golf and something quite new. I am certain that players of the caliber of Braid, Vardon and Taylor—the order in which I put these great names matters little—had all the shots, and used them to exercise their superiority over their contemporaries. That they tried out this shut-faced method, I am sure. Braid, in fact, due to his left hand being more on the top of the shaft than the other two, was at times a big hooker because of this tendency.

The shut-faced player can play very straight shots, of course—the records of those using this method prove it—but the records also show that very few of them escape periods, and for some long periods, when a disastrous hook has put them off their game. Many never recover their youthful form, for shut-faced golf is young man's golf, and they pursue the same method in the hope of recapturing that something which once gave them their greatest golfing days. The shut-faced player fights a hook as his "bogey," the open-faced player generally has the "slice" as his nightmare—to be a good golfer, anyway, it is necessary to have one side of the course to play towards. Although the rubber-cored ball of the era about which I am writing was a good prod-

uct, it needed flighting all the time to get the most out of it, just as would a floater if used today. In those days, with a wind from the left it would be necessary to fade the ball in order to steal a few yards, and likewise to hook with the wind when it came from the right. The modern powerful tournament player can ignore almost any wind except a gale. Today players repeat one swing monotonously, finding that it is "plenty good enough" for the vast majority of occasions.

Although the three heroes of the triumvirate I mentioned were by no means weak men, sheer power in golf as such was not worshipped then as it later was to become. Skill reaped its reward—skill at conceiving the shots and skill in executing them. When the century opened and the gutty was the ball, a whippy shaft was prized; but it was found that, for control under pressure, a somewhat firmer type of shaft was preferable and hence the straight-grained steely hickory shaft became in demand. This demand grew as the game developed in popularity. Hickory wood used in the construction of wheel spokes and tool handles, grew scarce and good hickory shafts became more and more difficult to find. When the war ended in 1918 players were using very mixed bags of clubs, and it was one of the joys of golf to search the racks of the professional's shop at each golf course visited to find a new "super" club. Then the next task was to learn to know that club, to adjust one's game to the club, and to remember when playing it how it had to be timed and if the shot could be forced or not. Some shafts would not take an all-out hit—they had to be timed, and this timing learned. With a big bag of clubs it was more than likely that every club in action would behave differently, due to the different weight and balance. Even a good club would soon be rubbed away with emery cloth by conscientious caddies, and the nonrustless soft iron heads got lighter every day they were cleaned. So golfers had many more problems than the 1951 players.

1921-1929

I TAKE these years following World War I as another definite period in golf, because in 1921 a standard golf ball of "not less than 1.62 in. in diameter and not more than 1.62 oz. in weight" came into being. This ruled out all the added complications of having to choose your ball for the day and the course according to local conditions, and meant that golfers had one problem solved for them. There were some faint objections, of course, but this was a sound move, for players could now set about learning to master one ball.

From this moment mechanical golf, as we were later to see and read about, was created, for all over the world golfers began to practice hard in order to learn all about this new standard ball. There were no outstanding methods of play differing widely from earlier ones, although Mr. R. T. Jones, Jr., of Atlanta, Georgia, the top golfer in the game through this period and, apart from Walter Hagen, well out on his own, set the whole world trying to play golf with such a narrow stance that at times the heels were touching even for full shots. Only Walter Hagen's wide sprawly stance reminded golfers that there could be champions with other stances. Bobby Jones—as he will ever be to British golfers, although he curiously enough dislikes being called Bobby and his letters are always signed Bob—turned professional after his great "Grand Slam" of wins of 1930. This period of narrow stance experiments by the golfing world—I used a narrow stance and persevered with it with mixed success like many others at the time—came to an end in due course, and I think that, like the "Naughty" nineties or the fabulous twenties, it will never return. Jones's long lazy swing was copied, photographed in slow motion, watched on cardboard flickers and analyzed by writers and students throughout the world, and had its effect on the world's golf game.

Overlapping (yet not overlapping but interlocking) the latter part of this period and the following few years, taking one into the thirties, came a best-selling golf book by Alex Morrison from California, in which the interlocking grip, index finger of the left hand and little finger of the right hand intertwined and with the left thumb outside the grip, was put forward as the latest in golf. This so-called *new* grip—Vardon referring to his own grip in 1904 said: "My grip is overlapping not interlocking"—clutched the golf world and it took quite a long time for each and every golfer to spend his quota of practice time, in the vast majority of cases without profit, in testing out the new false freedom of the wrists felt when swinging clubs with the interlocking grip. Many golfers have used this grip successfully: the Whitcombes, Sarazen, and Ouimet come to mind right away, but it was not the grip for everyone, and, like a Wall Street boom, its wave of popularity did not last.

Since scores and records began to be noted, it has been obvious, in Willie Park's oft-quoted remark, "that a man who could putt was a match for anyone." Although, for example, Arnaud Massy and Jack White, two Open Champions, were celebrated for their putting, it was not till this period, 1921-29, that the good putters began to be very much noticed. Players who, on the gradually improving putting surfaces, could regularly rely upon getting by with brilliant putting when the rest of their game was below first-class average, became more numerous, and golfers with inferior "long games" began to win big events through skillful performances on the putting greens. How could this happen all of a sudden? Well, I should say that competition and analysis gradually showed more clearly the supreme value of good putting, and the model round with thirty-six putts, two per green, was soon out of date. Thirty-three putts at the most it soon had to be, and today thirty, twenty-nine, twenty-eight, and even twenty-six putts is the standard aimed at, and required in order to win.

In addition, the postwar conditions found courses easier than before. Less rough had been kept because of the golf ball scarcity, and history repeated itself some twenty-seven years later—with the great difference that courses were already easier to start with. When courses are easy (whether they are short or long matters little) and with insufficient rough to punish erring shots, everything hangs on the putting. You cannot win through on a superlative long game as is possible on a punishing course. Players today are inclined to grumble about bad rough on a course, complaining that it ruins their scores—what will people think if their average is ruined? This may sound pathetic, but some professional players will actually cut out a tournament on a tough course for fear that their average will be spoiled.

As the chances of a lost ball in the wilderness became less with the building of courses on open land—for with the fast growth of the game in this period courses sprang up everywhere and ground with natural features could not always be found—the day of the recovery player (down in two from anywhere) arrived. Walter Hagen was the first of a line of great golfers who did not rely on mechanical skill like Vardon and Taylor to win and halve holes—he became a master of rolling three shots into two. He had no sand wedge to help him. He had to use, as did other players (such as Ted Ray and James Braid), who had earlier reputations for making fabulous recoveries, ordinary niblicks with "thin" soles. Hagen, while including the explosion shot in his repertoire, had much faith in his ability to flick the ball clearly off the sand, a shot very little used today. Even from a very teed-up lie in sand, the modern professional will blast the ball on to the green, a much safer shot which has been made so for him by the broad sole of the sand iron.

I feel that the golf game owes one particular debt of gratitude, amongst many, to James Braid, and that is for the way he has kept the courses at Walton Heath as such fine tests of golf. Their popularity has in no way diminished because of the fact that a bad shot is *always* punished to the maximum—a state of affairs fast disappearing from a game which is developing into a test of strength.

During this period, the matched set of clubs appeared as yet another step towards mechanical golf. The theory advanced was that you buy your set and use one swing only—get a good caddie to give you the right club and hey presto! The matched set, numbered 1-9, at first blew in from America and so did the ballyhoo with it, and our golfers wanted to learn the American swing that went with the set. This swing, under Bobby Jones's great influence at the time, was a long one, a real swing at the ball once again. I went to America towards the end of this period, in 1928 it was, in order to see why they were beating our home players so regularly, and found that steel shafts were already legal and one type of bigger ball was in use. This was the time when twenty-year-old Horton Smith was cleaning up on the winter circuit—he hardly knew golf with anything else but steel shafts and had knocked all the fancy shot-making

frills off low scoring. He used a slow deliberate three-quarter swing, which he repeated mechanically for every shot, letting the ball hook slightly—even for his short mashie-niblick shots. He never took three putts, and he holed a lot of "good" ones. It was rather like the way Bobby Locke plays today, though his swing is longer and faster. Seeing Horton Smith play was quite a revelation, for I saw straight away that the day of learning to play all the shots was over—the steel shaft had made golf an easier game. Only one swing was necessary, and I had to find out as soon as possible the swing which would suit me.

The soft watered greens—a necessity in a country where the fixed fine weather periods of spring, summer and autumn meant many sunny days and no rain—showed that one shot, if you could repeat it, was good enough to win any event. This fact did not really register at home till the steel shaft was legalized in Great Britain, and then we too all hunted for one swing to go with our new matched sets which had steel shafts in them. At last everyone could have the exact set used by his favorite champion.

THE STEEL SHAFT DAYS—1930 ONWARDS

GRADUALLY the top golfers began to realize that golf was a more simple game with this new standard link between the hands and the clubhead. It was not necessary to know or practice all the shots as in the hickory shaft days, though some of the older players never quite adapted themselves to steel. Abe Mitchell, whose play I have always admired and who was a wonderful striker of the ball, never got to like steel. He could not make himself play just one stroke. He liked to fade the ball up to the flag and found that the steel shaft let him down when he attempted to play a controlled fade or any special stroke. He missed the torsion of the hickory shaft. George Duncan was also too much of an artist to enjoy steel. As the leading players of the day were, of course, all brought up on the hickory shaft, it was only natural that there should be, for a time, a search to produce a steel shaft with the same qualities of the hickory one. This led to a series of shafts being produced which had torsion. These experiments turned out to be failures. Then it was realized that a shaft with no torsion was nearer to the ideal one. Whip it could have, but the less torsion the better. There have been various sorts of shafts from the "limber" type built to feel like a piece of cord, through the various "master" ranges from "pokers to average whip," right up to the "dynamic" range, the range of to-day which has given us a nearly torsionless type of varying degrees of whip which has contributed to lower and lower scoring.

As golf became an industry, and a big one at that, exploiters of golf courses realized that in order to make the turnstiles click healthily, the number of players using a course per day had to be increased. The rough began to disappear faster than ever to enable quicker rounds to be played and to give the customer a greater feeling of enjoyment. Then came World War II—with again a shortage of golf balls, making a lost ball nearly a tragedy—to finish off the trend, and when the war ended in 1945 so many golfers had got used to playing "around the park" that the days of rough as we used to know it were ended. This open field trend has had such an effect on golf that long driving has come to be worshipped. All the top players, particularly in the U.S.A., hit the ball "full out" all the time and do not pay much penalty for errors of direction or expect to do so. I find open park courses tedious and boring to play. I do not mean only that I find them easier to play than good courses or that I score lower on them, but that they do not inspire me and I feel all the time that my good shots are not sufficiently rewarded. I seem to score the same on the good as on the bad. Betting, now a big part of golf in the U.S.A., has developed to provide interest whilst playing in monotonous conditions.

In one recent U.S. Open Championship, I read that players—and the Press were backing them—were objecting to a fringe of rough around and behind the putting surfaces, because lies were poor and accurate chipping was impossible. This rough might have been extra heavy, but rough should always exist on a golf course—it is part of the game.

Courses are easier today. The extra yardage added does not seem to compensate for this, and now there is a definite leaning towards the use of forward tees for some rounds in order to encourage low scoring for publicity purposes.

Since 1941 there had been a general trend to use and recommend a more shut-faced action in play, and this fashion was a la mode up to 1945. Since then, players have moved their left hands back on the shaft, opened the hand to show two knuckles, which is what I have always recommended and used. The value of this change is to make more use of the hands and to cut out some of the body unwind which had a tendency to be exaggerated and which was more than the human frame could stand up to. Practicing with the steel shaft was easier because full pressure could be applied all the time without spoiling the shaft, and, given enough energy and practice, an unusual swing could be made to give results—at least while the confidence held. The larger ball, which naturally tends to fly higher, needed to be knocked down to get a boring flight and the maximum control, and so this led to the strong players closing the clubface much more than British golfers had been doing for some time. The only long driver of modern times who kept his wrist under the shaft like Harry Vardon has been Jimmy Thomson, the North Berwick boy, who went to the U.S.A. and he, in consequence, hit a very high ball.

Up to 1929, I always had a practice set and a tournament set, saving the latter so as not to wear them out; since those days, one set was enough. Then, of course, the restriction in the number of clubs permitted a player in competition golf was an obvious legislation, for as breakages were almost unheard of, it was silly to carry over twenty clubs round a course. Fourteen became the limit, but this had no effect on the scoring or club sales. The tendency with steel shafts had been for divots to get bigger and deeper, for no strain was too much for the steel shaft. If wrists could stand it, the shafts could. Players like powerful Sam Snead, one of the game's great players, were taking platefuls of earth with their iron clubs in order to get the maximum grip on the ball, for the USGA ruling that face markings were to be almost decorative caused the leading players to hit the ball steeper in order to grip it well on the clubface. This ruling came about because for a short time there was a sort of competition as to how rough a clubface could be made, and a cold chisel and hammer were employed to deepen the face grooves on standard markings. The very slotted club-faces, apart from ruining a golf ball at almost every stroke, caused the ball to fly lower, and so there came into being a low-flying pitch to the pin, which had much backspin on it caused by these face markings, and which was christened a "wedge shot" because the club generally used was a "wedge"—a broad-soled niblick with a flat sole, the back edge of this club not riding high as in the "sand wedge" or "dynamiter."

The sand wedge which came out in the thirties was a sensation at the time. The first models were egg-shaped, hollow-faced clubs, with a high back edge so that the club skidded and did not dig into the earth or sand. The hollow face, which it was soon ruled "hit the ball twice," was deemed illegal, but the form of the club has remained with us today and is to be found in the bag of every serious competitor. The technique for playing this club is to hit well into the sand (for it is primarily a bunker recovery club) behind the ball, using a full shot all the time but judging the distance the ball is to travel by the number of inches below the ball the club is made to enter the sand. All the world's leading players are experts with this type of club. This is understandable, for to be a good player in the first place, it is necessary to be an accurate hitter and a little regular practice in sand soon shows how far exactly it is necessary to enter the sand behind the ball for a given distance. Bad players are so because they are inaccurate strikers, and so they are never good bunker players and cannot expect to be until they improve their precision. The leaders of today are gifted players and can compare with any past champions, in every department of the game. Modern day writers naturally enough only extol their own generation and point out that as scoring has improved by so many strokes a round it must, therefore, be better. The experimental Royal and Ancient rules of 1950-51 caused improved scores also. But, much as I allow for the need to play better today owing to greater competition, I must claim for older generations that courses were tougher and equipment in general was poorer. I will "bump up" the scoring by at least two shots a round if you let me provide graded rough through and around the greens, and putting surfaces which are not "puddings to pitch into."

I do not propose to argue here about players of today and yesterday, for comparisons are odious. But it is specialization alone which has helped to raise the general standard, as today tournament players, both professional and amateur, if they expect top honors, do nothing else but take part in competitions. The club pro rarely steps out from home and cleans up the tournament players.

Style as such is not much appreciated these days. In fact, the public in general does not seem to be educated up to recognizing if a player is an artist at his job. Only figures on the scoreboard count. A successful shot, struck as the balance is lost, is just as valuable, we know, as the same shot played with perfect poise and balance; but for myself I enjoy seeing a real artist at work on a great course.

The Grip
Holds Your Swing Together

by

TOMMY ARMOUR

1953 — FROM *HOW TO PLAY YOUR BEST GOLF ALL THE TIME*
(DRAWINGS BY LEALAND GUSTAVSON)

THE FIRST THING that determines how well you're going to be able to play is the way in which you hold the club.

The coupling between you and the club has to be right *for you,* or you haven't a chance of being able to put yourself into the shot.

I've seen some golfers become quite good despite bad grips to which they adjusted themselves by long and unnecessary practice. I've also seen some experts devise ingenious methods of holding the club to compensate for physical abnormalities. But far more than these exceptional cases, I've seen golfers who might have improved greatly absolutely destroy their chances of doing their best because they never learned how to hold the club in a physically and mechanically sound coupling of player and implement.

Innumerable times I've had golfers come to me complaining about some fault that is ruining their swing. In some instances, they'll have made their own diagnoses of the troubles. Of course, each diagnosis is as complex as it possibly can be made by the victim's profound deliberations in clinics at the club bar with others equally unqualified to analyze or instruct.

A goodly number of these victims will begin telling me what's wrong with their swing. They don't seem to realize that if they knew what was wrong, they wouldn't be coming to me and paying me for an expert diagnosis and cure.

Generally, in such cases I find that the cause of the trouble is an incorrect grip which makes it utterly impossible to get any element of the swing correct. The situations have a parallel in your own automobile. If the transmission isn't right, everything else can be O.K., but the car won't go.

When you haven't got the connection (the hands) functioning properly, your arms, elbows, shoulders, body, legs, and feet can't work in the correct manner.

The basic factor in all good golf is the grip. Get it right, and all other progress follows.

The quickest and most encouraging improvement I have been able to effect in my pupils' games has come from teaching them how to hold the club so there will be neither looseness nor dead stiffness as the ball is hit.

To hold the club properly, let the shaft lie where the fingers join the palm of the left hand. The last three fingers of the left hand are closed snugly to the grip.

A good tip is to keep the little finger of the left hand from being loosened; then the next two fingers will stay firm.

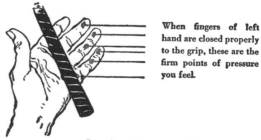

When fingers of left hand are closed properly to the grip, these are the firm points of pressure you feel.

Grip placed along roots of fingers

The left thumb is placed down the right side of the grip.

Where a mistake in the left-hand grip frequently is made is in having the shaft lie from the root of the forefinger diagonally across the palm, about to the heel of the hand.

After the club is placed at the roots of the fingers of the left hand, and the fingers closed snugly against the grip, the grip is pressed up slightly toward the heel of the hand, although it continues to lie in its original position against the left forefinger. Therefore, some make the mistake of believing that the proper placement at the beginning is diagonally across the palm.

What you always should do with the left-hand grip is to keep it just as near to the roots of the fingers as possible.

The position of the left hand on the shaft definitely must be slightly over to the right of the shaft so the V of the thumb and forefinger points to the right shoulder. That's old advice, but still the best.

THE LEFT-HAND GRIP

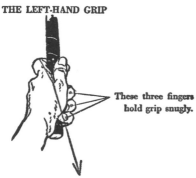

These three fingers hold grip snugly.

The V of thumb and forefinger points to your right shoulder.

Your right hand should be put on the grip with the club lying in the channel formed when the fingers are bent, and with your left thumb fitting snugly under your right thumb.

The right little finger goes over the forefinger of your left hand, or curls around the exposed knuckle of the left forefinger. It doesn't make any difference which of these two positions the right little finger takes—whichever one you like.

The right hand is placed slightly to the right of the top of the shaft.

The right thumb is in a natural position to the left of the shaft. It is important that the

THE GRIP
WITH BOTH HANDS

The V of the right thumb and forefinger also points to your right shoulder. Forefinger of right hand is against side of shaft in strongest position for hit. Hands fitted compactly together. Pressure of right-hand grip one-half that of the left-hand grip.

right thumb and forefinger be as close as comfortably possible because these two parts of the right hand are a vital combination in a grip for power. The right thumb-forefinger combination enables you to whip the club through with all possible speed. The club is held in the right hand with about half the pressure of the left-hand grip.

Keep both hands fitted compactly together. They must coordinate the essential factors of left-hand control and right-hand power, and unless they're working closely, your hand action will be faulty.

There are occasions when a deliberate hook or slice may be required, but to play these shots with control is a job for the expert who knows just what combination of grip and stance to employ. Reducing a tendency to slice by putting the right hand more underneath the shaft is not a correction, it's a distortion. That is the method sometimes recommended (but not by me) to the chronic slicers. The opposite tendency, that of hooking, also is sometimes reduced by putting the right hand more on top of the shaft in the weaker position. Obviously, in the latter case, the more logical thing to do would be to strengthen the left-hand grip and retain the full power of the right. But, as I've previously said, failure to think simply and directly is the cause of most faults in golf.

What you are seeking and must have in your grip is the utmost effectiveness in power and control. You need to keep the face of the club in correct alignment with the path of the swing at all times, until the ball has left the clubhead.

The most serious and most frequent deviation of the clubface from its proper position occurs at the top of the swing.

What very few golfers—outside of the experts—understand is the difference between holding the club tight and not letting it get loose at the top of the swing. When I see a player hold the club tightly at address, I know that the odds are about ninety to one that the firm grip of the last three fingers of his left hand is going to open at the top of the swing, and he'll never be able to regain control of the club for his downswing.

The big idea—the essential one—is to hold the club at address with easy security rather than grim, tightening intensity. You can keep that kind of hold on the club throughout the swing. The last three fingers of the left hand hold the club firmly. The right-hand grip is relaxed, and not at all tight throughout the backswing and the early stage of the downswing. When your right-hand grip does get firmer, just before and at the moment of impact, the tightening action will be spontaneous and precisely timed without conscious effort. The action must take place with such lightning speed that there is no possibility of deliberate application of the muscular strength that's available in the hands.

The correct left-hand grip at the top of the swing. Note how last three fingers make the firm coupling with the club. This is absolutely essential and must not be relaxed.

Here is the most serious frequent error at the top of the swing—loosening the left-hand grip. That compels you to make the mistake of starting to hit from the top of the swing, and to hit with the body instead of the hands. Then anything can happen—slicing, hooking, topping, hitting under the ball, or missing it altogether.

A few very good golfers have the interlocking grip, with the little finger of the right hand entwined with forefinger of the left, but I prefer to go with the majority who use the overlapping grip which is called the Vardon grip. Although the great British champion wasn't the first good player to use it, he did popularize that element of golfing style in winning six British and one U. S. Open championship among his many victories.

THE OVERLAPPING GRIP

The right little finger curls around the exposed knuckle of the left forefinger.

There are several grip variations which a few of the experts use. They can get away with these deviations because of considerable practice and play, enabling them to adjust to abnormal arrangements for combining power and control. But don't try these. The unorthodox methods usually are matters of desperate experiment which the experimenters don't use too long for the reason they eventually discover their golf isn't as good as it used to be.

The exceptions to standard technique which are employed once in a while by proficient players invariably are confusing to the average golfer. He may try these unusual grips which can't be used with safety, and go from bad to worse.

There isn't a first-class golfer in the world who doesn't have excellent hand action. Plainly, nobody can have a fine quality hand action without a grip ideally fitted to his kind of hands.

Golf is a game to be played with two hands. Your left guides the club and keeps the face in the desired position for the hit, and the power pours through the coupling of the right hand and the club.

Your hands must be together and work together to get the utmost leverage, balance, precision, and speed that can be applied.

Always have your mind made up that you are going to whip your right hand into the shot.

That is a "must."

Any time you hear an argument advanced against the right hand whipping into the shot, you may be sure that the objection is fallacious.

Something about the right hand that must have your thought and practice is having that part of the right forefinger, which is nearest the palm, functioning positively in the hitting action. When the right-hand grip lies firmly between the forefinger and the thumb, it is in perfect position for a fast, firm, lashing action.

THE RIGHT-HAND WHIP

The lashing action springs from the joint functioning of the forefinger and thumb.

What seems to make the left-hand position and function a mystery to some is the simple fact that the left hand, not being as conspicuous as the right hand is, doesn't get enough studious attention.

When your left hand retains control of the club as it should, you will not suffer the usual error of the higher handicap player. This is the mistake of wasting the hand action too soon.

Usually this mistake is made by straightening the wrists almost immediately after the downswing starts. Then, the ball is contacted by a stiff-arm push instead of with a vigorous whipping action.

You probably won't be able to observe in the fast action of the experts' play how their hands are over the ball or slightly past it before their wrists start to uncock. But, when you look at photographs of the stars in action, you will see how they get the right-hand whip precisely at the most effective time—and much later than the average player does.

When the grip is correct, there isn't an in-clination to let the right hand whip in too soon. What causes the right hand to throw from the top of the swing is that the left hand is loose, and the right hand tries to take over the function of control as well as power. Therefore, the right hand is in frantic action in a spontaneous effort to do the whole job.

By becoming acutely conscious of the necessity of a right-hand whip when the club is getting close to the ball, you will be pleasantly surprised at how your shoulders, hips and footwork are naturally disposed to coordinate with the hand action.

There's another detail of the swing that you won't have to worry about much when your grip is correct, and that's wrist cocking. When you retain a snug grip with the last three fingers of your left hand on your backswing, your wrists are easily cocked at the top of the swing, and they're cocked in the proper, nearly horizontal plane beneath the shaft.

With a half-palm grip of the left hand, you just can't cock your wrists correctly and retain control of the club.

The uncocking of the wrists as the clubhead nears the ball is greatly facilitated—almost assured—when you have the proper grip.

In my teaching, I eliminate every possible detail that might confuse the pupil when he's actually playing. That's no time for him to be disturbed by having to make some conscious effort. He should be free from the interference of the consciousness.

I have found that one of these disturbing points is the tendency of the right elbow to get far away from the body during the swing. This fault is definitely a result of an improper grip. When the club is held correctly, the right elbow is sure to stay comfortably close to the body and pointing down. Thus does the correct grip eliminate the pupil's becoming distracted by paying attention to the elbow position during the swing. When the grip is good, that becomes good automatically.

The correct grip, which is the governing component of hand action, is certainly the greatest single detail towards achieving direction and distance of the golf shot.

When you get your grip right, you have automatically eliminated many of the bothersome details which may confuse you and prevent proper execution of shots.

How Hogan Picks
His Clubs

by

JIMMY DEMARET

1954 — FROM *MY PARTNER, BEN HOGAN*

WATCHING Hogan pick his club amounts to watching one of the greatest club selectors in golf. He knows precisely what each stick in the bag will do for him. Although this is just another of the many things he does to perfection, he has always particularly impressed me in this department. He does everything that the average person should do and usually doesn't. He takes into consideration the wind, the distance, the obstacles, the condition of the course.

To begin with, here is a rough table that can be used as a general guide toward selecting the right club:

CLUB	DISTANCE
Driver	From 240 to 275 and up
Brassie	From 220 to 265
3 Wood	From 200 to 250
4 Wood	From 200 to 225
1 Iron	From 180 to 215
2 Iron	From 175 to 205
3 Iron	From 165 to 200
4 Iron	From 155 to 190
5 Iron	From 145 to 180
6 Iron	From 135 to 170
7 Iron	From 125 to 160
8 Iron	From 115 to 150
9 Iron	From 105 to 140
Wedge pitch	Edge of green to 105
Sand wedge	Edge of green to 40

That is, I repeat, just a rough guide. In many cases, you may find that a No. 2 iron just isn't enough club for you to hit for 190 yards. You may not command that kind of power. It's a simple matter then to go to your woods. Each player must choose his club according to the distance he gets when hitting naturally. When Hogan picks a club, he doesn't have to force himself to make distance with it. Nor does he baby himself on a shot in order to remedy overclubbing.

The weather and wind have a lot to do with the choice of a club. Other things, such as the texture of the grass and the amount of moisture both in the air and on the ground, count heavily. Take clover, for instance. If you see Hogan getting set for a shot from a clover patch, you'll note that he takes two clubs less than usual. That's because a ball skids or slides from a clover lie. The oily texture of the small leaves greases the club face when it contacts the ball, making it impossible to impart backspin. The ball will loop and float through the air with very little control. You might compare it to a spitball thrown by a baseball pitcher. It is because of such factors that we usually place club selection and course charting in the same category.

Ben has one technique in his club selecting which brands him as a conservative. On an approach shot, he tries to make certain he is short of the green, rather than over it. At Carnoustie in Scotland, all the trouble lies behind the greens, as it does in 90 per cent of the courses here in America. Time after time during the British Open, Ben's caddie would finger a No. 4 iron but Ben would take the five instead and plant his shot a bit short but in a safe position. The caddie thought Ben was wrong in playing it safe this way, and he wasn't the first one to have that idea. I remember a round with Ben at the Colonial Country Club in Fort Worth after which his caddie told the other boys in the yard that "I know more about this course than Hogan does."

During the round, from first to eighteenth hole, this bag-toter kept touting Ben on that one extra club. Each time Ben asked for the one under it. "You'll be dead to the pin with the four," the caddie said on one hole.

"I'll take the five," Ben answered, and planted his shot at the edge of the green.

"He would've been right up to the hole with the other club," the caddie muttered to me. "This guy is a champ and this is his home course, but he keeps using the wrong club!"

I just laughed. Ben Hogan knows only too well that trouble lies behind those greens. He'll take the club less and shoot for the front, and a sure two-putt green. Who's to say this conservative approach is the wrong one? Not I, certainly.

Course charting is automatic for the careful fellow who selects the proper club. When Hogan goes into the bag for a certain stick, it is a safe bet that he has looked over the area

he is shooting for with a telescopic eye. He plans his shot carefully before swinging. A number of times he has been criticized for taking too much time with his shots. They call him the surveyor, and Ben resents it.

"That's a brutal word to tag on a golfer," he says. "When I look a course over, I'm trying to figure it out. I want to know what's going to happen when my shot hits the ground. I want to check the grass as well as the distance to the green or my particular objective. Now what's wrong with that?"

Absolutely nothing, is the answer, when a golfer is simply going about his business thoroughly and not just wasting time. It's one of the elements which makes a great golfer. Ben knows grass thoroughly—from the Bermuda grass greens we have in Texas to the turf of a seaside course. He knows what the ball will do on each type. He is the master attacker of even our toughest layouts, because of this ability to think out a course. If necessary, he'll pace off the distance from where his ball lies to the spot where he thinks it will come down. While he's doing that, he'll investigate the grass and every shrub, tree, bunker, and depression along the way. In the 1953 Open, he strolled 250 yards uphill on the seventeenth, to get an idea of what would happen when his ball hit the ground. If he's trying to whack that ball over trees to save ground on a dog-leg hole or he feels that he can drive over a bunker, he always makes sure just what's behind these obstacles. He knows what's going to happen on the other end of the shot.

The Woods

by

SAM SNEAD

1946 — FROM *HOW TO PLAY GOLF*

THE TEE-SHOT is probably the most important in golf, for a good start is half the battle. Being able to use the wood off the tee gives the player confidence, to say nothing of the satisfaction and thrill he gets in seeing the ball gradually climb from the tee and travel straight down the fairway until it seems that it is about to roll out of sight. A good shot off the tee will put the golfer in a proper mental attitude to play the second shot well. If his woods are off and he is always forced to make recovery shots, his interest in the game soon wanes and he becomes careless. Playing shots half-heartedly, he soon falls into bad habits. The shorter woods should also receive their share of attention. With them the golfer can often make up yardage that would be lost if he had to rely on an iron to hit the ball with any amount of success. The woods are the clubs to use when distance is required.

When playing a wood shot, remember a straight ball pays off over the one that is slugged farther but winds up in the rough. Instructors will always warn the novice against trying to hit too far. To achieve distance, the player should try to swing more freely; then the movements will be more accurately made. The more accuracy, the farther the ball will travel. Any form of pressing will cut down distance.

There is no question that the shot off the tee is an easier stroke than one made when the ball is lying on the fairway. When the ball is set up well on the fairway, the stroke used off the tee is the one to use—striking the ball well in the back so that it will run. There are times, however, when the golfer will find that his ball is not setting up well, and that he cannot rely on the stroke he used off the tee. If the lie is close, he should study it to see if a wood shot is justified. The chances of failing are great, if the lie is too close to use a wood; the player would then be better off to use an iron. For a wood, there should be a clear path for the clubhead to swing into the ball. If the lie is cupped, the iron should be used, for with its more upright swing, the clubhead can be brought down sharper and the ball can be more solidly hit than if a wood were used with a blow that has a longer arc.

The golfer confronted with a close lie should hit down with the brassie. To get a brassie shot up, the same rules apply as in getting an iron shot into the air. It is the loft of the club and a downward blow, plus backspin, that will cause the ball to rise. The ball will not rise as quickly as when hit with an iron, so be sure there is enough room in front. If there is not, the player should use the spoon or No. 4 wood. Needing a longer stroke than the iron, the brassie rarely takes a divot, but just strips the sod in front of the ball.

If there is any doubt as to whether the

brassie should be used on a particular shot, it is better to use the spoon. The spoon, being a shorter club, will bring the golfer closer to the ball and the swing will be more upright. Naturally the ball will have to be played slightly more toward the right foot so that it can be caught while the clubhead is still descending. A good position for the ball is at a point between the center of the stance and the left heel.

It is important when playing shots off the fairway to start the backswing smoothly, and not to hurry the downswing. Free the body of any tension that may have crept into it by the thought that you are going to miss the shot; have the same confidence as you would off the tee, where the ball is teed up. It is true the latter is easier, and that swinging is much smoother and a more simple matter, but if you will remember the important thing about golf—to get the ball up in the air, hit down on it—you will soon gain the necessary confidence, and shots off the fairway will cease to worry you.

Balance is the very beginning of any golf shot. Stand with your weight evenly divided and your legs not too far apart. Turn the toes of both feet outward because this helps you retain good balance throughout your swing. Have your arms hanging freely so the movement of your body doesn't interfere with your arms. The ball and the hands are practically in the same vertical plane.

I drive with a slightly open stance, with the left foot a bit farther away than the right one from the line of intended flight. Others prefer a square stance, with both feet equidistant from the line, and there are many excellent players who use a closed stance with the right foot farther away from the line. This, so the champions of the closed stance maintain, makes it easier to hit from inside the line of flight out into the ball. Such an arc, of course, is proper, except in the cases of deliberate slices and "cut" shots.

A few waggles to get loosened up, and to get the flow of the swing started without a jerk, are really an important part of the swing. They help you to feel the beginning of a smooth swing. A slight lift of the left heel starts the hips rotating away from the shot. The left arm is held straight, practically as an extension of the shaft. There is no effort at all

made to lift the club from the ground. The clubhead is kept low. The left knee begins to bend slightly toward the right and there is a noticeable straightening of the right leg, although there should be no feeling of the right knee locking. In this initial stage of the swing, the prevention of tightening up is highly important. You can make many perfect swings clipping dandelions and scraps of paper, but when a golf ball is before you, you're apt to become tense to a degree that completely destroys your precision. Take it easily and lazily, because the golf ball isn't going to run away from you while you're swinging.

THE BACKSWING

IF THE golfer wishes to achieve a certain amount of success and desires to lower his score, he should pay particular attention to the backswing. This highly important item will not take care of itself, as so many mediocre golfers think. These players wonder what is wrong when scores mount and shots go astray. It would be to their advantage to concentrate on executing a good backswing, and let the downswing take care of itself. Such thoughts as power needed in the downswing to make the ball travel a needed distance down the fairway should be excluded from their minds. If the backswing is not properly performed, there can be little hope for a successful downswing. The player must be in a good position to accomplish the hitting part of the stroke.

Get set mentally before starting any motion. Think in terms of smoothness, excluding the desire to rush and hurry. Remember, one can, and should, spend twice as much time on the backswing as on the downswing. After mental assurance is gained, the golfer should think of starting the club back with a push from the left side through the left hand and arm as the body turns. The club will be the last thing to move and will be dragged away from the ball, lagging behind the hands. This start will help toward a correct pivot. Allow the right hip to turn so that it will not block the hands and arms. The hips and shoulders should turn until the back of the player is presented to the hole. Guard against breaking the wrists too quickly, for such action will hinder the success of the pivot and the top of the swing will be reached before the pivot is completed. If the player will start the club back low and close to the ground, controlled by the left hand, breaking of the wrists too soon will be avoided.

THE PIVOT

THE pivot is probably the least understood of all golf actions. It is not just the twisting of the waist; neither is it the action of dropping the left shoulder toward the ball, as the duffer does. Pivoting is the swinging of the club to the top of the backswing in a wide arc, with the left foot, knee, hip and shoulder turning toward the right. It is through this turning of the hips and shoulders that some golfers outdrive others who have more strength and weight. Harry Vardon once said: "Golfers find it a very trying matter to turn at the waist, more particularly if they have a lot of waist to turn. But they must learn to do so if they would acquire any proficiency at all; it is the only way to success at golf."

A turn of the body is necessary, because there is no other way to get into position to hit the ball with power and force, yet with ease and rhythm. The pivot places the body behind the swing and gives freedom to the hands, wrists, and arms to do their part of the job. The turn of the body should be made naturally and comfortably, letting the hands swing fairly close to the body. When the left shoulder drops and the golfer fails to complete the prior pivot, the right shoulder is swung too low in the downswing and the clubhead hits the ground. This fault can be traced to failure of the golfer to shift his weight to the right leg in the backswing.

The pivot isn't an artificial action; it is a natural turn of the body. Without holding a club, stand upright and turn the shoulders and hips from left to right and back again. This is simply the pivot action. Notice that in order to get the shoulders at right angles to the starting position, the left knee bends and the left heel leaves the ground.

THE RIGHT ELBOW

To INSURE control at the top of the backswing, the right elbow must not be allowed to wander too far from the right side. Never should the arm be lifted higher than the shoulder. When it is, the golfer can look for a faulty pivot. If

the turn of the body has not been completed, it is impossible to get the club to the horizontal position in the backswing without committing this error. When this fault takes place, the golfer can be sure that the right hand has played too great a part in the backward movement and you can look for it to dominate the downswing by hitting as soon as the forward stroke gets under way. A hook or a badly smothered shot can easily result. When the right arm is kept close, the right hand will not overpower the left.

THE TOP OF THE BACKSWING

IF THE actions of the backstroke have been made correctly, the golfer will feel a pull at the left shoulder, with the right arm and shoulder relaxed. The left side will be taut, for it will start the action back toward the ball. If the right side is in control here, there is an irresistible desire to hit from this position, with a tendency to turn the shoulders as soon as the downswing is started. Therefore, be sure control is in the left hand.

The greater portion of the weight should have been shifted to the right foot. If it has not, the backswing has been checked and is working against a resisting force. The shoulders then cannot swing around, and the hips bend in a sideward action to the left rather than turning in a rotating manner toward the right.

At the top of the backswing, the grip on the shaft must be firm. Often golfers open the hands here, with the result that the grip is altered in the downswing. Then when contact with the ball is made, the grip is not the same as it was at address.

TIMING

IT IS an odd fact, but true, that no two golfers swing alike. This is remarkable, considering the number of fine professionals and amateurs. Yet all good golfers, through experience and practice, have developed timing suited to the movements of their individual swing. Timing is the coordination of all actions into one continuous, easy, flowing movement. This is the secret of the long accurate hitter.

A baseball pitcher cannot show his usual

speed and control in throwing, if he jerks his arm back quickly. Whenever possible, he takes a slow, easy windup, and then puts his full power into the throw. Neither can the golfer control the club by quickly raising and lowering the clubhead. He must start slowly and then gradually accelerate in the downswing so that the clubhead is traveling at its greatest speed at impact.

When you have reason to believe your timing is off, slow down the backstroke. Do not pick the club up in a hurry, tossing it over your shoulder. Wait for the backswing to be completed before starting the club down, and avoid rushing the right shoulder around before the clubhead has reached the hitting area. Lead the club down with the left hand and arm so that the clubhead will be brought to the ball on an inside arc.

Turning the body too quickly in the downswing can only result in a badly timed shot. This is called hitting too soon. Eagerness to hit hard is the common fault of the ordinary player. The experts delay the complete turn of the body toward the hole to allow the hands and arms to come through. Better control and distance will be obtained if the player will keep his body out of the swing until he wants the final punch, coordinating with the wrists, arms, and hands. However, don't be misled by thinking that the body stays out of the shot entirely. Good timing necessitates the natural turn of the body on both the backswing and the downswing.

SPEED OF CLUBHEAD

THE length of a drive depends on the speed of the clubhead. The faster it travels, the farther the ball travels. The clubhead should be swung as rapidly as is accurately possible, and speed is dependent on correct wrist action.

Most golfers hit too soon; that is, they begin the uncoiling of the wrists long before the hands have moved two-thirds of the way down from the top position. Hitting force then has been expended before the clubhead reaches

the ball. From the cocked position at the top of the backswing, the wrists remain in the same relation to the shaft of the club until halfway through the downswing. Here is little change, except that the forward wrist action of the right hand, which until now has stayed out of the swing, takes place. The hands may then travel only a few inches while the clubhead moves three feet or more. The clubhead now is reaching the maximum speed as the right hand snaps it through the ball. Viewed from in front of the player, the correct action of the wrists brings the shaft of the club and the left arm in a straight line at impact.

THE FOLLOW-THROUGH

THE follow-through plays just as important a part in golf as it does in other sports. It results in an easy, rhythmical swing that is so all-important to good golf. It is that part of the swing in which the clubhead travels for a few inches low and close to the ground after the ball is struck. If the player gives this part of the stroke a little thought, he will be aided in correctly executing those parts of the swing that precede it.

Maybe you are one of those golfers who say, "Why bother with that part of the swing that takes place after the ball is struck? Nothing can be done to alter the ball's flight after it has been sent on its way." This is a fair question. It is answered by the following fact. By trying to make the clubhead follow out after the ball, the golfer will find that the hit has been from the inside. The left arm has stayed firm, and the hands have been kept in the correct path.

After the follow-through takes place—but not before—the head may be raised. Now the player is ready for the finish of the stroke. The follow-through continues with the right arm straight and the right knee bent. The body turns until the golfer faces the hole. At the finish, the right arm is fairly straight, and the wrists break. The finish should closely resemble the top of the backswing, but in reverse.

Playing the Irons

by

ROBERT T. JONES, JR. and O. B. KEELER

1927 — FROM DOWN THE FAIRWAY

IT SEEMS to me that the more loft there is on a club, the harder it is to play. Why, I don't know. For years I have been wishing I could play a mashie-niblick shot the same as a mashie shot. But I can't do it. I'm not so bad with a mashie. But it seems the mashie, for me, is one of the irons and not one of the pitching clubs. Now, the No. 4 iron, which is just over a mashie in strength, and the mashie-iron are my favorite clubs. I will have some kind words to say of them somewhat later. I can say right here that I'd far rather be left with a shot to the green needing a No. 4 or a mashie-iron—say 160 to 180 yards—than a shot needing a mashie-niblick, of from 100 to 120 yards. I'm more likely to be near the pin from the longer range. That is why I perform better, as a rule, on a long course. The drive-and-pitch courses which offer those alluring scoring opportunities to golfers like Walter Hagen, a veritable wizard with the pitch, are anything but friends of mine. Take the best round I ever played in important competition, the first qualifying round at Sunningdale, England, in the British Open championship of 1926. There was next to no pitching to be done at Sunningdale. It wasn't a back-breaking course for length, but the holes were so arranged that, with acceptable driving, you needed either iron shots or wood shots or tiny pitches or chip shots to the green. I remember I used my

mashie only three times there in thirty-six holes.

A sort of club-sketch of this celebrated course may not be out of order here. I liked it so much I wished I could carry it around with me, it suited my game so delightfully.

The holes are given with their length, the American par, the clubs I used, and the score of my best round in competition.

No. 1, 492 yards, par 5. A drive and a brassie. Two putts. Score, 4.

No. 2, 454 yards, par 5. A drive and No. 1 iron. Two putts. Score, 4.

No. 3, 292 yards, par 4. What is called a mongrel length. Drive and wee pitch to five feet from the pin. Missed the putt for a 3. Score, 4. This was not the type of pitch I dread.

No. 4, 152 yards, par 3. A mashie, 25 feet from the pin. Two putts. Score, 3.

No. 5, 417 yards, par 4. Drive and No. 4 iron to 25 feet from the pin. One putt (the only long one of the round). Score, 3.

No. 6, 418 yards, par 4. Drive and No. 4 iron to 18 feet from the pin. Two putts. Score, 4.

No. 7, 434 yards, par 4. Drive and No. 4 iron over hill to ten feet from the pin. Missed putt. Score, 4.

No. 8, 165 yards, par 3. The others were using a mashie here. I used the No. 4 iron and an easy swing, shooting for the center of a dangerously guarded green 40 feet from the pin. Two putts. Score, 3.

No. 9, 270 yards, par 4. Another mongrel, very interesting. A drive that rolled over the back of the small green. A chip to five feet from the pin. Missed the putt. Score, 4.

This put me out in 33 with 17 putts and 16 other shots and not a pitch except the wee one at No. 3. It was three strokes under par, based on the yardage.

No. 10, 469 yards, par 5. A drive from a hillside tee to a valley and a stiff iron shot to an upland green. My shot with a No. 2 iron was 30 feet from the pin and I was down in two putts. Score, 4.

No. 11, 296 yards, par 4. Apparently too short for a good hole, but very interesting; a blind drive with much grief if off line. I chipped to seven feet from the pin and got the putt down for a birdie 3.

No. 12, 443 yards, par 4. A drive and iron to 30 feet from the pin and two putts. Score, 4.

No. 13, 175 yards, par 3. A No. 4 iron and my first mistake of the round; I think the only one. I shoved the shot out a bit to a bunker at the right, chipped six feet from the pin and holed the putt. Score, 3.

No. 14, 503 yards, par 5. A drive and brassie to the left edge of the green, pin-high. Two putts. Score, 4.

No. 15, 229 yards, par 3. A driving-mashie 12 feet past the pin, well in line. Missed the putt. Score, 3.

No. 16, 426 yards, par 4. A drive and iron to 40 feet from the pin. Two putts. Score, 4.

No. 17, 422 yards, par 4. A slight dog-leg to the right. A drive into the angle and the short rough and a No. 4 iron 30 feet from the pin. Two putts. Score, 4.

No. 18, 415 yards, par 4. A drive and mashie 30 feet from the pin. Two putts. Score, 4.

This gave me a score of 33-33—66 against a par of 36-36—72, with 33 putts and 33 other shots, only three of them being pitches of any description, and not one of them a pitch of the type that has come to be something like a *bête noire* to me. The Sunningdale course is 6472 yards on the card as we played it that day, and the setting of the tee-markers made it a good deal longer at some of the holes than the figures given, which are taken from the card. The only round I have had approaching it in important competition was my second in the Southern Open championship at East Lake the following year, when I shot a 66, with two approximate mistakes in it. But the East Lake course is perhaps three strokes easier, and I had a 2 and a 5 in that round, where I had nothing but 4's and 3's in the Sunningdale 66. I love a round with only 4's and 3's in it. The implication of such a round is that you are shooting golf and not carrying horseshoes.

I love the irons. And knocking about a good deal I have gradually accumulated a set which seems to fit. They've been copied by Tom Stewart at St. Andrews and by Victor East, of the Spalding company. Mr. East, a designer and golf club engineer, told me the micrometric measurements and the scientific weighings and testings showed that in my own crude and purely instinctive way I had assembled, all unknown to myself, a perfectly coordinated set of clubs. All but the mashie-niblick, said Mr. East. It was a sort of maverick. I have felt for some years that there was something wrong with that darned club!

My set is not at all a regular series. Like my wood clubs, they tend less to loft than the models generally accepted as standard. I carry, in the descending order of power, a driving-mashie, a No. 1 iron, a No. 2 iron, a mashie-iron, and a No. 4 iron. The mashie, which comes next, also seems like one of the iron series to me. I do not carry a No. 3 iron. The mashie-iron, which I like better, takes its place.

Club nomenclature has changed much in recent years, and I may explain that the old driving-iron now is classed as a No. 1. The driving-mashie, a somewhat stronger club, is deeper and shorter in the face, and is a shade heavier. The No. 2 is what used to be called a midiron, but mine is straighter in the face than the usual No. 2 and is nearly like a No. 1 out of stock. My mashie-iron is nearly as straight as the old-fashioned midiron. My No. 4 perhaps is nearest the conventional model, being only a shade straighter. The widest gap in my series is between the mashie-iron and the No. 4.

It is next to impossible to assign a range of shots to these clubs, because the choice of a club depends less on range than on the character of the shot, and all shots are subject to almost infinite variation, due to terrain, wind, and other circumstances. If there is such a thing as a normal range under normal conditions, I should say that for me the No. 4 is good for about 160 to 175 yards; the mashie-iron up to 190 yards; the No. 2 something like 200 yards; and 210 to 220 yards for the No. 1 and the driving-mashie, though you may be sure that if my spoon is in working order I rarely call on the irons for a shot of that length unless the lie or other circumstances indicate an iron.

Yes—I love the irons, even if sloppy play on the second hole at Skokie was costly in the National Open of 1922, and looseness at Worcester ruined me in 1925. I've studied the irons a lot, and listened to many a lecture. The last one I listened to was the shortest, and it seems to have done the trick—for the time being, at any rate.

Genius or no genius—remembering the delicate compliment of Mr. Harold Hilton—I got away fairly well in Britain with iron play that was never really satisfactory except at Sunningdale, which was a matter so exceptional that now I feel I must have been hypnotized. At Sunningdale, with its profusion of iron shots, I had the feel of the clubs to an extent that made it seem utterly out of the question to be off line.

But I wasn't satisfied with the somewhat compromised style in which I was hitting the irons, and when I got home to Atlanta after the big journey of 1926, I went out and had a little talk with Stewart Maiden, who to me will always be the first Doctor of Golf. I suppose I did a little confessing.

Stewart said:

"Let's see you hit a few."

I hit a few. Stewart seemed to be watching my right side. He is a man of few words.

"Square yourself around a bit," said he.

I had been playing a long time with a slightly open stance, my right foot and shoulder nearer the line of the shot than the left side.

"Move that right foot and shoulder back a bit," said he. I did so, taking what is called a square stance.

"Now what do I do?" I asked Stewart.

"Knock hell out of it!" said he, concisely.

I did. The ball went like a ruled line.

That is Stewart Maiden's method of teaching or coaching. In this imperfect and complicated world I have encountered nothing else as simple and direct. Stewart saw that my swing was bringing the club on the ball from outside the line of play. He didn't bother with explanations or theories. He never does. He settled on one single thing by way of adjustment. It worked. That is a prime feature of his adjustments.

In a general way this is my method with the irons.

I try to hit the shot straight, that is, without fade or drift to the right or draw to the left, except when a cross wind indicates the desirability of what is known as "holding up" the ball. Even in that case the result is a line shot, if it is properly executed.

My stance for the irons is approximately square, that is, with my feet equidistant from the line of play—not from the ball, which is opposite the left heel. My left arm is straight, not theoretically but actually, from the moment the turning motion away from the ball is well started until sometime after impact. I try always to turn well away from the ball in the backswing. In this motion I am conscious that the left side is pushing the right side away from the ball. At the risk of becoming tiresome let me repeat that this free body-turn seems to me the most important factor of my swing.

With no wind to consider, I try to play a straight and simple shot, using a club a little more than adequate to get the distance, rather than taking a full crack with a club just strong enough. I rarely knock the ball down with an iron or play what used to be called the push shot, a very popular shot with many fine players formerly.

With the wind off the right or against, I like to take a club appreciably stronger than the range warrants. It is a curious fact that a slower hit causes the ball to bore better into a headwind, perhaps by reason of carrying less backspin. And when the wind is off the right, the tendency being to impart a bit of cut to a shot with a stronger club, the ball is held up, in a manner of speaking, into the wind and proceeds in a straight line.

With the wind off the left, I like a weaker club than the shot indicates and a harder smash in the stroke. I play the ball a bit farther from me and hit it hard with a slightly freer turn of the body. My right shoulder, too, comes in a little higher, inducing a slight draw, a faint curve to the left which holds the ball up into the wind. It should be remembered, however, that unless the wind is very strong it has little effect, right or left, on a properly struck iron shot, and these refinements are not often essential. Of course the wind will increase or curtail the range of a shot, and that is taken care of by the selection of clubs. As stated, I like a stronger club and a slower stroke against the wind, with a lower trajectory and relatively more wind-jamming power. You are shooting against a fine cushion, so you don't need to worry about stopping the ball.

With a following wind I like a weaker club, swung harder. This adds elevation to the stroke, which is needed, as a following wind seems to take spin off the ball or, at any rate, minimizes its controlling effect on landing.

I am aware that these minor variations are likely to appear as affectation, and I trust the reader to believe that my game never was built up and developed with any such things in mind. I suppose they came along subjectively, instinctively; and I know that most of them are performed with perfect unconsciousness in playing the round, just as an outfielder in baseball cuts loose for the plate with no thought of the position of his feet or the juncture at which his wrist snaps, or anything beyond sending the ball on a proper hop to the catcher. It is impossible to describe most of these little refinements of the golfing stroke. You just do them, when your subjective experience tells you to, mostly without any objective thought. It is a fascinating sort of thing to try to analyze, and I hope earnestly that my analytical efforts will not result disastrously for some confiding reader.

Putting

by

BOBBY LOCKE

1953 — FROM *BOBBY LOCKE ON GOLF*

AMONG GOLFERS the putter is usually known as the pay-off club, and how right that is! Putting, in fact, is a game by itself. I am recognized as a good, consistent putter. From early in my career I realized that there was far more in putting than actually striking the ball, and I do not think any prominent golfer has devoted more time and thought and practice to this side of the game than I have.

I change my grip for putting. First of all, I grip the club in the left hand, and the grip is normal except that I position my thumb down the center of the shaft. The art of putting lies in the tips of the fingers. If you have a delicate touch, you are lucky. It helps a great deal. But remember you must not grip tightly. You must grip loosely and do everything possible to acquire a delicate touch. The shaft of my putter is much longer than the standard men's length. I find that this gives me what I call "better head feel." By that I mean I can feel more clearly the weight of the clubhead as I swing. I grip my putter at the very end of the shaft and I use the same grip for all putts. Never change the position of the hands up or down the shaft whether it is a long putt or a short putt, as that will cause inconsistency.

I now place the right hand to the club. I use the overlapping grip as for all other clubs, but again the thumb is placed down the center of the shaft. Having the two thumbs in this position enables me to follow the clubhead through dead in line to the hole, and also helps to put topspin on the ball. It is so necessary to put topspin on the ball when putting, as it makes the ball run through on the line to the hole.

At one time as an experiment I tried the reverse overlapping grip with the index finger of the left hand lying on top of the little finger of the right hand. I found it did not help my putting and it had a very bad effect on the rest of my game, making my grip for other shots feel most uncomfortable.

Having explained the grip, I will now describe my method of putting. First of all I sum up the putt, and this is vital. Most putts are missed not because they are mis-hit but because they have been started on the wrong line and at the wrong speed. I examine the line of the putt, concentrating particularly on a radius of about three feet around the hole. This is where the ball completes its run, and what happens here is going to make or mar the putt. During this quick inspection I remove any obstacles which might deflect the run of the ball, but, more important, I check the pace of the green, determine how closely the grass has been cut and whether the green is fast-, slow- or medium-paced. Also I check the lie of the turf around the hole to see whether the ball will be going slightly uphill or downhill or dead level as it approaches the hole. It is at this stage that I determine how hard I am going to hit the ball, always, of course, taking into consideration the length of the putt.

I work to the rule that if the green appears to be fast, I will aim my putt at an imaginary hole six to twelve inches short of the hole. If the green appears to be slow, and particularly if during the last two or three feet to the hole the ground is uphill, I hit it firmly for the back of the hole.

Having made up my mind how hard I am going to hit the putt, I now get behind the ball to examine the contour of the part of the green my ball will have to cross. Chiefly I am concerned with slopes and any hills or hollows. According to the slope, I make up my mind on the direction of the putt, whether it shall be dead straight or whether I should aim for the right or left side of the hole. Once I have made up my mind as to the line of the putt and how hard I am going to hit it, I never change my mind. It is fatal to let second or third thoughts intrude as you are putting. You must make up your mind before you begin to address the ball, and never alter it.

So many putts are missed because at the last second the player thinks to himself, "Perhaps I had better hit it straight," or "I think it would pay to aim a little further left." Hitting a putt in doubt is fatal in most cases. Make up your mind what you are going to do, then go ahead and do it.

Now for the actual putt. In the first place, the weight is evenly distributed on both feet. I place the feet about four inches apart, with the right foot three inches behind the left in relation to a straight line from the hole to the left toe. This is known as a closed stance, and I adopt this to prevent myself from cutting across the ball and imparting any sidespin. I position the ball directly opposite the left toe. This enables me to hit the ball slightly on the upswing, whereas if the ball were farther back towards the right foot, there might be a tendency to chop or jab it. I begin the address with the ball opposite the toe of the putter but actually strike the ball with the center of the blade. I do this to avoid cutting the putt. If one addresses the ball with the center of the putter blade, there is a tendency to swing outside the line on the backswing re-

sulting in a cut and the ball not running true. By addressing the ball near the toe of the putter blade it is easier to take the putter back "inside" the line of the putt, and in this way one is able to impart topspin at impact. Never hit a putt with the heel of the club. That puts check on the ball and it will not run as far as you expect.

I now start the backswing, keeping the putter very low to the ground, almost brushing the turf. I am careful to take the putter back on the "inside," and there is no wrist work at all. Throughout the swing, the putter blade stays square to the hole. I want to emphasize that the blade *does* stay square to the hole. There are people who say it is impossible to take a club back "inside" without opening the face. With a putter it is not impossible, and this is how I putt. I learned the method largely from Walter Hagen in 1937. The term he used for taking the club back and still keeping it square was that you "hooded" the face. He proved to me that this backswing applies true topspin to the ball and is in fact the only type of backswing with the putter that will apply true topspin. Hagen in his heyday was probably the world's greatest putter and I was happy to learn from him. It is essential in the method I am showing here that there should be no wrist work. Wrist work results in inconsistency—and missed putts. A point I stress in the backswing is that you must keep the putter low. Watch these points, and with practice you will find that you can take the club back "inside" and still keep the blade square to the hole.

At the completion of the backswing, the putter, left hand and left arm to the elbow, are in one piece. To make sure that the clubface does not open, the back of my left hand keeps pointing to the grass. I have now reached the "hooding" position. By "hooding" I mean keeping the putter face dead square, or if anything slightly closed, in the backswing. This will make sure of getting true topspin on the ball, provided the putter returns to the ball on the same line.

At impact, I keep the left wrist firm in relation to the forearm; the position of the left hand in relation to my putter is exactly the same. This means that the putter blade is kept square to the hole. My head is being kept well down until the ball has been struck.

There is still no wrist work in the accepted sense. I am concentrating all the time on keeping that clubhead square to the hole and on keeping my head well down. It is only necessary to follow through as far as the club went back in the backswing.

The putt is now completed. My method of swinging the putter is the same as the swing of a clock pendulum. The club goes as far through in the follow-through as it goes back in the backswing. Though my head turns to watch what is happening to the ball, it is still in the same position in relation to the body. It cannot be too much emphasized that the putting action must be slow and smooth, and above all the grip must be loose to maintain the most sensitive touch.

My putting is based on the fact that if a ball has true topspin, there are three entrances into the hole, three chances, providing the speed is right. There is the front door and there are two side doors. Obviously it is safest to use the front door, but with my method, if the ball catches the left side of the hole it will fall, and if it catches the right side it will also fall. By thinking of these three entrances, I always feel that I have three chances of sinking every putt.

It Takes Brains
to Play Golf

by

GENE SARAZEN

1950 — FROM *THIRTY YEARS OF CHAMPIONSHIP GOLF*

As I near the age when fans are beginning to regard me as a sort of elder statesman of golf, I find that I am expected to sit on a bench by a tee and give advice. Along with overcomplicated instruction, the average golfer's greatest handicap, as I see it, is his own impatience to run before he can walk, to score before he understands the fundamentals of the golf swing. The inevitable result, of course, is that he will never be a regular low scorer. The multifold compensations he resorts to in order to remedy a swing that is basically faulty do about as much good as anchoring a shaky house with yards of velvet. I think the Japanese clubs have something when they rule that novices will not be allowed onto the golf course until they have reached a certain degree of proficiency. The novices practice their shots on a large field, something like a polo field, until a committee passes on them as ready to play on the course itself. While the idea of having a committee dictate to a golfer what he is allowed to do and what he isn't allowed to do is a practice we would not want to copy in letter or in spirit, the new players in our country would benefit immeasurably if they voluntarily set aside a period of time in which they learned to hit their shots with some correctness before invading the course in search of scores. All players, not just the beginners, would do well to think of winter as the ideal season for disciplined indoor practice that will reward them with many summers of pleasure.

In my tours throughout the country I have observed that less than 1 per cent of our golfers know how to practice correctly. At every club there is a group of overeager beavers who bang hundreds of balls down the practice fairway and are muscularly tired before they actually tee off. You've got to be fresh to play good golf. Ben Hogan is the one player I know who has the physical and mental stamina to play his best golf after expending maximum power and concentration on the practice field. It exhausts me, and most of the other professionals, just to watch Ben practice, and there are occasions on which I think that even the super-disciplined Hogan leaves his finest strokes on the practice grounds. Before a round a player should warm up, not practice. At my age, preferring as I do to conserve my energy, my warm-up consists of fifteen or twenty shots with my No. 6 or 7 iron on which I can check my timing; four or five drives to unlimber my other muscles; and then five minutes or so on the practice green.

It does you no good to practice after a round when you are feeling tired, or at any time when your coordination is worn down. You should not practice all the clubs in the bag indiscriminately. You should concentrate on the one club you were playing the poorest on your preceding round. If your irons need attention, do not succumb to the lure of practicing your woods, your best shots, just because there are a few friends watching on the porch of the clubhouse. I know some pros, who are old enough to know better, who are 70-golfers with their woods and 78-golfers with their irons and will always remain so since they apparently cannot resist impressing the spectators on the practice ground with their exceptional length with the woods.

But the cardinal error which players commit today when they practice is to nudge each shot onto a perfect lie. You can never develop the proper hand action if you sweep the ball rather than strike it. You must practice hitting balls out of fair, poor, and downright bad lies. If you just want to go out and kid yourself, you would do your game as much good by staying in the clubhouse and playing a few hands of pinochle. I think it follows that I am against playing preferred lies on the course itself unless conditions truly warrant this. Our national infatuation with scores and record breaking lies behind this deplorable trend. One year the directors of the Miami Springs tournament allowed preferred lies on perfectly healthy fairways, and also put the markers on the ladies' tees and set the pins in the easiest position on the greens, all this to encourage a barrage of 61's and 62's. Well, they got a few 64's by such measures, and these "sensational scores" were a travesty on the honest 67's that golfers had played.

I can sympathize with the millions of golfers who read that the sand-iron shot is really a cinch but who encounter paralysis every time they step into a bunker. Few clubs provide facilities for practicing trap shots. After the golfer finishes a lesson on how to get out of traps, the pro admonishes him to be sure and practice that stroke. The next day the zealous pupil takes his wedge and a few balls out to a trap, but before he has played five shots some emissary from the pro shop dashes out to ask him what he thinks he's doing—doesn't he know that he's spattering the green with sand, and didn't he ever read the green committee's regulation that under no conditions will any member practice in a trap? The common-sensical solution is for clubs to build practice traps. While they are at it, it wouldn't be a bad idea if golf clubs made provision for

practice grounds which can accommodate more than three players at a time. They might think about erecting an inexpensive canvas awning, so that the industrious members are able to practice in all kinds of weather; lessons would not have to be canceled because of rain. I have expressed myself earlier as favoring practice greens which bear a vague resemblance to the eighteen greens the player meets on the course.

One last criticism of practice habits. When most golfers practice their putting, they start out with the thirty-footers and then work in. I think it is much more advisable to start a foot or so from the hole and gradually work back to fifteen feet or so. You are more likely to develop a smooth stroke. Golfers think too much about holing their practice putts. Great putters like Horton Smith concentrate on their stroke when they practice. They know that if they are stroking the ball correctly, they will get their share of putts.

A golf type that I run into with irritating regularity is the person who weeps in the locker room, "But I wasn't putting." Anybody can hit the ball. It takes a golfer to put his shots together, and a three-foot putt is every bit as much of a golf shot as a 250-yard drive. The putter is the dipper. It separates the cream from the milk. The great champions have all been beautiful putters—Walter Travis, Jerry Travers, Hagen, Jones, Nelson, and Hogan. Harry Vardon is the one exception to this rule, and when Vardon was winning, he wasn't a bad putter. A champion cannot remain a champion if his putting falls off. In the 1946 Open, Byron Nelson played immaculate golf from tee to green, the best in the field, I thought. Nelson failed to win not simply because he three-putted the seventy-first and made a miserable putt on the seventy-second, but because on his full four rounds his putting was not coordinated with the pitch of the rest of his game.

I have never seen a consistently able putter who used a club with a rounded edge to the sole. For that matter, you must be sensible about all of your equipment. Get on intimate terms with your clubs, so that none of them are strangers to you. Maybe you're carrying too many. I think a principal reason why we developed such solid shotmakers in the early days was that golfers played with only eight or nine clubs and got to know them all. When I won my third PGA title, I had five or six irons in my bag, no more. Any club that cut into my confidence, I threw out. Whenever I pulled a club out during that tournament, I knew I was working with an old friend. "Here's a fellow I know," I would feel as I gripped my mashie, for example. "I've had a lot of dealings with him. I can depend on this fellow."

One club that the average golfer does not need is the No. 1 iron. Only players of the caliber of Nelson, Snead, and Hogan can play the temperamental No. 1, and they have to practice it assiduously. Hogan and Nelson, who are the finest long-iron players golf has known, realize that the No. 1 iron must be played with a swing that's a bit on the upright side. Snead is not quite as effective with the long irons as Hogan and Nelson. Sam has a tendency to flatten them out and hook them. He plays them with his wooden club swing, and I would much rather see him hit a wood. Instead of playing his No. 1 iron, the average golfer is far better off playing his No. 4 wood.

Another club I cannot endorse for the average golfer is the straight-faced driver. I believe it throws a man off to see the heel of his club. He is much better off with a driver that has a slight hook face. Then, when he addresses his tee-shot, he will see the face of the club and this creates the necessary feeling in a golfer that he will pick the ball up and get through it. He will hit that shot with confidence. You can help yourself to get this feeling—that you are going to get through the ball easily—by taking a little time on each tee to select a level spot, or if anything, a slightly uphill lie. The experts all do this. You will never see them making the error common among week-end golfers of teeing up on a low spot and struggling from a downhill lie.

I am an outspoken advocate of shallow-faced fairway woods. I like to see the top of the ball over the top of the club. That ball is going to get up with no effort, I know, and there are no bunkers in the air. I have yet to see the occasion when I needed a deep-faced brassie to keep the ball low. My match against Henry Picard in the 1940 PGA was played after a torrential downpour, and the thick clover fairways of the Hershey Country Club were soggy, almost morassy. I managed to pull that

match out because Henry couldn't get his brassie and spoon shots off the ground. The other players marveled at my wood shots off the fairway until they saw that my clubs had extremely shallow faces, and then they realized that the woods they were using were faulty for those particular conditions.

For a similar reason, the jigger is a club that has an enormous appeal for me. The ball always rides well over the top of the shallow blade at address. I hit my first golf shot with a jigger, and from that day on I never forgot how easily I got that ball off the ground; I have always had a definite partiality for that club. In my opinion it was the finest golf club that was ever in a duffer's bag. The jigger passed out of the picture when the clubs began to be numbered. The week-end golfer wanted to use numbered clubs like the pros he read about, and he felt he was being old-fashioned in relying on his jigger when none of the stars were reported to be playing jigger shots. The jigger has a very strong personality which overpowers the dull personalities of the No. 3 iron and the No. 4, and it would make sense to me if the jigger were given a number and incorporated in the modern set, possibly as an alternate for the No. 3 and the No. 4. My old jigger was the most responsive club I ever owned. I used to play it for everything from a No. 2 to a heavy 4. I could instinctively get just the height I wanted, lofting it over trees and banging it low beneath the limbs. I liked to chip with it. Every time Bobby Locke sees me, the first question he asks is, "Where are your jiggers, Gene?" He is as fond of the club as I am.

There would be a much larger percentage of confident iron players if golfers today weren't so hungry for distance, at the wrong time. A golfer gains nothing by trying to reach a green with a No. 8 iron from 165 yards out when the No. 5 iron is the club—nothing but the vain satisfaction of telling the boys about the tremendous distance he gets. He doesn't add that the ball rolled half the way, and he never narrates the gloomy tales of what happens twenty-four out of twenty-five times when he tries to impress himself with his own strength. You never hear of the wide hook, the fast slice, the look-up, and the fluff. When Babe Didrikson was first turning to golf, her desire to be a sensationally long hitter retarded her development. Babe would close the face of the seven and toe it in and belly the ball 170 yards. When Babe stopped kidding herself and began playing a seven like a seven and not like a two, she started to develop a grooved swing and a glorious golf game.

If I were asked which clubs are the most important for scoring, I would say the pitching staff—Nos. 7, 8, 9, and the sand-iron. These are the weapons that can set up a one-putt green. The leading players today use the sand-iron or wedge not only in traps but in the rough and on the fairway for playing shots 100 yards and under from the green. I see no reason why the average golfer should not do likewise, for the manufacturers have modified the sand-iron so that it can be played from rough grass and fairway lies. These modifications, narrowing the sole of the club, have, however, made the present models less efficient in traps than their wide-soled ancestors which came out in the thirties.

The sand-iron stroke remains the same on the fairway as in the trap. The club is picked up rather than swung, and picked up quite vertically, well on the outside of the normal line. You then come down on the same line as the backswing, cutting across the ball with an open face—hitting two inches or so behind the ball on the average explosion shot. Natu-

rally, the longer the shot, the less sand you take. The most common fault among poor trap players is that they take the club back on the inside. They have two chances of getting out —slim and none.

The sand-iron is a club that demands many hours of practice, but once mastered it is the greatest stroke saver in the game. I'm proud to have invented it.

It takes some intelligence to play good golf. An ambitious player must think clearly about his practice habits and his equipment. On the course he must know his limitations and not expect to hit eighteen perfect tee-shots. Middlecoff and Mangrum don't. He mustn't destroy his concentration before a shot by wondering if thirty-three anatomical parts are going to perform their appointed functions. If he falls into an error which he does not understand, that's what qualified professionals are for.

He must remember that a good grip is the foundation of a good golf swing. If your foundation is right, your house will stand firmly down through the years. If the foundation is faulty, it doesn't matter how well you have decorated the rooms, the house will collapse anyway. I am sincerely convinced that if the average player approaches the game sensibly, he will soon discover that he is well above average.

Discoveries That Helped My Golf Game Most

by

BYRON NELSON

1948 — FROM THE JUNE ISSUE OF *GOLFING*

I was just like a lot of other young touring professional golfers several years after my transformation from amateur to pro—lean at the waistline more from hunger than exercise. What made this situation just twice as bad as it might have been was that my wife, Louise, was also a victim of my lack of the means with which to provide many items in the "necessity" category.

Aggravating that perpetual financial pinch through my first three years as a play-for-pay boy was my penchant for blaming my lack of success not on myself (as I should have done) but on my clubs. Unfortunately, they couldn't speak up to let me know what a fool I was making of myself. As wonderfully patient and understanding as she has always been, Louise couldn't contain her thoughts any longer, when, in 1936, I was about to cast aside my 'steenth set of clubs and plunk down a sizable portion of our meager means for a newer set which I prayed and trusted might somehow cure my shot-making ills. "Byron, honey," she started (the crackling of her eyes took all the sweetness out of the "honey"), "why don't you quit kidding yourself? It just can't be entirely the clubs. Your trouble is YOU!"

Louise had hit it right on the nose, and I knew it. I had been afraid to admit this very truth to myself. But I couldn't argue against her. That colossal and strictly out-of-the-money 317 I had hacked out in the 1935 National Open had precipitated this incident. My immature and false sense of pride had prevented me from putting the finger on myself.

I quit butchering my clubs with chisels, knives, drills, and files, as I had been doing for some time in a blind search for improvement. I resolved to let the clubmakers worry about my clubs and to concern myself with my own use of the implements. I faced only two alternatives, at least in my own mind: (1) To quit the game (2) To start an intensive study of myself and the game of golf.

My golf game as I finally "grooved" it, began right then and there a five-year transformation. Rather than taking any one of the topnotchers of the day—Harry Cooper, Horton Smith, Ky Laffoon, Denny Shute, Johnny Revolta, Henry Picard, Paul Runyan, Gene Sarazen, Walter Hagen, or Craig Wood—as a model, I studied all of them, trying to figure out what each swing had in common with the other. The time I had wasted in trying to reshape clubs and in confused practice, I now put into purposeful experimentation. I seemed to be all balled up at first, but Louise wouldn't let me get too discouraged. A couple of times when I was ready to give up she kept me going by saying, "Just keep on working as hard as you are. Some day you'll be successful. I know you will."

The "new Nelson" (with hours on end of practice under his belt) turned up as one of the many unknowns in the field of the 1935 Metropolitan Open at the Quaker Ridge Country Club, New York. To my amazement and unbounded elation I put together a 283 total for the seventy-two holes to take the first money of $750. It was the best score I had ever posted for four consecutive rounds. Incidentally, it came none too soon for I had exactly one $5 bill to my name at the moment I stepped up to receive my check—and most of the clothes I owned were on my back.

Definitely more important, though it didn't seem so at the moment, was the "boost" this success gave me in my search for an efficient style. One of the changes to which I could definitely attribute some of my improvement at this point was in standing up to the ball. At various times I had reached perceptibly for the ball. This unnatural leaning forced me into a flat swing. I have since found overstooping to be a common fault. I early proved to my own satisfaction that it is next to impossible to stand too close to the ball. I discovered in time that I got my best results by bending just enough at the waist to allow my arms to hang freely from the shoulders at a sufficient distance from the body so that there will be complete clearance for arms and hands in carrying the club back and through in the process of swinging.

During my hours of trial-and-error on the practice tee the "new Nelson" experimented a great deal with hip motion—and in so doing stumbled on a discovery that I still consider one of the most important factors in helping me to achieve accuracy. Like many others I had for some time started my backswing with a turning motion of the hips. This caused the club to cut too sharply inside as it was drawn away from the ball. When I got to using my head and analyzing the game, I arrived at the deduction that it should improve my accuracy if I started the clubhead straight back from the ball and in a low arc. I found that I could facilitate this straight-back trajectory of the clubhead by shifting my hips laterally from left to right. I had previously proven to myself that the best way to insure a well-timed swing

was to start the clubhead, hands, and shoulders back in a single motion. It seemed that when I did this, my timing turned out to be O.K. throughout my swing.

While this lateral shifting of my hips in unison with the start of my backswing is in my opinion one of the most important improvements resulting from my newly-inspired search for winning form (particularly for the increase it effected in accuracy), an alteration in my hand work contributed to the same effect—namely to keep that ball going straight down the middle.

You needn't go back so many years to find pictures of leading amateur and professional golfers "rolling their wrists"—that is to say, with the right wrist going over the shaft and the left wrist turning under as the clubhead nears the ball and then follows through impact with the ball. As the result of a series of experiments with the various motions of wrists and hands I discovered that by keeping the back of my left hand toward my objective —from the time the clubhead entered the "hitting area" about thirty inches before impact, until it had completed the early stages of the follow-through—I materially increased my accuracy. This proved to be a sure way of preventing my wrists from varying or turning. In this device I had the answer to the old bugaboo of wrist-rolling which drives so many golfers to desperation via the roughs and other hazards lurking to right and left. I believe I have been down the fairway about as consistently as any of the tournament golfers since hitting upon the idea of "aiming" with the back of my left hand.

I'll mention briefly the matter of the "straight left arm." Like a lot of others I thought I was keeping my left arm pretty straight—that is, until I began the serious and intense analysis of my mechanical weaknesses. I then learned that my assumption had been erroneous. When I finally got around to keeping that appendage really straight I found that I became more firm at the top of my backswing, and consequently more consistent in my shot-making. I gained better control throughout my swing, particularly at the top where I am now very firm in the control of my club. Today in studying pictures of myself "in action" I note that my left arm is as straight as a ruler.

Of the improvements I have made in my game, I'd say that these I have mentioned and now repeat in review—(1) Standing closer to the ball (2) Replacing the direct pivot with a lateral shifting of the hips followed by the pivot (3) Keeping the back of my left hand toward my objective as much as possible— were the most important I made in trying to perfect and simplify my swing.

I do not mean to claim that these ideas are original with me. I can assure you that they are factors that I worked out by myself and incorporated into my game on my own initiative after weeks, months, and years of trial, error, and hard work.

Permit me to add a final word of advice. It's the easiest thing in the world to blame your golfing mistakes onto factors other than yourself, but the usual truth of the matter lies right under the skin of the alibi expert. I'm plenty thankful that Louise forced me to pin my golfing shortcomings on myself. It was definitely the turning point away from oblivion for me. My only regret today is that I didn't get wise to myself a lot sooner. If you have golfing ambitions, don't make the same mistake.

Golf Fashions,
Not Fundamentals, Change

by

HORTON SMITH

1948 — FROM THE MAY ISSUE OF *GOLFING*

WHEN I was about fifteen I began studying the styles of great golfers as I saw them in pictures, and once in a while in play. Then I had the usual boyish ambition to imitate the stars and the accompanying handicap of not realizing the reason for actions I noticed and tried to copy. That start developed into a habit of appraising the styles of the stars and the reasons for these styles when I became a professional and could see the paragons in actual play and discuss with them their ideas of effective playing methods.

For almost nineteen years I've had the interesting and valuable experience of getting a close-up on the methods of the experts. I saw Harry Vardon play when he was past his competitive prime and have talked with him about his observations of the fundamentals and the mannerisms of the stars with whom he played. From Vardon through the field of promising newcomers on the tournament circuit today I've watched the fashions in playing the game.

And fashions is the right word in describing the changes I have seen. There has been no radical change in the golf swing for two decades. There has been evolution but not revolution.

Certainly there have been improvements in teaching and playing and beyond any doubt the best golf that's ever been played is now being played by the professionals and amateurs—men and women—in the United States.

But these improvements haven't been the result of discoveries that differed from basic principles that were evident in the games of Vardon and his contemporaries. The improvements have come from application of these principles by patiently practicing and experimenting players who brought an era of specialization into the game and with it the American reign.

As the incentive of big money prizes has grown in American golf naturally emphasis on scoring rather than on the element of classic form has grown. Pitching, chipping, trap play and particularly putting have received more attention from more studious players.

Other factors have changed the style of play but not the fundamentals of playing. The watering of fairways and the shorter cutting of rough has placed a premium on long tee-shots and reduced the penalty of wildness. Heavy watering of greens also has diminished the former necessity for accuracy off the tee. If the drive is off line the soft greens usually leave a comparatively simple and safe shot with a No. 4 iron or less on the par 4 holes.

The multitude of tournaments and the attraction of prize money have brought into professional golf an athletic type of player who keeps in good physical condition. These men, constantly playing, have developed golfing muscles beyond the standard of previous generations. The conditions of play also account for stronger muscles of legs, back and shoulders. These factors combine to place accent on power instead of accuracy to the green. Incessant study and practice have been applied to the search for putting methods that will offset the uncertainties of nerves.

As in every other phase of life there are changes in styles and trends of the times in golf, but as an example of how the cycles never get far out of the circuit you can compare the swings of Macdonald Smith and Bobby Locke. I did not see Macdonald Smith play until late in his competitive career. He tied for the U.S. Open Championship in 1910. Older golfers told me that Mac's style was the same twenty-five years later when I saw him in action many times as it had been in 1910. Locke has most of Mac Smith's swing characteristics. Locke's full, unhurried, smooth swing is almost precisely in the Mac Smith pattern. Locke is a keener putter and seemingly has more competitive fire than Mac had.

The development of competitive attitude that generally is under quite steady control is an inevitable result of more competition for more money. Concentration, composure and coordination have become more habitual. With this improvement there has come greater confidence and that's a tremendously important element in scoring. The confident player isn't thrown out of his stride by the bad shots he is bound to make now and then.

There has been no change in the striving to play shots with a swing as fluid and as beautiful as that Jones had in his prime and which has fairly well stayed with Johnny Dawson who, when he was younger, had a swing that often out-Jonesed Jones, to repeat a statement made by Mrs. Tommy Armour. What we have seen are changes in individual styles and general fads and sometimes we've been misled by hearing the same sort of a swing described in different words. We have seen the punching hitters and the swinging strokers all through the modern period of the game and have seen in Hagen and Sarazen a "swinging hit" blend of styles.

Chick Evans was a pioneer stylist in combining the swing with control, and the swing school reached a high point during the days of the Jones conquest. Jones, Mac Smith, Johnny Dawson, Ed Dudley, Glenna Collett, Virginia Van Wie and Mrs. Leona Pressler were the glasses of that fashion. Hagen and Sarazen headed the aggressive hitter school. Johnny Farrell and Joe Turnesa modified that style. Tommy Armour and Harry Cooper established a style that was a highly effective compromise between the swing and the hit. However there was very little question of the full free-flowing type of swing being the ideal.

It didn't work for me, though, and probably not for others of my type of build. I retained the essentials of my predecessors but worked out a relatively short swing which began giving me excellent results during the tournaments in 1929. Apparently that experiment in changing a fashion influenced many. Bob Jones has said that my shorter swing served as an example in revising his shorter shots so he hit the ball with crisp, positive action.

The major influence in changing fashions in golf has been that of variations in physique. We see the results in the actual swings or in motion pictures but, particularly in the pictures, we are liable not to see the reasons for the departures from what we have been regarding as the ideal pattern. When we do eventually discover that some individual feature of physical makeup accounts for the variation from what we consider a normal method, further investigation shows us that there has been no departure from basic points that experts have maintained through the years.

Some have commented that Worsham and other of the younger stars have introduced something new in having the left wrist in line with the arm at the top of the swing instead of having it under the shaft. Hagen played many shots with the left wrist in line with the arm. Alex Morrison has advocated that position for years in his instruction book. Look at the pictures of Sam Snead in his book and you'll observe that this position is nothing new. Leo Diegel called attention to the weak undershaft position and the desirability of the strong straight position years ago. Lawson Little at his prime was a fine example of the straight arm-wrist position and so was Sam Byrd when he was a tournament contender.

Older Scotch-born American professionals have remarked that the trend toward using more of a palm grip with the left hand and which recently had been called the "new

American grip" was in vogue forty or more years ago.

Nearly twenty years ago I was playing with belated wrist action which kept my wrists cocked on the downswing until they were getting into what we now call "the hitting zone." Byron Nelson's employment of the same detail has been regarded by many as something new. For years Al Watrous has emphasized that action by teaching his pupils to "keep the club behind the hands on the way down."

There has been talk lately of "rerouting" the club. It has been caused by a quite obvious loop in Locke's swing and some who have noted this loop have thought they've discovered a note that Bobby has introduced. The same discovery was made in Jones's clubhead path and some maintained that the Jones loop was a grave fault requiring superfluous movements that allowed more of a chance for error. Possibly there could still be debate on whether Jones played great golf because of that loop or despite it.

However, Ky Laffoon and "Jug" McSpaden when they were top-ranking tournament players had outside-inside loops in their swings. Both of them broke their wrists more fully coming down than during their backswings, although that feature generally is regarded as a comparatively new procedure of tournament headliners.

Feel of the clubhead and control of the clubhead still are main objectives, and timing continues to be the all-important factor in good golf. The fundamentals involved in mastering these three factors haven't changed either. Modifications probably have resulted from the introduction of the steel shaft and other improvements in club design and construction but the essential remains the same and we not only understand these fundamentals more clearly but can express our observations more lucidly.

We have learned to learn from our mistakes in experimenting. Tommy Armour once said he copied more than twenty-five swings before settling on his own. I know that I made some experiments on my swing that were harmful temporarily although most of them were carefully considered in advance and produced some durable improvements. I found that there are numerous deviations allowable in attaining quite effective results but that I dared not stray from the fundamentals. Any time there was a deviation from the standard pattern in my swing I had to introduce a compensating and correcting detail.

During my best play I had a slight dip of my left shoulder during the backswing and a compensating lift as I came into the ball. The dip was a peculiarly individual affair but the fundamental which was retained and which saved my swing was the benefit of a full shoulder turn and thrust which gave the correct position and the power to my swing.

My swing of 1928-30 when it was getting set as somewhat of an innovation in style had features which definitely were improved upon by Nelson. It is my belief that the same thing holds true in comparing Snead's style during his greatest years and the Jones style of that triumphant year of 1930. Snead made some improvements.

Primarily these improvements made by Nelson and Snead I believe are the result of the highly specialized heavier competitive schedule of later years. Later players have developed a more direct and mechanical type of stroke in which as little as possible is left to chance or the uncertainty of touch. Golf is less a "finger game," even in putting, than it was ten years ago. There was more striving for complete freedom of action and "throwing the clubhead" before the newer crop of tournament winners appeared on the scene. Although compactness of the swing certainly was recognized as a most desirable point years ago the predecessors of Nelson, Hogan, Demaret and Snead didn't attain it as admirably as these men have.

The changed style apparently has helped somewhat to reduce the uncertainties of the human element although the stars still have their hot and cold rounds unaccountably. One of the possible explanations for there being fewer "off" rounds by the newer school of star golfers is that they've had to practice longer and harder in developing the new style's accent on leg, body and shoulder action and that arduous practice has set the style more firmly than the arm and hand action routine that formerly was in general favor.

I think that O. B. Keeler made an accurate observation in noting that main attention now is paid to "form" instead of to "style."

Changes in describing the ideal procedure

that I happen to call to mind include the following:

Head steady and spine in line has replaced the admonitions to "keep the eye on the ball and the head down."

Smoothness has replaced slowness.

Leg and body movement have replaced the "heel lift."

And in playing tactics it is the desire now to want to pitch the ball dead as near as possible to the hole and trust to bounces or rolls only in emergency. That desire accounted for the eagerness to indent clubfaces for backspin.

Notwithstanding the changes in style I don't see drastic revisions in the fundamentals of form that I had rather clearly in mind about twenty years ago.

There still is the necessity of feeling the clubhead through the hands. That continues to involve proper order of movement—gripping the club, taking aim, adjusting stance to line up the shot. This of course calls for proper placement of hands and correct pressure for control without making muscles rigid. The grip still has to be firm enough for control and light enough for "feel." The left hand and arm still have a backhand function and the right hand and arm a forehand performance in properly delivering the blow.

There has been no change in the fundamental requirement of using the body and weight to coordinate and reinforce the hand and arm swinging or hitting with the club. Posture, balance and weight position still call for the head position, shoulder turn, shift and turn of hips that every good golfer of twenty years ago knew he should have.

There has been no change in the fundamental of moving the clubhead in a "groove" that could be most easily maintained for accuracy and power. The fundamentals involved in pacing all action of the players so the clubhead will reach and go through the ball at desired speed and smoothness haven't changed a bit.

The necessity of concentration and composure so the player will have a sense of security, comfort and confidence and a clear mental picture of the shot required is just the same as it ever was.

Progress in the game has been made by applying the fundamentals with greater understanding. Progress will continue along the same line while the same fundamentals continue as the platform of modern golf.

Tournament Golf

by

ROBERT T. JONES, JR. and O. B. KEELER

1927 — FROM *DOWN THE FAIRWAY*

EARLIER I made the statement that there were two kinds of golf—golf, and tournament golf; and that they were not at all the same. Here I shall try to go a little into the difference, with special reference to tournament golf, because, whether justly or unjustly, a golfer in these days is judged principally upon his tournament record and his tournament achievements.

I think a man may be a truly great golfer and not be a great tournament golfer; and I do not think that the customary implication, that a great golfer who fails to shine at formal competition lacks courage, is justified. Matters of physique and mere physical stamina have a profound effect, as do also personal inclination and taste. Then there is that curious and little understood factor of temperament, which is so convenient an explanation either of the successful tournamenteer or the unsuccessful one.

In any event, I maintain that golf and tournament golf are two different things; and it may be that I can speak with a little show of authority from acutely personal experience, since for a number of years I was regarded as a great golfer, and most certainly not a great tournament golfer. I had a remarkably good opportunity to study the difference, which was increasingly heavy upon me in those years while I was competing in eleven major championships, and never winning one.

A great golfer—but he can't win championships. That was what they said; kindly, but with a sort of conviction.

Now, I did not lack confidence, in my earliest championship tournaments. I was very young and brainless; I didn't know enough to fear the competition or to worry about it. And even then tournament golf was different. Especially the big tournaments. There was something about it; something that seemed to key me up, not unpleasurably. I began to notice that I seemed to play better when nervous. This is true today. The most unpropitious symptom I can experience before an important round, of match or medal play, is absence of nervousness. It is a rare thing for me to be able to manage even the restricted tournament breakfast, the morning on which the big show starts.

Digressing a moment, I might explain here that I play better fasting. That is one of the changes since I grew up. As a boy I loved to eat; I still love to eat, but not on the days of tournament play, until after the second round. I used to eat plenty of breakfast of my accustomed kind: oatmeal, bacon and eggs, all too frequently cakes or waffles, and coffee. And at luncheon between rounds, hungry from the exercise, I would not think of denying myself something substantial, topped off by pie a la mode. Pie and ice cream—with an afternoon round to play!

Not any more. For breakfast, when I can eat, a strip of bacon and a small chop and a cup of black coffee. For luncheon, between rounds, a slice of dry toast and a cup of tea.

There is another difference between just golf and tournament golf. Playing an exhibition match, I eat—and drink—whatever I please between rounds, and seem to play none the worse for it. In fact, I could tell you the story of a match Max Marston and I played against two professionals, where our host took us to his home for luncheon between rounds —we were all square at the end of the morning round and having a hard battle—and administered to my unsophisticated palate five or six pleasant-tasting cocktails, whose bland guise concealed a mighty kick. When I reached the club for the afternoon round, I had to get very carefully out of the motor car, and while teeing my ball I was concerned with my balance. This state of affairs, of course, should have been ruinous. But such are the vagaries of golf, when the tournament strain is not on, that instead of disgracing myself hopelessly in the matinée round, I led off with a 3 at each of the first three holes, finished with a 66, and our side won the match, 6-5.

Not in tournament golf. I have a good, big dinner in the evening in my room, prefaced by two good, stiff highballs, the first taken in a tub of hot water, the finest relaxing combination I know; and then a few cigarettes and a bit of conversation, and bed at 9 o'clock. And usually I sleep well, despite the curious strain that is always present in championship competition.

Some of the best informal rounds I have played followed closely on the heels of dietetic eccentricities that would cause the coach of a football team to faint in his tracks. But, according to our little maxim, there is golf— and tournament golf. And in the latter I try to take no more chances than I have to. There are chances enough, at the best.

It must be a sort of subjective nerve-tension, this difference in tournament golf. Years ago I discovered that the best preparation for a big tournament, for me, was as much rest as I could acquire, in the twenty-four hours before the opening gun. In my younger days I liked to play a lot of golf, right up to the day the competition began. Often I'd play

36 holes the day before it started. Now I try always to schedule the little preliminary practice season, of three or four days, so that the last day I can rest. In bed, often, with a book. I remember the day before the National Amateur championship at Flossmoor, I stopped in bed and read Papini's *Life of Christ,* a book with an odd fascination for me. If I can avoid it, I never touch a golf club the day before a big competition opens, and I prefer to play only 18 holes a day the two days preceding.

The fair success of this plan induces the opinion, then, that the strain of championship golf is mostly mental; and certainly the mere physical strain would not burn one up as has been my experience in so many tournaments. Could anyone make me believe that six days of just golf, 36 holes a day, would have stripped eighteen pounds off me, as that six days at Oakmont in 1919, did? At Worcester, in the Open Championship and play-off of 1925, I lost twelve pounds in three days, and I wasn't much overweight when I went there. Perhaps these physical symptoms help to explain the furious toll exacted from the spirit, under the stress of tournament competition. I know that tournament golf takes a lot out of me; the photographs, before and after, sometimes are rather shocking in contrast.

Now, my career to this writing, which includes the year 1926, is divided with so extraordinary a balance as regards tournament golf and championships that it would seem there must be a good opportunity to offer something in the way of a solution of the difference between a good golfer and a good tournament golfer. In the seven years between 1916 and 1922, inclusive, I played in eleven national championships, and did not win one. In the four years including 1923 and 1926, I played in ten national championships, winning five and finishing second three times.

Something, then, seems to have happened, to fatten the run of what one fanciful writer termed my seven lean years. And here it seems I have worked up to a climax, without the climax—excepting a negative sort.

There has been a change in my tournament attitude; of that I am sure. It was not an improvement in shot-making. Leaving off the minor refinements, I had as good an assortment of shots in the seven lean years as I have today. I think I never played particularly badly in any of those tournaments, before I broke through to win. I know that in the amateur competitions I never was beaten by a man who was not playing first-rank golf. And as I began to read more and more, to hear more and more, the dictum that I was a great golfer, but I could not win a major championship, the sorry option seemed forced upon me that either I was jinxed—a wretched sort of plea—or that I didn't have the tournament stuff. I pondered that miserable option more than I would care to have people know.

There must have been a change in my tournament attitude, then. But I cannot say surely when it came about, or how. Certainly I did not go to Inwood in 1923 for the National Open with any fresh access of confidence. I think I never was less confident. I had been beaten until I was expecting it. I was not well, and I was playing wretchedly.

Yet I won that championship, after tying with Bobby Cruickshank; and I think that perhaps it was in that tournament my attitude began changing. I saw Jock Hutchison leading after the first round and the second, collapsing midway of the third round. I saw Bobby Cruickshank, going to the fourteenth tee of the final round in a dazzling burst of golf—he went through seven holes, beginning with No. 6, in 23 strokes—break down even as I had broken down in my own finishing round, and tie me by shooting a wonderful birdie 3 at the seventy-second hole. And I managed to beat him in the play-off.

So I suppose I began to understand that the other fellows all had their troubles, too; that I didn't have to go out and shoot four perfect rounds to win a major open championship, or even one perfect round, if I could just keep four decent rounds sticking together. I suppose I began instinctively to understand that one lost stroke did not necessarily have to be redeemed at once; perhaps it was not ruinous; perhaps the other fellows were losing a stroke, too.

Now, if this was a change in mental attitude, it was not complete by the time we played the National Amateur championship at Flossmoor that year, and Max Marston put me out in the second round. But I do think the alteration crystallized between Inwood, 1923, and Merion, 1924. Perhaps at Flossmoor.

I got a severe lesson and a drubbing in the second round. I had played well enough in the qualifying rounds to tie with Chick Evans for the medal score, and as he also was retired early from match competition, we played off the tie the following day. At the fifth hole Chick, playing grandly, was leading me by two strokes—medal play. Now, on the previous day when Max Marston had got me two down in the afternoon round, I remember thinking I must get those holes back right away—*right away*. And I never could get them back, hard as I tried.

In this play-off with Chick, at medal competition, I was two strokes down. But I had a different attitude. Some way, I wasn't in that frantic hurry about getting those strokes back. It was as if something deep in my consciousness kept counseling patience. Patience! Somewhere lately I heard or read that the greatest asset of Harry Vardon was his perfect realization of the cold fact that no matter what happened, there was only one thing for him to do—keep on hitting the ball. I hadn't heard or read that, at Flossmoor; and I cannot say that such a plan was in my mind. Indeed, I had no plan. Instinctively or otherwise, I managed to keep on hitting the ball, and not trying to wrench back those strokes immediately. And presently—presently they came back to me, in a sort of normal and ordinary manner, and some more with them.

So maybe that is the answer—the stolid and negative and altogether unromantic attribute of patience. It is nothing new or original to say that golf is played one stroke at a time. But it took me many years to realize it. And it is easy to forget, now. And it won't do to forget, in tournament golf.

Mostly I've had to run behind, in the major championships. The only important medal competition in which I went into the last round with a comfortable lead was the Southern Open championship of 1927, at my home course, East Lake, and I hardly knew what to make of the situation—being eight strokes ahead of the field. But in the major championships I've managed to win, I've usually had to run behind. At Inwood I fancied I had a good lead in the closing round—and I did not run well in front. Maybe that taught me something; that when I was behind, I did not need to load myself with additional worries about the man who was setting the pace, because he probably had his own troubles. Anyway, I was running behind right up to the closing holes of the British Open and the United States Open of 1926, and if anything pulled me through it certainly was not courage, but just patience, and managing to keep on hitting the ball. At Scioto, in the United States Open, indeed, I was so far behind there was no use going out to pick up strokes. As I stood on the seventh tee of that last terrible round, if someone had come to me and said: "You will have to do these last twelve holes in two under fours to win," I should have known surely that it could not be done. Yet that is precisely what *did* have to be done, to win. And by managing to play those twelve holes one hole at a time, and one shot at a time, I scraped through.

Maybe that is the answer—patience. Whatever I may possess of it now must have been cultivated, as I assuredly did not have it at first, and the number of years required to hammer it into me is a sorry commentary on my native intelligence.

It's a long way from that first round of 80 at East Lake, when I was a skinny kid, running to show my card, which I made Perry Adair sign, to Dad; my first real bout with Old Man Par, and, I suppose, the first glimmering notion that here was the real opponent. After all, it's Old Man Par and you, match or medal. And Old Man Par is a patient soul, who never shoots a birdie and never incurs a buzzard. He's a patient soul, Old Man Par. And if you would travel the long route with him, you must be patient, too.

I really think that is good advice. I hope I may be able to follow it, occasionally.

Tournament golf! It's different from just golf in other ways, especially when it leads at last into the cage of championship. I read a line somewhere, or a title, "The Cage of Championship." It *is* something like that. Something like a cage. First you're expected to get into it, and then you're expected to stay there. But of course nobody can stay there. Out you go—and then you're trying your hardest to get back in again. Rather silly, isn't it, when golf —just golf—is so much fun?

Still, championship has its compensations. There was that sight of New York harbor, in 1926, when I was bringing the British Open championship cup home; New York harbor, and the *Macom* coming out, with the home folks aboard, and the band playing "Valencia."

I've been awfully lucky. Maybe I'll win another championship, some day. I love championship competition, after all—win or lose. Sometimes I get to thinking, with a curious little sinking away down deep, how I will feel when my tournament days are over, and I read in the papers that the boys are gathering for the National Open, or the Amateur. Maybe at one of the courses I love so well, and where I fought in the old days. It's going to be queer.

But there's always one thing to look forward to—the round with Dad and Chick and Brad; the Sunday morning round at old East Lake, with nothing to worry about, when championships are done.

The Controlled Golf Swing

by

PERCY BOOMER

1946 — FROM *ON LEARNING GOLF*

EVERY TEACHER has to keep continually in mind the fact that the natural thing for any golfer to do, if he thinks first of hitting the ball to the hole rather than of making the shot correctly, is to swing the clubhead down the desired line of flight. The urge to do this is so strong that a merely academic knowledge of where the clubhead ought to be felt to go cannot stand against it. William James said that where there is a conflict between the Will and the Imagination, the Imagination *always* wins. So no will to make a correct swing—unless reinforced by our conscious control—can resist, when imagination of the ball flying straight for the hole supervenes. What usually happens is that before the backswing is completed, the player *transfers his attention from the matter of making the correct swing to the matter of where he wants to hit the ball,* i.e., somewhere at the top of his swing he switches from a correct in-to-out swing to one along the desired line of flight. Consequently he comes down *outside the ball.*

The player who comes down outside is almost invariably thinking of where he wants to put the ball, and the only effective way of overcoming his trouble is by getting him to concentrate on the swing that experience tells him will *place* it there. If this is done, his conscious control—his feeling for the right movements, plus a steady intention to follow

them out—will inhibit his natural desire to take disastrous short cuts.

This desire to take the short cut can only be defeated by building up a swing which can be accepted by the mind as well as the muscles as a satisfactory means to the end desired, and then concentrating on the production of that swing. With a properly felt swing, *the swing becomes the aim* and the matter of where the ball will fly is left (as it should be) to take care of itself.

And finally, the good golfer feels his swing as *all one piece.* It is produced by a psychophysical unison and its control is outside the mind of the player. Any control that is *within* the mind is subject to the state of the mind and is therefore unreliable.

In whatever class of golf you play, you will agree that the quality which enables the fellow just above you to give you strokes is not so much his ability to make shots which you cannot, as his knack of keeping his average shot nearer his best than you can. And this prime virtue of consistency is commonly credited to concentration.

And concentration is taken to mean such a pulling of oneself together, such a fixing of the mind on the task in hand, such a tight-lipped determination to do one's best, that golf becomes a trial of nervous strength rather than a game.

Now my own observation of many thousands of golfers from neophytes to tigers is that this form of concentration does *not* assist the production of one's best game. In fact I think the whole "concentration" doctrine a perversion of the truth, almost a reversal of it. I say that a golfer can only produce his true quality when he can play *without* concentrating (in this sense), when he can make his shots without clenching his teeth.

Nothing makes a simple physical action so difficult as does "concentration." Consider this odd fact about walking. We pay less attention to walking down a street than to walking over a plank across a stream—and *because* we pay less attention to it, we walk at least as straight and with much better balance, greater firmness, and greater ease.

Simply because the penalties of deviating from the straight are so much greater when crossing the plank, we feel we have to concentrate our attention on the job. And it is this attitude of overtense attention that makes the simple and familiar act of walking straight so suddenly and curiously difficult.

Now we can translate that directly into a common golfing experience. Put the average good golfer on a tee with a fairway fifty yards wide before him, and time after time he will drive slap down the middle of it. Yet reduce the width of that fairway to fifteen yards and he will become so conscious of its narrowness —so concentrated on the importance of keeping dead straight—that time after time he will put himself well out in the rough. That is why a course with wide fairways is commonly more popular than a narrow one; the average golfer feels more comfortable about it and *because* he feels more comfortable, plays better.

Hitting a golf ball is not difficult, nor is walking straight, *so long as the penalties of failure are not great.* But introduce the plank bridge or the narrow fairway and the difficulties follow.

The desire to *guide the ball* dead straight increases with the need for a dead straight drive, and the greater the desire the greater the difficulty! So when we stand on a tee with a narrow fairway before us, we must use our will power to inhibit the desire to *guide* the ball and simply perform the swing which our golfing sense tells us will send the ball straight. In fact we must forget that the plank is a bridge and simply walk across it!

This is true about the longest shot in golf, the drive; it is equally true and even more obvious about the shortest, the putt. What a simple operation is the five-foot putt on a good green *when there is nothing hanging to it—* and how exasperatingly difficult when it will decide the hole, the match, and the half-crown!

So I repeat that if concentration means focusing all our mental attention and capacity on the problems and penalties of the shot in hand, then concentration is destructive of good golf. Good golf, consistent golf, depends upon being able to shut out our mental machinery (with its knowledge of the difficulties of the shot, the state of the game, etc.) *from those parts of us which play golf shots.*

If you want my idea of the ideal mental attitude to the game, I will give it you in two words—Walter Hagen's! Walter Hagen was not only one of the greatest golfers, he was one of the most buoyant. Wherever he played he simply oozed with the joy of life. The more he was up against it, the better he played. He really enjoyed a fight, and the harder it was, the more superb his confidence.

The general verdict is that the Haig had a "marvellous temperament for the game." And what do we mean by that? My own interpretation is that the Haig had perfect psychophysical equilibrium, that his mind and body were perfectly balanced and perfectly correlated for the purpose of the game of golf.

Walter Hagen had found by trial and error, as most of us do, how he could best hit the ball. He had got the *feel* of his shots thoroughly into his system and could pull them out whenever he wanted. While he was playing he inhibited any extraneous matters in the most effective way possible—*he refused to let them into that part of himself that was concerned with his golf.* So he could play his best in circumstances that would have turned gray the hair of any less perfectly adjusted player.

Please note that the Haig did *not* concentrate in the accepted sense. He did not shut extraneous matters out of his mind; he merely shut them out of his golf. While he was playing he would talk intelligently about any subject that cropped up, stocks and shares, eating and drinking, politics or puritanism. *Nothing,* neither wind nor weather, bad greens, tight corners, or unduly chatty opponents, ever made the Haig *tense*. Consequently golf never exhausted him; he was as fresh at the end of a championship as he was at its beginning.

Incidentally this mental limberness was not left behind on the last green. I remember talking to him at Sandwich on the day he won the British Open. He had finished and we sat and chatted for a long time while waiting to see if George Duncan would deprive him of the title which otherwise he had won. Well, George very nearly did it, but Walter Hagen never batted an eyelid. He was as chatty, as cheerful, and as untense as ever—at the end of a week's competitive golf with the whole issue of a three-thousand-mile trip in the balance.

I suppose everyone would agree that "self-control" as effective as that possessed by men like Hagen and Harry Vardon is a priceless quality. But how achieve it? It can only be done by building one's golf into a closed, self-controlling circle, and then keeping extraneous matters outside that circle.

Too much thought about the mechanics is a bad thing for anyone's game. Now the reason why golf is so difficult is that you have to learn it and play it *through your senses*. You must be mindful but not thoughtful as you swing. You must not think or reflect; you must *feel* what you have to do. Part of the difficulty arises because, apart from simple things like riding a bicycle, we have never learned to do things in this way.

Now no teacher can tell in exact words how it feels when you make a certain movement correctly. You will have to use your imagination to interpret what he says, and if he is wise he will encourage you to use it.

Let me give you an example. I want to teach you to pivot from the hips. Now I can show you how it is done and issue the usual mass of detailed instruction, but that does not call up your imagination and it gives you no conception of how it *feels* to pivot correctly.

So, instead of explaining all the mechanical and anatomical details of the pivot to you, I show you how to pivot and then tell you to do it yourself *imagining that you are standing in a barrel hip high and big enough to be just free of each hip but a close enough fit to allow no movement except the pivot.* At once you get the *feeling* of the pivot. Incidentally

nine out of ten golfers would improve their games if they would use this image to the fullest degree in practice.

So far so good; we can learn to feel the body turn to the right and round to the left, beautifully fixed in space by the hips. Now carry the image a stage further: first, as you pivot, *sink down from the knees*—you will feel that if you sink down, even ever so little, you will become stuck in the barrel. *This will not do*, so you must feel that you keep your hips *up* on a level with the top of the barrel. Do this and you will develop the feel of keeping your hips up as you pivot—a thing which, unfortunately for our golf, very few of us do.

Now do not think that we use *imagination* in teaching golf in order to evolve new theories. Oh, no—there are too many theories already! What we use imagination for is to translate theory into *feeling*, and to keep our minds awake and our circle of golfing sensations expanding. Every new golfing sensation (if it is to be deliberately induced and not left to happen by accident) may need an introduction through the imagination in this way—but once the image has done its work of introduction, it can be put on one side and the *feel* that it has made known can be relied on. But put your images on one side—do not abandon them, because if you *do* lose the feel, the image through which you learned it will bring it back.

Now the golf swing is a connected series of sensations or feels, and when you get all these *feels* right and rightly connected, you will swing perfectly. I have just given you the *feel* of the pivot—the movement on which the modern swing is based.

Now to that one basic feel, the pivot, we will add other feels, and every new feel gives you a new *control* until your whole game is controlled and you can play it as you will. But do not think you cannot play until you have this whole series of controls established. Lots of players go through their golfing lives and get a lot of fun out of the game without building up any controls at all! But the more controls you can build up *and link together*, the better for your game, the finer the conception of the swing you will evolve.

Let us get back to the visualizing of our swing. We have laid our foundation by getting the *feel* of the pivot from the hips. This movement goes up through the body to the next control point—the shoulders. And here I believe that wrong imagination does a great deal of damage to many people's swings.

We think that in the fine swing we see the left shoulder come down as we come back and the right shoulder come down as we come forward; so we feel that this shoulder movement is *right* and tend to encourage it—to the detriment of our swings because it is *wrong*. And I say it is wrong, cheerfully certain that it *is* wrong in spite of its almost universal acceptance. How much the shoulders actually dip depends upon how erect we stand when addressing the ball. We should stand as erect as possible and I contend that we should *not* feel our shoulders go down but should feel that we are keeping them fully up.

As we address the ball we look at it a little sideways—we *peep* at it. The head is fixed (because you "keep your eye on the ball"), and the movement of the shoulders is not an independent movement of the shoulders at all, but is due to the shoulders *being moved around from the pivot*. We can only keep the shoulder movement in a fixed groove and make it *repeatable* time after time, by keeping the shoulders at the limit of *upness* in whatever position the turn from the hips may have placed them. Any *excess* of upness (that is, actual shoulder lift) will result in the ball being lost sight of. In short, the fixed head determines the limit of lift and dip of the shoulders.

You will see that this is why you must feel you keep the shoulders up to the same degree with, say, a driver and a full swing and a mashie-niblick (a more upright club) and a half swing. The closer you stand to your ball the more upright the swing and the more directly downward your sight of the ball—also, the less extensive the swing you can make without losing sight of the ball.

Now try this conception of the shoulder action without a club, and *link it to your feel of the pivot from the hips*. Feel how the two become connected. This is the first connection in our building up of a controlled swing—and a very important one. You cannot take too much trouble in understanding it and building it up.

From the shoulders our power travels down through the arms, and as to arm action also

I believe the common conception to be erroneous. Most people think they lift their arms to get them to the top of the back swing. With a modern controlled swing, they do *not* lift them—the arms work absolutely subjectively to the shoulders, that is why they *are* controlled.

But, you may say, if I do not lift my arms how do I get them up to the top of my swing? To find the answer, think this out. As you stand to the ball with the wrists slightly up, there is a straight line practically from the clubhead up the shaft and along your arm to the left shoulder, and as your hands are already waist high it needs only the inclining of the shoulders as we turn (on the pivot) to bring them *shoulder high,* without having altered their relative positions at all. They have not been *lifted;* they have gone up in response to the shoulder movement. This accounts for the curtailment *and* the control of the modern swing.

Naturally, the more flexible we are the more we can get our hands *up* without breaking up this connection, that is, without moving the arms independently. The triangle formed by our arms and a line between the shoulders should never lose its shape—it should be possible to push a wooden snooker triangle in between the arms and to leave it there without impeding the swing back or through.

Now to my mind, the foregoing are the three basic *feels* of the golf swing—the pivot, the shoulders moving in response to the pivot, and the arms moving in response to the shoulders. These are the basic movements of a connected and therefore *controlled* swing, and they must all be built into the framework of your *feel* of the swing.

Of course there are many additional nuances and supplementary *feels* which you will build up and recognize as your game develops, but though you will *add* to these three fundamentals, you will never alter them. Therein lies much of their value. You will get used to taking a sly look at them occasionally as you go round the course, and so long as you keep these three primary *feels* right, nothing much will go wrong with your game.

And if your game does go wrong, if the shots which you thought you had mastered desert you, all you need to do is go back to the *feel* of these three basic points. You just take a peep back at them, and then with one or two shots your mechanism will feel familiar again —and all the other supplementary feels which you have built up by practice will be enticed back.

Now we might break off this chapter at this point. I realize that I have already given you plenty to think of and to work at. But there is a development in your game or in your way of playing it that I want to prepare you for; so, for that reason and for the sake of analyzing the matter out to its logical conclusion, I add the following.

After a while by dint of pivoting correctly, not dipping our shoulders (i.e., not lifting with the arms), we begin to play some good shots, nice and straight and reasonably long. We have arrived at this stage by building on the basic trinity—pivot, shoulders up, and width— and by occasionally taking a sly peep at how they are going. *So far we have never consciously produced a good shot;* we have merely made certain mechanical movements which we have been taught will result in good shots.

But now we begin to realize how we should feel in order to produce a good shot. We are on the other side of the fence. We know now what it feels like to produce a good shot, and now, instead of preparing for a shot by sly looks at our pivot, etc., we instinctively get into the position which we feel will produce a good shot. And as we go on, the *feeling* of this preparatory state comes more and more into the foreground.

Also because we are working from a secure basis we can now begin to notice the nuances and subtleties. We find that we produce purer shots from one sensation than from another

only slightly different. We are enticed to arrange our backswing according to the type of shot we wish to produce; an extra pivot if we wish to pull or a restricted pivot if we wish to slice. But please notice that this will not be a conscious, mechanical control—you will not say to yourself, "I wish to slice slightly so I will restrict my swing to an arc of so many degrees," you will simply alter your swing unconsciously in response to your *feeling* of what will produce the shot you want.

In other words, the control of your shots has now been placed outside your *conscious mind and will.* You have built up a feel that a certain swing will produce a slice—so you can produce a slice by getting that feel into your swing. This is only the beginning of control by feel to the very good golfer. He begins to hit a variety of shots, with little difference in flight or character and yet each subtly different and with its individual feel. He files away in the "feel cabinet" in his unconscious memory all these subtleties. Consequently he never has to "think out" a shot on the course—he sees the lie and the flight required, and these produce, by an automatic response, the right feel from his cabinet and so the right shot from his club.

I hope that this chapter is easier to read than it was to write. I like it as well as any in the book, because it does condense what I take to be the essence of the golf swing into a reasonable space, readable in a reasonable time, so that the beginning should not be forgotten before the end is reached.

But it is a vast field to cover and much compression had to be exercised—so it might be as well if you turned back now and read it again!

Golf's Greatest Teacher— Who?

by

HERB GRAFFIS

1952 — FROM THE APRIL ISSUE OF *GOLFING*

BILLY BURKE came in after a morning on the lesson tee and sat down with fellows who were discussing the greatest golfers they'd ever seen play.

"What's the matter, Billy, are you weary?" one of the grillroom authorities asked.

"Yes, I am," Burke admitted, "and I don't mind it. I treated six tough cases this morning and I did them all some good. That's bound to tire your brains more than your back, but I love it. This afternoon I'll rest up, playing."

"Billy, is teaching golf harder than playing championship golf?" one of the group queried. It was a leading question to put to Burke who'd won the National Open Championship in 1931 by one stroke from George Von Elm after the longest play-off in golf history: 144 added holes.

"Certainly it's tougher," Burke replied. "When you teach you have to play your good shots through the pupil. What's more you defeat yourself and your pupil too if you ever let your pupil know you are doing hard work. You have to build up the pupil's belief that you are delighted to see that the pupil isn't as hopelessly bad as he thinks he is. That helps him to relax and begin to let his muscles work without tightness, strain or embarrassment.

"It isn't as difficult, psychologically, to teach women as it is to teach men. A woman isn't under the mental handicap of thinking that she was a great athlete or is supposed to be an athlete now. Almost every man thinks that he should be muscularly perfect for his age. He is inclined to feel almost humiliated because he doesn't have a good golf swing. Then you have to get him into a hopeful mood of realizing that considering his muscular handicaps, how seldom he plays, how late he took up golf and how he's just beginning to learn what he's supposed to do, he actually is performing quite well."

That last remark cheered the fellows at the table, and in relief they resumed their debate about the game's greatest player.

"Billy, who's the greatest player you ever saw?" Burke was asked.

"I've listened to a thousand arguments about that question," Burke replied, "but what we've been talking about reminded me that never once have I heard any golfers discussing who was the game's greatest teacher."

"That's strange," said one of the golfers, "but I've been around the game for more than thirty years and I've never heard anybody talking about the greatest golf teacher they'd ever seen. No, Billy, since you've brought up the question for the first time, who's your choice?"

Burke reflected.

"I've seen a lot of good ones, but in being careful about naming the greatest I think I'll

have to give the decision to Willie Mac-
Farlane. I haven't seen all of them who might
have claims to top rating, but of those I've
seen teach different types of pupils from beginners to champions, MacFarlane has been
the best."

"But, why?" Burke was asked.

"He went at his job like a good doctor does.
His diagnosis was expertly made and he
wasn't deceived by any surface indication of a
fault that was really deeper.

"He gave a simple explanation of the cause
of the trouble, and he straightened out one
thing at a time.

"Willie gave a fine lesson in ten minutes,
if ten minutes was all that was required for
the fault that most urgently needed treatment.
He didn't keep talking after the lesson was
effectively taught, just to use up the half-hour
lesson time. When the lesson was learned so
well that MacFarlane was satisfied the pupil
got what he needed and wanted, that one lesson was over."

Burke's reference to MacFarlane's disregard
of the customary half-hour length of a golf
lesson moved a listener to ask why a half-hour
was the standard period for a golf lesson.

"I've never been able to find out," Billy
said. "It's just become a custom that seems
to be too deeply set to be altered by good
common sense. The custom is just as illogical
as expecting every visit to a doctor to be a
half-hour long. Some lessons to some pupils
can be given perfectly in ten or fifteen
minutes. The pupil will get the right way so
it stays with him. Then, because the lesson
time is the standard half-hour the professional
is expected to stand around and watch for
something else that may be wrong. Then the
lesson that has been learned may be undone
and new confusion aroused. Spreading out
the lesson time, unless the pro knows teaching
and his pupil, may result in something like
trying to teach algebra and Greek at the
same time.

"One of the improvements that could be
made in golf instruction would be throwing
out that accidentally established custom of the
half-hour lesson and make the single lesson
just as long or just as short as the pupil and
instructor need together to show definite,
satisfying results that will sink in and stay."

After Burke had brought up the interesting

and unique subject of "the best teacher" I
took the question to other professionals. At the
PGA's National course at Dunedin, Fla., I
asked Emil Beck, chairman of the pro association's course committee, whom he'd name as
the best golf teacher.

Beck said his answer, like that of any other
professional, would depend a great deal on
geography as well as personality. "You can
name your choice only on the basis of the professionals in the sections where you've worked
and watched men teach. In the Detroit area
I know at least a half-dozen professionals who
probably would have to be considered when
great golf teachers are named, but in due
respect to them, I'll say the greatest teacher I
ever saw was Norman Sommers who was in
Nebraska when I was fairly new in pro golf.

"What made Sommers great to me was the
simple and easy way he got results. He didn't
have much to say. He showed his pupils what
to do and got them doing it. He'd explain a
point, maybe adjust the pupil, then let the
pupil's feeling, instead of Sommers' talking,
do the teaching.

"His instruction was as interesting and enjoyable to most pupils as their playing rounds
were."

Then, at lunch with Gene Sarazen, the
"greatest teacher" question was asked. Gene
is seldom reluctant about expressing himself
even when it means getting into an argument
that he feels will benefit golf. But he did hesitate before he came out with Alex Smith as
the greatest golf teacher he'd ever seen.

Sarazen said "Alex knew how to teach them
how to get the most out of what they had.
From what I saw of him he was the best in
making the teaching fit the pupil instead of
having a certain system that the pupil had to
be fitted into. He got them all transferring
their weight correctly by sliding the hips in a
lateral shift, although he'd get the idea across
to the fat ones, the thin ones and the medium
ones, in different ways. He got them so they'd
make good use of the body without swaying
out of balance, and by keeping that axis steady
made it possible for them to use their hands
effectively.

"Smith taught Glenna Collett who's been
the greatest 'taught' golfer we've ever had
in this country—and probably the best synthet-
ic golfer the game ever has had. When you

get right down to it, how can you rate the greatness of a golf teacher except by the greatness of his pupils?"

Alex Smith also was among those chosen by George Jacobus, former president of the PGA. Jacobus told of asking Smith, one time when George was an aspiring young pro, if Smith wasn't the greatest of all golf teachers. Jacobus says he can remember Smith's surprise, then his laugh. "I don't think I'm great but I know I'm good," Smith answered.

"What made Smith a great teacher was simplicity," Jacobus remarked. "He'd see the detail in which improvement was most necessary and work on that so effectively and simply that soon the pupil was ready to graduate into some other phase of instruction. He loved golf and he didn't want any part of it, especially instruction, to be made so awesome people would be discouraged and scared away."

Jacobus said he couldn't name any one as the "greatest" golf teacher because where one was great in some respect another might be superior in another way. "When you're naming the 'greats' of golf instruction you have to include Jim Barnes," Jacobus declared. "His book *Picture Analysis of Golf Strokes* which was published in 1919 is a basic work of modern golf instruction.

"Vardon was a great teacher of handwork. During a visit of his over here I learned from him his ideas on the coordinated work of the hands. Those ideas have stood up through the years and his developments in golf instruction have been invaluable to my pupils and to me.

"And when the exceedingly important phase of psychology in golf instruction is considered, anybody naming great instructors must headline Tommy Armour."

Summers at Wheatley Hills and winters at La Gorce have kept the veteran Willie Klein still playing with the sharpness of youth and teaching with zest and effectiveness. Willie was asked whom he regards as the greatest teacher he ever saw. Willie remarked that if he thought about the question at length he wouldn't want to answer but in making a quick decision he'd name Frank Bellwood of the Garden City Golf Club and Bob Mac-Donald as two of the greatest who'd have to be figured in.

"Frank is a product of Vardon who, in my opinion, was the first great professional student of teaching. Bellwood knows golf so thoroughly that he can see and explain the difference between sound principles and fads or individual peculiarities. That's an essential quality of a great teacher because it means protecting the pupil against complexity and confusion.

"Bob MacDonald is a great teacher because he is such a master of the fundamentals. He goes directly to the basic requirements and is a genius at seeing clearly what the deviations are from sound methods and what's the simplest, surest way of putting the pupil on the right track. Bob thoroughly understands the theories, old and new. In an easy, natural, authoritative way he analyzes them and explains them so they are clear to the enthusiastic young pro who thinks he has discovered something entirely new. And, just as clearly, he explains them to the high handicap player who has only a vague idea of what it's all about.

"One difficulty in learning to teach is that most good playing professionals come along by themselves," Klein pointed out. "They don't go through the experience of being on the receiving end of another's teaching such as the club member gets on the lesson tee. Then, there's the danger of being misled away from the first principles. For instance, there have been some adjustments in application of the essentials of golf play because of change in conditions under which the game is played. Seldom now are there fairways hard as concrete sidewalks, greens that are brick-hard and slippery, or are there many bare patches on, or alongside fairways, from which full shots or chips must be made. The improvements in course condition haven't meant a revision in the style of shot-making.

"The great teacher, at any period, is the one who knows how to get down to the essentials where he can give his pupil the only sound foundation for development."

From Klein I went to get Tommy Armour's opinion. Almost every time there's a discussion about golf teaching and teachers Armour is mentioned. Armour gets the highest teaching fee in golf during the winter season mornings he spends seated beneath his umbrella at Boca Raton's lesson tee.

He'd finished his morning's schedule of

tutoring and was holding court in the Boca Raton locker room. Afternoon matches were being arranged with the handicap lawyers in full-tongued eloquence. Armour was applying his golfing psychology as he listened to the others tell how bad they were and how Armour was on the magnificent crest of his game, hence he should give them . . . you know how that sort of talk goes.

"The way I have to give strokes to you fellows convinces me I am the only pro in the world rich enough to be able to afford to be the professional here," said Tommy. That made them all feel happy, including Tommy.

"What'll it be, you ink-stained menace to society?" was Tommy's affable greeting.

"All I want is you to answer—who is the greatest teacher of golf, present company excepted," I asked in due respect.

"Count the present company in, and save your needle, for I can take oath that there are no great golf teachers. I have to answer that honestly in self-defense and in defense of my colleagues in pro golf who are sweating away their brains on the lesson tees.

"How can there be any 'greatest' or even 'great' golf teachers when the task itself is too great to permit greatness?

"Can anyone name the 'greatest' atomic energy scientist? Yet, designing, engineering and constructing an atomic bomb is simple compared to trying to teach a fellow how to stop shanking. The atomic energy scientist deals with factors that are subject to exact mathematical calculation. The golf instructor has to deal with the unpredictable variables of the brain and the unknown qualities of the muscles. I'd like to know how he can get great when he must contend with those mysteries.

"The best the golf instructor can do, and it's astonishing how well some of them can do it, is to use extensive knowledge of the game and inherent ability to impart some of that knowledge in vivid one- or two-syllable words. And at that, I believe that the highest achievement of the golf instructor may not be in teaching but in getting the pupil to learn.

"I see golfers from all over the world come here and I can tell where they come from almost every time I see one of them swing. That is an indication that they have been taught but it doesn't necessarily mean they've learned much more than a chimpanzee would have to learn in learning how to ride a bicycle in a circus act. It takes great 'learners' to make great reputations for teachers, in golf and other studious fields.

"When you're talking about great golf teachers, talk about fellows who have done the great service of getting pupils so they really want to learn even if it means a slight mental effort and inconvenience."

So spoke The Great Armour.

· VI ·

GOLF COURSE ARCHITECTURE

From St. Andrews to the
Modern American Courses

by

ROBERT TRENT JONES

Robert Trent Jones is generally regarded as America's outstanding golf-course architect. An excellent golfer who prepared himself expressly for his career at Cornell's graduate schools, Jones has been associated over the past twenty-five years with the construction or remodeling of over two hundred courses in the United States, Canada, Brazil, and the Caribbean. His original courses include Peachtree in Atlanta, the United States Military Academy's course at West Point, and The Dunes at Myrtle Beach, South Carolina. Jones has remodeled a number of the courses on which our national championships have been held, most notably the venue of the 1951 Open, Oakland Hills, which many authorities believe to be the finest test of skill ever devised for that event.

GOLF WAS started in America in a very primitive manner. John Reid, of Scottish descent, played what was probably the first game of golf in this country in a meadow behind his house in Yonkers, New York, in 1888. From that Sunday afternoon diversion the first golf club in the United States developed, St. Andrews Golf Club—its name indicating the true reverence the Old Course inspired even across the sea.

As we are indebted to the Scots and English for the game, we are also indebted to them for our principles of architecture. There is no doubt that early golf and its growth in the United States owed much to the interest, en-thusiasm, initiative and fine conception of design of Charles Blair Macdonald, our first Amateur Champion, who learned the game when he was being educated at St. Andrews, Scotland. Macdonald was responsible for the first course in Chicago, in 1893, but it was not until the National Links at Southampton, Long Island, New York, was built by Macdonald in 1907 that our golf began to come out of the "cow-pasture" stage of golf-course architecture.

Macdonald became obsessed with the idea of building a truly classical golf course in America, incorporating in this course the best features of the most famous holes of England

and Scotland. In this way he felt that he could obtain an eighteen-hole golf course with each hole of outstanding quality, for although certain holes on most English and Scottish links were outstanding, these did not usually exceed two or three per course, with the remaining holes falling into the "fair" category. In 1902, Macdonald went abroad to gather material. This consisted of playing on most of the courses, observing them studiously, and discussing them with golfing friends. From these investigations he decided that his plan was entirely feasible.

For four years he proceeded to gather ideas, and in 1904 he made a second trip to study foreign courses. This time he made a detailed survey of the more famous holes, such as the Alps at Prestwick, the Redan at North Berwick, the Eden and the Road Hole at St. Andrews. He also drew twenty to thirty sketches of holes that embodied distinct features that in themselves seemed misplaced, but which could be utilized in principle to harmonize with certain characteristics of undulating ground, and so serve as the foundations of outstanding holes.

The work of Macdonald and his disciples was unquestionably one of the chief factors behind the spread of golf throughout the United States. Many of the holes that Macdonald brought over were copied at other places. In addition, the emigration of English and Scottish professionals added to the growth of golf in this country. While many of the professionals laid out mediocre courses—"eighteen stakes on a Sunday afternoon"—some did very fine work, such as the late Donald J. Ross, who became nationally famous in the United States as a designer of golf courses.

The influence of British architecture was also felt in the next era of our golf-course design, when the course at Pine Valley in Clementon, New Jersey, was built by George Crump, a Philadelphia sportsman. With the advice and assistance of the English architect, H. S. Colt, Crump laid out one of the world's ranking golf courses.

In the twenties American courses fell into the "penal" pattern of architecture which punishes the golfer for the slightest error. This undoubtedly was produced by attempts to emulate Pine Valley, a basically penal course.

As a result, our fairways became overcluttered with traps and our greens became extremely small target areas. The high cost of maintenance necessary to keep such a course well groomed, as well as the dissatisfaction felt by the average golfer, led to the next revolution in golf-course architecture in the United States.

In the late twenties Dr. Alistair Mackenzie, the Scottish golf architect, came to America and began designing golf courses. The main principle of Mackenzie's design was to revert from the "penal" to the "strategic" theory of design implicit in the best British courses and to bring about the elimination of the overabundance of traps. (In this same period, Stanley Thompson, a well-known Canadian golf-course architect, was paralleling the Mackenzie idea at Jasper Park in the Canadian Rockies. It was at this time that Thompson and I became partners, because of our basic agreement on this philosophy of golf course design.) It took the greatest name in American golf, Robert Tyre Jones, Jr., to give this new theory impetus. With Dr. Mackenzie, he created the Augusta National golf course. Jones had some theories of his own which modified some of Mackenzie's extremes. Jones believed that a course had to require thought as well as sheer technical skill to test a player's true ability. Furthermore, it was his conviction that a really great course must be a source of pleasure to the greatest possible number of players, giving the average golfer a fair chance and at the same time demanding the utmost from the expert who tries to break par. Jones' theory of design was influenced by his love for the Old Course at St. Andrews.

In the next decade, the post-depression thirties and early forties, very few new courses came into being in the United States. Those that did were built under Government programs for states, municipalities, counties, and the like. These courses were the finest public courses built during any period in the history of American golf-course architecture, but they were, of necessity, modified somewhat to meet their special mass-play conditions.

Since the war, golf has been on the upswing, and our golf-course architects have been busy from coast to coast developing new courses. During this period, I have had the opportunity of working with Robert Tyre

Jones, Jr., on the second Jones course, the Peachtree Golf Club in Atlanta, Georgia, Jones' home town. Since it exemplifies, we believe, the best principles of modern golf-course architecture, I should like to describe it in some detail.

Peachtree differs from the Augusta National particularly in the basic principle of green design. Each green has five or six definite pin positions, of which at least four are ideal for tournament play. These pin positions represent the target area for the better golfer, whereas the whole green represents the target area for the average golfer. The greens are undulating in character, but not as severe nor as continuous as the slopes at Augusta, the undulations at Peachtree being folds between the various pin positions.

Another feature of Peachtree is exceptional flexibility, brought about through the extreme length of the tees and the numerous possible variations in pin positions. In some cases the tees are as much as eighty yards long. The course can fluctuate from 6,300 to 7,400 yards in length, and yet, by the proper positioning of the pins, the holes are never made tricky in character. By combining these two factors, the number of green positions and the number of tee positions, it is possible to give an infinite variety to the layout.

While there is no hole on the course that a golfer would recognize as a copy of one of the classic English or Scottish holes, some British holes did play a part in the design. For example, Bob Jones asked if we could not work in a Sahara-type trap (after the one at Sandwich) on one of our holes, and this we were able to do on the tenth, which we consider has now become an excellent par five. The hole plays from the top of a hill into a valley, then up to a green nestled punch-bowl-like in the hillside. The left-hand side of the green is guarded by an awesome-looking trap about eight or nine feet deep, and the green is well undulated and large, being about 11,000 square feet. The left side of the fairway is clear. At the right side of the fairway we devised a long Sahara-like maze of trapping, which the bigger golfer, attempting to get home in two, must carry.

On the sixteenth hole of the course Bob Jones said that he would like to have the principle of the fourteenth at St. Andrews developed into the strategy, as he had always found that hole very fascinating to play. The tilt of the green was the point he wanted to bring out, and we worked this in with a plateau-type green at the crest of a hill. The green is elevated on the left, behind a mound that protects the left-hand pin position, and then drops to the right through two foundation mounds. The tilt of the green is not continuous, but is broken by two little valleys, one running out through the right, the other through the front.

THE OLD COURSE, ST. ANDREWS

As you can see, the Old Course at St. Andrews is still very much with us when we build our courses today. And it is also very much alive in its own right, remaining one of the world's greatest tests of golf. There it is as it has always been, winding out and back along the narrow thumb of linksland between the Firth of Forth and the Firth of Tay. There is only one Old Course, and nature built it.

It would be outright folly for any architect to attempt a duplication. The Old Course is only right at St. Andrews.

If you are an ardent golf fan and have dreamed for years of visiting St. Andrews, your first look at the Old Course will result either in exhilaration or let-down. The let-down is the more common reaction—at least for Americans who are used to courses which divulge all their secrets and present all their beauty at first sight. St. Andrews doesn't. The aspect from its first tee is not impressive nor is there any other visible hint of its right to its honored position. Perhaps one should never play the Old Course at St. Andrews without first getting the spirit of the town. It is like no other town in the world. The very backbone of the town is golf, the spirit of the town is golf, and it is supported by its four golf courses, its beach, and its University. What delightful sources of revenue! The spiritual feeling for golf is matched only by the spiritual feeling for religion. Sunday is the one day on which you cannot play the Old Course. The Royal and Ancient clubhouse lies but a block from the main street. Bordered by the sea, it sits there monumentally, a thing apart, which is as it should be, for the Royal and Ancient is the oldest and most respected club in the world, celebrating its two-hundredth season in 1954.

The first few rounds a golfer plays on the Old Course are not likely to alter his first estimate that it is vastly overrated. He will be puzzled to understand the rhapsodies that have been composed about the perfect strategic position of its trapping, the subtle undulations of its huge double greens, the endless tumbling of its fairways, which seldom give him a chance to play a shot from a level stance. Then, as he plays on, he begins to realize that whenever he plays a fine shot, he is rewarded; whenever he doesn't play the right shot, he is penalized, in proportion; and whenever he thinks out his round hole by hole, he scores well. This is the essence of strategic architecture: to encourage initiative, reward a well-played, daring stroke more than a cautious stroke, and yet to insist that there must be planning and honest self-appraisal behind the daring.

Of all the splendid holes at St. Andrews, the most renowned are the eleventh, or the Eden; the fourteenth, or the Long Hole; and the seventeenth, or Road Hole. The strategy of the eleventh, which measures 164 yards, is developed by its key hazard, the Strath bunker, a deep, heavy-lipped bulldog that patrols the access to the right-hand side of the green. The Strath sets up perfectly the function of Hill bunker to the left of the green

and of the green itself, which slopes back-to-front at a very severe angle. When the wind is out in full force and blowing down the slope, it is next to impossible to keep a downhill putt from running off the green, no matter how gently you tap it. (I feel that at no other place but St. Andrews would such a slope be countenanced.)

The seventeenth, the famous Road Hole, is a par five, as we would rate it here, which measures 467 yards. It is a very possible 4 and a very possible 7. To be in a position to reach the green in two, the golfer must take his courage in his hands on the tee and drive over Auchterlonie's drying sheds, which are situated in an out-of-bounds area that noses into the direct line between the tee and the choice side of the fairway. The long second shot must be played with true precision. A deep trap at the left of the green forces the player to hew to the right; there, running diagonally behind the green, is the road, and behind the road a stone wall. They play as part of the course, and any guess at how often they have proved to be the difference between a match that was won and a match that was lost would be an almost astronomical figure. (Here again I feel that at no place but St. Andrews would such hazards be acceptable; on the Old Course, they are as natural as the gray stone of the houses which line the closing hole.)

As for the fourteenth, the Long Hole, the longest on the course, a brute of 527 yards, we have here the apotheosis of one cardinal tenet of golf architecture: a great hole always offers the golfer an alternate route to the green. The fourteenth, in fact, offers the golfer a choice of three alleys: left, center, and right. The intelligent golfer will wait until he arrives at the tee and take into account how the wind is blowing at that moment, and the other immediate conditions, before he chooses his route for that particular round. By any of the routes, he must tack his way skillfully to the green, avoiding the bunker-groups that lie in wait to change his peaceful sail into a hapless Odyssey. To cite just one famous shipwreck here, Sarazen lost the 1933 British Open when he took three to get out of Hell bunker and ultimately wound up with an eight.

The OLD COURSE, St. ANDREWS

Surveyed & Depicted by
A. Mackenzie
Golf Course Architect
March 1924

Length of Holes on the Old Course.

Hole Nº	Name	Yards	Hole Nº	Name	Yards
1	Burn	374	10	Tenth	314
2	Dyke	400	11	High coming home	163
3	Cartgate going out	347	12	Heathery coming home	316
4	Ginger Beer	424	13	Hole o'Cross coming home	409
5	Hole o'Cross going out	522	14	Long	513
6	Heathery going out	370	15	Cartgate coming home	404
7	High going out	354	16	Corner of the	351
8	Short	153	17	Road Dyke	466
9	End	310	18	Tom Morris	356

REPRODUCED BY PERMISSION OF W. C. HENDERSON & SON, LTD., UNIVERSITY PRESS, ST. ANDREWS.

SCALE

The NATIONAL GOLF LINKS of AMERICA

MAP
Shinnecock Hills L.I.

LEGEND

- Green
- Fairway
- Rough
- Bushes
- Sand
- Tees
- Bunkers
- Mounds
- Sand mounds
- Water hazard

Arrows run with downward slope

BULL HEAD (SEBONAC) BAY

E.J.Rausz Columbia University N.Y.

Hole	NAME	Champ	Regular	Short	Par
1	Valley	310	300	290	4
2	Sahara	262	252	228	4
3	Alps	418	398	357	4
4	Redan	185	172	143	3
5	Hogs Back	478	460	420	5
6	Short	135	125	100	3
7	St Andrews	480	465	410	5
8	Bottle	386	366	286	4
9	Long	542	527	505	5
	Out	3196	3065	2739	37

Hole	NAME	Champ	Regular	Short	Par
10	Shinnecock	435	412	371	4
11	Plateau	434	405	383	4
12	Sebonac	385	374	348	4
13	Eden	170	162	125	3
14	Cape	355	337	236	4
15	Narrows	383	370	360	4
16	Punchbowl	419	380	360	5
17	Peconic	360	338	323	4
18	Home	482	467	448	5
	In	3423	3245	2944	36
	Total	6619	6310	5683	73

PINE VALLEY GOLF CLUB

CLEMENTON, NEW JERSEY

HOLE	YARDS	PAR	HOLE	YARDS	PAR
1	415	4	10	130	3
2	353	4	11	387	4
3	175	3	12	330	4
4	446	4	13	439	4
5	217	3	14	167	3
6	372	4	15	584	5
7	554	5	16	422	4
8	314	4	17	335	4
9	416	4	18	410	4
OUT	3262	35	IN	3204	35
			OUT	3262	35
			TOTAL	6466	70

FEET

0   200   400   600

PREPARED BY ROBERT TRENT JONES

HOLE	YARDS	PAR	HOLE	YARDS	PAR
1	385	4	10	405	4
2	480	5	11	380	4
3	355	4	12	185	3
4	325	4	13	380	4
5	160	3	14	555	5
6	502	5	15	406	4
7	110	3	16	400	4
8	425	4	17	218	3
9	450	4	18	540	5
OUT	3192	36	IN	3469	36
			OUT	3192	36
			TOTAL	6661	72

OCEAN

PACIFIC

PEBBLE BEACH GOLF COURSE

PEBBLE BEACH, CALIFORNIA

PREPARED BY ROBERT TRENT JONES

0 200 400 600
FEET

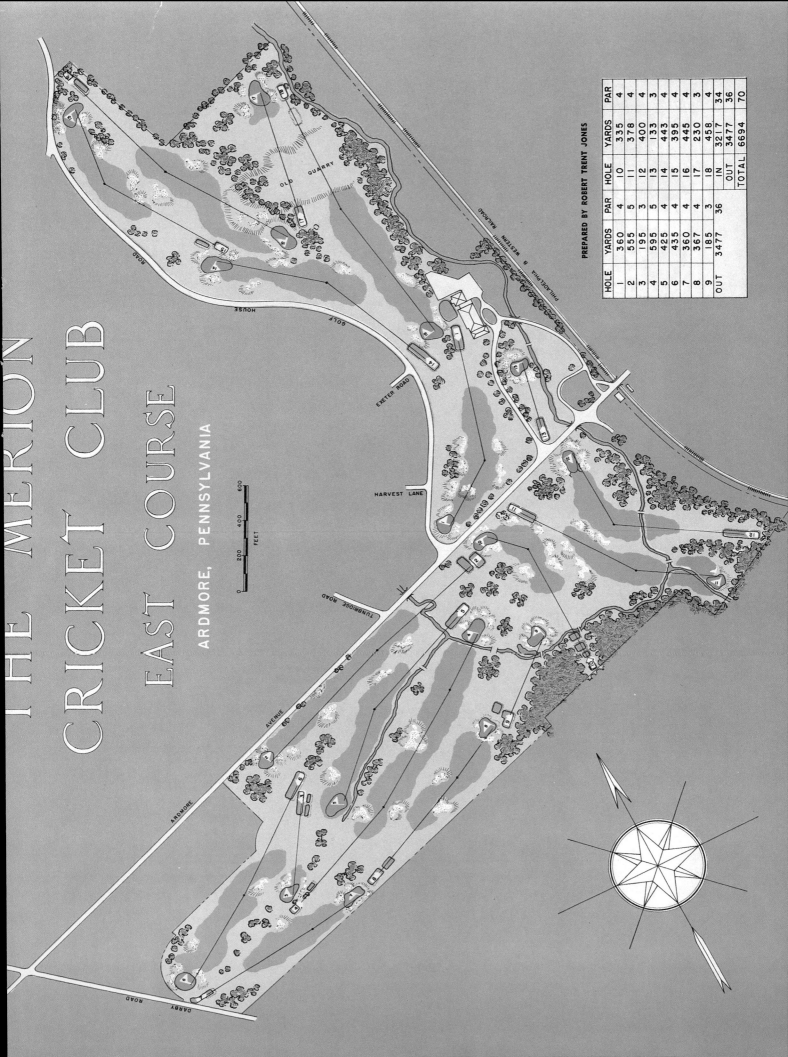

THE MERION
CRICKET CLUB
EAST COURSE

ARDMORE, PENNSYLVANIA

PREPARED BY ROBERT TRENT JONES

FEET
0   200   400   600

OLD QUARRY

HOLE	YARDS	PAR	HOLE	YARDS	PAR
1	360	4	10	335	4
2	555	5	11	378	4
3	195	3	12	400	4
4	595	5	13	133	3
5	425	4	14	443	4
6	435	4	15	395	4
7	360	4	16	445	4
8	367	4	17	230	3
9	185	3	18	458	4
OUT	3477	36	IN	3217	34
			OUT	3477	36
			TOTAL	6694	70

PHILADELPHIA & WESTERN RAILROAD

EXETER ROAD

HARVEST LANE

TUNBRIDGE ROAD

AVENUE

ARDMORE

GOLF HOUSE ROAD

DARBY ROAD

PINEHURST NO. 2

VILLAGE OF PINEHURST

TO RALEIGH

TO SOUTHERN PINES

TO ABERDEEN

CLUBHOUSE

HOLE	LONG TEE	PAR	HOLE	LONG TEE	PAR
1	427	4	10	593	5
2	448	4	11	433	4
3	340	4	12	419	4
4	528	5	13	378	4
5	440	4	14	444	4
6	211	3	15	206	3
7	394	4	16	492	5
8	488	5	17	186	3
9	156	3	18	424	4
OUT	3432	36	IN	3575	36
			OUT	3432	36
			TOTAL	7007	72

FEET
0   160   320   480

PREPARED BY ROBERT TRENT JONES

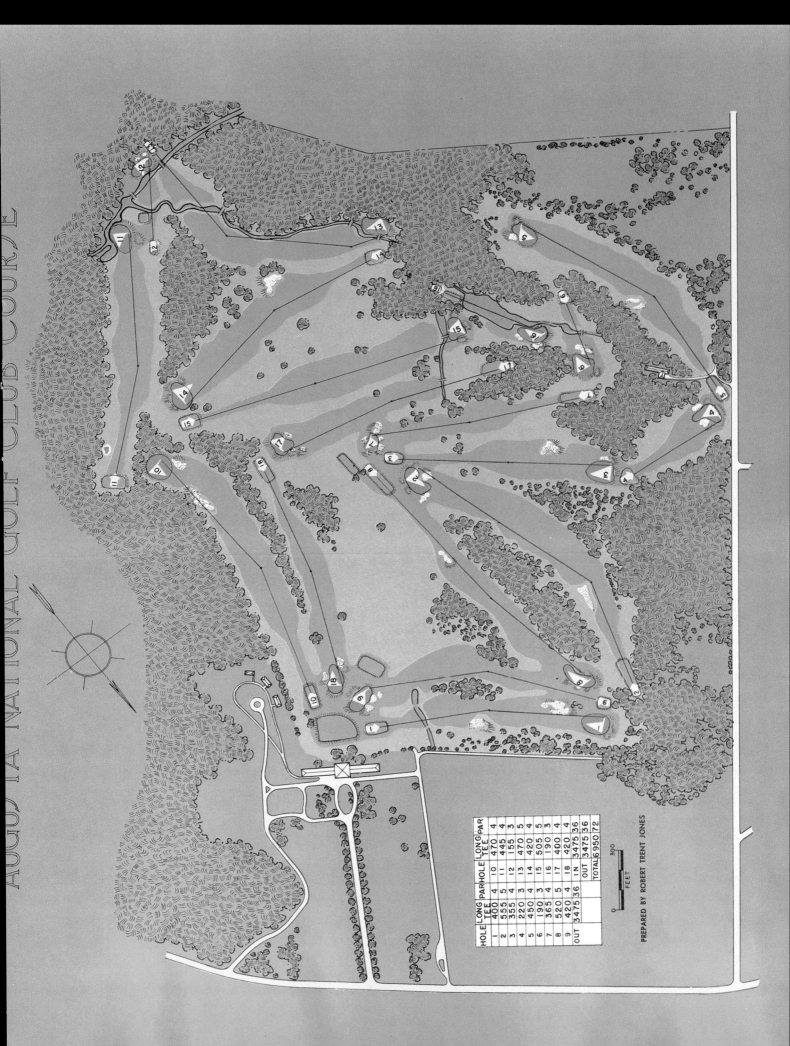

AUGUSTA NATIONAL GOLF CLUB COURSE

HOLE	LONG TEE	PAR	HOLE	LONG TEE	PAR
1	400	4	10	470	4
2	555	5	11	445	4
3	355	4	12	155	3
4	220	3	13	470	5
5	450	4	14	420	4
6	190	3	15	505	5
7	365	4	16	190	3
8	520	5	17	400	4
9	420	4	18	420	4
OUT	3475	36	IN	3475	36
			OUT	3475	36
			TOTAL	6950	72

300

0 FEET

PREPARED BY ROBERT TRENT JONES

OAKLAND HILLS COUNTRY CLUB

BIRMINGHAM, MICHIGAN

NO.	YARDS	PAR	NO.	YARDS	PAR
1	440	4	10	448	4
2	510	5	11	407	4
3	200	3	12	566	5
4	448	4	13	169	3
5	437	4	14	447	4
6	350	4	15	392	4
7	381	4	16	405	4
8	458	4	17	194	3
9	216	3	18	459	4
OUT	3440	35	IN	3487	35
			OUT	3440	35
			TOTAL	6927	70

PREPARED BY ROBERT TRENT JONES

THE NATIONAL GOLF LINKS

BYPASSING an examination of such other enduring courses as Muirfield, Carnoustie, Troon, Prestwick, Sandwich, Hoylake, Westward Ho!, and other British courses of championship caliber, let us now turn to the National Golf Links, at the east end of Long Island, where, as was noted earlier, Charles Blair Macdonald sowed the seed of modern golf-course design by transplanting what he considered to be the most successful features of the superior British courses. While the terrain on which Macdonald developed his British-type holes was in marked contrast to the holes' original sites, the principles embodied in these translations were sound, and the new holes held up. It is my feeling that to copy holes in detail, moving mountains of earth in trying to parallel the originals, is a waste of time and effort; the copy never lives up to the original. However, to adapt the principles of an excellent original to a suitable piece of topography can at times produce a hole equal to or better than the original. This is true of many holes at the National. I think Macdonald's Redan at the National is the peer of, or possibly a better hole than the Redan at North Berwick (see page 304). On the other hand, I think his Alps a weaker hole than the original at Prestwick. As for the Road Hole at the National, while fairly good, it does not at all engender the threat that goes with the St. Andrews original, for in the place of the road, which can mean complete catastrophe, Macdonald substituted an orthodox trap.

Strangely enough, the analysis, the study, the discussion, the playing, and the mental mixing of all these factors bred in Macdonald the creative sense that made it possible for him to conceive holes of his own design that in many ways surpass his successful copies of British holes. Such a hole is the fourteenth, or the Cape—a truly splendid golf hole which Macdonald returned to many times thereafter at his other courses and which has been frequently copied by other men since. So, too, the tenth, called Shinnecock, and the seventeenth, Peconic, two holes which demonstrate Macdonald's mastery of the strategic values of the links abroad that he revered.

From another point of view, Macdonald initiated the modern era of scientific architecture: while he had a good eye for "golf country," he was not at all hesitant to call in machinery to construct features he wanted that the landscape did not supply him. American architects have since followed his lead. They have built whenever possible on land that was congenial for golf—not the billy-goat terrain erroneously favored by our fumbling turn-of-the-century architects, but on gently rolling slopes—and they have also availed themselves of the latest models in earth-moving machinery, tractors and bulldozers, to knock their fairways into shape and to mold the delicate contours of greens.

To comment on all the wonderful courses that have been built in America over the last four decades would be an impossible assignment. It strikes me that the best alternative would be to discuss the diverse charms and merits of five of our other leading courses—the Augusta National, undoubtedly the last word in meadowland courses; Pebble Beach, that unusually dramatic layout over the uniquely beautiful Monterey Peninsula; Pinehurst Number Two, the prime example of the "American-type" shut-in fairway courses; Pine Valley, perhaps our finest example of heroic architecture; and Merion, the most durable of the courses over which our national championships have been played. I should also like to say a few words about one other layout, Oakland Hills, another veteran course which I had the privilege of remodeling before it served as host to the 1951 National Open.

PINE VALLEY

GEORGE CRUMP started to cut Pine Valley out of the thick pine forests of western New Jersey in 1912. The course was finished ten years later. Pine Valley fills you with dread and delight . . . it takes your breath away . . . it's a monster, but it's beautiful. It is frequently alluded to as the most difficult course in the world, and this reputation is justified. To my way of thinking, it also possesses more classic holes than any other course in the world—ten of the eighteen. Of the remaining holes, five are outstanding, two are good, and one, the twelfth, is ordinary, which, at Pine Valley, is tantamout to being a misfit.

What makes Pine Valley a course unlike any other on the globe is the basic principle of its design: the island. From the tee, the fairway targets are islands of grass surrounded by sandy wastes and forests. The sandy wastes are terrifying, for, unlike ordinary trap-land, they bristle with small pines, low-growing juniper, and other troublesome bushes and shrubs. Moreover, the sand is mottled with footprints. Since there is too much sand at Pine Valley for all of it to be raked, none of it is. If you do not hit the fairway island off the tee, you must play brilliantly to finish the hole only two strokes over par. The greens are islands too, smaller ones, of course, and they rank among the best-molded, best-textured greens on the continent. Like the fairways, the greens are surrounded by sandy horrors. There is no compromise house on the approach shots: you either make or break. One must really see Pine Valley to appreciate it, play it to enjoy it, assault it to relish the combat, laugh at one's own desperation, thrill with one's pars, be satisfied with a "bogey," and continue on far from downcast after a "double bogey."

There are four holes at Pine Valley that I find particularly enjoyable to play: the second, third, thirteenth, and fifteenth. The second, a par four, 350 yards long, demands a drive with a minimum carry of 175 yards to clear the badlands between tee and fairway. However, you must be out about 220 yards in order to have the percentages with you when you play the approach to the green. The green

sits at the crown of a mesa-like ridge that climbs some thirty-five feet above the level of the fairway. It is understatement to say that there is no framework around the green to give it a receptive feeling. What you are really faced with, as you look up at the green from the fairway below, is the fearful incline of the ridge—yards and yards of heavy, raw sand on all sides. That, too, strikes me as understatement. The second is a Vesuvius in contour and it causes as many eruptions as any hole on the course.

To pick one short hole as better than another at Pine Valley is something like judging a beauty contest: it's all a matter of taste. If I were to continue with this analogy, I would label the third a "redhead." The tee on the third is elevated, the green is below you, about 175 yards away, and there is nothing between you and the green, and nothing around the green but sand, a veritable lake of sand. The front deck of the irregularly-shaped green has a treacherous tilt, downhill from right to left. When the pin is positioned on this front deck, to find the green and hold it requires a shot played with the finesse of a Ryder Cupper. If you miss the green island . . . well, it is a good idea to count to ten after fluffing your first "out"; it may save your counting to ten when you are subsequently asked for your score.

The thirteenth, 439 yards long, presents one of the most challenging second shots you will ever encounter. After a good drive you will usually have a 3-wood or 4-wood left—rarely anything shorter than a 3-iron under any conditions—and all you have to do is produce a shot that defeats the long, menacing crescent of sand-land, depressed below the level of the green, which curves with the dog-leg fairway for some eighty yards before the green. It is up to the player to think out in his mind how much of this junior desert he believes he can carry. To reach the green, he must carry it all. The thirteenth is a nonpareil of "heroic" design. It requires great length, great control, and audacity. If your gamble fails, of course you are far worse off than the cautious golfer who has veered his ball away from the challenge, but the player has the privilege of deciding on the exact amount of his wager.

The fifteenth is a par five that has never been reached in two by any player; 584 yards long, its fairway becomes narrower and narrower as it climbs a long, gentle, thicket-bordered slope to the small, tight green area. In other words, three excellent shots must be played—a rare requirement today in America where we are presently faced with a dearth of honest par fives. Along with its golf-packed character, the fifteenth has immense beauty. I remember playing a round at Pine Valley not so long ago with Lowell Thomas, who, as you know, has traveled the world as widely as any man. On this fifteenth, after we had driven across the lake that separates the tee from the start of the fairway, Thomas turned and looked back across the water, then quietly gazed at the rest of the scene around us. "In all my travels," he said, "I do not think I've seen a more beautiful landscape. This is as thrilling as Versailles or Fontainebleau."

PEBBLE BEACH

THIS IS probably as pertinent a place as any to speak of Pebble Beach, the spectacular course on the Monterey Peninsula. If Pine Valley is the most dramatically beautiful pine-and-lakeland course in this country, Pebble Beach is its unrivaled counterpart among our oceanside courses. I say "oceanside" and not "seaside," because "seaside" has come to imply low-lying linksland, and Pebble Beach is quite the reverse. It is routed along the craggy headlands that drop abruptly into Carmel Bay. I think you can best visualize the superlative qualities of this setting if we briefly describe the eighth hole. The simple deceptive facts are that it is a par four, 425 yards long. Strategically, it is a cousin of the thirteenth at Pine Valley, a dog-leg to the right this time, instead of to the left; in the place of the sandy waste, an elbow of Carmel Bay commands the tactics for the second shot. The tee sits at the base of a hill, and it is only after one has driven (blindly) and scaled the slope that he realizes what a tartar he is tackling. From his perch at the top of the headland, after his drive, he sees the green in the distance, and yawning between his ball and the green is an elbow of Carmel Bay, 180 yards wide, lined with precipitous cliffs. Here again, it is up to the golfer to decide for himself how much of the hazard he wants to bite off. The fairway curves around the rim of the cliffs to succor the conservative. For my tastes, this second shot on the eighth is every bit as awesome, and wonderful, as the tee-shot on the more famous sixteenth hole at the neighboring Cypress Point course.

Unfortunately, the "inland" holes at Pebble Beach are not in the same class with the holes that follow the bay. The course is, in fact, a complex of ordinary holes and thrilling stretches. The first three holes—they are "inland"—are adequate, and so are the fourth, which skirts the bay, and the fifth, a difficult par three which cuts away from the water. Pebble Beach, however, really begins at the next tee. A run of five spectacular holes begins there—six, seven, eight, nine, ten—each utilizing the grand terrain along the cliffs to splendid advantage. After the tenth green, the course leaves the bay and becomes somnolescent again, for none of the next six holes is above average and their difficulty is not organic. With the seventeenth and eighteenth, the course returns to the bay and regains its character. These last two holes comprise one of the great one-two finishing punches in all of golf.

While the architects of Pebble Beach deserve acclaim for the intrepidity with which they seized the opportunities the headlands afforded, it remains an enigma to me why they did not invoke the same shot values for the interior holes. The interior holes could not have been bequeathed the gorgeous excitement of the holes along Carmel Bay, but the same grandeur of design could easily have been sustained.

15TH HOLE

NORTH BERWICK

"REDAN"

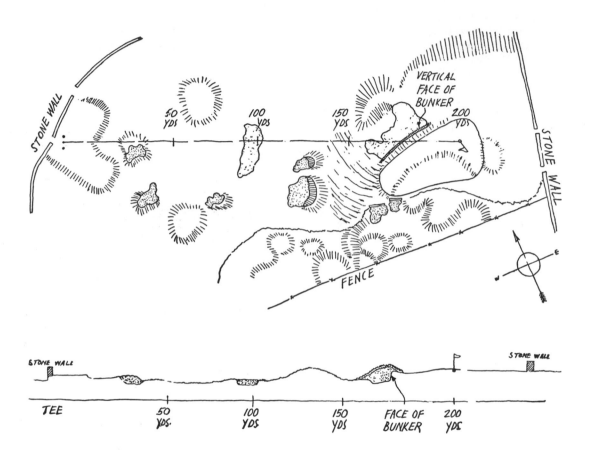

THE REDAN—the fifteenth hole at North Berwick—takes its name from the famous redoubt at Sevastopol, which the British stormed in 1855. It is a redoubtable hole, and the incredibly steep face of its key bunker gives it a truly combative appearance. But more than this, the Redan holds a salient position in the development of golf architecture. It was one of the first holes to demonstrate the beauties of strategic design so forcibly that it was copied and adapted at many other courses, and it became a touchstone for golf-course layout.

As this rough sketch indicates, both the green and the key hazard of the Redan are positioned diagonally to the line of play. The result is that the golfer is forced to choose whether he will play conservatively to the right and away from the hazard—by which route a 3 can only be gained by a brilliant chip or putt—or whether he will go boldly for the pin in quest of a 3 or a possible 2, despite the mental and physical hazard of the greenside trap. In other words, the transverse principle leaves it up to the golfer to bite off as much as he thinks he can take care of, and rewards him in proportion to the audacity and skill of his shot.

MERION

ON THE OUTSKIRTS of Philadelphia, on the city's Main Line, lies the Merion Golf Club. The charm and dignity of the colonial clubhouse blend admirably with the parklike golf course. Over its rolling, wooded, brook-bisected slopes has been routed one of America's great courses, the venue for the 1916 National Amateur Championship, the 1924 Amateur, the 1930 Amateur, the 1934 Open, and the 1950 Open. Of all the courses that form the American championship rota, Merion has held up best against the onslaught of modern equipment and the modern ball, and this without any major change being made over the last twenty-five years. In the interim between the Open Championships of 1934 and 1950, an interim in which improvements technical and otherwise radically changed the quality of the scoring, Merion held the golfers to within less than two shots a round reduction of the 1934 scoring averages. It is my feeling that the two-shots-per-round improvement could be attributed to one club, the wedge.

Merion is an inland course, but the framework of its greens with their combinations of multiform mounds, oriented with sand and sod, give it somewhat the appearance of a seaside links. It is these well-shaped, artistically appealing green areas that make Merion characteristically different from most American courses and, further, explain to a considerable extent why Merion remains a vital test of golf, whereas most other courses of its pre-World War I vintage have long since lost their snap and crackle.

Merion's greens set up the target—they are a challenge to play to. The demands of the individual holes are brought out by Merion's famous "white faces"—the sand flashed on the faces of these greenside mounds. They also imbue Merion with its psychological terror. To see a pin nipped in close against a face of sand is a challenge so brutally frank that it makes the spine quiver. The problems are set before you. Handle them with all the skill that you have.

From the very first hole, Merion confronts you with genuine golf. The first hole is just 360 yards long, relatively short for a championship course. There are two factors that make this hole amazingly effective, particularly for one built on flat terrain. First, it entices the player to drive as far as he can in order to get the most advantageous angle of entrance to the green, especially if the pin is on the right-hand side. Second, after a short drive or a pushed drive, the approach shot must carry over traps to get in close to the pin when it is set on the right. A hole which encourages the golfer to drive far increases the possibilities of a hook, and there is a trap at the 250-yard mark that will surely catch a long stray hook. If the tee-shot is hit too hard to the right, there is a fairway trap to contend with. Unless the tee markers are forward or the wind is behind, it is out of the range of even the long hitters, but players of professional caliber would do well to yield their power and play this tee-shot discreetly, taking their chances on the accuracy of their second shots.

The second hole—which, for me, is one of the best par fives in the country—is 555 yards long, bringing it within the range of the power hitter's ability to reach in two. But with what consummate accuracy these two shots must be executed, if they are to escape the threat of the out-of-bounds stakes, which hug the narrow fairway from tee to green on the right. Yet if one does not hit his two most powerful shots and get as close as possible to the green, the third shot, especially when the pin is in the back left-hand corner of the diagonal green, is one of the meanest little pitches you can imagine.

The third hole, 195 yards in length, has the elements of the Redan but is not a copy. Both the tee and the green are plateaued with a valley between, and a deep trap on the diagonal protects the green at the right. Three traps flank the left-hand side of the green. The green is shaped like a pear, with the small end toward the front, and a pronounced tenace divides the upper and lower levels.

Hole after hole, Merion restates challenges of this order, requiring the golfer to place his tee-shot but never insisting that he knock the cover off it, then throwing at him a succession of second shots to all kinds of green sites—a green that tilts forward at a sharp angle, a green that is best approached by a pitch-and-run played off an incline at the right of the apron, a green that is long and narrow but not too sternly trapped, a green that tilts backward to a central hollow and is further fortified by tough frontal trapping (which is eminently fair since the shot to the green is usually an 8-iron or a 9-iron), a green that is flanked with five traps in back and guarded in front by a lake, here a green that sits below you, there a green that sits above—a wonderful variety, each of them making the most of natural features of the terrain and geared to the golf sense of the individual hole. The eleventh hole is an excellent illustration. It is only 378 yards long, but even those golfers who have gone to pieces on it speak of it as one of the best holes of its length anywhere. It is the second shot that makes the eleventh. The green, small in area, lies just across a creek which, after bordering the fairway on the left, curves across the fairway before the green, then twists again and continues around the right-hand side of the green. If you hit this green with your second shot, you heave a sigh so deep that it is usually audible a mashie shot away.

Among its other distinctions, Merion possesses one of the strongest finishes in golf, a stretch of five holes that sustains a proper pitch of solvable difficulty. The fourteenth, which starts this finish, is a 443-yard dog-leg to the left, flanked along that side by Golf House Road—out of bounds. There is a trap at the right at the 240-yard mark, and the urge to veer away from the road brings it frequently into play. While the green is on the same level as the fairway, the sharp lines of the greenside trapping make it seem a very tough target to hit and hold. The green surface is contoured with mild rolls that can be exasperating since their actual negotiation is far more slippery than the eye first perceives.

The fifteenth is a dog-leg to the right. While the card gives the yardage of this hole as 395, during the championships the tee can be pushed back into the part of the sixteenth fairway which serves as the alternate route on that hole. From this back tee, it takes a first-class shot to carry the traps at the angle of the dog-leg. There is not too much to be gained by this short-cut route except that, as usual, power is its own reward and sets up the chance to use a higher lofted club on the approach. The deep trap in front of the green, at the right, makes the approach most hazardous when the pin is positioned on the right-hand tongue of the green.

The sixteenth is perhaps Merion's most celebrated hole. This is the famous Quarry Hole, and the quarry has been used ingeniously. Following an accurately placed drive, the second shot—a strong 4-iron up to a 4-wood for the bigger players—must carry the quarry, as terrible a piece of wasteland as one would want to see. Trees have been allowed to grow wild and jungle-like at the base of the quarry, and sand has been flashed there. Across the quarry, the green area has been placed astride a hilltop. The green itself, with its double terrace, is a perfect complement to the general ruggedness of this hole.

The seventeenth hole is a par three, 220 yards long, and when the wind is slightly against you, even the professional stars will use woods. The green is situated well below the tee, framed by four traps which are handsomely shaped and oriented. The main strength of the green, however, is in the boldness of its contours. The front deck lies about four feet below the upper deck, and the break between the two decks is severe.

The eighteenth hole, 458 yards long, is a grand finishing hole. The tee-shot is played over another arm of the quarry, and, from the back tee, it takes a reasonably good hit to carry the quarry and reach the fairway. Then it is either a long-iron or a controlled fairway wood home. The green takes conscientious reading.

Analyze Merion closely. It has something. It keeps the pressure on the tournament golfer all the way through to the home hole. It is harder on the average golfer than a course like the Augusta National, but its variety of fairway contours, the angles of its green surfaces, its contiguous "white faces," and the intelligence of its routing have made for a course that age has not withered nor custom staled.

PINEHURST NUMBER TWO

THERE HAS NEVER been a better example of the sow's-ear-to-silk-purse metamorphosis than the miracle that James Tufts and Donald Ross wrought in changing a worthless piece of sandy wasteland in North Carolina into Pinehurst. The beginnings of Pinehurst, some fifty years ago, were not impressive—the buildings were modest boarding houses, the golf course barren and sparsely covered fields with flat sand greens—but this modest set-up was a magnet that drew from all over the United States sportsmen who were interested in learning about the new game. The Tufts family and Ross were skillful missionaries. They sold the game to thousands, and Ross was retained to go back to the visitors' home towns and develop courses for them. As the result, Pinehurst has had a tremendous influence on American golf, an influence that has always been in keeping with the game's finest traditions. The architecture of its courses was crude at first, since Ross was mimicking as best he could the linksland of the Scottish seaside from whence he came. His copies, as was inevitable, were not always successful. Ross' architectural flair improved through trial and error, and as he accumulated knowledge and experience, he constantly improved Pinehurst.

By the early thirties, Pinehurst had become a Mecca for golfers. It had its famous North and South Championships, both amateur and professional, but the courses had not yet reached their pinnacle. The trapping was good and the strategy was fine, but one could not at that point say that there were any great courses at Pinehurst. This did not come about until the mid-thirties when Ross made a complete revision of his famous Pinehurst Number Two course. When he finished it, he stated that this was his masterpiece.

In the early spring, which is the resort's peak season, Pinehurst's four courses are a hubbub of the most golf-happy golfers one can find in America. A thousand players a day trudge over its four courses, tiring the unused muscles that have become flabby over the winter. Pinehurst in the spring is delightful. The big open, barnlike clubhouse is a beehive of conversation and one can hear nothing but golf talk. In a sense it is somewhat like St. Andrews. This is golf, golf, golf.

Pinehurst's most famous course, Number Two, is routed over more or less level land, with only one pronounced change in the conformation of the terrain, a dip at the fifth hole. One of its most striking aspects is the isolation of the separate holes. Each becomes an individual unit, due to the fact that the pine trees planted early in the development now frame the holes completely. This framing accords the holes a third dimension which adds immensely to their character and creates as well an aesthetic background that emphasizes the flowing lines of the architecture. The thick pine woods also offer a comforting protection when the cold winds sweep down from the north, as they are bound to do on occasion.

Americans, unlike the British, are not given to playing in the rain, but at Pinehurst they make what is perhaps their one exception. I dare say that more people play in the rain at Pinehurst than at any other golf course in America. In fact, if you can have a windbreaker and an umbrella, it's a rather pleasant thing to do, because the sand underfoot makes for relatively dry walking. In the rain, the pine trees seem to glisten, making each hole an individual jewel.

As to the character of the architecture of Pinehurst Number Two, the most striking feature is that the greens are extremely small, perhaps the smallest of any on our championship layouts. They are nicely formed, with their rhythmic sweeps carrying well out into the approach areas. This particular type of architecture makes the greens difficult to hit and at the same time makes for a chipping course that has no equal, since one is apt to be chipping more often here than at any other place I know. It is my feeling that Pinehurst is a more difficult test of golf for the nearly great golfer than it is for the truly great golfer, for here the big hitter carries all the fairway trapping, and his power, of course, brings him within closer range of the green. With small greens as the targets, that edge in distance is important, because the nearer one gets to any target in any sport, the more often he is apt to hit it. It has been my feeling that a half-dozen cunningly placed pot traps at the 250-yard mark (measured from the back of the tees) could make Pinehurst a truly formidable test for golfers of championship caliber.

THE AUGUSTA NATIONAL

THE FATE of a great golf course, of a great golf club, and a great golf tournament was determined by one look. In 1931, when Bob Jones was asked if he would be interested in building a course which would incorporate his ideas on the strategy and the shot values and the principles of design a golf course should embody, he indicated that he was definitely interested but that it would depend upon his visiting the property and looking it over before making his decision. That Jones was mightily impressed after one look at the Berckman's nursery property and its lovely ante-bellum mansion house, outside of Augusta, is now a well-known fact to anyone who follows golf. That same view has become known to many thousands of people who visit the Augusta National to watch the Masters, yearly, in April. Augusta reaches its peak at that season, for then the nursery stock planted by the previous owners of the plantation reaches its full glory and the course is a maze of color. Azalea, dogwood, and redbud, are in full bloom. The setting is the last word in skillfully nurtured natural beauty.

From the clubhouse hilltop at Augusta, one peers down into the natural amphitheater over which the course is laid out. One can see to the far end of the property. There, a sharp escarpment rises, defining the course's border. This bank, covered with pines, blue-green in the spring sun and towering high into the sky, is an impressive backdrop to a natural stage on which some of the greatest drama in American golf is annually enacted. This incline, from clubhouse pinnacle to its lowest point at Rae's Creek, is 120 feet. The conformation of the terrain plus the routing of the course have made it possible to develop within the amphitheater some of golf's most wonderful holes, modern classics.

The Augusta National is the epitome of the type of course which appeals most keenly to the American taste, the meadowland course. From tee to green there is nothing but closely cropped green turf. These broad expanses of fairway, punctuated with pines and dotted with flashes of white sand, give Augusta a clean, sprightly appearance. The Jones conception, incarnate in Augusta, was that the course should be a true test of championship golf, but, more than that, that it should be a pleasure for all classes of golfers to play. The width of its fairways allow for latitude from the tees. Missed tee-shots are not punished drastically, either by trapping or rough. In order to offset this freedom from the tee and the minimal use of traps both at the target area from the tee and around the green, the plateau principle of green design has been employed. On these plateaus, the sinuous rolls have struck fear in the hearts of the finest golfers in the world. It is that constant pressure to get in close to the pins and so reduce the chance of three-putting a green that makes the golfer edgy and his nerves taut during the Masters Tournament.

While the first nine has some interesting holes (such as the third, fourth, fifth, and seventh), it packs nowhere near the punch of the second nine. This second nine is probably the nerve-testing run of championship golf in America. Starting with the tenth, an absolutely stirring par four, one continues on to the eleventh, with water flanking the left-hand side of the green; to the short twelfth, with its tricky whirlpool winds; to the par five, creek-guarded thirteenth green that has ruined many a champion's hopes; to the fifteenth, where the ambitious second shot must carry over a pond to the crowned green; to the short sixteenth with its two-level, contoured green across its fairway of water; and on to the two finishing holes which, even without the benefit of water, are sturdy enough to keep the pressure on the competitor. One is never sure at Augusta that he is "in" until that last putt drops to the bottom of the cup.

The Augusta National keeps up with the times. Almost every year, upon the conclusion of the Masters Tournament, and after things have been mulled over, changes are made in one or two holes to increase their playing value. Undoubtedly the two most thorough overhaulings took place on the eleventh and the sixteenth, and my work in developing these two holes has been my loving contribution to Augusta's greatness. Over a period of years these two holes have been transformed from the easiest par four and the easiest par three on the course to perhaps the most difficult. The eleventh, for instance, was originally a shortish four, about 365 yards long, which called for a controlled fade on the drive; an efficient drive left the player with a simple pitch over the mounds to the green below him. It was decided to strengthen the eleventh. A new tee was built in the pine grove to the left of the tenth green, as one walks off that green. From this new tee, the hole now plays relatively straightaway and measures 450 yards. The tee is elevated and there is a hollow between it and the crest of the tee-shot target area. The fairway is edged by woods on the left-hand side its full length to the pond, which was created by damming up the creek that trickled innocuously to the left of the green. The green itself was reshaped and a new cape projected to the left, there to be surrounded on three sides, virtually, by the waters of the new pond. The big hitters now play anything from 4-irons to 3-woods into the green on their seconds, and when the pin is set on the cape, the shot they face is terrifying indeed. More often than not, discretion is the better part of valor and even the professional titans prefer to play wide, to the right, relying on a chip and a putt for their par. Since the hole has been changed, the Masters has twice been lost on it, once by Hogan and once by Snead. Knowing that they had to cut a few strokes from par on their last round and that holes were rapidly running out, they felt they could not afford to play safe, went all out for the pin, and found the water in their bold ventures.

The Augusta National has one further virtue that should be underlined: the club has always kept the needs of the spectators in mind, and, in my experience, the course is unmatched in the physical facilities it affords for watching a major tournament.

OAKLAND HILLS

The most pungent remark made during the controversial 1951 Open Championship at Oakland Hills Country Club, near Detroit, came from that patriarch of professional golf, Walter Hagen: "The course is playing the players instead of the players playing the course." In this comment, Hagen summed up the psychological shock suffered by the world's ranking golfers when they encountered the remodeled course, for these modern players had been getting away with murder for years, and didn't know it. They had been playing over courses that, with few exceptions, had been laid out in the 1920's, or earlier, and which had been tailored for the equipment and the ball and the playing conditions of that era. Courses that had tested the masters of that day—Jones, Hagen, Sarazen, Armour—had lost their testing abilities. Steel shafts and the improved ball had enabled the players of later decades to develop a swing pattern that would not have been possible with wood shafts; their added length carried them beyond the trapping that was intended to punish poorly hit shots from the tee. Their power hitting, on-line or not on-line, brought them so close to the greens that they had little trouble dropping a niblick or a wedge shot onto them. As a result of the combined advantages, par lost its significance, as was bound to happen when correct shot-making had lost its intended meaning.

In the 1951 Open, for the first time in many years, the course the Open was played on completely caught up with the players. That was, at least, our intention when we set out to revamp Oakland Hills. From having conducted tests at several previous Opens, I had accumulated sufficient data to arrive at values which related truly to the playing skills of the modern professional leaders. These values were introduced into the remodeling.

Our first move was to fill in all the obsolete traps situated at the right and left sides of the fairway 200 to 220 yards from the tees. These traps had made the 1924 Open field keep down the middle or be penalized, but the modern pros would have cleared them with yards to spare, even when they did not hit first-class tee-shots. We then replaced these traps with new ones which flanked the fairways, starting some of these traps at the 230-yard mark and extending others to the 260-yard mark. This presented the 1951 professional with a task no harder and no easier than the 1924 professional had been confronted with: no leeway was allowed for a missed shot on either side of the fairway. After this, we tightened the greens, protecting the tongue areas with additional trapping. The green surfaces had originally been molded with good contours, and these, for the most part, we left as they were. On one or two greens, we softened contours we deemed too harsh or tricky.

The players arrived and met the new course. After playing the circuit layouts where a sprayed tee-shot followed by a wedge shot left them putting for birdies, they found themselves on a course that demanded accuracy and imposed a penalty for error. From playing a card and thinking in terms of one under par, two under par, three under par, they suddenly were playing a course that sent them over par to the same degree. The field was thrown into utter confusion. Golfers of reputation staggered home with rounds high in the 70's, occasionally in the 80's. They yelled the golf equivalent of "Foul!" But there were no trick holes at Oakland Hills. There was no particular hole on which all the players did badly. Each did badly on any hole where he missed a shot, and the scores reflected exactly the extent of his errors.

The first reaction of most of the players was to adopt cagey tactics for their ensuing rounds. The way to play this course, they figured, was to play it safe—club down, be short of the trouble. They started using 2- and 3-woods off the tee, and even in some cases irons. This was true of the great Ben Hogan. On his first two rounds, he refused to attack the course. As a result, he scored high. His first round was a 76. It was not until the end of the third round that the players realized that they could not play Oakland Hills "safe." In order to conquer it, you had to assault it. Clubbing down off the tee had only made for longer second shots. The longer the second shots, the higher the incidence of error. No wonder the boys were not scoring.

During the last round, Hogan attacked. He used his driver off the tee on every par four and par five. He played his approaches for the pin. His last round, which he has called the greatest round he ever shot, was a magnificent 67 and brought him victory.

The most satisfying thing about Oakland Hills was that at the end of the tournament the great players' names were at the top, where they should be. To me, that was the real proof of the honest character of the layout. It has always seemed to me that if I were a Hogan, a Snead, or a Locke, the more difficult the course, the better I would like it, knowing that the extensiveness of my repertoire of shots would work to my advantage. Such a course, I would know, was not a scrambler's course—a scrambler could not win. Look at the record and the basic truth stands out: when a championship is played on a great golf course, you rarely get a winner who is not a great golfer.

* * *

EACH OF the famous courses we have discussed is markedly different from the others. Each has its own distinct personality—and if it did not, it would be safe to say that it would not be a successful course. But above and beyond their individualities, these courses possess in common certain fundamental characteristics. They are situated in lovely natural settings. They are routed so that there is an interesting, varied sequence of holes. The strategy of the individual holes derives from the natural features of the terrain. And, last, they punish or reward the good shots and poor shots of golfers of all classes in proper proportions, since the design of the holes is based on true shot values. A course which combines these qualities is assuredly a great golf course.

PHOTO CREDITS

The photographs on the endpapers are used by permission, as follows:

1. Sam Snead at the Masters, at Augusta. (*International News Photo*)
2. Byron Nelson, 1939 U.S. Open champion. (*U.S.G.A.*)
3. The incomparable Joyce Wethered plays a mashie. (*Wide World Photos*)
4. Francis Ouimet in 1913. (*U.S.G.A.*)
5. Bobby Jones at St. Andrews. (*Photo-Illustrations Co., London*)
6. Walter J. Travis, with his Schenectady putter. (*U.S.G.A.*)
7. Bobby Locke lines one up. (*Country Life Limited and the Daily Mail, London*)
8. President Dwight Eisenhower at Quantico, Va. (*International News Photo*)
9. Harry Vardon, six-time winner of the British Open and U.S. Open champion in 1900, at the top of his backswing. (*U.S.G.A.*)
10. Babe Didrikson Zaharias swings into her tee shot. (*Private collection*)
11. Driving across an elbow of the Pacific to the green of the 16th hole at Cypress Point. (*International News Photo*)
12. The Walker Cup match at St. Andrews in 1926, with Bobby Jones putting on the 18th green. (*Photo-Illustrations Co., London*)
13. Glenna Collett, the six-times National Women's champion (*International News Photo*)
14. Tommy Armour at his winter home, Boca Raton, Florida. (*Rotofotos, Inc.*)
15. Henry Cotton, three-time winner of the British Open, holding the cup after his second triumph at Carnoustie in 1937. (*Newsphotos*)
16. Gene Sarazen and Walter Hagen flip for the honor. (*Fotograms*)
17. Ben Hogan, last round, last hole, in the U.S. Open at Merion in 1950. (*Life magazine*)
18. The 1953 U.S. Walker Cup team: (Standing) Venturi, Jackson, Cherry, Capt. Yates, Coe, Campbell, and Westland. (Crouching) Urzetta, Littler, Ward and Chapman. (*New Bedford Standard Times, Mass.*)
19. Bing Crosby practices as Jimmy Thomson, Jimmy Demaret, Enrique Bertilino, and Bobby Locke pick up a few pointers. (*International News Photo*)

INDEX

PUBLISHER'S NOTE

In the original edition of "The Complete Golfer" the eight golf course maps were presented in fold-out form. In this edition, as you have already noticed, the maps are printed on the same size paper as the text. They are identical to the original fold-out maps with the exception of being slightly smaller in size.

Some preliminary material relating to original title page, copyright references, and acknowledgements which was in the beginning of the original edition has been moved to the end of The Classics of Golf edition and follows this note. At the very end of our edition is Frank Hannigan's new Afterword.

An effort was made to resecure permissions to reprint copyrighted material which was not always successful. Any requests sent to The Classics of Golf, Ailsa, Inc., 67 Irving Place North, ninth floor, New York, N.Y. 10003, will be promptly taken care of.

R.S.M.

The Complete
GOLFER

Edited by

HERBERT WARREN WIND

with an Introduction by

ROBERT T. JONES, Jr.

19 — 54

SIMON AND SCHUSTER, NEW YORK

"The Clicking of Cuthbert" from *Golf Without Tears*, New York, 1924. Reprinted by permission of author and author's agents, Scott Meredith Literary Agency, 845 Third, Ave., N.Y., N.Y. 10022.

"Mr. Frisbie" from *Round-Up* by Ring Lardner. Copyright, 1929, by Charles Scribner's Sons. Used by permission of the publisher.

"The Sweet Shot" from *Trent's Case Book* by E. C. Bentley. Copyright, 1938, by E. C. Bentley and 1953, by Alfred A. Knopf, Inc. Used by permission of the publisher and (for Canada) the author.

"The Ooley-Cow" from *Fore!* by Charles E. Van Loan. Copyright, 1918, by Doubleday & Company, Inc. Used by permission of Virginia Van Loan Updike for the author's estate.

"Golf Is a Nice Friendly Game" from *Golf Is a Friendly Game* by Paul Gallico. Copyright, 1942, by the Curtis Publishing Co. Used by permission of Alfred A. Knopf, Inc.

"The Birth of the Linksland Courses" by Sir Guy Campbell from *A History of Golf in Britain*, Cassell & Company, Ltd., London. Used by permission of the author.

"Some of the Humors of Golf" by The Rt. Hon. A. J. Balfour from *Golf* by Horace G. Hutchinson, Little, Brown & Company.

"Hints to Golfers of Riper Years" from *Hints on Golf* by Horace G. Hutchinson. Used by permission of William Blackwood & Sons, Ltd., Edinburgh and London.

"How to Go About Buying a Putter" from *Concerning Golf* by John L. Low. Used by permission of Hodder & Stoughton, Ltd., London.

"The Old Apple Tree Gang" from *Fifty Years of American Golf* by H. B. Martin. Copyright, 1936, by Harry B. Martin. Used by permission of Dodd, Mead & Company.

"Across the Street from the Country Club" from *A Game of Golf* by Francis Ouimet. Copyright, 1932, by Francis Ouimet. Used by permission of Houghton Mifflin Company.

"Golf in Four Acts" by George Ade. From the Chicago *Record* of September 27, 1897, and *The American Golfer* of April, 1926. Used by permission of *The American Golfer*.

"Caddying at Edgewater" from *Chick Evans' Golf Book* by Charles Evans, Jr., Thomas E. Wilson & Co. Used by permission of the author.

"Mr. Dooley on Golf" from *Mr. Dooley at His Best* by Finley Peter Dunne, edited by Elmer Ellis. Copyright, 1910, 1938, by Charles Scribner's Sons. Used by permission of the publisher.

"Merion—First Visit" from *Down the Fairway* by Robert T. Jones, Jr., and O. B. Keeler. Copyright, 1927, by Minton Balch and Company. Used by permission of G. P. Putnam's Sons.

"How I Kept My Wait Down" by Walter Hagen. Copyright, 1954, by Hagenwise Enterprises.

)n Diegeling" from *Second Shots* by Bernard Darwin, George Newnes, Ltd., London. Used by permisison of the author.

he Prospect for 1930" by Grantland Rice. From *The American Golfer* of May, 1930. Used by permission of the author.

"Two Niblicks" from *Playing the Like* by Bernard Darwin, Chapman & Hall, Ltd. Used by permission of the author and publisher.

"The Fabulous Commodore Heard" by Grantland Rice. From *The American Golfer* of August, 1934. Used by permission of the author.

"Golfers with a Past" by Noel F. Busch. From *The New Yorker* Magazine of July 17, 1937. Copyright, 1937, The New Yorker Magazine, Inc. Used by permission of the author.

"The Dr. Livingstone of Golf" by Harry Robert. From *USGA Journal and Turf Management* of November, 1951. Used by permission of the magazine.

"Francis Drives Himself In" by S. L. McKinlay. From the Glasgow *Herald* of September 20, 1951. Used by permission of George Outram & Co., Ltd.

"The Hong Kong Golf Club" from *Hong Kong: The Island Between* by Christopher Rand. Copyright, 1952, by Alfred A. Knopf, Inc. Used by permission of the publishers.

"Watching My Wife" by John L. Hulteng. From an August, 1950, "In Perspective" editorial column of the Providence (R.I.) *Journal-Bulletin*. Reprinted in *USGA Journal and Turf Management* of September, 1953. Used by permission of the author.

"*Le Bing et le Golf*" from "18 Holes with Bing Crosby" by Art Buchwald. From the New York *Herald Tribune* of May 31, 1953. Copyright, 1953, by the New York Herald Tribune, Inc. Used by permission of the newspaper.

"The Golfomaniac" from *Laugh with Leacock* by Stephen Leacock. Copyright, 1930, by Dodd, Mead & Company, Inc. Used by permission of the publisher.

"Golfmanship" by Stephen Potter. From *The Atlantic Monthly* of September, 1948. Copyright, 1948, by The Atlantic Monthly Company. Used by permission of A. D. Peters.

"The Triumvirate" from *Out of the Rough* by Bernard Darwin, Chapman & Hall, Ltd., London. Used by permission of the author and publisher.

"The First United States Amateur Championships" from *Scotland's Gift—Golf* by Charles Blair Macdonald. Copyright, 1928, by Charles Scribner's Sons. Used by permission of the publisher.

"How I Won the British Amateur Championship" by Walter J. Travis. From *The American Golfer* of March, 1910. Used by permission of the magazine.

LIBRARY OF CONGRESS CATALOG CARD NUMBER: 54–9796
DEWEY DECIMAL CLASSIFICATION NUMBER: 796.35
MANUFACTURED IN THE UNITED STATES OF AMERICA
BY H. WOLFF BOOK MFG. CO., INC., NEW YORK. THIRD PRINTING

ACKNOWLEDGMENTS

P. G. WODEHOUSE *dedicated one of his collections of golf stories,* The Heart of A Goof, *to his daughter Leonora "without whose never failing sympathy and encouragement this book would have been finished in half the time." It is a classic line and I came to appreciate its full meaning during the period when this anthology was being prepared. Thanks to the interest of friends who were continually turning up new source material they felt should be considered, the book took many more months to assemble than I had first gauged—and became, en route, a far better collection in every respect. I am particularly indebted for their multiple courtesies to Joseph C. Dey, Jr., the Executive Secretary of the U.S. Golf Association, and to his right-hand men, John P. English and Edward S. Knapp, Jr. "Golf House," where the USGA maintains its headquarters in New York, possesses not only a wonderfully comprehensive library but an atmosphere that exudes the fine feel of the game. I would also like to express my gratitude for their sizable aid to Fred Corcoran of the PGA and John Derr, the sports director of CBS, and to the following friends here and in Britain who dug up much of the material, lent books from their personal libraries, and generally made their erudition available: Glenn McCrillis, Jr., B.O.B. Gidden, Howard J. Fine, Charles Wintour, William E. Rae, C. L. Fuller, Sr., Mrs. Mildred Long, C. Edmund Miller, Arthur and William Tarlow, Robin Cater, Donald Doyle, Roger Starr, Frank Duane, Dr. Samuel Sherman, Harry O. H. Frelinghuysen, James D'Angelo, Archie Compston, Tom and Arthur Schlesinger, Miss Amy Loveman, and William Shields. I am genuinely beholden as well to Mrs. John M. Flagler, Mrs. Cameron Moseley, and Miss Kathryn Ritchie, who bore the brunt of the photostatic and stenographic work; to Peter Schwed, an editor's editor; and to my colleagues at the* New Yorker Magazine, *none of whom can tell a mid-iron from a midwife but who were always ready to lend an attentive ear.*

H.W.W.

ABOUT THE EDITOR

HERBERT WARREN WIND has played golf on every continent except Africa, and has been writing about the game for the past twenty years. A good enough golfer himself to have competed in the British Amateur at St. Andrews in 1950 (where he made his way into the first round), he is particularly well fitted to have put together this collection of the best golfing literature that has been written on either side of the Atlantic. A native of Brockton, Massachusetts, and a graduate of Yale University, he took his M.A. at Cambridge University.

Since 1948 he has been a writer of Profiles for the New Yorker *Magazine, and has contributed a number of articles, the overwhelming majority of which have been on the subject of golf, to other magazines. He is presently on the staff of* Sports Illustrated. *He collaborated with Gene Sarazen in the writing of Sarazen's autobiography,* Thirty Years of Championship Golf, *and he is also the author of the book,* The Story of American Golf.

Afterword
by
Frank Hannigan

I wonder what Bernard Darwin would have made of the Skins Game or the Sony ranking system? Or, for the matter, the emergence of an entity known as the Volvo PGA European Tour as a force to be reckoned with by Darwin's own R & A in deciding what golf is in Great Britain and the rest of Europe.

There's no way of knowing how Darwin, who died in 1961, would have reacted to the phenomenon of big money golf. It's likely he would have scorned and then ignored it. But it's also possible he might have opted, like many of us, to take a comfortable ride on its economic zephyr.

Money was something Darwin had to think about. Leonard Crawley, himself the golf correspondent for the London Telegraph, once whispered to me that Darwin never made more than a thousand pounds a year from the gray and penurious Times of London. So who knows? Given the opportunity, Darwin might have become a client of Mark McCormack's and earned what he should have earned as the greatest of writers on sport.

These thoughts came to mind when I noted, after re-reading Herb Wind's happy anthology, that "The Complete Golfer" was first published in 1954. That's just about the time when golf was beginning its inexorable slide from a position as the most engaging of recreations into another form of sport-as-commerce. Most of Herb's choices came from magazines. What's so striking about the collection, apart from the consistent quality of the writing and art, is the absence of the staples in contemporary golf periodicals.

There's nothing about television, which has changed the way we perceive golf and is now routinely discussed in golf magazines although seldom perceptively.

The U.S. Open Championship was first televised nationally in 1954. Golf on television is now a year-round weekly entertainment. The golf writer who sits down at his word processor had better understand that television is his competition. Every golfer has access to every event of the slightest consequence.

Darwin, on the other hand, tells us that between 1894, when he became a Cambridge student, and 1908, when he gave up the practice of law ("I sold my wig"), he had relatively little opportunity to see golf played other than his own.

When Bob Jones retired from competitive golf in 1930, he was a hero as great as Palmer or Nicklaus in the television age, but only a small percentage of golfers had actually seen Jones swing a club. That's one of the reasons the instructional films he made for Warner Brothers in the early 1930s were so successful. The moving images of Jones, combined with his appealing drawl, were a stunning novelty.

"The Complete Golfer" is virtually devoid of golfers attempting to explain themselves. That's left up to the writers. Modern golf writing depends too much on the stultifying institution of the mass press conference even though the interviewee has little to say and what is said is inevitably self-serving.

Not one bureaucrat is mentioned by name in "The Complete Golfer"—not the commissioner of the PGA Tour (a role that did not exist until 1969), not the executive director of the U.S.G.A., not even the secretary of the R & A.

There is no mention of litigation in this book about golf. Litigation, especially the prospect of alleged violations of the Sherman Anti-Trust Act, is a must for today's golf editor. Indeed, during my stint as executive director of the U.S.G.A., I understood that the individual whose judgment mattered most in terms of the U.S.G.A. being able to function effectively was not myself or the U.S.G.A. president, but the special counsel retained on anti-trust matters. It is not a coincidence that the commissioners of Major League Baseball, the National Football League, and the National Basketball Association are lawyers.

Above all, there is nothing about the tiresome business of golf, of the all-pervasive deal-making that decides who gets what while the getting is good.

"The Complete Golfer", then, is a reminder that the game doesn't have to be about profit. The book is full of good humor. Just in case you missed it, I jump at the chance to close with its funniest lines. It's Henry Longhurst citing Harry Vardon's response to an attempt to conscript Vardon as a backer of the Women's Christian Temperance Union; "Moderation in all things is essential, madam, but never in my life have I lost to a teetotaler."

Frank Hannigan